Communicating Gender Diversity

This book honors the memory of our mothers:

Victoria DeFrancisco Leto (1924–2004)

Maj. Helen Mary Finks Palczewski (1921–1999)

Communicating Gender Diversity

A Critical Approach

Victoria Pruin DeFrancisco • Catherine Helen Palczewski

University of Northern Iowa

SAGE Publications

Los Angeles • London • New Delhi • Singapore

For information:

Sage Publications, Inc.
2455 Teller Road
Thousand Oaks, California 91320
E-mail: order@sagepub.com

Sage Publications Ltd.
1 Oliver's Yard
55 City Road
London EC1Y 1SP
United Kingdom

Sage Publications India Pvt Ltd
B 1/I 1 Mohan Cooperative
Mathura Road, New Delhi 110 044
India

Sage Publications Asia-Pacific Pte Ltd
33 Pekin Street #02-01
Far East Square
Singapore 048763

Printed in the United States of America.

Library of Congress Cataloging-in-Publication Data

DeFrancisco, Victoria L. (Victoria Leto)
Communicating gender diversity : a critical approach / Victoria Pruin DeFrancisco and Catherine Helen Palczewski.
   p. cm.
Includes bibliographical references and index.
ISBN 978-1-4129-2559-4 (pbk.)
   1. Sex role. 2. Gender identity. 3. Communication—Social aspects. 4. Communication—Sex differences. 5. Sexism in language. I. Palczewski, Catherine Helen. II. Title.
HQ1075.D43 2007
306.44082—dc22   2006103537

This book is printed on acid-free paper.

07   08   09   10   11   10 9 8 7 6 5 4 3 2 1

Acquiring Editor:	Todd R. Armstrong
Editorial Assistant:	Katie Grim
Marketing Manager:	Amber Erzinger
Project Editor:	Astrid Virding
Copyeditor:	April Wells-Hayes
Typesetter:	C&M Digitals (P) Ltd.
Indexer:	Juniee Oneida
Proofreader:	Gillian Dickens
Cover Designer:	Candice Harman

Contents

Preface

Welcome to our view of the state of the scholarship on communicating gender. We say *our view* to make the point that this textbook represents our best effort to be critical reviewers of existing knowledge on the topic, and because we want to clarify that our view is uniquely tied to the materials we have chosen to include, to our worldviews, and to the ways in which we make sense of the material. This view may differ from yours or from other textbooks' views. In fact, we hope it does.

Our purpose with this textbook is not to provide any final conclusions about communicating gender. Because gender is a constantly evolving concept, both in terms of individuals' gender identity development and the larger culture's predominant notions of gender, such absolute claims are not possible. Instead, our intent is to better equip readers with tools with which they can examine and make sense of the intersections of communication and gender.

To do so, we have attempted to write this book as an extended conversation in which we interact with the research on gender in communication that has most excited our own scholarly imaginations. As such, this book is not simply a review of research but rather an attempt to place the research in the context of larger theoretical, social, and political issues that we see emerging in the study of gender in communication. We hope this makes the material presented in the book more meaningful and useful for readers and relevant beyond the life of this publication.

This does not mean we only present research that is consistent with our preexisting views or academic disciplines. In fact, we believe people learn most by stepping outside their academic or personal comfort zones to consider other perspectives. We value engaged and vital disagreement, the push and pull of argumentation. We believe readers will be able to glean more from our presentation of substantiated arguments than they would if we pretended to present the research as if we were objective and value free. We will express our views of the material, and we hope this encourages you to do the same. Agreement is neither a necessary nor a preferred requirement for learning from this book, and disagreement is not a sign of disrespect.

Our approach to writing this text is the same as our approach to learning, teaching, and life: We advocate feminism. We believe that sex as a social category is one of the most important nexuses of power that are used to organize contemporary societies, and we believe that discrimination on the basis of gender and sex is one of the most violent forms of oppression. However, we also believe that many other social categories intersect within an individual's sex identity and with social relations of power.

That we subscribe to feminism does not mean we necessarily define it in the same way. In fact, this diversity is a quality of feminism. Feminism was proposed as an alternative to thinking in absolute, patriarchal truths. Consequently, it is important to make room for diverse feminist theories. For example, we honor the contributions of Black womanist theory, we celebrate the contradictions of third-wave feminism, and we happily navigate the tensions between global and postmodern feminisms, which you will learn about throughout the text.

While no single definition can represent all of feminist thought, we can offer some common qualities that we perceive as central. Feminisms challenge common cultural assumptions, such as the assumption that men should be mechanically inclined but women should not, and the assumption that women should be nurturers but men should not. Feminisms recognize the contributions of persons and groups historically undervalued, such as the contributions of women, LGBT (lesbian, gay, bisexual, and transgendered) people, and persons of color. Feminisms reveal related cultural oppressions, such as the feminization of poverty and the racing of welfare dependency. Feminisms create new ways of thinking, such as appreciation of the value of narratives as opposed to ostensibly objective scientific methods. Feminisms work toward social change and social justice. Thus, our ultimate goal in writing this book is nothing less than *intellectual activism*. These two terms often are perceived as opposites, polarized along the lines of theory and action—but we see them as inextricably involved in the creation of a world that is more welcoming of women *and* men who diverge from expected sex roles and gender norms.

We do not shy away from complex and controversial subjects. We foreground a rejection of the sex binary, recognizing the existence of intersex people. We see heterosexuality, homosexuality, bisexuality, and queer sexualities as equally valid sexual orientations. We incorporate the insights of queer theory. We reject the differences and the two-culture approaches to communicating gender, making clear that one cannot understand how communicating gender operates without also recognizing the power dynamics involved. Finally, we make clear that one can never study gender or sex in isolation. How a particularly sexed body performs gender always intersects with other identity ingredients. Our hope is that even as we grapple with complex issues, we do so in an approachable way.

Given the complexity of the issues involved, this book is intended for upper-division undergraduate or lower-level graduate courses focusing on gender in communication. Our approach is interdisciplinary, in terms of both method and the literature cited. We meld humanistic/critical and social scientific approaches. Although we highlight communication studies literature, we also integrate scholarship from anthropology, literature, philosophy, political science, psychology, sociology, and gender and women's studies that has served as the foundation of communication scholarship.

Organization of the Book

The book is divided in two parts. "Part I: Foundations" includes five chapters that describe the theories and methods that guide the study of gender in communication. These chapters are meant to provide a heuristic vocabulary that enables people to study gender in communication with more subtlety and nuance. "Part II: Institutions" includes an introductory chapter to explain our focus on social institutions, followed by five chapters on the social institutions we think make most evident the intersections of gender and communication: family, education, work, religion, and media. In each chapter, we examine the ways in which individuals experience and enact gender within the institution (micro) and the ways in which the structures and predominant ideology of the institutions influence the experience and enactment of gendered lives (macro). The concluding chapter draws links between the preceding chapters and presents visions for future study.

To cover the topics in depth, the chapters are longer than may be customary in textbooks. Gender in communication is necessarily complex when approached from an intersectional gender diversity approach; thus, easy lists of differences are not an option. This is not meant to detour the reader. Instead, we anticipate that classes will spend multiple days reading and discussing each chapter. The headings in the table of contents and within each chapter provide ways to divide the reading. The instructor's manual offers further direction.

We also have chosen to forgo numerous illustrations, sidebars, diagrams, and insets. Although such additions almost seem de rigueur in textbooks, we would rather operate under the assumption that students will be engaged because of their interest in the topic. We also have attempted to keep our writing lively and to offer more and longer quotations from others so that the reader gets a sense of participating in a conversation populated by more than the textbook authors.

Distinctive Features

If we had to summarize our approach to communicating gender in one sentence, we would say this: We study the variety of ways in which communication of and about gender and sex enables and constrains people's intersectional identities. We believe that people are social actors—and that, as such, they create meaning through their symbolic interactions. Thus, our emphasis is not on how gender influences communication but on how communication constitutes gender. We also believe that people are capable of being self-reflective about communication processes and creative in generating new ways to play with symbols. To study how people perform and construct genders and what factors influence these performances, we draw on seven principles that compose our approach to the study of communicating gender:

1. *Intersectionality.* Persons are not just female or male, feminine or masculine. To more accurately study gender, we must study gendered lives in the context of

other social identities, particularly race, ethnicity, social class, sexual orientation, and national origin. Although research embracing this approach is still limited, it continues to grow, and we make a concerted effort to recognize diverse social influences on gender.

2. *Interdisciplinarity.* We seek to fuse and balance social scientific, humanistic, and critical methods. Thus, we rely on quantitative, qualitative, rhetorical, and critical studies. As coauthors, we have the benefit of drawing on two fields of communication studies that often are seen as independent of each other but that we believe are inextricably linked: rhetoric and social science. Palczewski, trained as a rhetorical scholar, is an active debate coach who studies political controversies and social protest. DeFrancisco, trained as a social scientist, uses qualitative research methods to study how gender and related inequalities are constructed in interpersonal relationships and individuals' identities. Most texts on gender in communication focus on social science studies of gendered interpersonal interactions and thus fail to recognize the ways in which broader, public discourse can influence gender. Not only do we bridge methodological chasms within our own discipline, we do so between disciplines. We purposely look at each topic from multiple disciplinary and activist perspectives. The result is a richer, fuller understanding of the topic that stretches the boundaries of what is commonly considered relevant for a communication text.

3. *Gender diversity, not sex differences.* We do not subscribe to typical conceptualizations of gender as a form of difference. Instead, we problematize the differences view by showing how it ignores power, reinforces stereotypes and related oppressions, fails to account for intersectionality, and is inconsistent with meta-analyses demonstrating that sex does not consistently account for differences in communication. However, our rejection of the differences approach does not mean that we deny differences exist. Instead, we seek to recognize an even richer diversity as a result of intersectionality and in the form of a gender diversity approach.

4. *Masculinity.* The study of gender is not just the study of women. However, the study of gender has traditionally been considered a "women's issue," hence researchers and textbooks often have focused almost exclusively on women and femininity, underemphasizing men and masculinities. Thanks to the recent growth in men's studies, we have at our disposal a rich literature base that considers gender and masculinity. In this textbook, we make a concerted effort to include masculinities, particularly in the chapters on work, media, and family.

5. *Gender is a performed social institution.* Gender is something a person does, not something a person is. Gender is not something located within individuals; it is a social construct that institutions and individuals maintain (and occasionally challenge). Thus, we examine the microlevel—how an individual might perform gender—and the macrolevel—how social understandings of gender are performed on individuals. Given this attention to institutions, we also pay attention to the ways in which institutions intersect, not just to the ways identity ingredients intersect.

6. *Violence.* To study gender in lived experiences means to study the darker side of gender: oppression and violence. We do not avoid or limit the discussion of gendered violence to one chapter. Rather, a range of specific social injustices are made visible in each chapter. We do so not to bash males (not all men abuse, and not only women are victims) but to more fully recognize the consequences of the prevalent gendered society in which most people live. Gendered violence is systemic in the form of domestic abuse, rape, and violence against LGBT people. By linking seemingly innocent, gendered practices to more overt forms of gendered violence, we are better able to move beyond superficial generalizations about gender differences and to make visible the struggles many women and men face in their unique cultural contexts.

7. *Emancipation.* Even as we recognize violence, we also want to recognize the emancipatory potential of gendered practice. Gender identity need not be oppressive and limiting to persons. For each social institution addressed, we offer examples of how diverse groups of people have created strategies to free themselves of stereotypical gender and other cultural expectations.

We recognize that these guiding principles might require a substantial retooling of many courses. Thus, this textbook is accompanied by an instructor's manual that includes sample syllabi, possible assignments, and teaching aids. For each chapter, we provide a chapter outline, discussion questions, class activities, additional examples, full texts of significant paraphrased quotations, and media and Web resources. The manual also includes special "hot topics" essays that enable students to see how one might apply concepts introduced in the text to current issues.

Some Author Admissions

Writing this book was challenging, exciting, fun, enlightening, frustrating, and hard, joyful work. DeFrancisco has taught courses and conducted research related to communicating gender since 1981; Palczewski has done so since 1987. Despite our collective years devoted to feminist studies of communication, we continually struggle to do it right. It is difficult to talk about gender without reinforcing stereotypes about it. Language and cultural perceptions of gender (the primary resources we have to communicate) fail us! As we discuss in Chapter 5, the very words *female* and *male, woman* and *man,* and the connotations associated with them encourage perceptions of individuals as only one *or* the other sex and as different and differentially valued in the predominant culture. The words also ignore intersex persons and the fact that men can be feminine, women can be masculine, or both. Additionally, there is no word to identify a person who marks all of her or his intersecting identity ingredients, making it difficult to constantly keep in mind that when one studies gender, one also must consider the ways in which multiple identities intersect and influence persons' lives. We have adopted the following strategies to try to compensate for some of the limitations of language and gendered cultural perceptions:

1. One often sees lists of multiple cultural group identities, such as race, class, gender, sex, and sexual orientation, as a reminder that the topic of study is not gender alone. However, it is impossible to recognize all group identities each time (e.g., physical ability, age, urban/rural, religion). Hence, the categories in the list shift across chapters according to the point we are trying to make.

2. We use language that is inclusive of women and men throughout this text (e.g., *people, persons, she and he, women and men, spouses*). We take this a step further, adopting the suggestion of linguist M. J. Hardman (1999) to reverse the commonly used order of men first and women second, as in *boys and girls*, until, as Hardman says, the order "doesn't matter anymore" (p. 1).

3. We try to avoid overgeneralizing about women and men. When we report on a study, we use phrases such as "the women and men in the study," rather than "women and men" to make the point that claims cannot be generalized beyond the scope of the particular participants in the study being reported.

Ideally, our book embodies the changes currently emerging in the ever-transforming field of gender in communication. We hope it challenges the very way in which readers think about gender and sex, as well as the ways in which gender and sex intersect with race, class, sexual orientation, and nationality. Instead of providing simplistic answers, we hope this textbook provides guidance on how to ask good questions. We also hope this book will inspire present and future researchers to contribute to the study of gender in communication, further stretching the boundaries of culturally gendered perceptions.

Acknowledgments

This book could not have been written without the assistance of our colleagues. People too numerous to list have helped us as we wrote this book, but a few deserve special note for the extra time they spent sharing resources, reading chapters, and providing invaluable research assistance. The chapters would not have been as grounded in current scholarship, and the examples would not have been as rich, had it not been for the following people: Nathan Epley, Michael Fleming, Tom Hall, Susan Hill, Kristin Mack, Karen Mitchell, Martha Reineke, and Mary Beth Stalp. We also thank M.A. students who worked as research assistants: Ruth Beerman, Danielle Dick, Danelle Frisbie, and Eric Short. Other students and colleagues served as universal resources, offering ideas and examples, checking facts, and other support: Rob Asen, Judith Baxter, Harry Brod, Dan Brouwer, April Chatham-Carpenter, Jeanne Cook, John Fritch, Shoko Hayashi, Kyle Kostelecky, Maria Mastronardi, Gayle Pohl, Alimatul Qibtiyah, Vickie Turner, Donna Uhlenhopp, Atun Wardatun, and Jayne Morgan Witte. We recognize that no book is created in isolation. We thank Julia Wood (*Gendered Lives*), Diane Ivy and Phil Backlund (*Gender Speak*), and Karlyn Kohrs Campbell (*Man Cannot Speak for Her*) for helping pave the way in gender/sex in communication textbooks, as well as scholars whose work has informed the development of our own gendered lenses: Judith Butler, Patricia Hill Collins, Celeste Condit, bell hooks, Cheris Kramarae, Judy Pearson, Dale Spender, and Anita Taylor. We thank our life partners, Arnie Madsen and David Pruin, for their willing honoring of our need to have room of our own in which to write. We especially thank our SAGE editor, Todd Armstrong, for his continued trust. We also want to thank the skilled professionals who worked with us through the final stages of the publication process: Katie Grim (editorial assistant), Astrid Virding (project editor), and April Wells-Hayes (copyeditor). Support for the development of this book was provided in part by the University of Northern Iowa's Graduate College, the College of Humanities and Fine Arts, the Department of Communication Studies, and the Women's and Gender Studies Program.

SAGE Publications gratefully acknowledges the following reviewers:

Cynthia Berryman-Fink, University of Cincinnati; Derek T. Buescher, University of Puget Sound; Sandra L. Faulkner, Syracuse University; Lisa A. Flores, University of Utah; Jeffrey Dale Hobbs, The University of Texas at Tyler; Charlotte Kroløkke, University of Southern Denmark; D. K. London, Merrimack College; M. Chad McBride, Creighton University; and Lynn H. Turner, Marquette University.

PART I

Foundations

 **CHAPTER 1**

Developing a Critical Gender/Sex Lens

No doubt about it, in the United States and many other parts of the world, gender in communication is a *hot* topic. You can turn on a television or radio almost any day of the week and hear some version of the following: A woman complains that her husband never listens to her, then another person complains that the women she or he works with gossip and are not to be trusted; finally, audience members or experts react with recognition of these anecdotal experiences and readily diagnose them as examples of common "gender communication problems." Given most people's ability to generate such a seemingly obvious explanation, you may wonder whether you even need a course on gender in communication. After all, you have been engaging in and observing gendered communication practices all your life.

Popular assumptions abound regarding gender differences between the sexes such as the ones just mentioned. Research suggests, however, that women and men alike use gossip to build group solidarity; it's just that society usually does not derogatively label men's talk as gossip (Coates, 1996; Pilkington, 1998). Similarly, researchers suggest that differences in listening are likely influenced by socialization more than by biology (Johnson, Weaver, Watson, & Barker, 2000). Researchers find that the listening goals of women *and* men tend to be influenced by socialization toward masculine or feminine stereotypical preferences in terms of what captures their attention. As with the sexist labeling of gossip, people tend to expect the listening goals and abilities of women and men to differ more than has actually been documented by research.

A key point in this text is that, more than actual differences in communication patterns, *perceptions* of women's and men's behaviors are gendered. In *Same Difference: How Gender Myths Are Hurting Our Relationships, Our Children, and Our Jobs* (2004), psychologist Rosalind Barnett and journalist Caryl Rivers critique social myths of gender differences. They and others compellingly argue that the predominant cultural belief in gender differences has created a self-fulfilling prophecy in which people's beliefs actually create the differences.

To say that most gender and sex differences are socially created rather than purely biological does not mean that no differences exist or that the perceived differences do not matter. According to the research gathered and analyzed for this book, there are many, often subtle, nuances in behavior and experience tied to *gender*, one's psychological identity (feminine and masculine), and *sex*, one's biological identity (genitals, hormones, and chromosomes). This is partly why, in this text, we refer to *gender/sex*. Ask parents who are struggling to raise their children in less gender-specific ways. Many will likely tell you that the differences, whether biologically or socially constructed or both, are real to them. No matter how hard the parents try, some children cling to gender-specific identities and related sex stereotypes. Similarly, as you will learn in this chapter, scientists have found no dependable biological markers of race—yet members of society continue to construct and employ racial identities, sometimes to prejudge others and sometimes as a way to name and celebrate group identity. Unfortunately, people who are labeled African American, Muslim, Chicana, woman, and so forth, often face discrimination solely on the basis of placement in that category. The experiences of difference and discrimination are interconnected and real, whether or not they are biologically false.

Because of these issues, the approach we take in this book is not to merely summarize current research on the topic but to go a step further and attempt to equip you with the critical analytical tools to develop your own informed opinions about society's gender expectations, about existing research, and about prevailing cultural views, as well as about future research needs. To do that, it is necessary to understand the ways in which predominant cultural views about gender and sex create a *gendered lens* through which people view reality. This lens can become so embedded that a person doesn't realize how it might limit her or his perceptions of reality. In place of the predominant culture's gendered lens, we hope to help you construct a more critical gendered lens by providing analytical tools with which you can examine common assumptions about gender, sex, and communication.

In this chapter, we first take on the question of why it is important to examine how gender is communicated. A big part of the answer is tied to unpacking prevalent popular cultural messages about gender, as in the foregoing examples. We then define and examine some basic vocabulary used throughout this text, to help equip the reader with the critical tools we find useful for this closer examination. Because these terms are so interrelated, we necessarily use some terms before we have an opportunity to define them. If you come to a concept that is unfamiliar to you, read on.

Gender Differences: A Cultural Obsession

Popular culture portrays gender as a series of "differences," often more dramatically presented as "gender wars" between the sexes. Out of curiosity, we searched the

Internet using the key words "gender wars." During the last year, the phrase appeared 70 times in the 50 major English-language papers indexed by LexisNexis. A Google search generated more than 10,700,000 hits. The term *gender wars* is used to frame discussions about health, education, business, marriage, sexuality, child care, brain structure, the military, war, sexual harassment, athletics, computer use, emotions, acting, toilet seat norms, computer marketing, clothing, and even camping equipment. The "gender wars" are a primary topic for joke lists, and there is even a downloadable game called Gender Wars.

We probably do not have to tell you, as communication students, that words matter. However, even as people recognize the importance of communication, they sometimes are unaware of its influence on them. Metaphors, in particular, can be especially influential because they frame thinking about an issue even when people do not realize they are using metaphors. Metaphors become *dead metaphors* because they are no longer recognized as overt metaphors; instead, they come to denote what they are used to describe. According to the metaphor categories created by linguist George Lakoff and philosopher Mark Johnson (1980), *gender wars* is a structural metaphor, meaning that the phrase structures one concept in terms of another: Gender relations = war. Structural metaphors often are extended by a series of additional metaphors stemming from the initial equation, as in "the latest skirmish in the war between the sexes" (Blustain, 2000, p. 42). If one thinks of gender and sex relations as a constant battle, with casualties, assigned sides, enemies, and weapons, the ultimate goals of surrender or annihilation become inherent.

The war metaphor is not a coincidence. It reinforces differences and highlights opposition. The assumption is that there are two very different views of reality, with sides assigned at birth, and they conflict. As in actual wartime, both sides use propaganda to demonize the enemy. Thus, women often are demonized as being relationally demanding, emotionally unstable, and needy. Men are often demonized as being withdrawn, unemotional, and aggressive. With contradictory descriptions such as these, gender wars seem inevitable and never ending.

Although it is true that the gender wars metaphor sometimes is used humorously to poke fun at women and men, this humor is actually part of the metaphor's power. It helps to popularize the metaphor of gender wars and render it seemingly innocuous. This humor is harmful, as well, because it can trivialize real issues of sexual violence, such as sexual harassment, domestic violence, and rape.

It is important to examine the ways in which this view of gender and sex as oppositional, pitting women and men against each other, limits an understanding of the issues involved. Imagine, instead, if the popular metaphor of gender relations were *gender union* (as in European Union, workers' unions, student unions, the United Nations, the United States). How might predominant depictions of women's and men's communication differ from what is typically reported? Indeed, although the predominant culture continues to assume that women and men are extremely different and therefore communicate in different ways, actual research does not support such a clear distinction (Anderson & Leaper, 1998; Edwards & Hamilton, 2004; MacGeorge, Graves, Feng, Gillihan, & Burleson, 2004; Yaeger-Dror, 1998). Research suggests that gendered behavior variances among women and among men are actually greater than those *between* women and men (Hyde & Plant, 1995; Wood & Dindia, 1998). Think about it. Why would anyone assume that all women or all men around the world and across ethnic groups and through the generations communicate the same way?

Interestingly, as researchers continually disprove the existence of generic gender differences, media and popular culture seem to spread the myth of difference even more pervasively. It seems to be a message many people want to hear. The magnetism of this simplistic view is incredibly compelling. Why might this be so?

First, sex and gender are primary social categories in most cultures. When a child is born, what is the first question most people in the United States ask? It is not about weight, length, hair color, or even whether the baby and mother are healthy. Instead, people ask, "Is it a boy or a girl?" From then on, they tend to talk about, interact with, and dress the infant accordingly. It is no surprise, then, that one of the first things toddlers learn about their identities is whether they are categorized as girls or boys. Society sexes and genders infants based on their genitals, under the assumption that there are only two sexes and two corresponding genders. In Western cultures, since the 1900s pink has been designated for girls and blue for boys. Many a parent won't dress an infant in the color designated for the other sex for fear that people will misidentify the sex of the child, as if such a mistake would be a horrible embarrassment.

The preference for a male firstborn remains true for many in Western cultures. In other parts of the world, such as Papua New Guinea, Tamil Nadu in India, and some areas of rural China, the cultural and economic bias toward boy children sadly still leads to the infanticide of girl babies or to orphanages filled with them. Tradition allows only boy children to carry on the family name; thus, boys also inherit the family assets and, with their future wives, provide for their aging parents. Girl children are often expected to marry, to provide dowries upon marriage, and to care for their husbands' families. Given this, it becomes more understandable why boys still may be preferred. Lest you think the preoccupation with babies' sexes has dissipated in the United States, a new test was released in the U.S. market in June 2005. The Baby Gender Mentor determines the sex of a fetus as early as five weeks after conception. This test has caused serious concern among bioethicists, who fear it will be used for sex selection purposes (Goldberg, 2005).

Even for adults, sex is a prominent identity marker. Just look at any survey. One of the first demographic questions asked is whether you are male or female. If you do not think you stereotype people based on their sex, just try talking to a person whose sex you do not know. For most people, it is awkward. The topics raised, the tone of the conversation, and the use of sexual innuendo all tend to vary with the speaker's perceptions and expectations of the sex of the other person. Interestingly, men's studies scholar Michael Kimmel (2000) notes that only within the last few decades have we come to recognize that "gender is one of the central organizing principles around which social life revolves" (p. 5).

Second, the assumption of difference is tied to the assumption of heterosexual romance. It is not a coincidence that popular self-help literature links gender/sex differences to heterosexual relations (DeFrancisco & O'Connor, 1995). Communication scholar Robert Hopper, who studied gender and talk for 30 years, concludes that the cultural belief that everyone should be in a heterosexual relationship feeds into the focus on gender differences (Hopper, 2003). Early on, boys and girls are encouraged to see each other as the "opposite sex" and to vie for the other's attention. Heterosexual dating is a primary means to popularity for many in U.S. middle and high schools. And heterosexual weddings are seen as the ultimate social rituals (Ingraham, 1999), so much so that states are moving rapidly to amend their constitutions to bar marriage among gays and lesbians.

Whether or not one accepts alternative forms of romantic relations, the focus on heterosexual relations and the presumption that oppositional gender/sex differences exist combine to create expectations that everyone should be in such relationships, thereby decreasing the value of other types of platonic or romantic relationships.

Third, in Western capitalistic cultures, sex, differences, and conquest sell. When popular writers, television directors, and advertisers put the word *sex* in their presentations, sales and ratings go up. People are immediately interested and want to hear or read more. If emphasis were placed on recognizing the ways in which the sexes are similar, as in the *gender union* metaphor, there would be no challenge, no mystery, no threat. As we live in a culture in which heterosexual romantic relations are stressed so much, an interesting question to ask is why authors and the media do not focus more on identifying and celebrating the similarities between women and men. This omission is very telling about the predominant culture and its political tools.

Fourth, the focus on difference is political. It helps reinforce the notion that women and men are different, that women and men are in a series of "gender wars" with each other, and that women and men will never understand each other. As noted previously, the problem is that opposites in society are rarely considered different *and* equal. Rather, the emphasis on differences becomes a tool to mask or justify social inequalities based on race, sex, class, and other social categories (e.g., Barnett & Rivers, 2004; DeFrancisco, 1997; West & Zimmerman, 1987). A differences focus leads to portraying one group as deficient and maintaining the other as the norm (Weatherall, 1998).

As linguist Mary Crawford (1995) explains, if communication problems were due solely to differences and not to group power or status, women and men could borrow each other's styles with similar effectiveness. But in reality, what works depends on the social status of the speaker and the power relations between the speaker and listener. The same communication features do not perform the same for all speakers. A female who adopts a more autocratic style of management may be labeled overbearing, whereas a male manager using this style may be seen as a strong leader.

The negative political effects of presumed differences show up in everyday life. The assumption of presumed differences creates conflicts, persistent inequalities, false expectations, and disappointments. As Barnett and Rivers (2004) explain, "These [differences] theories hurt male-female relationships, undermine equality in schools and the workplace, adversely affect the division of labor in the home, and deprive our children of the opportunity to develop their full human potential" (p. 2).

In sum, a view of gender/sex as difference is popular, and so people raised in the predominant culture tend to focus on differences rather than similarities. It is as if each member of society wore glasses, and the lenses were refracted so that each person saw gender and sex in a culturally limiting way. What follows is an adjustment in your prescription. The following concepts make clear why a focus on differences between women and men as homogeneous groups is impossible and, in fact, produces inaccurate descriptions of human communication.

A Critical Vocabulary or a New Lens Prescription

Welcome to our view of gender analysis. These are the concepts without which one cannot talk meaningfully about gender, sex, and communication. The vocabulary is grouped into three categories: (1) intersectionality, which is a way to understand the ingredients of cultural identities; (2) communication, which refers to how these identities are constructed, maintained, and changed; and (3) systems of hierarchy, which refers to the social structures of oppression. You will find that we have not provided simple dictionary definitions for these terms but rather indicate why these concepts deserve critical analysis and must be discussed in relationship to each other.

Intersectionality

Writing a book about *only* gender in communication is impossible. So, we need to explain what we have written. Gender is not the only thing that influences communication patterns, whether in interpersonal, group, or public settings. One's identity and how one expresses it are determined by a number of intersecting factors. African American feminists were among the first to recognize this. They developed the theory of intersectionality to explain how gender is not a separate part of identity but is related to all other parts of a person's identity.

Legal scholar and critical race feminist Adrien Wing (1997) explains the theory of *intersectionality* as the notion that identity is "multiplicative" rather than additive (p. 30). Instead of understanding identity as the addition of one element on top of another, as in woman + White + heterosexual + second-generation citizen, and so forth, identity makes more sense if you think of each identity element as inextricably linked with another, as in woman × White × heterosexual × second-generation citizen. All facets of identity are integral, interlocking parts of a whole. What it means to be a woman or a man influences one's class, which influences one's race, which influences one's gender, which influences one's nationality, and vice versa. In other words, you cannot understand what it means to have a certain gender/sex without examining these other identities simultaneously.

Kimberlé Crenshaw, a lawyer and legal scholar, was the first to use the word *intersectionality* (1989). She explains, "because the intersectional experience is greater than the sum of racism and sexism, any analysis that does not take intersectionality into account cannot sufficiently address the particular manner in which Black Women are subordinated" (p. 59). However, one should remember that "it is not just the marginalized who have a gender, race, and so on" (Harding, 1995, p. 121). Intersectionality explains the complexity of all people's identities. And just as any analysis of subordination relating to gender in communication is incomplete without taking one's multiple identities into account, so, too, is any analysis of empowerment.

Research that assumes that a person's identity exists in removable, separable layers leads to overgeneralized conclusions. Such research does not recognize that identity actually occurs as a complex, synergistic, infused whole that becomes something completely different when parts are ignored, forgotten, and unnamed (Collins, 1998). Author Audre Lorde (1984) offers an example of why the intersectional approach is also important to the individual:

> As a Black lesbian feminist comfortable with the many different ingredients of my identity, and a woman committed to racial and sexual freedom from oppression, I find I am constantly being encouraged to pluck out some one aspect of myself and present that as the meaningful whole, eclipsing or denying the other parts of self. But this is a destructive and fragmenting way to live. My fullest concentration of energy is available to me only when I integrate all the parts of who I am, openly, allowing power from particular sources of my living to flow back and forth freely through all my different selves, without the restrictions of externally imposed definition. Only then can I bring myself and my energies as a whole to the service of those struggles which I embrace as a part of my living. (p.120)

Lorde's use of the metaphor *ingredients* is quite apt when explaining intersectionality. For example, a cake is an object with ingredients such as flour, eggs, oil, sugar, and milk, which can exist separately from each other. The combined result contains all the ingredients, but none are recognizable in their separate forms. A cake is not just flour and eggs and sugar and oil and milk. A cake is only a cake when the ingredients are so fused together that they cannot be separated again.

An intersectional approach allows scholars to avoid falling into the trap of overgeneralization, such as in *biological determinism*. This trap is the belief that, because a person is born a female or a male, or of one race rather than another, she or he has some predetermined, essential, or innate characteristics. Another related overgeneralization is *essentialism*, the presumption that all members of a group are alike because they have one quality in common, such as when one attempts to speak about all *men's* communication, or *Black women's* communication, or *LGBT* (lesbian, gay, bisexual, and transgendered) communication, or any identity element's role in communication. Author Angela Harris (1997) advocates the avoidance of essentialism, explaining that "fragmentation of identity and essentialism go hand in hand" (p. 11). One cannot study a person as if her or his gender or sex or race exclusively defined the person completely. To do so risks essentializing and stereotyping.

Intersectional identity theories do not absolutely reject the existence of identity categories and the social reality they produce, nor do they celebrate identity politics with an uncritical acceptance of identity categories. Instead, they embrace what sociologist Leslie McCall terms the "intracategorical approach to complexity" that "seeks to complicate and use [identity categories] in a more critical way" (2005, p. 1780). Like McCall, in this text we seek to "focus on the process by which they [categories of identity] are produced, experienced, reproduced, and resisted in everyday life" (p. 1783).

GENDER AND SEX, GENDER/SEX

In the late 1970s, researchers started using the term *gender* instead of *sex* to identify attributes of women and men (Unger, 1979). This was heralded as an important breakthrough for research and for human rights. No longer were authors essentializing all men as acting one way and all women another based solely on their genitals. In contrast, *gender* refers to one's self-identity—that is, how much a person associates herself or himself with the masculine or the feminine or both, as prescribed by society. Because the characteristic is cultural rather than biological, the assumption is that a person can identify to varying degrees with masculinity and femininity, rather than just one or the other.

However, the attributes of masculinity and femininity are drawn from predominant cultural assumptions and expectations, replacing one set of generalizations based on sex with another based on gender. You can probably name these attributes easily. Masculine characteristics include independence, strength, and decisiveness. Feminine characteristics are typically considered the opposite (although most people do not openly acknowledge that "the opposite" means that femininity includes dependency, weakness, and irrationality). In a more positive light, femininity is also recognized as compassionate, supportive, and relationship oriented (e.g., Bem, 1974; Gilligan, 1982).

Although similarities in the definitions of masculinity and femininity emerge across many cultures of the world, surveys show that cultures differ in terms of how much each is valued (Hofstede, 1998). Cultures also differ in terms of how their current notions of masculinity and femininity emerged historically. In the United States, current conceptions of these terms primarily evolved out of the Western Industrial Revolution, beginning in the mid-18th century. Paid productivity left the home, and women's and men's work became dichotomized. White men mostly claimed the better-paying jobs outside the home in business and government. It was assumed that White men were more inclined to have the skills the work demanded: leadership ability, assertiveness, physical strength, and independence. In contrast, the home was popularly heralded as women's domain and area of expertise. The work there demanded caretaking, supportiveness, empathy, and a relational focus. Heterosexual nuclear families were emphasized more than they had been previously, and women became more economically dependent on men. Before this time, women and men tended to share more of the tasks of productivity and caretaking in their homes (Cancian, 1989). Today, people see gender roles changing before their eyes as more U.S. men than ever are choosing to be stay-at-home dads, and more girls and women than ever are participating in athletics, including professional athletics (Barnett & Rivers, 2004; Coontz, 1997).

This history demonstrates not only that the meanings of masculinity and femininity change over time and thus are not innate but also that they are influenced by a predominantly White, capitalistic marketplace. The concepts were never neutral or free of social influences. They prescribed who should do what work and thus who should have what personal qualities, creating an artificial split between women's and men's abilities and lives. Women and children who were African American, immigrants, or poor Whites did not share this history. Because of slavery, prejudice, and poverty, women and men from these groups have always worked outside the home in positions in housekeeping, food preparation, and factories and as sexual laborers (Andersen, 2006; Burn, 2000).

Although focusing on gender instead of sex was meant to be a step away from overgeneralizing women's and men's identities, masculinity and femininity are still stereotypes, prescribing how women and men are supposed to behave. In the United States, the stereotypes are based on White, heterosexual, upper-class standards. This explains an ethical dilemma in studying gender. By putting the focus there, we risk reifying the stereotypes (Young, 1997). Intersectionality is a useful tool to help address this dilemma.

The term *androgyny* emerged with the concept of gender in the 1970s. It was expected to be another step toward equality of the sexes. Psychologist Sandra Bem (1974) used the term, which combines two Greek words: *andros*, meaning "male," and *gyne*, meaning "female." Bem developed a questionnaire called the Sex-Role Inventory (SRI) to identify a person's gender orientation as highly feminine, highly masculine, androgynous (both), or undifferentiated (low in both masculine and feminine traits). Persons who are androgynous are said to have more behavioral flexibility. Although the concept of behavioral flexibility certainly seems admirable and is consistent with the flexibility needed to be a competent communicator, the concept of androgyny is still limiting.

Researchers who use the Sex-Role Inventory are limiting descriptions of persons according to the two stereotypic concepts of masculinity and femininity, or are engaging in what some refer to as a *gender binary*—a system having two distinct and exclusive genders. Androgyny merely collapses the two stereotypes together and thus inadvertently helps to maintain them. Because of this criticism, in recent use of the SRI, researchers have dropped the terms *masculine* and *feminine*, relying instead on measures of dominance, nurturance, orientation toward self versus others, and so forth, but the stereotypical inferences are still present. There is no ideal means to study gender identity.

To add to this problem, researchers often do not use the concept of gender correctly. If you read the research, you will find that many claim to have found gender differences or similarities, when in actuality they never assessed the participants' self-identities. They merely asked participants to label themselves as biologically female or male.

This blurring of sex and gender concepts raises another question. The longtime distinction between sex (as a biological given) and gender (as a social construction) may not be as clear as once thought. Judith Butler (1993), a professor of rhetoric and comparative literature, argues that sex is as much a cultural creation as gender and that bodies have no meaning separate from the meaning language gives them. She identifies the belief that there are only two sexes as one of the most vivid examples of this linguistic framing of bodies. This belief does not recognize inter-sexed persons.

Intersexuality is the term used to describe a person who has ambiguous or non-congruent sex features. *Ambiguous* means that the person has mixed genitalia of females and males. *Noncongruent* or *transgender* means that the person feels that her or his biological sex and genitalia do not match her or his gender identity. Lest you think these are extremely rare medical phenomena, consider that "recent medical literature indicates that approximately one to four percent of the world's population may be intersexed" (Greenberg, 1999, pp. 267–268). One percent trans-lates into 2.7 million people in the United States. Four percent would translate into approximately 10 million people in the United States. Despite this, the very way society talks and legislates about sex in the United States constantly reinforces the idea that there are two and only two distinct sexes. Law professor Julie Greenberg (1999) explains how this works:

> Implicit in legislation utilizing the terms "sex" and "gender" are the assump-tions that only two biological sexes exist and that all people fit neatly into either the category male or female. In other words, despite medical and anthropological studies to the contrary, the law presumes a binary sex and gender model. The law ignores the millions of people who are intersexed. A binary sex paradigm does not reflect reality. Instead, sex and gender range across a spectrum. Male and female occupy the two ends of the poles, and a number of intersexed conditions exist between the two poles. (p. 275)

One's understanding of the body and its relationship to identity is always medi-ated by language, the words each person uses to talk about the body, and therefore one can never comprehend the biological entity without the meanings language attaches to it. In Butler's (1993) terms, "there is no reference to a pure body which is not at the same time a further formation of that body" (p. 10). The notion that our so-called biological sex is itself influenced by communication is not to deny the existence of a material body, "but to insist that our apprehension of it, our understanding of it, is necessarily mediated by the *con*texts in which we speak" (Price & Shildrick, 1999, p. 7). When the predominant culture calls a body a par-ticular sex, male *or* female (and nothing else), the culture has already engaged in an act of communication that has "normative force," as it recognizes some parts of a person but not all (Butler, 1993, p. 11).

It is important to understand that the terms *sex* and *gender* refer to different aspects of the self but are deeply interrelated. A simple example should demon-strate this point. Biologist Anne Fausto-Sterling (2005) conducted an exhaustive study of human beings' bones, a part of the body you would think would be most biological and least cultural. In an attempt to answer the question, "How does experience shape the very bones that support us?" (p. 1495), she explores the way osteoporosis was identified and treated. Her discovery shows: "Osteoporosis is a condition that reveals all of the problems of defining sex apart from gender" (p. 1499); in fact, the widely held belief that women are more susceptible to osteoporosis depends on "how we define osteoporosis, in which human populations (and historical periods) we gather statistics, and what portions of the life cycle we compare" (p. 1500). The differences between men's and women's bones may not be as different as first thought. "Our bodies physically imbibe culture" (p. 1495).

In another example, men's studies scholar R. W. Connell (1995) argues that men cannot escape their bodies. The social significance placed on men's bodies as large, strong, and agile heavily influence many men's gender identities. The struggles many transgendered persons experience with self-acceptance and social acceptance illustrate the undeniable relationship between mind and body.

Accordingly, we want to recognize that people experience their gender and sex together. By using the phrase *gender/sex* in this textbook, we are able to constantly emphasize the cultural interrelations of the concepts of gender *and* sex. When we discuss gender in communication, we always discuss sex in communication, because communication that is about gender, that is influenced by gender, and that differentiates gender also always is about sex, is influenced by sex, and differentiates sex.

SEXUALITY

One's identity as a gay, lesbian, heterosexual, bisexual, or transgendered person is also often confounded with the terms *gender* and *sex*. Part of the confusion is due to social stereotypes: Gays are assumed to be effeminate, lesbians are assumed to be masculine, and so on. But sexual orientation is not the same as gender or sex. *Sexual orientation* refers to whether one is physically and romantically attracted to or has sex with persons of the same sex, the other sex, or both (as in the case of bisexuals).

However, sexuality is more than orientation. It also involves what one does when one is sexual. Even those who might be labeled heterosexuals can be *queer*, meaning they may not abide by heteronormative sex practices. *Heteronormativity* describes the way in which, in the United States, social institutions and policies reinforce the presumption that people are heterosexual, that gender and sex are binaries. It is important to note, however, that challenges to heteronormativity are not challenges to all norms. As English professor Michael Warner explains (2002), "To be against processes of normalization is not to be afraid of ordinariness. Nor is it to advocate the 'life without limit'" (p. 197).

Our goal is to make clear the distinctions between sex, gender, and sexual orientation as we discuss sexuality, recognizing that each affects the other. The way culture communicates about sexual orientation constructs and maintains not only differences but heterosexuality as the norm (Rich, 1980). Persons who are discriminated against because of their sexual orientation are not being oppressed simply because they are behaving as "bad women or men"; they are also being discriminated against because they are perceived as sexual deviants (Rubin, 1984). Sociologist Gayle Rubin (1984) states, "The system of sexual oppression cuts across other modes of sexual inequality, such as racial, class, ethnic or gendered inequality, and it sorts individuals and groups according to its own intrinsic dynamics. It is not reducible" (p. 22). Conversely, discussions of gender and sex are intricately tied to sexual orientation and sexuality.

RACE AND ETHNICITY

As the concept of intersectionality suggests, one cannot adequately study gender without studying race and ethnicity. Like gender/sex, race in particular is a primary social category used to identify people. Like the other social identifiers discussed in this chapter, race and ethnicity are largely constructed through words and actions.

Most scientists long ago abandoned the idea of using race as a valid indicator for categorizing human beings. Races do not exist in the biological sense, and there is extensive research to suggest that "purely" distinct races never did exist (Orbe & Harris, 2001, p. 31). More genetic variations occur *within* groups of people than *between* them (Tobin & Dusheck, 1998). However, in daily life, people tend to identify a person's race by examining a few physical traits, such as skin color, hair texture, eye color, and the shape of eyes and nose. Groups of people do vary in these physical appearances from one geographic area to another, but when these physical traits are looked at together, researchers find no consistent identifiers shared within a group of people. The huge variances within a group of people mean, for example, that persons who are considered White can have darker skins than some persons who are labeled Black.

Ethnicity refers to a group of people who share a cultural history, even though they may no longer live in the same geographic area (Zack, 1998). They may share values, a language, and a way of life. Race and ethnicity are generally seen as connected. In the United States, people within a given ethnic group tend to be identified as the same race, with origins in the same geographic area. But the link between race and ethnicity is becoming less predictable as the world becomes more transnational. Although most Jewish people are considered White, many are Black; French people are expected to be White, yet many are Black. Furthermore, both race and ethnic labels are subject to cultural change. Germans and Italians are now considered White, but this was not always so. In 1751, U.S. founding leader Benjamin Franklin wrote of his fear that the Germans would take over Pennsylvania and how they would "Germanize us instead of our Anglifying them, and will never adopt our Language or Customs, any more than they can acquire our Complexion" (para. 23). Similarly, immigrants of the early 1900s from Ireland, Italy, Russia, and Spain were generally thought of as "colored" until the 1960s (Martin & Nakayama, 2004).

Additionally, the intersections between races often are ignored. Even though racial purity is a myth, when you fill out forms, you often are asked to identify yourself as one race and only one race. Not until the year 2000 did the U.S. census allow people to identify themselves as belonging to more than one racial category. Individuals and social institutions, such as government census takers, accept the biological fiction of race and continue to use it to classify people.

Consequently, we cannot offer a precise definition of race in this text. At its simplest, race is a way in which groups of people are socially identified. When society constructs arbitrary racial categories, these categories are rarely different and equal. Rather, race has been used as a primary tool of social oppression. In the United States, fair skin is socially preferred, even among many African Americans and Mexican Americans. A fairer-skinned person of color is more likely to be perceived as attractive and successful than is a person of darker skin (hooks, 1995). This bias toward Whiteness is spreading as a result of the globalization of Western values, products, and images (Lont, 2001). For example, in Japan and China, women's magazines carry advertisements for products to whiten the skin. Whiteness has become the norm to which all other racial identities are compared, and the comparisons are rarely different and equal.

This central position of Whiteness allows it to become normalized to the extent that most White persons do not even realize their race is a cultural category. They can readily list stereotypes of other races of peoples, such as the expectation that Asians should be smart and that African Americans should be good at sports, but they have difficulty naming a quality that applies to their whole race.

Racism and violence prevention educator Paul Kivel (2002) argues that Whiteness is "a powerful fiction enforced by power and violence. Whiteness is a constantly shifting boundary separating those who are entitled to have certain privileges from those whose exploitation and vulnerability to violence is justified by their not being White" (p. 15). Kivel's approach is consistent with that of communication scholars Thomas Nakayama and Robert Krizek (1999). They identify six cultural norms that form a "strategic rhetoric of whiteness" (p. 96) that maintains White privilege: Whiteness is closely tied to power or status, Whiteness is the norm, Whiteness is natural, Whiteness is indicative of nationality and citizenship, Whiteness is beyond the necessity of racial identity labels, and Whites are descendents of White European ancestry.

When race is conceptualized as natural rather than as culturally created, the conceptualization helps hide the power of this category. In particular, it is important to recognize Whiteness and the strategies of Whiteness in the study of gender, because if one does not, race remains a concern only for non-Whites, and gender, when studied alone, remains implicitly an identity owned solely by Whites.

Throughout this book, we capitalize the words Black and White to clarify that we are referring to racial categories and the politics of skin color rather than to hues on the color wheel. Authors often use other terms, such as *Northern European* and *Euramerican* to refer to Whites and *African Americans* to refer to Blacks. We, too, will use the more specific term *African American* where relevant or when used by an author we are quoting, but we feel that *Northern European* does not clearly indicate the White race, because, as noted, Blacks can also be born in Northern Europe.

NATIONAL IDENTITY

As the foregoing examples illustrate, national identity also is linked to race and ethnicity. Interdisciplinary feminist scholars have begun to explore how national cultural identities are gendered/sexed and how citizens tend to experience their national rights differently based on gender/sex (e.g., Enloe, 1989; Mayer, 2000;

Yuval-Davis, 1997). Theorists posit that "control over access to the benefits of belonging to the nation is virtually always gendered" and that "the ability to define the nation lies mainly with men" (Mayer, 2000, p. 2).

This means that, ideally, national identities should be included in the study of gender/sex. Gender and national identity are related, not just for persons in economically disadvantaged countries or in countries with more visible internal violence, but for U.S. citizens, too (Mayer, 2000; Mohanty, 2003). And it means that gender/sex issues happening around the world *are* extremely relevant to this study. Placing the study of gender in the context of national identity prevents an overgeneralized gender differences approach that assumes universal differences between women and men or, worse yet, assumes that research primarily conducted in the United States represents gendered lives around the world. Gender and ethnic studies scholar Nira Yuval-Davis (1999) explains, "Essentialist notions of difference . . . are very different from the notions of difference promoted by those of us who believe in the importance of incorporating notions of difference into democracy. In the first case notions of difference replace notions of equality—in the second case they encompass it" (p. 131). Including analyses of national identities is an important part of creating a gender diversity approach to the study of gender/sex in communication.

When national identity is included in the study of gender, the focus has usually been on the citizens of economically disadvantaged countries. The influence of the United States as a nation has not been a primary focus in gender in communication research. Instead, most of the research has focused on the one-to-one relationship level, as if it existed independently of national identity.

One way feminist scholars have attempted to talk about the mix of race, gender/sex, economic, and national privilege is to refer to the North and the South. *North* tends to refer to countries in Europe and North America, which tend to share economies developed on the capitalist model. *South* tends to refer to countries in Africa, Central, South America, and South and Southeast Asia, the economies of which are not considered developed according to the capitalist model. *North* and *South* are not meant to refer to geographic areas as much as to economic, racial, and nationality issues. Thus, for example, even though Australia is geographically located in the Southern hemisphere, it is considered part of the North.

The phrase *developed country* often is used as a synonym for *North*, and *developing country* is used as a synonym for *South*. We will try not to use *developed* and *developing* as designators, because they tend to imply that the North is farther along the evolutionary path than the South, and they fail to recognize the limits of economic development (see Esteva, 1992; Latouche, 1993). We use it on occasion, however, for lack of a better term. Similarly, *East* and *West* are used to refer to a mix of ethnicity, religion, culture, and geography. *West* tends to refer to the same nations as does *North*, although the connotation of *West* has less to do with economics and more to do with culture. *West* tends to refer to those nations that are predominantly Christian, capitalist, European, and North American. *East* refers to those countries of Asia and the Middle East that tend to be non-Christian, predominantly Buddhist, Hindu, Muslim, Shinto, Sikh, and Taoist. *Middle East* tends to refer to those countries that are predominantly Muslim. Like North and South, East and West are geographic fictions, as there are no absolute east and west on a globe. After all, Japan and China are west of California.

Socioeconomic Class

Politicians and media refer to social class all the time, but it is difficult to provide a succinct definition of this concept. Usually, people use it to refer to income. In the United States, the upper class is the wealthiest, the lower class is the poorest, and the middle class is somewhere in between. The exact income levels of each change with the economy, and class distinctions are clearly different in other countries. Although there is no set definition of middle class, in the United States it usually refers to those whose pretax income is between $25,000 and $75,000. A person defined as middle class in the United States would be extremely wealthy in other parts of the world where a middle class may not even exist. However, income alone does not adequately define class. Neither do education level nor profession, yet they are a part of the concept. For example, a person with a graduate degree may be making only minimum wage.

One's social class includes predominant cultural ideologies, values, beliefs, and ways of viewing the world. For example, middle-class people in the United States are expected to value affluence and strive for its material markers, such as nice homes, cars, toys, and travel. Many have extreme credit card debt yet may still be considered middle class according to income, education, job, or material possessions.

Perhaps because social class is difficult to define, the field of communication studies has been slow to examine the ways in which it may affect communication. However, research in women's studies and intersectional analyses has shown that social class is important to include in the study of gender. Distinct class experiences influence how people perform gender. For example, historian Glenna R. Matthews (1992) explains how working-class women were able to enter the public realm as labor activists more easily than upper-class women because they were already present in the economic sphere. Economic necessity required them to work and hence to violate the social demands of the time that White women remain domestic. The additional violation of being politically active presented no unique violation of gender/sex expectations. As a result, the history of labor activism is replete with women leaders: Mary Harris "Mother" Jones (Tonn, 1996), Emma Goldman (Kowal, 1996; Solomon, 1987), Voltairine de Cleyre (Palczewski, 1995), and Lucy Parsons (Horwitz, 1998).

Class affects not only how gender is performed but also how gender/sex is perceived. *Classism* is discrimination toward persons of lower socioeconomic class. Men of lower classes face the stereotype that they are less intelligent, immoral, and prone to criminality. Women of lower classes are stereotyped as sexually promiscuous, easily duped, and dependent on state assistance. This discrimination and related stereotypes help maintain separation and oppression (Ehrenreich, 1990), which can be multiplied by oppressions due to racism, sexism, and so on.

In sum, our attention to the intersectionality of identities and oppressions is meant to highlight the way cultural identities and inequalities are embedded in political systems and social structures, not only in people. Philosopher Sandra Harding (1995) explains that sexual and racial inequalities "are not *caused* by prejudice—by individual bad attitudes and false beliefs." In fact, she believes that focusing on "prejudice as the cause of racial (or gender, class, or sexual) inequality tends to lodge responsibility for racism on already economically disadvantaged whites." It keeps the focus on individuals rather than on the larger culture in which their attitudes were created. Clearly, prejudice does contribute to racism, sexism, and other forms of inequity, but Harding argues that people should view inequalities as "fundamentally a political relationship" that manifests itself through cultural strategies or norms that privilege some groups over others (p. 122).

Communication

In contrast to many communication texts that implicitly focus on a sender–receiver model of communication, we focus on the central role communication plays in the construction of meaning and consequently in the construction, maintenance, and change of social identities such as gender/sex. This much broader view of communication lends itself to a more interdisciplinary approach. The social construction approach to communication is why the textbook focuses on "gender *in* communication" rather than on "gender *and* communication" (Taylor, personal correspondence, January 2003). *Communicating Gender Diversity* locates gender *within* the communication process. Instead of examining how gender influences communication, we explore how communication creates gender (Rakow, 1986). This statement is not meant to deny possible biological influences but to put a spotlight on the profound role communication plays *in* the construction of gender/sex identities. To say that gender is socially constructed clarifies that it does not simply exist on the individual level. Rather, it is a *system* of meaning constructed through interactions that govern access to power and resources (Crawford, 1995).

"Communication creates gender" is a simple statement, but it holds other important implications. Individual gender identities and cultural assumptions about gender can and do change over time, and each individual plays a role in maintaining and changing gender constructions. Each person, therefore, can play a role in bringing about gender/sex equality.

A communication studies approach provides a unique vantage point for studying gender/sex. It views gender as dynamic and ever changing, informed by multiple perspectives and experiences. This approach avoids essentializing gender because it treats gender as a verb, not a noun. Gender is a process, not a thing. Accordingly, this book examines how people "do" (West & Zimmerman, 1987) or "perform" (Butler, 1990a) gender.

Thinking of gender as a system of meaning constructed through communication rather than as merely an individual attribute allows one to study the effects of gender on at least three communication levels: individual, interpersonal, and societal (Crawford, 1995, pp. 13–17). At the individual or intrapersonal communication level, persons develop gendered identities through the interactions of biology, personality, and internalized social expectations. To varying degrees, they come to see themselves as masculine, feminine, or both. They internalize messages of privilege, status, inferiority, or subordination and behave in ways that help to create, maintain, or change them.

At the interpersonal communication level, persons influence each other's gender identities through their interactions with each other. For example, parents who treat young children in stereotypical gendered ways, such as protecting girls and pushing boys, can influence the development of their children's gender identities. Such treatment can encourage self-fulfilling prophecies about gender, self-confidence, physical ability, and more.

In the United States, at the societal level, White men as a social group still dominate most social institutions, such as business, politics, law, health, and academics. Although the statistics are changing, the reason for the domination is not that more White men are in these fields (they are not). Rather, the norms of these fields tend to be based on White, masculine values. This generally privileges the White men who perform their gender in a way that fits the norms of such masculinity. It does not mean that all individual White men intentionally oppress others. Gender/sex implications are contained within the systems or structures. This is why we dedicate the second half of the textbook to a close analysis of the ways in which primary social institutions contribute to the construction of gender/sex—both in terms of imposing gender expectations and in terms of liberating persons from them.

Gender identity and experiences are not affected by one of these three communication levels at a time; rather, one experiences them simultaneously. For example, rape is a crime of power and domination. A person who is attacked experiences the crime on all three levels. It is an attack on the individual, it is an attack on an interpersonal level, and it is an attack that tends to happen to women because of the social system of masculine domination and communication forms that normalize sexual violence. The phrase from the 1960s women's movement, "The personal is political," refers to this interaction of levels. What happens to people on a personal level is inherently tied to social norms supported by political structures.

Rhetoric. As we examine the societal level and the larger discourse formations that happen there, an understanding of rhetoric is essential. The study of rhetoric enables explorations of how gender/sex influences the way individuals engage in public rhetoric and how public rhetoric genders/sexes individuals. Aristotle defined *rhetoric* as the discovery of the available means of persuasion in any given situation. Other scholars have advanced more complex definitions (Campbell & Burkholder, 1997). Typically, rhetoric is composed of complete thoughts with the sentence as the basic unit; it is planned and structured discourse, not random comment. Its focus tends to be on solving problems. The substance of rhetoric is not facts but the interpretation, elaboration, and evaluation of data. Rhetoric does more than transmit information; it is addressed to others in order to provide practical solutions. Finally, rhetoric is poetic. It plays a ritualistic or aesthetic role, displaying dramatic or emotive qualities that may influence others. More recently, scholars have begun to study visual rhetoric and body rhetoric, noting the ways that visual units and the body function like verbal units (Palczewski, 2002). This is useful in the examination of nonverbal contributors in gender/sex construction. Ultimately, we want to help you understand how public rhetoric about gender/sex influences the way each person expresses her or his gender/sex (Sloop, 2004). Throughout this description, note that we have been defining the practice of rhetoric; however, the term *rhetoric* also is used to refer to the study of rhetoric. *Rhetor* refers to one who uses rhetoric, and *rhetorician* tends to refer to one who studies rhetoric.

The most complete way to study gender in communication is to try to keep all three of these levels—individual, interpersonal, and societal or public—in mind. Doing so makes it easier to recognize that the gender/sex norms that influence individual and interpersonal communication also influence the range of rhetorical choices available to people giving public speeches. Similarly, the way politicians or popular culture stars speak may influence one's expectations of how people in daily lives will interact. The way a person talks influences the ways the person and others are gendered/sexed. This text examines ways in which different communication contexts and levels create, maintain, and change gender/sex in people's lives. This multilevel approach also helps one avoid the trap of essentializing gender/sex communication.

CONTRADICTION

Another tool that will help render a more complex and realistic view of gender/sex is the concept of contradiction. *Contradiction* refers to the tensions commonly present in one's communication, identity, relations with others, and relations to the larger culture. It is part of what makes these dynamic and ever changing. Communication scholars and psychologists have long recognized that individuals, relationships, and the larger society are filled with apparent contradictions or inconsistencies in their values, behaviors, beliefs, identities, and so forth. This does not mean that people are necessarily aware of the contradictions, or that individuals would agree with what outsiders might label contradictory. It means that humans are amazingly complex, resilient beings and that social life is largely about coping with, balancing, or redefining apparent contradictions. Strategies for coping with contradiction are not necessarily about overt efforts to resist oppressive forces such as society's gender/sex expectations. Such strategies are more commonly about "attempts to work within perceived or internalized structural constraints," not attempts to resist them (Bloustien, 2003, p. 12). Austrailian communication scholar Gerry Bloustien (2003), in an ethnographic study with 10 young women, found they used play as a strategy to try out seemingly contradictory images of femininity and masculinity to find ones that worked for them.

The idea that we need to recognize contradictions as we study gender/sex in communication came to the forefront of our thinking through the writing of U.S. third-wave feminists (e.g., Dicker & Piepmeier, 2003). Third-wave feminism generally refers to feminists born in the 1960s and 1970s. The concept of contradiction has helped many younger people more comfortably place themselves in the feminist movement. The classic illustrations of people embracing contradiction are young women wearing baby-doll dresses and combat boots and young goth men wearing makeup, dyed hair, and black leather pants with chains; these contradictory symbols represent how they might see themselves as capable of being feminine or masculine *and* stylish warriors.

Contradiction emphasizes how people live with multiple (apparent) inconsistencies contained in their singular, coherent bodies. Because intersecting identities affect people simultaneously, it is understandable that these complex, multiple identities may at times be in tension with each other. Being masculine may at times conflict with being homosexual or bisexual, which may conflict with being of Japanese descent, and so on. Yet, one person's identity can contain these contradictions.

We include contradiction as a part of our critical vocabulary because it resonates with many related concepts and goals in our study of gender/sex in communication. First, it encourages readers to remember that no group of people is homogeneous. Thus, it can help prevent generalizations such as "men do this" and "women do that." Second, it reminds readers that life is about choices, even if these choices are somewhat limited by socialization influences and cultural taboos. Everyone faces contradictions in seeking to balance the many life tensions related to these choices. In the study of gender in communication, the concept of contradiction makes visible the diverse rhetorical choices people make when faced with similar dilemmas. The notion of contradiction reminds one of the range of choices available, as well as the pressures of social norms and the need to be tolerant of the variety of choices others make.

Third, the concept of contradiction and the related choices involved can help create spaces for a variety of ways of living and a diversity of identities. This is especially important for persons in oppressed and marginalized groups. When cultures value contradiction and complexity, persons no longer have to fully subscribe to the way of life of the dominant culture. They can carve out their own ways of living. For example, immigrant women and men do not have to fully assimilate a dominant culture's notion of gender/sex; they can create identities based on the contradictions of the cultures they left and the ones they have joined.

Fourth, you will find the concept of contradiction present at every level of communication. Recognizing this can be personally and professionally liberating. It is present at the intrapersonal level, defining the self. For example, psychologists note that the seemingly contradictory desires for agency (self-achievement and independence) and communion (forming connections with others) exist in all people. These needs are not reserved only for masculine or feminine persons as social stereotypes suggest. Both are necessary for good mental health (Helgeson, 1994).

Contradiction is present at the interpersonal level, as communication scholars Leslie Baxter and Barbara Montgomery (1996) make clear in their popular dialectic tensions theory. The theory suggests that relationships consist of tensions between seemingly opposite interpersonal needs, such as autonomy/connection and desires for openness/closedness in self-disclosure. It is through communication that people successfully or unsuccessfully negotiate these tensions, hopefully to their mutual satisfaction.

Contradiction is present at the group and cultural levels as well, which is one reason why generalized statements describing an entire group of people, such as a nation or even a family, are stereotypes at best. To help recognize this limitation, when we make statements about the values of a given culture in this textbook, we refer to *predominant* cultural values rather than assuming that such values are true for all. In fact, because cultures—like communication, relationships, and people—are always evolving, tensions and contradictions are necessarily present. Therefore, to study a culture completely, one must study all groups and all aspects of the contradictions at the same time (Martin & Nakayama, 2004). These should not be studied separately. One cannot fully understand the concept of femininity without studying the concept of masculinity, and one cannot study gender within a specific community, such as Mexican American immigrants to the United States, without taking into consideration the predominant White community in which they try to coexist.

Fifth, revealing contradictions can be an important step toward personal and group survival. It can reveal ways people can become trapped within seemingly inconsistent truths, and it can identify coping strategies. Contradictions can create double binds that may be harmful to mental health; they can also put persons in subordinate positions in interpersonal relations and in dominant cultures (Taylor & Perry, 2001).

Communication researchers Valerie Renegar and Stacey Sowards (2003) eloquently explain that an analysis of contradiction can create

> a coherent, unifying, ironic feminist rhetorical theory that demonstrates the importance of language and rhetoric, eliminating pain and humiliation from our language, demanding solidarity among all sorts of humans, highlighting social hope and optimism, and providing a theory that tolerates, mediates, respects, and encourages differences. (p. 332)

By studying contradiction, we are not reverting to a binary way of thinking about gender/sex in communication but rather attempting to make other ways of thinking more visible.

Systems of Hierarchy

This is the last and broadest level of analysis necessary for our critical gender/sex lenses. The phrase *systems of hierarchy* refers to our earlier discussion that gender/sex is not simply located within individuals but exists within the larger predominant culture. Gender/sex, together with race, class, sexual orientation, and other cultural identities, lives in the ideology, norms, laws, worldview, traditions, popular culture, and social institutions that sustain a society. The institutionalized nature of these systems of hierarchy makes their influence more implicit and pervasive, as we discuss in Part II of this book.

CULTURE

Gender must be studied in its specific cultural contexts in order to best understand the unique gender identities created there. Culture is difficult to define because it is everywhere and includes so many things. Culture is composed of conceptions of knowledge, experiences, beliefs, values, attitudes, meanings, hierarchies, religions, time, social roles, worldviews, land, and even the material possessions or artifacts acquired by a group of people. More simply, it is "learned patterns of behavior and attitudes shared by a group of people" (Martin & Nakayama, 2004, p. 3). Together, the primary function of culture is to create shared meanings, shared views of the world, and a group identity. Through these characteristics, cultures also serve to help reduce uncertainty and chaos largely by socializing their members to behave in prescribed ways. Cultures can exist on many levels, in families, neighborhoods, towns and cities, ethnic and racial groups, religious groups, regions of a country, and nations.

All this is not to suggest that there is one uniform cultural view for any group of people. Rather, within a given larger culture there are predominant views and predominant social groups, as well as contested, or minority, views and groups. Intercultural communication researchers Judith Martin and Thomas Nakayama argue that cultures are by nature "contested zones" (2004, p. 58). That is, there are multiple power inequalities within a given culture, including gender/sex.

HEGEMONY

The term *hegemony* designates the systems of hierarchy maintained by the predominant social group's ideology that comes to dominate other social groups (Gramsci, Rosenthal, & Rosengarten, 1993). Philosopher Rosemary Hennessy (1995) explains that hegemony is not a form of power that controls through overt violence; rather, it controls subtly by determining what makes sense: "Hegemony is the process whereby the interests of a ruling group come to dominate by establishing the common sense, that is, those values, beliefs, and knowledges that go without saying" (pp. 145–146). People willingly belong to cultures for the protection and order those cultures provide, even though predominant cultural ideology may control them in some ways. By following society's norms of behavior, members uphold the culture's ideology.

Cultural ideology refers to the ideas, values, beliefs, perceptions, and understandings that are known to members of a society and that guide their behaviors. For example, capitalism is not only an economic system but also a dominant ideology in Western culture. This ideology undergirds the values and behaviors that support competition, individualism, consumerism, status, money, and power. This does not mean that every person in Western culture embraces such ideology, but it does explain the predominant system and culture in which all members must try to survive. Stuart Hall, a British scholar in cultural studies, says that dominant cultural ideology influences how we come to perceive reality (1989).

POWER

The word *power* can simply mean "the ability to get things done" (Kramarae & Treichler, 1992, p. 351). It is not an innately evil concept. However, feminist theorists make an important distinction between "power to" and "power over"

(Freeman & Bourque, 2001, pp. 10–11). *Power to* is the ability to get things done that do not infringe on others' rights and may actually lead to the emancipation of others. *Power over* refers to coercive misuses of power. If one is in a position of *power over* others, then one can dominate and coerce others and in the process subordinate or oppress them. If one lacks *power over*, one is more likely to be in a subordinate position. The interesting point is that to respond to any instance of *power over*, or to get out of a situation in which one is suppressed by those who have *power over*, one needs *power to*.

Power is a social phenomenon. People have power in relationship to others. Social power is embedded in the communicative negotiations of gender/sex, race, class, sexual orientation, and other identities. For each of these social groups, multiple differences are socially created. The important point repeated throughout this text is that differences are rarely constructed equally. Rather, the groups that have more say about the construction are privileged over others. Thus, in the study of gender/sex in communication, one must include the concept of power and related concepts such as domination, subordination, oppression and privilege, as well as responses to power such as accommodation, individual empowerment, resistance, and group emancipation. Through communication, people, groups, and social structures can dominate and empower others and themselves.

Studying power does not mean blaming individuals. Power can exist at the interpersonal level in one's ability to control or dominate others in the negotiation of personal or professional relationships (Weber, 1947). More important, power is systemic. You cannot see power. It is usually implicit or sanctioned by cultural norms and ideology. It exists at multiple levels in society at one time. Thus, it is difficult to study, and yet the implications of power are omnipresent. It can exist at the larger institutional level, such as in the norms of competition for giant corporations, in power differences ascribed according to social categories that oppress some groups to benefit other groups, and in the general hegemonic relations the dominant culture has with individuals (Foucault, 1980).

People who hold social power possess social privilege. *Privileges* are unearned freedoms or opportunities. Often, privileges are unconscious and unmarked. They are socialized through cultural hegemony, which makes them easy to deny and more resistant to change. Most people enjoy some degree or type of privilege. U.S. citizens enjoy certain freedoms that they may take for granted but that those in countries with dictatorships or military regimes cannot. At a more personal level, when violence prevention educator Jackson Katz asks men in his workshops what they do to prepare to walk alone on campus at night, most of them respond with an unknowing stare. When he asks women this question, they readily offer several strategies they use to keep safe, such as phoning roommates ahead to tell them they are leaving, carrying their keys pointed out between their fingers as a weapon against would-be attackers, or looking in their cars before they open the doors (see Katz, 2003). Gay, lesbian, bisexual, and transgendered persons often try to pass as straight to avoid possible verbal or physical violence. Heterosexuals usually do not have to consider such acts. Where there is privilege, there is unspoken power and the ability to misuse that power to oppress others.

Violence. We cannot adequately study gender communication without addressing abuses of power manifested in psychological or physical violence. Communication studies scholar Robert Hopper (2003) writes: "There is one undeniable sex difference in social behavior: men sexually harass, assault, and rape women, whereas women rarely do comparable acts" (p. 55). Hopper proceeds to note that cultural norms regarding flirting, men as sexual aggressors, and masculinity "bear a troubling relationship" to violence (p. 55).

We note this troubling relationship to highlight how many other gendered social practices contribute to a culture that normalizes the violence committed by many men against many women, feminine people, and persons perceived as homosexual. These practices include the seemingly innocent standard that girls and women should be more polite, ladylike, and willing to smile, and that they should take sexist remarks, street calls, and whistles as innocent jokes or flattery whether they like it or not (Kramarae, 1992). Those who speak up risk criticism or physical retaliation. Such gendered social practices also include the expectation that all men should be aggressive, sexually active, and unemotional or risk abuse of some kind.

Sociologist Charlene Muehlenhard and associates point out that social pressures can be coercive and that *coercion* is violence. People who are coerced feel they have no choice but to comply, such as when married persons and young teens have sexual relations even though they do not want to (Muehlenhard, Goggins, Jones, & Satterfield, 1991). The coercion can be verbal or nonverbal, direct or indirect. Dutch linguist Teun van Dijk (1995) notes that talk is not the alternative to physical force; it, too, can be violent insofar as "discourse may enact, cause, promote, defend, instigate, and legitimate violence" (p. 307).

A tool that helps conceptualize the relationships between coercive gendered norms and violence is what feminist communication scholars Cheris Kramarae (1992) and Elizabeth Arveda Kissling (1991) call a *violence continuum*. They suggest viewing all forms of such gendered/sexed practices and the degree of violence within each of them on a continuum. By locating seemingly innocent gendered norms (such as that men should be virile and that women should play hard to get) on a common line with more overt forms of violence (such as rape and physical abuse), the observer is better able to see that such social practices create a culture in which gendered/sexed violence becomes normalized. The violence continuum reveals that violence can be overt or covert; intentional or unintentional; and verbal, emotional, or physical. The connections between all forms of violence expose that the responsibility for violence lies not just in the individual violator but in all who maintain the cultural ideology and structure.

Putting It All Together

Hopefully, we have demonstrated why we must go beyond a differences approach to the study of gender/sex in this text. As anthropologist Nancy Henley and communication scholar Cheris Kramarae (1991) write, "Most importantly, cultural difference does not exist within a political vacuum; rather, the strength of difference, the types of difference, the values applied to different forms, the dominance of certain forms—all are shaped by the context " (p. 40). When two people communicate, there are never just two parties present in the interaction, but multiple social groups are represented, such as race, class, and gender, each with varying degrees of privilege and oppression. We seek to study gender/sex in communication in a more dynamic way that allows for multidimensional, contradictory, and simultaneous influences. We seek to recognize the inherent, potentially political nature of gender/sex in communication.

The inclusion of power issues in the study of gender is not a radical new idea. Countless researchers in gender in communication have included similar discussions of power in scholarly books and articles (Eckert & McConnell-Ginet, 1992), but communication textbooks, like popular relationship books, often downplay this issue. Why? Perhaps it is an effort not to offend some readers or to avoid the discomfort people feel when inequalities are discussed and privileges are exposed.

To us, the risk is necessary. Learning comes from taking risks and allowing oneself to receive and consider information that may be inconsistent with one's values or beliefs (Freire, 1972; hooks, 1994). If you reflect on times in your life when you learned the most, you will know what we mean. Leaving home for the first time, going away to college, getting a job, having a child, going to another country, entering a committed relationship or leaving one all involve risk, but the potential rewards of self-understanding and analytical skills are well worth it. Power is central to explaining social realities that a focus on gender differences alone cannot, and it helps to construct a more realistic, complex picture of gender/sex dynamics that has relevance across cultures.

As we examine power and privilege issues and challenge common assumptions about gender/sex throughout the book, we offer one additional tool useful in constructing a critical gendered/sexed lens, *reflexivity*. It is a research analysis method used by qualitative and feminist researchers. Ethnographer Bud Goodall (2000) provides an excellent definition: "To be reflective means to turn back on our self the lens through which we are interpreting the world" (p. 137). Reflexivity encourages one to pay attention to, value, and critically analyze subjective (positive or negative) reactions to a topic of study to help reveal further personal and academic insights and to produce more ethical, rigorous conclusions. Reflexivity encourages open examination of your relationship to what you are studying. Such efforts can be informative and can promote self-growth.

In many ways, this textbook is a "how to" book. It explains *how* to study gender/sex more than it explains what already has been discovered in gender/sex research (although we'll do a good bit of that as well). Given that the discipline's understandings and people's performances of gender/sex continually evolve, it is more important to know how to read, hear, understand, and critique gender in communication than it is to know what has already been discovered. Our goal is not to tell you the way things are, for the state of knowledge changes. Instead, our goal is to teach you *how* to see *why* things are the way they are. That way, you can consciously choose to embrace that which is liberatory and work against that which denies the full measure of your wonderfully unique, distinct, and idiosyncratic humanity.

CHAPTER 2

Alternative Approaches to Understanding Gender/Sex

T hus far, we have addressed why it is important to study gender/sex in communication from an interdisciplinary and multilevel perspective (individual, interpersonal, and societal) to gain the most comprehensive, informed view. In this chapter, we examine the primary approaches used in the study of gender/sex. The purpose of doing so is threefold: (1) to provide a more comprehensive view of the topic, (2) to critically identify researchers' and laypeople's underlying assumptions, and (3) to assist in developing a more informed gendered lens for the study of communication. Before one can construct a more critical gendered lens, one must first examine one's current gendered "baggage"—one's assumptions—and better understand the underlying premises of alternative approaches.

By *approach,* we mean the worldview a researcher applies as she or he develops knowledge on a topic. This includes how the researcher believes knowledge is best created, whether through scientific laboratory methods of data collection, through rhetorical examinations of speakers' verbal and nonverbal choices, or through ethnographic work in which a researcher lives in a specific culture to attempt to learn how members define gender identities. This worldview also includes the theories a researcher develops to explain gender/sex–related phenomena and the underlying assumptions about the origins of gender/sex.

In its simplest form, a theory is only an attempt to explain something. A theory is not an absolute truth but an argument to see, order, and explain the world in a particular way. Whether you realize it or not, you probably have a theory about every aspect of your life, including gender/sex identities in communication. The primary difference between everyday theories created for one's own benefit and academic theories is a matter of formality and rigor. Academic theories generally are expected to be systematically developed and tested.

To visualize how a research approach influences knowledge construction, it is helpful to think of the research process as circular. At their inception, theories and research are based on hunches and assumptions influenced by personal and social values (Caplan & Caplan, 1999). The worldview and theories researchers choose influence the types of research questions and methods they select; these in turn influence interpretations of the results, which then affirm, extend, or disprove the original theory and worldview. If research is found to confirm an assumption, the original assumption will likely go unchecked.

No theoretical approach can be fully inclusive. The approach chosen necessarily causes a person to focus on one aspect of the topic while at least momentarily ignoring other aspects. Thus, theories and research methods are persuasive. They exhort persons to direct their attention in one way rather than another. When researchers construct research approaches, they frame the way people think about a particular topic. Additionally, the act of observing alters the reality being observed. As recent work in the rhetoric of science demonstrates, science itself is political, and the language involved in the description of scientific findings is rhetorical.

The power of researchers' approaches is heightened by the fact that people tend to assume that researchers are authorities and thus may not question their underlying assumptions. We are *not* suggesting that researchers intentionally attempt to mislead. Instead, we want to make clear that all researchers (including us) are products of their cultures. Cultural influences that generate bias lead researchers to find certain topics important, such as detailing how women and men, Blacks and Whites, gays and straights *differ,* rather than detailing similarities or acknowledging power differences and related inequalities.

Generally speaking, researchers across academic disciplines seem to subscribe to three basic worldviews or beliefs about how knowledge is constructed (West & Turner, 2004). The first is called an *empirical* or *positivist* worldview. This is the view most used in the physical sciences and the one adapted initially by researchers in the social sciences, such as communication scholars studying gender/sex. Positivism is the belief that truth is objective, exists prior to the researchers' efforts, and thus can be discovered; knowledge is not created. A theory's goal is to explain and predict behaviors, and the research methods used focus on controlling possible subjective influences, using laboratory experiments and surveys, and seeking to make larger generalizations through the use of statistical analyses where truths are generated based on laws of probability. Although the other two views described next are different from the empirical view, this scientific way of knowing has been predominant in U.S. culture and has influenced the other two views in subtle ways. The views are not as independent as they might seem, and increasingly researchers are realizing the value of combining approaches.

The second worldview is called an *interpretive* or *humanistic* worldview. This view is most used in the social sciences and humanities by researchers who believe that knowledge or truth is not objective but can be known only through people's perceptions. Therefore, knowledge is by nature subjective, and people play an active role in the creation of what they come to see as truth. The goal of theory and research methods is not to predict or to control as much as to describe and understand the perceptions of the people in the study. Thus, researchers in this worldview use more qualitative research methods, such as in-depth interviews, ethnography, analysis of conversations, textual criticism, and field observation, which better reveal the unique influences of context.

The third worldview is called *critical studies* or *cultural criticism*. This is the worldview of knowledge construction to which your authors most subscribe. It is the view that researchers do not leave their personal politics at the library or laboratory door. Rather, knowledge is by nature subjective and political. Knowledge is constructed in the context of predominant cultural ideology and beliefs. Research results that become accepted as *facts* often are accepted because they fit predominant cultural beliefs. The methods used in this worldview may vary but are probably most closely aligned with those of the interpretive and humanistic view, in which qualitative and critical methods are used more frequently.

Based on these worldviews of knowledge construction, the current approaches to gender/sex in communication generally fall into three areas: biological (empirical worldview), psychological (empirical and/or critical worldviews), and cultural (interpretative and/or critical worldviews). Those who locate biology as the primary determinant of gender/sex in communication are likely to see gender differences as a natural consequence of differences in one's sex genitals, hormones, and chromosomes. They tend to use quantitative approaches to conduct research. Those who subscribe to a psychological perspective are likely to see gendered communication as influenced by one's personality development, in which the experiences of early childhood leave a strong and fairly permanent imprint on one's development of a feminine and/or masculine identity. Their worldview also turns to an empirical view of knowledge, although more recent feminist work has turned a critical lens on psychology. Those who subscribe to a cultural/critical perspective are likely to see gendered communication as constructed by one's interpersonal interactions in the context of larger societal influences such as White privilege, patriarchal culture, language structures, and stereotypes about masculinity and femininity. Their worldview encourages an interpretive and/or critical focus on how researchers construct and influence what counts as knowledge.

We should caution you that these three approaches are not so distinct in actual practice, and it is difficult to separate the three influences from one another (Caplan & Caplan, 1999; Fausto-Sterling, 1992). If you are like most people, your views of gender are probably influenced by a combination of them. Some gender phenomena do seem strongly influenced by psychological gender/sex roles, some by broader social influences and institutions, and some by biology. However, we want to make clear that you should be wary whenever biology is presented as absolute or immutable. Throughout history, appeals to biology have been used to justify unequal treatment of women, Native Americans, African Americans, and others. Also, just because scientists may determine that a particular gender attribute is influenced by biology, it does not mean they know how to value that gender attribute; data are just data until people imbue them with meaning.

In this chapter, we review these three approaches. At the end of each, we provide examples of how the approach informs historical and contemporary understandings of women's and men's rhetoric. The purpose of these examples is to demonstrate how understanding the particular approach can help readers identify and examine the underlying assumptions and worldviews governing speech norms and rhetorical theory. The examples help document the influence of the approach on communicators' lives and practices. They also explain why the fields of biology, psychology, anthropology, sociology, and others matter in the examination of gender/sex in communication.

Given that it is difficult to separate the variety of influences on gender/sex in communication, we embrace a multidetermined social context approach (Henley & Kramarae, 1991). This approach suggests that researchers stop fighting over which theory is the best and instead recognize the value of alternative views and move on to examining the social consequences of gendered/sexed lives. Research approaches do not have to compete with each other; they may complement each other and together provide a wider perspective on the topic.

Biological Approaches

When you read research, theories, religious doctrine, or popular literature that infers that the feminine/masculine gender binary is naturally derived from sex, and places an emphasis on differences, the underlying assumption of the author is likely *biological determinism.* This does not necessarily mean that the author completely denies any psychological or cultural influences, but the author does attribute primary causation to genetics, and the assumption of two opposing sexes leads to an emphasis on two opposing genders (Fausto-Sterling, 1992; Tavris, 1992). Most of this research focuses on three areas of difference: chromosomes, hormones and genitalia, and brain development.

Chromosomes

The sex of a fetus is determined by its chromosomes. Something you rarely hear about is how males' and females' chromosomes are more alike than different. Humans have 23 pairs of chromosomes; males and females share 22 of 23 of the pairs. Furthermore, a fetus's sex is undifferentiated until the sixth week of gestation. Until the seventh week, all XX and XY fetuses are identical (Carroll, 2005; Strong, DeVault, & Sayad, 1999). You may recall from biology classes that generally males and females have an X chromosome, but only males have a Y chromosome. The XY pair is what determines a male child. Females generally are XX. We say "generally" because, although discussions of sex do not usually recognize variations beyond this, there are persons who have sex chromosome combinations of XO, XXX, XXY, or XYY. In all cases, if a Y chromosome exists, the child is usually identified as male. As discussed in Chapter 1, the presence of intersex persons proves there are more than two sexes.

Although chromosomes may determine the sex of the person, the question ✳
remains, can the sex chromosome determine one's gender identity? Research thus far "gay
has not established this link. There is, however, research associating maleness with gene"?
greater physical strength. It is the Y chromosome that develops variances in internal
and external sex organs and differences in fatty tissue. The differences in body fat
translate into differences in muscle mass, with men generally having less fat and
greater capacity for muscle strength. Men also tend to have greater strength because
they have a larger capacity for oxygen, lower resting heart rate, higher blood pressure,
and the ability to recover from physical activity more quickly (Stockard & Johnson,
1980). Women's body fat averages about 10% higher than men's (Bailey & Bishop,
2001). On the question of physical endurance, sex differences become less clear.
Women's child-bearing abilities often are pointed to as an example of extreme
endurance. Also, male fetuses have more developmental difficulties and birth defects,
their deliveries average an hour longer, and the death rate of male fetuses is higher
than that of female fetuses (Davis, Gottlieb, & Stampnitzky, 1998; McLoughlin,
Shryer, Goode, & McAuliffe, 1988). Women also tend to live longer than men, but
this difference may be lessening as more women engage in risk-taking behaviors such
as cigarette smoking (Charchar, 2003).

How are genitalia related to gender identities? The answer may have more to
do with society's portrayal of sexuality and genitalia than with any actual genital
functions. Long before psychologist Sigmund Freud celebrated the male penis as
a sign of strength and power, every walk of life, from artists, journalists, and historians to religious leaders, heralded the penis as an outward sign of men's virility and right to assert their strength over others. The virile penis has become an
essential characteristic of masculinity. Diane Ivy and Phil Backlund (2004), communication studies specialists in gender, suggest that the more obvious, external
nature of males' sex organs makes the strength of it more overt than females'
less overt sex organ: "Social interpretations of women's sexual organs identify
women as reactors, receivers, followers, and beneficiaries of men's decisions"
(p. 64).

Although similarities exist between the penis and the clitoris, the comparison is
not perfect: No urethra runs through a woman's clitoris. Pulitzer Prize–winning
science author Natalie Angier notes, "The clitoris is simply a bundle of nerves: 8,000
nerve fibers, to be precise. That's a higher concentration of nerve fibers than is found
anywhere else on the body, including the fingertips, lips, and tongue, and it is twice
the number in the penis" (1999, pp. 63–64). Remember, scientific fact means little
until people attach meaning to it through symbol use. So, is a woman's clitoris
smaller than a man's penis? In terms of external exposed tissue, yes. But in terms of
its function as a pleasure organ, is a clitoris smaller? Not if you measure size by the
number of nerve endings. The meaning of sexual organs is rhetorically constructed.

Not surprisingly, reproduction also commonly influences conceptions of gender;
it seems as though she who births also must give care. Ivy and Backlund (2004)
argue, "The reproductive capabilities of men and women have more profound social
translations than any other biological property or function" (p. 64). The fact that

women bear children has led them to be associated with nurturing and caregiving. Breast-feeding alone extends that role beyond the birth of the infant. Males' provision of sperm to the egg in order to create an embryo is seen as virile and in control. To demonstrate how much reproduction affects gender, Ivy and Backlund suggest that traditional gender roles likely would not have been the same had the reproductive process been reversed. Imagine a world in which men bear children.

Hormones

Hormones affect sex distinctions as early as seven weeks after conception. They are related to chromosomal differences. If the fetus has a Y chromosome, it will produce an abundance of androgens, hormones that then develop the internal and external sex organs of males. Fetuses with no Y chromosome will only produce a small amount of androgens and will develop genitalia more consistent with female sex organs. It is commonly assumed there are clear distinctions in female and male hormones, but this assumption is false. To label estrogen and progesterone as strictly female and androgens and testosterone as purely male is to maintain a false dichotomy. Rather, they all exist in human beings but to varying degrees within and across the sexes (Caplan & Caplan, 1999). Some women produce more testosterone than some biological men, and some men produce more estrogen than some biological women.

Hormones affect people throughout their lives. At puberty, testosterone stimulates the development of lower voices, increased body hair, and increased sex drive, and the development of sex organs for females as well as males (Gadpaille, 1975). Higher levels of testosterone often are thought to explain why many men tend to exhibit less nurturing and are physically and sexually aggressive. Testosterone has been linked to attempts to dominate, gain power over others, and express anger (Schwartz & Cellini, 1995). In a quantitative study of 4,462 male military veterans, James Dabbs and Robin Morris (1990) found that unusually high levels of testosterone were associated with delinquency, drug use, multiple sex partners, conduct disorders, abusiveness, and violence. Other research suggests that young female and young male children alike show signs of aggressiveness. As children learn what is expected of them, girls ease off the aggressiveness, and boys demonstrate more of it (A. Campbell, 1993). In an analysis of research on sex aggression and hormones, medical science professor Anne Fausto-Sterling (1992) found inconsistent results. Hormones alone cannot explain aggressive behavior.

Estrogen stimulates menstrual cycles and related changes for most women. Prior to the groundbreaking research by Estelle Ramey (1976) linking many women's emotional swings to hormonal cycle changes, the medical profession largely attributed women's menstrual discomforts to hypochondria. Additional work substantiates many women's physiological struggles with menopause (Fausto-Sterling, 1992). Substantial research confirms that many women's emotional and physical pains are physiologically induced by hormonal fluctuations during menstrual cycles, but the stereotype that all women are emotional time bombs and physically diseased is false. Not all women suffer with what is called premenstrual syndrome (PMS) or difficult menopause. Those who do are not "sick"; they are generally experiencing normal biological processes (Tavris, 1992).

Brain Development

Brain structure has been examined for sex and gender differences. Some evidence indicates that females and males tend to specialize in one hemisphere of the brain, although they each use both hemispheres. For most people, the left hemisphere is responsible for language skills, abstract thought development, and linear, logical, mathematic abilities. The right hemisphere is responsible for more holistic and intuitive thinking, artistic activity, nonverbal processing, and spatial ability. Some biologists argue that men tend to specialize in the left hemisphere and develop stronger skills tied to it, such as the traditional masculine abilities in mechanical processes, and women tend to specialize in the right hemisphere and develop stronger abilities tied to it, such as the traditional feminine relationship skills and intuition. Interestingly, however, over the years, researchers have bounced back and forth regarding which hemisphere of the brain accounts for which gender/sex (Tavris, 1992), suggesting that the conclusions are flawed.

Furthermore, some argue that women tend to be better at using both sides of the brain because the corpus callosum, which bridges the two hemispheres, is larger in women. This has been used to explain many women's tendency toward stronger language skills (actually a left hemisphere specialty), the ability to identify others' emotions more quickly (Begley & Murr, 1995), and the ability to use both hemispheres for listening. However, neurons travel quickly across the two hemispheres regardless of the size of the corpus callosum. Psychologist David Meyers (2004) cautions against assuming that people use only one hemisphere for individual tasks. Instead, they almost always use both hemispheres because there is a constant exchange of information. Social psychologist Carol Tavris (1992) writes, "The two hemispheres of the brain do have different specialties, but it is far too simple-minded (so to speak) to assume that human abilities clump up in opposing bunches" (p. 49). The two hemispheres have the ability to compensate for each other and to cooperate. For example, if one hemisphere is damaged, the other hemisphere takes over its tasks. This demonstrates that both sides have the neurological ability to perform the other side's tasks. This plasticity decreases with age, but it never disappears. The two hemispheres are interdependent (Meyers, 2004).

Researchers have found more consistent links between sex differences and responses to mental disorders, stress, hormones, and memory (Cahill, 2005). These findings have raised awareness that research and medical treatment procedures performed on men cannot be generalized to all women or even to all men. Additionally, the National Academy of Sciences reports that sexual orientation may be influenced by brain differences. A band of fibers called the anterior commissure, which connects brain hemispheres, tends to be larger in gay men than in heterosexual women and men (Elias, 1992). Other researchers have found that twins raised apart tend to have the same sexual orientation (Whitam, Diamond, &

Martin, 1993), and lesbians are consistently different from heterosexual women in self-reported sexual orientations across cultures (Whitam, Daskalos, Sobolewski, & Padilla, 1998). Yet, we do not know whether the fiber band's size is affected by use and whether it can change. In addition, cognitive researcher William Byne (2005) points out that quantitative size differences alone cannot tell about qualitative differences in sexual orientation.

Although some evidence of biological influences exists, the links to gender are not as simple as some might think. Imagine trying to explain that a person's external genitalia determines whether she or he will be more skilled working under the hood of a car or cooking in the kitchen. Ultimately, biology alone cannot determine gender identities, and it certainly cannot predict gendered communication. Otherwise, all woman and all men in all cultures and all countries across the world would express masculine and feminine gender in identical ways. Biological links to gender are probably more realistically described as influences rather than as sole or direct causes (Reiss, 2000). Currently, the influence of biology is more correctly located in how assumptions about it continue to prescribe expectations for women's and men's communication activities.

Rhetorical Implications, Historic

Historically, women's biological differences were used to justify their exclusion from the public sphere. Rhetoric professor Karlyn Kohrs Campbell (1989) summarizes the arguments used in the early 1900s when women's brain size was used to prove that women were incapable of engaging in the "rational deliberation required in politics and business":

> Moreover, their smaller, and hence more delicate and excitable, nerves could not withstand the pressures of public debate or the marketplace. Menarche, the onset of menstruation, was viewed as a physical cataclysm that rendered women unfit for normal activity. (Vol. 1, p. 11)

In fact, some argued that educating women and allowing them to advocate in public would atrophy their wombs, "since the blood needed to sustain development of the ovaries and womb would be diverted to the brain" (p. 12).

In addition, women's supposed greater physical weakness was used as a justification to deny them suffrage rights. Interestingly, Black women were not even considered, but if one accepts the argument about to be described, then slave women most certainly should have had the right to vote, for they had demonstrated physical strength. Aileen S. Kraditor's (1965) history of the suffrage movement outlines the argument linking physical power to voting rights:

> If women were to vote . . . half the electorate would be incapable of enforcing its mandate and vicious elements would be encouraged to resort to violence. A vote was not simply the registering of an opinion; it was a demand and consequently

would be meaningless unless exercised only by the muscular portion of the community. (p. 28)

The New York Association Opposed to Woman Suffrage, in a circa 1910 statement presented to both houses of the U.S. Congress, noted, "To extend the suffrage to women would be to introduce into the electorate a vast non-combatant party, incapable of enforcing its own rule" (in Hazard, 1910, p. 88). In other words, physical power was needed in order for a vote to have any force. It is this legacy, whereby supposed scientific fact is used to justify unequal treatment, which makes us wary of attempts to paint gender differences as immutable biological fact.

Rhetorical Implications, Contemporary

The history in which biology determines men's and women's roles in society is not one confined to the past. Public debates about women's appropriate roles continue. In May 2005, the House Armed Services Committee sent to Congress an amendment to the 2006 defense authorization bill that would transform into law a 1994 Pentagon policy that prohibits female troops from serving in units below brigade level whose primary mission is direct ground combat. The bill also would have required direct congressional oversight of military decision making concerning the expansion of women's combat roles. The proposal was brought forth because, with the war in Iraq, women serving in military police and combat-support units are functionally on the front line, even though their units' primary mission is not direct ground combat. However, given that no real front line exists in a counterinsurgency war, even women who are not in combat units face combat situations. As a result, as of May 2005, when the bill was being considered, 34 women soldiers and army civilian employees had been killed and 260 wounded. Similar arguments about biology dominated the debate about women's admission to the military academies (e.g., Shannon Faulkner and the Citadel; see Schriver, 2003). However, the debate about this bill also points to progress. Leading army groups and the Pentagon opposed it, leading to the bill's eventual withdrawal from consideration (Tyson, 2005).

[handwritten margin note: proposed different PT tests for men & women?]

Appeals to biological difference are made not only by those who would keep women unequal but also by those who want to value women's contributions. Some eco-feminist activists and women's peace activists believe that women are biologically programmed to be closer to the earth because women's capacity to give birth makes them uniquely opposed to practices that bring death. One of the most prominent examples of a biologically determined approach to communication is found in Sally Miller Gearhart's "The Womanization of Rhetoric" (1979). Gearhart believes that the entire history of rhetoric is one that is premised on violence, for "any intent to persuade is an act of violence" (p. 195). Her idea is not that creating conditions that generate change in others is bad; rather, she offers that "[the] act of violence is in the *intention* to change another" (p. 196). Her core criticism of the "conquest/conversion model" is that it is a "very male chauvinist model" (p. 199). Thus, she offers the womanization of rhetoric as an alternative. The womanization of rhetoric views "the whole communication environment . . . as a *matrix,* a womb" (p. 199). Gearhart believes that communication should be understood "as essentially the womanlike process," for "in order to be nonviolent communicators, we must all become more like women" (pp. 200–201).

where/ when does bias play a role?

Extending Sally Miller Gearhart's work, communication studies professors Sonja K. Foss and Cindy L. Griffin (1995) propose an alternative rhetoric called *invitational rhetoric.* Accepting Gearhart's criticism of the conquer/conversion model, Foss and Griffin (1995) agree that rhetoric with the intent to persuade is a form of violence. In contrast, in invitational rhetoric, "absent are efforts to dominate another because the goal is the understanding and appreciation of another's perspective rather than the denigration of it simply because it is different from the rhetor's own" (p. 6). As an alternative to what they characterize as *traditional rhetoric,* "invitational rhetoric is an invitation to understanding as a means to create a relationship rooted in equality, immanent value, and self-determination" (p. 5). Foss and Griffin explain that even though their theory of invitational rhetoric is constructed from feminine qualities, it is not an approach that only women can use or that all women automatically employ. However, it is still essentialist to assume that all women are one way and all men are another. These gynocentric approaches, although their motives are to valorize women's contributions to humanity, often engage in a form of biological determinism that is problematic.

Psychological Approaches

When you read research, theory, or popular material that assumes gender is hardwired into one's personality, the authors are likely drawing from the field of psychology. They do not necessarily claim that biology and culture have no influence, but most focus on how one's identity becomes gendered through early childhood experiences. In fact, some argue that a child's gender identity is generally set as early as 1–3 years of age (A. Campbell, 1993). Although psychological theories vary, they all seem to focus on linking one's sex to gendered personalities via the influences of close relationships. Later theories also recognize the influences of culture in developing one's cognitive gender schema and implicit assumptions.

Psychoanalysis

Author Rosalind Minsky (1998) explains the general field of psychoanalysis:

Psychoanalytic theory is primarily concerned with how early bodily and emotional experience in infancy and early childhood is transformed symbolically into the unconscious ways in which men and women live out their lives as male or female, "masculine" or "feminine" within culture. (p. 6)

Sigmund Freud is probably the best-known contributor to the psychoanalytic approach to studying gender/sex identity formation. Freud theorized that children develop gender identity personalities based on their perceptions of sex differences in biological genitalia. Much of his work has since been criticized for reflecting a masculine bias and a misunderstanding of women's psyche. For example, his argument that all women have "penis envy" has been rejected (Tavris, 1992). He was also stringent about the development of masculinity. He argues that to develop normally, boys must experience severe anxiety toward and hatred of their fathers. The way boys then overcome the trauma is by identifying with their fathers. Boys who do not make a complete break in their dependence on their mothers will not likely become fully masculine (Brannon, 2005).

Feminist psychologist Nancy Chodorow (1978) built on his theory, except that she attributes most of the influence of early experiences to the mother as primary caretaker. According to Chodorow, because the mother is a gendered person herself, she interacts with boy and girl children according to her gender, forming distinct relationships. At the same time, each child experiences internal conflict in trying to construct a separate identity from the mother. Because the mother and daughter are overtly similar, the daughter resolves her conflict by identifying with the mother and thus emulates a feminine gender identity. The girl develops intimacy and relationship as a primary part of who she is. According to Chodorow, the mother treats a boy child differently from a girl child. The mother encourages independence in the boy earlier than in the girl and is less intimate in her talk with the boy. The boy child also recognizes that he is not like his mother in basic ways. To resolve his internal conflict, the boy must reject the mother as a part of his independent identity development. The boy develops independence and activity as a primary part of who he is and thus finds relationships potentially smothering.

Although these early psychoanalytic theories recognize the influence of communication, they essentialized gender/sex (Bell, 2004). All girls and all boys do not respond to gender development in the same way. Instead, children respond to gender identity in highly idiosyncratic and individual ways. Also, early theory recognized only heterosexual identities, not homosexual or bisexual ones, and did not consider cross-cultural variations. Furthermore, one wonders what happens to girls and boys now increasingly raised by fathers as the primary caregivers. Another criticism of this approach is that it often is used to justify blaming the mother for children's psychological problems. As psychologists Paula Caplan and Jeremy Caplan (1999) point out, even when the mother is the primary caregiver, children are exposed to a variety of other influences.

Another primary contributor to the psychoanalytic view of gender/sex and sexuality is French psychoanalyst Jacques Lacan (1998). He argues that the unconscious is accessible only through speech and writing, and thus communication plays a central role in personality development. Because identities are based on symbols, he believes that people have only a sense of their identities. One's identity exists only in language, and the thought processes through which we speak are both gendered and eroticized (meaning driven by an unconscious desire). Much of Lacan's theory is a reinterpretation of Freud's notion that identity is based on sexuality and the central role of the phallus. One difference is that Lacan does not embrace Freud's notion of men and masculinity as the norm of good health but rather attempts to explain how masculinity is used by men to maintain power over women.

Feminist theorists from diverse perspectives have criticized portions of Lacan's theory, but they also have drawn heavily on his language emphasis. French authors such as literary theorist Hélène Cixous (1991), linguist and practicing psychoanalyst Julia Kristeva (1977/1980), and philosopher and psychoanalyst Luce Irigaray (1985a, 1985b) have analyzed language, revealing how positive feminine qualities have been silenced and also how binary gender divisions of masculine/feminine are cultural constructions. Cixous explains that *masculine* or *feminine* has meaning only through its relationship with the other binary term, and the relationship is not equal. Masculine remains the norm, and feminine is devalued and silenced (Moi, 1985). The way to reclaim the feminine is through writing the feminine, or *écriture feminine* (Cixous, 1991).

These French scholars agree with Freud that gender identity is influenced by one's sexual identity and vice versa. Persons do not experience these in isolation but rather as related parts of the self (Bell, 2004). They agree that all meanings, conscious and unconscious, have their origins in early bodily and emotional experiences and the fantasies associated with them (Minsky, 1998). However, this does not mean that sex *causes* gender. These theorists emphasize the role of culture in gender development. By combining the influences of culture and the unconscious self, the authors are better able to explain why some persons fail to conform to cultural pressures of gender/sex expectations; why gender, sex, and sexuality are more fluid and diverse than cultural stereotypes suggest; and how race, class, and culture create multiple variations of gender, sex, and sexuality (Bell, 2004).

Interest in feminist psychoanalytic theory has grown in the last 20 years because of the theory's ability to explain links between gender, sex, and sexuality. One primary contributor to this effort is Judith Butler, a professor of rhetoric, comparative literature, and women's studies. Butler (2004) argues that sex is as socially constructed as gender and that gender is often as immutable as sex, given the way in which social institutions and language constantly reiterate and reinscribe it. One of the primary ways understandings of sex and gender discipline bodies is through the enshrinement of binary views (meaning you have only one choice or another) of one's sex, gender, and sexuality. These binary views cannot explain persons who are intersex, transgender, or bisexual.

As we discussed in Chapter 1, intersex persons are born with sex organs of both females and males or with the sex organs typically associated with one sex and the chromosomes typically associated with another. Current medical practice is to surgically alter infants' genitals to "normalize" them, usually as female, because doctors believe that the vagina is easier to construct. Butler points out that this practice tells us how narrowly defined "normal" is in society, and the failure to recognize that intersex persons are part of the human continuum prevents them from being treated with respect.

Furthermore, research shows that, after intersex persons' organs are surgically altered and they are heavily socialized to develop a gender identity consistent with their sex organs, many do so, but some do not. Some children with high levels of the male androgen who were treated surgically and hormonally and then raised as girls still preferred to play with trucks. Psychologist Melissa Hines (2004) reports similar findings on intersex children from studies done in other countries (p. 13). However, just because girls with high androgen levels like to play with trucks does not mean they are "really" boys. It may just mean they are children who like to play with trucks. The need to categorize is one we should resist.

Transgender persons are persons who identify psychologically with one gender but have the external genitalia of another sex. The standard diagnostic manual used by U.S. mental health practitioners still identifies persons who desire to be "another sex" or participate in the pastimes of the "other sex" as having a disorder (American Psychiatric Association, 2000, pp. 576–577). *Gender identity disorder* is the label given to this "dysfunction." It is used for individuals with homosexual or bisexual tendencies, and some practitioners attempt to alter the individuals' gender identities; however, psychotherapy rarely changes their gender identity (Unger & Crawford, 1992). Intersex, transgender, lesbian, gay, and bisexual activists raise the question of how medical professionals can ascertain a person's "real" gender/sex identity. Instead, social activists argue that gender should be a matter of personal choice.

[handwritten margin note: homosexuality was once in the DSM, when will G.I.D. be removed? Difference? (name changed in 1973, but removed from DSM in 1986.)]

People who cross sex, gender, and sexuality lines reveal a more fluid notion of gender, not limited to two binary (either/or) options. As Judith Halberstam (2005) explains in her analysis of transgender bodies, "The rise of alternative models of masculinity within gay, lesbian, and transsexual communities in this century has been part of an ongoing interrogation of models of manhood that were previously viewed as 'natural,' 'unimpeachable,' and even 'inevitable'" (p. 126). Theory development and research based on their experiences are important. Such work reveals that the link between biology and personality is complex. Psychology alone cannot explain gender identity.

Social Learning

Other psychological approaches focus less on what influences the child's mental processes and more on describing the social interactions that shape gender/sex identities. One of the oldest and best known of these is social learning theory, originally developed by Walter Mischel (1966) and later modified by Albert Bandura (2002). This theory examines the socialization process whereby children internalize many identities and norms of behavior, not just gender. Basically, the theory portrays socialization as a passive process in which children learn by watching and imitating others and by being rewarded for gender-appropriate imitations (Bandura & Walters, 1963; Mischel, 1966). Again, the parents' and/or primary caregivers' behaviors are most influential. When children are positively rewarded for mimicking them, children will more likely repeat the patterns and make the behaviors habitual. According to this approach, young girls tend to be rewarded more for being polite, neat, emotionally expressive, and well behaved. Young boys tend to be rewarded more for being independent and emotionally controlled and for participating in physical activity. Thus, girls will tend to develop feminine qualities, and boys will tend to develop masculine qualities.

The reinforcement of behaviors that are consistent with social norms of gender occurs across a lifetime. You can probably think of examples from your own lifetime that illustrate social learning. Perhaps girls in your family were rewarded more for writing neatly, dressing up, sitting quietly, or being sweet and loving. Boys more often may have been allowed to be aggressive, to get dirty, or to be defiant. As adults, women may still be evaluated according to their looks and men according to their success.

Social learning theory fares better than the psychoanalytic approaches in its ability to help explain interpersonal influences, and it is much easier to directly observe and test. However, it has stimulated fewer researchers to expand on the theory, tends to dichotomize gender/sex, and fails to explain why some boys and girls do not conform to cultural expectations.

Cognitive Development

The cognitive development approaches share some commonalities with the psychoanalytic and social learning approaches. Like psychoanalysis, cognitive development explains gender identity development as a mental process. Like social learning, it notes that children will behave according to social norms of gender. Cognitive development theory is different from social learning because the assumed motive for learning gender is not a desire to mimic others or to attain rewards from others but a desire for self-development and competency. Thus, unlike social learning theory, this approach recognizes the more active role children play in developing their own gender identities.

Swiss psychologist Jean Piaget (1965) is best known for identifying stages of cognitive maturity and moral reasoning. Psychologist Lawrence Kohlberg took this a step further to address gender/sex. He argues that the development of gender identity and moral reasoning is a process of increasingly complex thinking and moral reasoning, from highly concrete, extreme views of gender, such as "only boys can play football" or "only girls can play with dolls," to less stereotypical, more sophisticated understandings. According to Kohlberg (1966), only boys advance to the highest stage of moral reasoning. He argues that it is necessary for them to do so because this is where they realize they must and can separate their identities from their mothers' as primary caregivers. At this point, fathers become more central in boys' lives. According to Kohlberg, girls do not advance to this stage because they cannot separate themselves from their mothers' identities.

Although cognitive development theory has generated a great deal of research because it is more easily observable, as you might guess, most psychologists today do not agree with Kohlberg's theory. Researchers in cross-cultural studies point out that defining the highest morality as individualistic is reflective of Western cultural values and does not adequately account for Chinese, South African Blacks, and other cultures that place more value on collectivism (Chow & Ding, 2002; Ferns, 2000).

Researchers also point to limitations of the theory related to gender/sex. Like Freud, Kohlberg defined femininity as an absence of desired masculine qualities. Feminist psychologist Carol Gilligan (1982) challenged Kohlberg's moral development theory. She found that most of his research was based on the study of White males, using male actors in the moral dilemmas tested. In her studies of predominantly White young women and men, she finds that by not rejecting their mothers, girls tend to gain a sense of identity *through* relationships, whereas boys who differentiate themselves from their mothers tend to gain a sense of identity *outside* relationships. This distinction could play an important role in explaining some gender misunderstandings that arise from orientations toward relationships and independence. She further argues that from these different orientations, women and men have equally valid but different moral codes. Women's morality is defined as an ethic of responsibility/relationship and men's as an ethic of individual rights. Gilligan helped raise awareness that feminine attributes can be positive and that research on male adolescents cannot be generalized to females. However, feminists have since criticized Gilligan's theory for essentializing the two sexes and attributing the central influence/blame to the mother.

In sum, psychological approaches suggest that gender identity is not naturally set at birth but rather developed through early childhood interaction. However, different cultures raise children differently, some (in parts of South Africa) even raising children communally so that questions of attachment to one parent or the other are irrelevant. In general, the psychological approaches presume that all children are raised in Western, two-parent, heterosexual, nuclear, bourgeois families. These cultural complexities and others have led many to question the existence of psychological differences between women and men. Psychologist Janet Hyde (2005) conducted a review of 46 meta-analyses on gender and psychology research. She concludes that there is no foundation for the continued belief in prominent psychological gender differences: "The gender similarities hypothesis *emphasized* holds that males and females are similar on most, but not all, psychological variables. That is, men and women as well as boys and girls, are more alike than they are different" (p. 581). Even though cognitive development theories have been roundly criticized and are somewhat outdated, they have played a role in analyses of rhetorical action.

Rhetorical Implications, Historic

Historically, women were excluded from access to the public podium and the vote because they were thought incapable of the moral reasoning required to deliberate on important public issues. Additionally, White women's supposedly more delicate sensibilities meant that the rough-and-tumble world of politics was unsuited for them. An early 1900s pamphlet distributed by a group opposing woman suffrage provides some of the most powerful claims concerning women's psychology. Daniel Webster (lawyer, congressperson, and statesperson) decried, "The rough contests of the political world are not suited to the dignity and the delicacy of your sex;" Cardinal Gibbons (Catholic archbishop) worried, "If woman enters politics, she will be sure to carry away on her some of the mud and dirt of political contact" (Massachusetts Association Opposed to the Further Extension of Suffrage to Women, 1912). Arguments describing women's psychological makeup were used to exclude them from the public sphere.

However, White and Black women did speak in public to oppose slavery and to advocate for women's rights. Karlyn Kohrs Campbell (1989) studies these women and notes that their distinctive style "emerged out of their experiences as women and was adapted to the attitudes and experiences of female audiences" (Vol. 1, p. 12). Feminine style was a product of their psychological socialization.

White women were socialized to be a particular way: pure, pious, domestic, and submissive (Welter, 1976). However, White women were not passive recipients of this socialization. As the cognitive development theory notes, White women were active participants in the development of their identity as women rhetors, creating a feminine style of rhetoric. These characteristics include being "personal in tone"; relying "heavily on personal experience, anecdotes, and other examples"; structuring speeches inductively; "invit[ing] audience participation"; addressing the audience as peers; and having as their goal empowerment (Campbell, 1989, pp. 10–12). The values of connection that mothers taught to girls in the home was translated into a style that could be used outside the home. As we discuss later, this feminine style is not *the* feminine style but one feminine style used strategically.

Rhetorical Implications, Contemporary

Although Campbell's description of feminine style was deduced from studies of mostly White women's rhetoric from 1832 to 1920, its salience persists. Although the theories explored earlier examine the psychological influence of parenting on children (e.g., Chodorow), other scholars have explored the psychological effect of parenting on parents, particularly on mothers. Sociologist Sara Ruddick outlined this theory in *Maternal Thinking* (1989). Ruddick posits that the way people think is influenced by the activities in which they engage. Although maternal practice is one in which women and men can engage, women have been primarily responsible for it. Communication scholars Bonnie J. Dow and Marie Boor Tonn (1993) argue that mothering activities contributed to the successful speech of then-Texas governor Ann Richards at the 1988 Democratic National Convention. Richards's rhetoric demonstrates an alternative paradigm for political progress that reflects the values of maternal thinking and an ethic of care. Dow and Tonn argue that feminine style should be studied not only for its strategic value as an inventive response to the unique rhetorical problems women face as members of a less powerful group but also as a philosophical foundation for moral reasoning in political discourse. Feminist rhetorical action not only adapts to the situation but also provides an example of and impetus for changing the situation: It enacts the alternative worldview it calls for.

The writings of French psychoanalytic feminists also have influenced rhetorical theory. Barbara A. Biesecker (1992) explores how Cixous's concept of *écriture feminine* is a foundation for reconstructing rhetorical theory from a feminist perspective. Biesecker argues that Cixous's essay "The Laugh of the Medusa" is "first and foremost a call to women to discursively intervene in the public sphere" and "offers suggestions on how they might effectively go about it" (pp. 89–90). Cixous's primary suggestion is to "steal" back and recode particular signs—to resignify language, a tactic we will discuss in Chapter 5. A focus on language is important, according to Cixous (1981), because "no political reflection can dispense with reflection on language, with work on language. For as soon as we exist, we are born into language and language speaks (to) us, dictates its law" (p. 45).

For Cixous and Biesecker, *écriture feminine* offers an alternative, embraceable by women and men but not *automatically* embraced by women *because* they are women, for "to be signed with a woman's name doesn't necessarily make a piece of writing feminine" (Cixous, 1981, p. 52). Taking Cixous's feminine rhetoric seriously would create a future wherein "differences are celebrated and exchanged rather than seized as levers in a struggle for power . . . this would not just be a new theory of rhetoric. It would also be our new ethics" (Biesecker, 1992, pp. 94–95).

As this review reveals, researchers using psychological approaches acknowledge the influence of interpersonal communication and language. If it is true, as psychoanalysts argue, that language plays a central role in constructing gender/sex identities, then attention to language must play a central role in any theory that seeks to explain gender/sex.

Descriptive Cultural Approaches

In research, theory, or popular material that infers the social construction of gender, the authors likely see gender as a personal and cultural identity created through social interactions. Again, this does not necessarily mean that they reject biological or psychological influences but that they see them as being structured and given meaning by social influences.

Not all the approaches under this cultural framework agree, nor would their authors agree with how we have grouped them. In our view, there are two loosely defined groups of cultural approaches. The first group, labeled *descriptive cultural approaches*, subscribes to an interpretive or humanistic view of how knowledge is attained. This group focuses on describing how individuals learn gender (and other cultural identities) through cultural socialization. Such approaches do not critically analyze the type of socialization or recognize power inequalities.

Symbolic Interactionism

You may have studied this theory in sociology or interpersonal communication courses. It has a broad scope that attempts to explain all social behavior. The concept that communication creates gender and meaning, rather than that gender or preexisting meanings create communication, is rooted in this theory. Symbolic interactionism is based on the work of George Herbert Mead, philosopher and social scientist. Mead (1934) suggested that people construct their personal identities and views of the world only through their symbolic interactions (communication) with other members of society. Consequently, gender and other identities exist not in the individual but in interactions with others in the social order. Symbolic interactionism helps reveal how interactions encourage people to subscribe to predominant cultural views and roles. It suggests that the communication of social stereotypes and expectations of gender affect not only identities and people's actions toward others but also how people are likely to interpret the behaviors of others. Meanings such as gender are not predetermined and simply passed on in interactions; rather, people bring these meanings to the interaction where they are negotiated and possibly changed. Social expectations, such as those for feminine and masculine gender roles, constrain people's interactions but not completely (West & Turner, 2004).

The key point of the theory is that persons internalize the meanings created in social interactions. Thus, society plays a central role in how personal identities are constructed. Ultimately, the theory focuses on how persons as individuals are gendered; it is not as useful for explaining the political implications of the ways in which gender and related inequalities across groups of individuals are maintained and reinscribed.

Anthropology

Researchers in anthropology have provided evidence of the unique ways in which different cultures construct and define gender. Anthropological theory encourages a researcher to try to become a part of a given culture to better understand its norms, values, and identities, and posits that each culture will define its norms, values, and identities (such as gender) in unique ways. Gender/sex constructions have been observed in two areas: gender/sex exclusive language patterns and gender/sex preferences in communication style.

Exclusive language patterns refer to cultures in which women and men are expected to use different pronunciations, grammar, and/or vocabulary for similar words and ideas. The majority of the language is shared by women and men, and all speakers understand it, but usage is actually prescribed by sex and also often by age and class. The best-known example of this is Japanese. Japanese has multiple words that traditionally have been relegated to separate use by women or men. For example, wives were expected to refer to their husbands by the phrase *uti no hito*, or "person of the home." Husbands referred to their wives by the phrase *uti no yatu*, or "fellow of my home." Although these may not seem very different to English speakers, in Japanese culture the wife's usage is considered a polite phrase used to show deference to a person of higher status. The husband's usage is considered an impolite and informal phrase referring to a lower-status person (Bonvillain, 2003). Recent research indicates that younger generations do not adhere to these norms as closely (Mizokami, 2003).

Similar gender/sex differences in language use have been found elsewhere. In Kūrux (a language spoken in North India) and in Chiquita (spoken by native people in Bolivia), women and men traditionally are not allowed to use each other's language forms (Bonvillain, 2003). Research on gender/sex exclusive language patterns provides support for the anthropological view that gender is primarily culturally constructed.

Regarding behavioral gendered/sexed communication styles, in most cultures studied, women and men *both* show nurturant and aggressive behaviors, but cultures differ greatly in the degree to which women and men are encouraged to engage in these behaviors (Adler, 1991). Anthropologist Margaret Mead studied three tribes in New Guinea and found distinct gender norms for each (1935/1968). In the Tchambuli culture, women were domineering and sexual aggressors. Men were considered the weaker, more refined sex and spent much of their time adorning themselves to be more attractive to women. In the Mundugumor tribe, women and men alike were socialized to be aggressive, independent, and competitive. In the Arapesh community, women as well as men were socialized to be nurturing, passive, and mild.

In the work following Mead's, researchers generally have found that how a culture sustains itself seems to affect how gender/sex is defined. In hunting/gathering cultures, women do the bulk of food gathering and, for the most part, hold higher status. Cultures that survive on horticulture are similar, although other factors, such as matrilineal descent, also play a role. More marked gender/sex divisions and inequalities come into play in cultures with land ownership and pastoral and harvesting work. The most marked divisions occur in competitive, capitalist, industrial societies (Mascia-Lees & Black, 2000). It might seem surprising that the societies presumed most advanced are not the most equitable. However, as we discuss in Chapters 3 and 9, cultures that value industry and capitalism also tend to place higher values on the personal qualities of competitiveness, assertiveness, and leadership, which are stereotypically ascribed to men more than to women.

Today, many cultural variances persist in terms of gender (Mascia-Lees & Black, 2000; Nanda, 2000). Anthropologist Geert Hofstede, who does cross-cultural survey comparison research, has identified feminine/masculine as one of four primary value dimensions found in 50 countries, with large variances across those countries (Hofstede, 1998). In highly masculine cultures, men are expected to be assertive, tough, and focused on material success. In highly feminine cultures, women as well as men are expected to be tender, modest, and more concerned about the quality of life. While some critics of Hofstede have pointed out the limitations of assessing cultural norms using a survey instrument, he and others consistently have found that countless cultures embrace the concepts of femininity/ masculinity. Another limitation of Hofstede's work is that researchers have not found a relationship between his findings and other gender-related concepts such as sex stereotypes (Best & Thomas, 2004).

More recently, feminist anthropologists and geographers have taken the analysis of gender and culture a step further, theorizing that gender/sex and nation are intersecting identities that create unique lived experiences, and that to more fully understand a nation, one must include gender in the analysis (Elliston, 2000; Mayer, 2000). Gender and ethnic studies professor Nira Yuval-Davis (1997, 1999) notes that unique gender relations contribute to national reproduction, national culture, and citizenship, as well as national conflicts and war. She believes that, because women in most cultures traditionally assume nurturing and educational roles, it is women "who reproduce nations, biologically, culturally, and symbolically" (p. 2). Therefore, gender relations must be a part of national studies, and nations must be a part of gender studies. Anne McClintock (1997), who studies gender/sex in South Africa, argues that stereotypic gender differences are culturally created to define power symbolically between men and the boundaries of national differences and similarities. By distinguishing gender/sex differences between women and men, the national power of the men who dominate a given culture is more clearly defined. Gender and national identity research extends beyond traditional descriptive cultural research to include critical analysis and thus bridges the two cultural approaches to studying gender.

Scholars have published so many anthropological studies of gender (e.g., Bonvillain, 2003) that we cannot begin to report them all, but here are some examples of the unique manifestations of genders in cultures. Among Jaqi societies in South America, people are not ranked by sex or gender at all. Sex and gender differences may be recognized, but they are not commonly seen as unequal. Linguistic anthropologist M. J. Hardman (1986) explains that the Jaqi categorize by human/nonhuman distinctions rather than male/female or masculine/feminine. The Lahu people in a mountainous region of Southwest China hold an ideal of gender unity rather than gender difference. Gender unity and the need to have efficient household labor contribute to an extraordinarily high degree of jointly shared household tasks, including child rearing (Du, 2000).

Even within the United States, countless cultural differences occur in gender/sex identities. Researchers found that African American women studied tended to use more assertive speech styles than White women, and that the African American men tend to be more relationship oriented than the White men studied (Rothenberg, 2001). Many Native American societies were historically matrilineal prior to the invasion by Western Europeans (Gonzales & Kertesz, 2001). These were not cultures in which women held the power, but the lines of inheritance and social status were traced through mothers. Among the Iroquois, land could not be sold without the wife's consent. Women also had veto power in the decision to go to war (Gage, 1980). Although cultures have existed in which family descent is primarily matrilineal, these are not societies *controlled* by women. In matrilineal societies, more value is placed on sibling relations than on marital relations, and brothers and sisters may have more power than husbands or wives (Mascia-Lees & Black, 2000).

As many as 150 Native American societies have historically celebrated more diverse notions of gender and sexuality. "Two Spirit" people have long been recognized. White anthropologists labeled them *berdache,* but the label implies that all Two Spirit people are homosexual males, which was not the case. Instead, researchers have documented multiple variations with three to four recognized genders. These included men, women, male variants and female variants (persons who were biologically identified as one sex but who, due to their gendered activities and skills associated with the other sex, were reclassified) (Roscoe, 1987). Similarly, some parts of India have a history of cultural acceptance of *Hijras,* primarily men who are born intersexed or who choose to have an emasculation surgery to become intersexed (Nanda, 1996). Acceptance of the *Hijras* is based in traditional Hindu belief in the interchangeability of male and female qualities and in the transformations of sex, gender, and alternative sex and gender roles among both deities and humans. In most cases, the variety has been welcomed and revered (Nanda, 2000).

In sum, anthropologists' research shows that most societies identify with the notions of femininity and masculinity, but strong cultural variances appear in the ways in which these concepts are valued and ascribed to women and men. However, given increasingly Western capitalistic influences on other countries, it is becoming difficult for anthropologists to distinguish gendered practices indigenous to non-Western cultures.

Two-Culture Theory

This theory, also called the cross-cultural theory of gender communication, has been the predominant approach to understanding gender relations in popular literature as well as research for at least the last 20 years. It is largely based on sociolinguists Daniel Maltz and Ruth Borker's (1982) paper, "A Cultural Approach to Male-Female Miscommunication." Maltz and Borker apply a theory used to study communication problems between different ethnic groups to communication problems between women and men, arguing that communication problems between women and men are similar to problems that arise when persons from different cultural language groups attempt to communicate. The two groups have different cultural goals and rules for conversation. Based on their observations of U.S. girls' and boys' play, Maltz and Borker argue that girls and boys are socialized in different language groups, due in part to self-segregated childhood play. In these groups, girls learn a communication style for creating and maintaining close equal relationships, to be tactful when criticizing others, and to correctly interpret others' behaviors. In contrast, the researchers argue, boys tend to play in larger, hierarchal groups, in which the interactions involve competition and the emphasis is on action, not talk. Here, boys learn a style of verbal dominance. Consequently, when adult women and men experience "miscommunication," the researchers suggest it is due to incorrectly interpreting the other's behavior through her or his own frame of reference (or conversational style) rather than, for example, the malefic intentions of the speaker.

This view is popular largely because the assumption of two gendered cultures is consistent with predominant cultural stereotypes of two opposite gender roles.

Men are expected to be assertive, strong, and competitive, and to lead. Women are expected to be supportive, nurturing, and collaborative.

Variations of this view were popular long before Maltz and Borker's work. Linguist Robin Lakoff (1975) proposed a theory suggesting that women and men have two separate language styles, but unlike Maltz and Borker, Lakoff argued that the cause was social role inequality. She reasoned that women's language style reflected feelings of insecurity and weakness as second-class citizens in a culture where men dominate. She described women's style as *deficit,* using a specialized feminine vocabulary (e.g., more precise words for colors), less profanity, so-called empty adjectives (e.g., *sweet* or *cute*), and tag questions (statements made into questions to soften the assertion, e.g., "I think this is what we should do, don't you?"). Lakoff's theory drew a great deal of attention in the popular press (e.g., *Psychology Today* and *The National Enquirer*). Even though it was based on introspection rather than systematic research, Lakoff's theory helped spur 30 years of research as scholars dug for evidence to confirm that women and men speak differently.

In spite of the lack of research confirming different language styles, years later another sociolinguist, Deborah Tannen, was propelled into the public realm with her internationally best-selling book, *You Just Don't Understand: Women and Men in Conversation* (1990). She applied Maltz and Borker's two-culture theory to explain gender communication problems. Unlike most of her other writing, this book is based on anecdotal examples and introspection, not systematic research. She suggests that women's style of communicating is best characterized as *rapport* talk: talk that focuses on building relationship, connecting collaboratively with the other person, showing empathy, and so on. Men's style of communicating is best characterized as *report* talk: talk that focus on instrumentality or task orientation, asserting oneself, competitiveness, and the like. When persons from these two communication styles come together, the result is asymmetries in their conversation. They talk at cross-purposes. The practical implication of this theory is that if persons realize the presence of differing styles, they will have a better understanding of why gendered communication problems happen and will be more understanding of each other.

However, when the two-culture theory describes women as having a more accommodating, collaborative style and men as having a more independent, competitive style, it legitimizes the social expectation that relationship work is women's work and reinforces masculine culture as dominant. Consider the example of conflict management. Tannen suggests that men's style is to want to fix problems by themselves; in contrast, women's style is to talk out problems collaboratively. Thus, to resolve the conflict, women need more cooperation than men do, which necessarily places them in a more dependent position in which they are less likely to have their needs met.

Although the two-culture theory offers a description of participants' interaction intents and styles to which many people can relate, it does not examine the effects or social consequences of such contrasting styles. In Tannen's later academic work (1994a), she points out that one cannot study gender differences (or those of other social identities) separately from possible dominance. She suggests that group dominance arises out of group differences and that intent is not always the same as effect.

Several feminist communication scholars and linguists criticize the two-culture theory because it does not acknowledge inequitable effect and because it assumes there are two universal gendered cultures—thereby essentializing women and men. It does not take into account the gender differences anthropologists have noted across cultures. As you will read in Chapter 3, the two-culture approach has not been well supported by subsequent research. It also cannot be used to explain more serious problems between women and men. As linguist Mary Crawford explains, systemic violence against women cannot be the result simply of innocent communication style differences (1995). It is the result of power inequalities, not gender/sex differences (Dworkin, 1993). When scholars explain gendered/sexed violence as mere style differences, the violator's responsibility disappears. In sum, the interpretive/descriptive cultural theories presented here focus on gender as culturally constructed, but in general they do not attempt to critically examine this construction in terms of its impact on groups of people.

Rhetorical Implications, Historic

Two-culture theory found its expression historically in appeals to men's and women's different domains as separate but equal. For example, at the turn of the 18th century, Remonstrants (women who opposed woman suffrage) claimed as their motto "Home, Heaven, and Mother" (Jablonsky, 2002, p. 123). For Remonstrants, women of good character would be better able to influence public policy by means other than the vote. The public sphere, an "arena of business, politics, and the professions" was the world of men, whereas "the private sphere, the domain of love, the home, and family was the world of women" (Jorgensen-Earp, 1990, p. 84).

Although the Remonstrants' early arguments emphasized scriptural admonitions that women's appropriate place was in the home, from the 1890s to 1920, their arguments shifted, proclaiming that although women did, indeed, have a place in *public* life, they did not belong in *political* life (Thurner, 1993). In fact, Remonstrants argued that woman suffrage would undermine women's ability to be effective public advocates. Remonstrants did not believe that women were incapable of social influence. Instead, they believed that women's distinctive communication skills were best exercised through their relationships with men rather than through the instrumental use of public rhetoric. Women's and men's two cultures meant two realms: private and public.

Rhetorical Implications, Contemporary

The idea that women's communication styles represent a unique culture also informs some contemporary rhetorical analyses. Although not exactly a two-culture analysis, Karlyn Kohrs Campbell's (1973) article, "The Rhetoric of Women's Liberation: An Oxymoron," provides a relatively suitable example of how the cultural construction of gender/sex influences women's communication patterns.

Campbell's (1973) essay is one of the first analyses of the second-wave women's movement from a communication studies perspective. Her primary argument is that traditional theories and models of rhetoric fail to explain what was rhetorically significant in the early stages of the movement because they were based on masculine models of communication. She believes the movement represented a distinct form of communication, informed by (White) women's traditional cultural values regarding communication: "The rhetoric of women's liberation is distinctive stylistically in rejecting certain traditional concepts of the rhetorical process—as persuasion of the many by an expert or leader, . . . and as directed toward inducing acceptance of a specific program or a commitment to group action" (p. 78). Women leaders in the 1960s rejected persuasion and an instrumental focus; they instead relied on collaboration and empathy.

In particular, consciousness-raising groups were one way this relationship orientation to communication was expressed. They were meetings of small, leaderless groups in which each person was encouraged to express her feelings and experiences. The goal was to create awareness, through shared experiences, that what was thought to be a personal deficiency or individual problem was actually a shared result of one's position as a woman (Campbell, 1973).

Campbell makes clear in her description of this rhetorical style that it parallels the goals of what is considered typical of women's culture: "affirmation of the affective, of the validity of personal experience, of the necessity for self-exposure and self-criticism, of the value of dialogue, and of the goal of autonomous, individual decision-making" (p. 79). However, even as this rhetoric celebrated what might be considered women's traditional cultural values, it also represented a truly radical challenge to the patriarchal system.

Critical Cultural Approaches

Critical cultural approaches differ from descriptive cultural approaches in that they start from different points of analysis. In descriptive approaches, researchers focus on describing cultural distinctions and do not see the construction of difference as a tool of political power. At most, power inequalities are a consequence of gender/sex and other cultural identity differences. In critical cultural approaches, researchers attempt to deconstruct, or take apart and critically examine, the cultural creation of differences and inequalities. They focus on revealing possible explanations for socially created differences and similarities. These explanations emphasize hegemony, power, and status. Gender/sex and other social identities are not seen as belonging solely to the individual but rather as belonging to social systems and structures. Gender/sex is imposed on individuals by social systems (which are under human control). Given this, gender is not who a person is but what a person does. ⟶ current

Critical cultural approaches also are unique in that they attempt to navigate artificially created boundaries among biological, psychological, and cultural approaches. The work here is highly interdisciplinary. As such, it speaks to work in biology, psychology, communication studies, sociology, linguistics, and nearly every other academic discipline.

The critical cultural approaches described here draw from a plethora of academic and activist thought: postmodern theory, Marxism, feminism, men's studies, and more. Rather than getting caught up in a game of labels, we attempt to demonstrate how the approaches build on each other, contributing new insights. The sequencing of approaches here is purposeful. The first approaches, such as standpoint theory and social constructionism, take the existence of identity at face value. The latter approaches, particularly post-structuralism, problematize the concept of identity, viewing it instead as fluid and defined relationally through micro (interpersonal) and macro (institutional, cultural, social) practices. We present this group of approaches last because it is the current direction of the study of gender/sex and the intersecting identities of race, class, sexual orientation, and so on.

Standpoint Theory

This theory was developed by German philosopher George Wilhelm Friedrich Hegel to explain the social institution of slavery (1807). It has since been adapted by feminist and cultural studies scholars to explain African American women's unique cultural perspectives and the ways in which social class affects worldviews (Collins, 1986, 1990; Harding, 1998). The theory posits that the social groups to which one belongs affect one's perceptions of the world. Persons in different groups develop specific skills, norms of communicating, and values consistent with the needs of their lived group experiences. Therefore, the predominant culture in which all groups exist is not experienced in the same way by all persons or groups. The views of those who belong to groups with more social power (such as Whites, men, heterosexuals, or the middle and upper classes) are validated more than those in marginalized groups. Those in marginalized groups must learn to be bicultural, or to "pass" in the dominant culture to survive, even though that perspective is not their own. This is why African American feminist scholar bell hooks (1984) argues that one can learn more from the observations of persons living on a culture's margins than from members of its dominant groups.

The theory makes clear that research based on dominant groups within a culture cannot be generalized to the entire culture. A criticism of standpoint theory is that it, too, overgeneralizes, suggesting that all persons within a social category or group have the same identity and perspective. Persons belong to multiple social groups according to race, class, gender/sex, sexual orientation, and so forth, and the intersections of these groups create unique individual perspectives and experiences. The theory also does not question the concept of identity.

Social Constructionism

Like symbolic interactionism, social constructionism suggests that meaning is constructed, not passively given, and that the creation happens in and through interaction with others and the culture. The distinction between the two approaches is that symbolic interactionism is less socially critical. Social constructionism focuses on *how* individuals construct meaning and related inequalities by *doing gender.* In this case, gender is viewed as a social institution. As such, power and hegemonic relations become central foci for study (Marecek, Crawford, & Popp, 2004; Weatherall, 2002). Linguist Mary Crawford (1995) explains that

> the social constructionist views gender as a social construct: a system of meaning that organizes interactions and governs access to power and resources. From this view, gender is not an attribute of individuals but a way of making sense of transactions. Gender exists not in person but in transactions. It is conceptualized as a verb, not a noun. (p. 18)

This means that when one talks about a tendency for one group to dominate another, the speaker is not blaming every individual man, or White, or wealthy person, for being intentionally domineering, or blaming every individual woman, or Hispanic, or Black, or poor person for being submissive. The cultural systems of patriarchy, racism, and classism create an unequal playing field on which communication takes place. Individuals do play an active role in the construction of gender, race, social class, sexual orientation, and other identities, but they cannot fully control the direction of these constructions created and maintained by systems (Gergen, 1994). However, because members of dominant groups do benefit from unearned privileges, social justice depends on those individuals to rectify the inequalities.

Communication Strategies

This approach is different from the others in the critical cultural group because it focuses specifically on communication. We place it here because it reveals the ways in which even interpersonal communication is political. It demonstrates that communicators are not simply passive receivers of life circumstances; they play an active role in creating their realities.

Many researchers in sociolinguistics and communication studies suggest that style differences in communication are not simply the result of various group socialization experiences. Rather, they argue, communication is goal oriented, strategic (Kellerman, 1992). Penelope Brown and Stephen Levinson, linguistic anthropologists, use the word "strategy" in its broadest sense (1978, p. 91). People develop communication strategies to help them be effective in their unique life situations. Strategies can be conscious or unconscious (Kellerman, 1992). Strategies can become routine when the original rationale for the behavior is lost but the automatic behavior remains. The approach not only explains individual behavior but differences according to one's group identities and the relative privileges one holds. Because women and men, Blacks and Whites, lesbians, gays, bisexuals, transgendered persons and heterosexuals, rich and poor, as groups have differing degrees of social resources, they will develop different strategies to be effective. No one communication strategy serves them all.

If a person is a subordinate in a job or a female in a male-dominated organization, that person may use more indirect, polite strategies to try to obtain her or his communication goals than would a person who has more legitimate power in those situations. A person who has legitimate power, meaning that her or his right to speak in public is not questioned, can be effective using a more direct style of speaking (Jamieson, 1995; Kramarae, 1981). Men, who are expected to be assertive and strong, will likely be more effective using direct, assertive communication strategies, and men who do not may be seen as less masculine. Similarly, women who use strong, direct strategies may be seen as less feminine by White standards, and their message may be less effective. Of course, there are cultural differences. For example, Chinese and Japanese cultural styles tend to be more indirect, in general, but even within these cultures it is more acceptable for men to speak with a stronger style than it is for women. Thus, social status helps explain gendered communication.

Nondominant group members may adopt the style commonly associated with the dominant groups, such as immigrants who adopt the predominant language of their host countries, or persons of lower economic backgrounds who adopt the speech style of upper-class persons. This is called trying to "pass." Their efforts may or may not be received positively by those in the dominant groups. Persons who are attempting to create unique identities within the expectations of their group styles may develop combinations of strategies from within and outside their groups.

The communication strategies approach is useful because it no longer frames gender/sex differences as deficits or as passive socialization processes. Rather, people are considered rational speakers who are capable of using the communication strategies available to them to be most effective in resisting oppression. The limitation of this approach is that it is nearly impossible to identify distinct group power relations and make direct links between people's styles and their assumed goals in a situation.

Gender as Performance

We introduced the concept of gender as performance in Chapter 1 as central to the study of gender/sex in communication. Like the communication strategies approach, it suggests that individuals participate in the construction of their personal and group identities through daily enactments, or citations, of gender/sex. The focus on citationality reveals the power of seemingly unconscious performances of seemingly unimportant norms of gender/sex as well as the norms of other intersecting identities. Although the writings of philosopher Judith Butler (1990a, 1990b, 1993, 2004) have significantly contributed to raising awareness of this perspective, performance studies has most readily embraced the concept within the field of communication studies. An important difference exists, however, between Butler's notion of performativity and communication scholars' notion of performance. *Performativity* tends to refer to the daily, nonconscious doing of gender, in which agency and intent play a limited role and where the performance of gender is not interpreted as a performance. *Performance* tends to refer to conscious making of an event in which the creative, the playful, and the politi-cal are all overtly thematized (Conquergood, 1992; HopKins, 1995).

A multitude of articles, books, and interpretive performances, including the entire journal *Text & Performance Quarterly,* document the diversity of lived gendered/sexed experiences as tied to race, ethnicity, social class, sexual orienta-tion, nationality, and other identities. Because this approach locates the experience of gender/sex in the body, we explore it in Chapter 4, where we focus on the body.

Multiracial and Global Feminisms

Scholars and activists studying gender/sex through the lens of global feminist theory and multiracial feminist theory have crystallized the reasons that gender/sex must be studied from cultural and global perspectives. Their position is that no sin-gular gendered experience defines women or men, and the norms of one culture should not be imposed on another in an attempt to improve women's and children's human rights. Law professor Isabelle Gunning (1997) puts the challenge this way: Instead of being "arrogant perceivers" of the world who judge other cultures based on the ethnocentric view of their own culture as the norm, people should strive to be "world travelers" (p. 352). To be world travelers means to be ethnographers, to try to view other cultures from their members' perspectives rather than one's own, outside view. To be world travelers also means to recognize the interconnections between cul-tures. This requires not only observing the other culture but being willing to turn that same critical lens back on one's own culture, including examining the ways in which one's cultural practices contribute to the oppressions of other cultures.

Authors from this perspective emphasize the experiences and voices of multiple gendered/sexed experiences, particularly for racial minorities living in the West and those living in non-Western, nonindustrialized, noncapitalist countries. They argue that White, Western, educated feminists have had the most to say in defining women's experiences and have falsely assumed that their worldview represents all women, consequently portraying other women as passive, backward, unenlight-ened, oppressed, undereducated, and needing help.

In her profoundly influential book, *Feminism Without Borders,* Chandra Talpade Mohanty (2003) makes clear the failures of White Western feminists' studies of third-world women and women of color:

> To define feminism purely in gendered terms assumes that our conscious-ness of being "women" has nothing to do with race, class, nation, or sexual-ity, just with gender. But no one "becomes a woman" (in Simone de Beauvoir's sense) purely because she is female. Ideologies of womanhood have as much to do with class and race as they have to do with sex. Thus, during the period of American slavery, constructions of white wom-anhood as chaste, domesticated, and morally pure had everything to do with corresponding constructions of black slave women as promiscuous, available plantation workers. It is the intersections of the various

systemic networks of class, race, (hetero)sexuality, and nation, then, that positions us as "women." (p. 55)

Mohanty (2003) urges everyone to recognize "the application of the notion of women as a homogeneous category to women in the Third World colonizes and appropriates the pluralities of the simultaneous location of different groups of women in social class and ethnic frameworks; in doing so it ultimately robs them of their historical and political agency" (p. 39).

A sex-only approach misidentifies third-world men as the root cause of third-world women's oppression, not economic, colonial systems. This creates a dynamic that English professor Gayatri Chakravorty Spivak (1988) describes as "White men saving brown women from brown men" (p. 297). This is not a dynamic confined only to colonial times, however. Dana Cloud (2004) provides a trenchant analysis of images circulated by *Time.com* of Afghan people while the U.S. administration was building public support for the 2001–2002 war in Afghanistan. Focusing on the images of women as veiled and oppressed, the images appealed to White men to save Brown women from Brown men and evoked a paternalistic stance toward the women of Afghanistan.

So called third-world people and the colonization of them can exist in any country, including the United States. Chicana author and activist Gloria Anzaldúa explores the ways in which living on the U.S.–Mexican border shape *mestiza* (mixed-race) women. Throughout her work, she moves between English and Spanish, detailing the process and purpose of communication, constantly reminding the reader of her role as a person positioned on the border between two cultures. As part of her exploration of political and personal borderlands, Anzaldúa, like other Chicana feminists, creates a space in which to perform multiple identities (Flores, 1996; Palczewski, 1996).

Rhetorician Raka Shome (1996) explains why the study of communication and imperialism is important and how it can be done. *Postcolonialism*, "a critical perspective that primarily seeks to expose the Eurocentrism and imperialism of Western discourses" (p. 41), asks two related questions:

> How do Western discursive practices, in their representations of the world and of themselves, legitimize the contemporary global power structures? To what extent do the cultural texts of nations such as the United States and England reinforce the neo-imperial political practices of these nations?

Shome explains that a focus on communication is necessary because "discourses have become one of the primary means of imperialism" (p. 42). Although "in the past, imperialism was about controlling the 'native' by colonizing her or him territorially, now imperialism is more about subjugating the 'native' by colonizing her or him discursively" (p. 42) by forcibly changing gender and national identities and values. The tremendous reach of Western media, the universality of English (a legacy of earlier territorial imperialism), the way in which academics have named and defined the "native" as "other," and the creation of economic dependency all mean that attention to communication patterns are central to understanding how colonialism persists.

Queer Theory

Queer theorists challenge the very terms used in descriptive cultural approaches: *gender* (*feminine/masculine*), *sex* (*female/male, woman/man*), and *sexuality* (*homosexual/heterosexual*). As a form of study, queer theory is the "process by which people have made dissident sexuality articulate," meaning "available to memory, and sustained through collective activity" (Warner, 2002, pp. 17, 203). In the process of studying those who do not fit into the neat binaries just outlined, queer theory creates a language that names and makes present those who live outside the binaries.

This approach is overtly political in its aim, but is not meant to be an umbrella term for work on gays, lesbians, bisexuals, and the transgendered. Instead, it is meant to question all forms of sex and sexuality categorization as it addresses "the full range of power-ridden normativities of sex" (Berlant & Warner, 1995, p. 345), particularly heteronormativity, as discussed in Chapter 1. Queer theory makes clear the variety of ways in which heterosexuality is composed of practices that have very little to do with sex (Warner, 2002, p. 198). When it comes to thinking about sex, sexuality, and gender, queer theory calls for a "rethinking of both the perverse and the normal" (p. 345). For queer theorists, desire is a focus of study, including the "categorization of desiring subjects" and what allows some desires to "pass as normal, while others are rendered wrong or evil" (Giffney, 2004, p. 74).

By recognizing and examining connections between sexual desire, gender, sex, and sexual orientation, this approach broadens the study of gender/sex in communication in important ways. For example, English professor Judith Halberstam writes about transgender persons' experiences. She shows that studying women performing masculinity may reveal more about cultural assumptions of masculinity than studying men, for whom society assumes the relationship is normal (1998). Similarly, Halberstam's (2005) study of drag kings (women and men who expressly perform masculinity, like Mike Myers's performance in *Austin Powers*) exposes some of the absurdity of gender norms and how gender functions as a "*a kind of imitation* [or copy] *for which there is no original*" (Butler, 1991, p. 21).

Post-Structuralism

Post-structuralism builds on many of the critical cultural theories. It also is related to many other theories not addressed, such as postmodernism. These views are not independent of each other. Just as there is no one feminism, there are multiple forms of post-structuralism. At its most basic level, post-structuralism is an approach to examining texts and cultures. Because of this, we limit our discussion to what is common among these approaches and what is most useful for the study of gender/sex in communication. Drawing from linguistic psychoanalyst Judith Baxter's writing (2006), we identify four primary features:

1. Discourse, oral and written, is a form of social/ideological [hegemonic] practice, such as the assumption of universal gender/sex differences, and as such warrants critical cultural analysis.

2. The goal is to study discourse in small-scale, localized contexts.

3. Human identity is intersectional, multiple.

4. Speakers' identities are fluid. They are never exclusively powerful or powerless.

Speakers continuously, actively negotiate their identities. Baxter (2006) explains that "power is not a possession in somebody's hands, but a net-like organization which weaves itself discursively through social structures, meanings, relations, and the construction of speakers' identities" (pp. 155–156). Similarly, identity is not a property of the individual but an evasive and ever-changing concept that is always in flux, never fully realized or set. As Baxter says, this notion of identity in process means that "within any single speech event, both male and female speakers are constantly negotiating their subject positions within interwoven and often competing institutional discourses" (Baxter, 2006, p. 157). The goal of research done from this perspective is not to make sweeping generalizations but to identify and better understand the diversity of gender/sex as experienced at a given time and place.

Post-structuralists, like feminists, queer theorists, and men's studies, challenge universal assumptions. Feminist theorist Martha Reineke explains, "Post-structuralism looks at box making—how categories are created," such as "girl is what boy is not," and "It is a critical interrogation of practices of exclusion through which meaning happens" (personal correspondence, spring 2006). This is a radical move away from traditional psychological theories such as social learning and sex roles, which view gender as an individual development process. In post-structuralism, researchers constantly examine the interface between individual experiences and cultural structures.

Rhetorical Implications, Historic

Critical cultural approaches contribute to the increasing acceptance of diverse peoples in the public sphere. Once a group understands the way social structures have marginalized it, the group can challenge that marginalization, arguing that its subordination is not natural but political. Additionally, the unique perspectives generated by living at the margins enable rhetors creatively to carve out space in public discourse. Even as Campbell's feminine style was the result of socialization processes, it also was a conscious set of strategies adopted by women rhetors as the 19th century became the 20th. The women used the very characteristics that were meant to exclude them from public life to create a space in public life. As Campbell (1989) explains, "Many strategically adopted what might be called a feminine style to cope with the conflicting demands of the podium" (Vol. 1., p. 12). The fact that Campbell's concept illustrates a variety of theoretical approaches shows that multiple approaches can simultaneously inform the research conducted on gender/sex in communication.

Rhetorical Implications, Contemporary

Standpoint theory, social constructionism, and global feminism inform a wide range of contemporary research. They highlight the way strategic choices about social roles expand the communication options available to all people. Given that gender/sex differences in communication can be deployed as strategic choices, it should be clear that such strategies are open to all, regardless of their sex. Men may adopt a feminine style, as Jamieson (1988) argues contemporary politicians such as Ronald Reagan did, in order to adapt to the demands of the electronic age to produce more personal forms of communication. Similarly, women politicians may highlight elements of their femininity as part of running for office. For example, Patty Murray (D-Sen, WA) began her political career as a parent protesting budget cuts in a preschool program. When one state legislator dismissed her efforts because she was "just a mom in tennis shoes" (Murray, 2005), she was not demobilized by this comment but embraced it, eventually running as "a mom in tennis shoes" and winning a U.S. Senate seat. She also now holds an annual "Tennis Shoe Awards Dinner" to recognize people for their community service.

Although many assume that women candidates automatically campaign on issues that are in line with voters' gender/sex expectations for them, research tends to indicate that most candidates *do not* make this strategic choice. Kathleen Dolan (2005) studied male and female candidates' campaigns to determine whether issues conformed to gender expectations. Her findings: "Contrary to assumptions, women in 2000 and 2002 did not focus their issue priorities on a set of gender-stereotyped issues, but instead campaigned on a set of topics that were similar to their male opponents" (p. 31). The strategic choices once made by women candidates for political office may have changed. As Dolan explains, "Campaigns may make strategic decisions on how best to present women candidates in different situations—facing women vs. men opponents, running in more conservative or liberal districts—that can affect how issues are presented" (p. 42).

In sum, we have noted several variations in cultural theories. However, they all infer that the individual plays a more active role in the construction of gender and other social identities and suggest that, unlike biology and psychology, gender can and does evolve and change during one's life span. If individuals would like to become more behaviorally flexible, they can make efforts to utilize what society calls feminine and masculine behaviors. If groups and persons want to change the cultural systems of gender, race, class, and sexual orientation, change is possible (even if it is not easy).

Conclusion

In this chapter, we outlined the primary approaches used by researchers, popular media, and laypeople to explain gender in communication. Although these are not exclusively communication theories, they all reflect underlying assumptions about how people conceptualize and talk about gender/sex. Our goal has been to help readers better identify and examine their own assumptions as well as those of others.

Throughout this discussion, we have not been theoretically agnostic; we find some theories more persuasive than others. However, we have been theoretically promiscuous; we find multiple theories and research practices useful, depending on the precise question studied. Given that gender is complex and diverse, it makes sense that complex and diverse theories are necessary. For this reason, we embrace Nancy Henley and Cheris Kramarae's (1991) advice to quit arguing about whether gender is a product of nature *versus* nurture or cultural style *versus* domination. Their *multi-determined social context* approach recognizes the influences of intersecting identities (such as sex, gender, race, social class, and sexual orientation) and that biology, psychology, culture, and social hierarchies influence each other. The approach also cautions that one should remember that just because a difference exists does not equate to knowing what the difference *means*.

In this admittedly inconclusive review of the biological, psychological, and cultural approaches to studying gender/sex in communication, we do reach two conclusions: (1) that knowledge is culturally influenced, and (2) that a gender diversity, rather than a binary, perspective is best. Researchers bring their social and disciplinary assumptions and biases to the topic of study as well as to their choices of theories and research methods. There is more than one way to conduct research and build knowledge about gender in communication. How researchers define concepts such as gender and sex, difference, sexual orientation, ethnicity and race, and the methods they choose to study these concepts affect the conclusions formed about gender/sex in communication. Thus, one's perspective should recognize the existence of gender/sex diversity and not be limited by a gender/sex binary.

Given the multitude of variables that influence who persons are, it makes sense that there would never be just two gendered types of communication. Communication studies professor Celeste M. Condit (1998) outlines the four benefits of a gender diversity perspective. First, "The gender diversity perspective advocates respect and care for persons of all genders and gender types (as long as those types do not directly harm others or infringe on the human rights of others)" (p. 177). Like Henley and Kramarae's multi-determined social context approach, gender diversity "assumes that gender is a combination of temporally and locationally specific interactions among biological, social, and individual components" (p. 177).

Second, it allows people to stop feeling like failures in the "ideal woman" and "ideal man" game (Condit, 1998, p. 179). For example, the theories discussed earlier that celebrate the traditionally feminine attributes of nurturance, cooperation, and gentleness have much to recommend, yet "they ignore not only racial diversity, but class and regional diversity, as well as personal idiosyncrasy" (p. 180). They are prescriptive for how women should act, not descriptive.

Third, it makes clear that systems of patriarchy have costs for men, not just women, even though the form and size of those costs might differ. Some groups of men benefit from the system more than other groups of men, yet all men share the burden of upholding the myth of men's superiority.

Fourth, it reorients our research in an invigorating way: "Instead of trying to describe how men and women speak differently, we can begin to explore the range of gendered options available to people" (p. 183). It diverts attention from the study of how women's gender limits communication and directs it to the study of how a range of people have used diverse gender styles to speak passionately, ethically, and effectively to their audiences. A gender diversity approach provides a more realistic, more interesting, and wider scope for analyzing gender/sex in communication.

A more productive way to study the topic of gender in communication is to use a broader lens of analysis that recognizes that theory and knowledge construction are rhetorical and political acts, as are people's efforts to interpret, embrace, and reject them. This does not mean that there is no objective reality, but rather that reality means nothing until people give that reality meaning as they play active roles in its construction and deconstruction. Our perceptions *are* our reality. This is no less true for researchers. Understanding the link between expectations and reality brings with it an awesome ethical responsibility to attend to how one communicates and how one studies this topic. It also represents an exciting adventure through which we travel in the remainder of this book.

✺ CHAPTER 3

Gendered/Sexed Voices

Having stated in Chapter 1 that "communication creates gender/sex," we believe that it is essential to examine the verbal and nonverbal ways in which that process occurs. This is our goal in this chapter and the following one. We examine the use of verbal and nonverbal communication to continually create individual, relational, and group gender/sex identities.

The term *identity* refers to how people define themselves as individuals and as groups. As discussed in Chapter 1, identity includes concepts such as (1) unique individual qualities, such as personality; (2) intersecting group identities, such as gender/sex, race, class, sexuality, and nationality; and (3) contextual role identities, such as friend, lover, student, and supervisor. Thus, a person's identity has multiple (sometimes contradictory) facets that may be negotiated in a single conversation (Coates, 1996; Kroløkke & Sørensen, 2006). To make things even more complex, recall that critical cultural approaches theorize that identity is not fixed but rather is fragmented and in constant flux. Identity emerges in the process of repeatedly performing behaviors culturally recognized as feminine, White, heterosexual, educated, and so on (Kiesling, 2005; Whitehead, 2002). This does not mean that people can change their identities on a whim but that social constructions of identity shift across time. Although identity is in constant flux, it is perceived socially as stable. People are disciplined to perform identities in particular ways. Performance does leave some room for agency, as people can play with the ways they perform their identity. Ultimately, this approach theorizes that communication constructs gender/sex.

In contrast, if one presumes that "gender/sex creates communication," one would assume that identities are static and universal, and one would analyze talk simply by dividing speakers into two groups of females and males, noting sex patterns. This approach "assumes personal identity is an unproblematic category and that all social relations may be derived from it" (Livia & Hall, 1997, p. 6). It is the way in which gender/sex in talk mostly has been examined, via the descriptive cultural approach explained in Chapter 2. It is consistent with predominant scientific approaches to creating knowledge, and it is consistent with predominant assumptions about gender/sex as universal binary differences.

This approach to studying gender/sex in talk represents more than 50 years of research, but it has yielded few consistent results (Canary & Hause, 1993) and fewer differences than similarities (Dindia, 2006). Most of the research focuses presumptively on the interactions of White, middle-class, heterosexual women and men (Aries, 2006). Researchers also assume they are identifying gender markers in behaviors, but given that most do not ask for gender identity information, they end up focusing on stereotypical sex differences. Yet, knowledge of a person's sex has not been found to predict reliably how that person will behave (Aries, 2006). Researchers have investigated every tiny detail of interaction for possible sex differences in areas such as politeness, pronunciation, topic initiation, question asking, hesitancy, interruptions, and amount of talk. But it makes little sense to assume that sex differences dictate gender differences that are consistent across relationship types, personalities, races, sexual orientations, socioeconomic classes, and situational contexts.

Even though fixed gender/sex differences do not exist, studying talk still is important. Sociologist Barbara Risman (1998) explains that to create social equality, it is not enough to change social institutions such as the law, "for the gender structure exists not only on the institutional, individual, and interactional levels, but on all levels at the same time" (p. 157). Thus, an understanding of interaction in interpersonal and group situations is essential. This potential to reveal how power relations and inequalities are negotiated through every day interactions has drawn feminist, African American, and queer studies scholars to examine discourse.

The study of talk, or discourse, basically means analyzing multiple turns at talk in conversations, or multiple sections of written narratives, texts, or speeches. Conversation patterns, like language, are not random. Conversation consists of layers of rules and norms that create conversational practices and shared meanings. How speakers create and use these rules and norms can reveal much, not only about their identities but about the types of relationships they attempt to negotiate, such as cooperative/combative, subordinate/superior, romantic/platonic. The choices one makes in conversation also may influence the conversational partner's identity. This is what social psychologists call *altercasting*. "Altercasting . . . highlights how the way we talk to and act toward others (alters) puts them in roles (casts them)" (Tracy, 2002, p. 23). This does not mean that the other person has to accept the role cast upon her or him, but the potential for influence is there.

Thus, conversational work and identity work intertwine. Talk and nonverbal communication are ongoing ways in which persons make available to themselves and others who they are at a given time. Karen Tracy and other scholars call this "identity work" (p. 7). This work includes day-to-day maintenance efforts in which one presents one's self-concept to others. Sociologist Erving Goffman (1955) called this *face work*. Goffman emphasized people's need to present themselves to others in a particular way, which is influenced by individual as well as cultural expectations.

Because gender/sex is a primary way in which members in the U.S. culture categorize people, presenting one's gender/sex face becomes particularly important.

The word *work* points out that identity is accomplished primarily through the cooperation of the persons and groups with whom one interacts. Gender identity is not in a person but is performed in interactions between people. This is also true for conversation. Conversation requires the cooperation of the parties involved. Sociologist Pamela Fishman (1978) studied heterosexual couples' talk at home, calling conversational relationship work the "shitwork" of interaction (p. 405). Her point was that relational maintenance depends greatly on day-to-day interactions and on both partners' efforts to create mutually satisfying conversations. If one partner tends to do most of the work, her or his efforts may go unappreciated, and an inequitable, unsatisfactory relationship may emerge. Thus, behavioral patterns in discourse can provide a window for examining how personal, relational, group, and intergroup relations are negotiated. However, this analysis is complicated by the fact that behaviors (for example, interruptions) can have more than one function and meaning. The relationship between conversational cues and relational dynamics is not straightforward (Mills, 2003). In this and the following chapter, we explore how persons negotiate gender/sex identities through the microinteractions of talk (voice) and the body (nonverbals).

We begin by offering critical thinking tools one can use to examine the research and theory presented here, recalling that much of the research is based on the flawed assumptions previously noted. After reviewing this research, we conclude that a dichotomous view of gender as the differences between women and men is erroneous, overly simplistic, and risks reifying stereotypes and related inequalities. Instead, an intersectional, multidetermined, gender diversity view that recognizes multiple influences on differences *and* similarities is more useful. Our approach recognizes that power is implicated in discourse and gender, and the feminine gender is often a lower-power role. Accordingly, we conclude this chapter by looking beyond differences to explore the range of gender options available to communicators as strategic resources.

Constructing a Critical Gender/Sex Lens

To assist in treading through the multiple complexities involved in studying talk, we employ the theory of post-structuralism described in Chapter 2. Baxter's (2003) *feminist post-structuralist discourse analysis approach* provides a nuanced means to study discourse. Briefly, this form of discourse analysis uses the following practices and principles:

1. *Deconstruction*, recognizing that meanings of speech, identities, and relationships are not fixed.

2. *Self-reflexivity* on the part of the researcher and the participants.

3. *Close analysis* of the discourse in its immediate context, including insider views and relational, institutional, and power influences.

4. That *process* (as in conversation) *produces structure* (as in gender/sex identities and expectations); sex does not produce conversation.

5. *The use of multiple methods* to analyze discourse because there can be multiple interpretations of the same act.

Researchers can use this as a checklist to confirm that they truly are doing a poststructuralist analysis.

Baxter emphasizes studying the *process* of identity construction rather than an assumed product such as gender (Kr[o]løkke & Sørensen, 2006, p. 147). Her approach is a useful component of a critical gendered lens that can reveal the limitations of most previous research. We describe these limitations before reviewing the research, to assist in developing your critical analysis abilities.

First, most studies identify only participants' sex, not their gender. Researchers who do so assume that sex determines gender or that sex and gender are the same thing. They attempt to identify *gender* differences by comparing how *women* and *men* communicate. Women are studied, and conclusions are drawn about feminine communication; men are studied, and conclusions are drawn about masculine communication. In one of the few studies to examine communication style, gender, and sex identities, there was no statistical interaction between sex and gender. One did not relate to the other (Kirtley & Weaver, 1999).

Communication researchers Dan Canary and Kim Hause (1993) synthesized 15 meta-analyses of research on gender/sex differences in communication covering more than 1,000 recent studies. They found that sex accounted for a scant 1% of the differences that were present; the unique interactions and contexts better explained differences found. In detailed analyses of linguist Deborah Tannen's (1990) claims about gender/sex two-culture styles (discussed in Chapter 2), researchers found that virtually none of her claims were adequately supported (Goldsmith & Fulfs, 1999). Actual research conducted to test the two-culture gender theory shows gender differences of small degrees rather than of kind (Edwards & Hamilton, 2004; Michaud & Warner, 1997). When researchers asked for the gender identities of the primarily White college student groups studied, they found that the students' behaviors were influenced not only by gender but by other identities, such as whether the student saw herself or himself as a joker, an adviser, or a nurturer; the student's interest in cross-sex communication; and the student's beliefs about cross-sex communication differences.

The risk of research that claims gender/sex differences is that it essentializes gender/sex (Stokoe & Smithson, 2001). It falsely reduces an individual's complex identity to mere sex identity. Although only limited research exists on gender and discourse in non-White groups, this research offers important indicators suggesting that the assumption of only two gendered communication styles is racist, classist, and ethnocentric.

Sociolinguist Patricia Nichols (1983) conducted a classic study of two different African American communities on an island off the South Carolina coast. The women who gained employment in service positions on the mainland used Standard English (non-Creole). Their language style was directly connected to their employment opportunities and to the language requirements of their jobs in a sex-segregated, predominantly White marketplace. The other group of women who stayed on the island used less Standard English, like the men in their households. The men were better able to find employment in fishing industries and to stay on the island and so had less need to learn or speak Standard English. Thus, sex-based economic opportunities and geographic boundaries, not gender/sex alone, affected language use.

Communication scholar Bonnie J. Dow (1995) extends this caution against overemphasizing gender/sex differences to the study of public speakers. Instead of noticing how cultural and social conditions required women to craft unique responses to their rhetorical situations, many researchers have assumed that women's rhetorical styles are innate. However, feminine style is not biologically tied to sex; instead, it is "as much a product of *power* as it is a product of *gender*" (p. 109). If researchers look only for differences between women and men, differences will be all they find.

A part of the difficulty is that researchers possess no adequate way to identify gender ethically and adequately. As discussed in Chapter 2, psychological measures are based on stereotypes of masculine and feminine, and most infer that a person's gender is a permanent trait even as post-structuralist theories compellingly demonstrate the fluidity of genders. Although little discussion of this dilemma has taken place, our observation is that discourse researchers' more recent works do not attempt to place gender labels on individual participants. Instead, they observe the process by which persons coconstruct multiple masculinities and femininities tied to the unique contexts of interaction (e.g., Baxter, 2003; Cameron, 1997; Coates, 2003). Some also ask the participants about their interpretations of the discourse. By doing so, researchers are no longer inferring that sex differences produce consistent gender differences. Instead, the focus is on multiple contradictory genderings in a given interaction.

Second, much research has been based on outside observers' interpretations of behavior. When researchers interpret this way, they necessarily base their interpretations on their own gendered/sexed views and predominant cultural norms. For example, you could have a mutually satisfying conversation with a friend that an outside observer might consider rude or adversarial. The observer does not know the unique ways in which you and this person communicate. Similarly, psychologists Elizabeth Stokoe and Janet Smithson (2001) note that the researcher might impose gendered labels on your behavior that you would not accept. Others might label your tendencies to be gruff or abrupt as masculine behavior, whereas you might attribute these tendencies to other influences, such as your working-class background or simple dislike of the person to whom you are talking.

Third, it is difficult to identify the function of a specific component of conversation, such as talking at the same time as or longer than another person. Each component can have multiple functions in the interaction (Crawford, 1995; Tannen, 1994a). Behaviors can even play seemingly contradictory functions at the same time. For example, two people talking at the same time could mean that they like each other, that they are enthusiastic about the topic, and/or that they are competing for the talk floor (Henley, 1977, 1995). In fact, the multiple functions can serve as tools to make acts of domination or affection less obvious. To compensate for this uncertainty of meaning, researchers look for patterns of behavior. Identifying the functions of isolated parts of interaction, such as simultaneous talk (two or more persons talking at the same time), is much less meaningful than when researchers focus on patterns, such as how the simultaneous talk interacts with who talks longer, who makes more eye contact, and who successfully develops a topic of interest (DeFrancisco, 1991; Eckert & McConnell-Ginet, 1999). If one participant interrupts more and is more successful developing the topics she or he raises, dominance may be at play.

Fourth, the focus on two-culture gender/sex differences infers that behavior is inflexible, that people always act in the same ways across contexts. Such inflexibility is inconsistent with what scholars think of as characteristics of a good communicator. Communication competence is the ability to adapt one's communication to the needs of the context (Crawford, 1995; Weatherall, 1998). One prevalent assumption has been that men always tend to interrupt more than women because of their assumed right as men and in an attempt to control situations and relationships (Tannen, 1990; West & Zimmerman, 1983). However, although the men studied tended to interrupt more in multiple contexts (Johnson, 2000), in heterosexual relations, participants perceived such behavior not as intrusive but as indicators of participation (DeFrancisco, 1991). Furthermore, in a statistical meta-analysis of 43 previous studies on women and men interrupting, the reviewers found, across situations, that the men in the studies did interrupt the women slightly more than the women interrupted the men (Anderson & Leaper, 1998), but a more complex model helps explain the interruptions better than the speakers' sex alone. More intrusive interruptions were especially apparent when the settings were natural rather than in a laboratory and when three or more persons participated in the discussions. The context, not just gender/sex, affected the participants' use of interruptions.

These limitations on gender/sex in talk research explain why we cannot provide an uncomplicated list of gender/sex differences in discourse. Furthermore, such a list would not explain why such differences and similarities exist, nor would it recognize the social and personal impact of such behaviors—for example, the gender/sex stereotype that relationship work is women's work, and the injustices of sexual harassment and acquaintance rape. Instead, we have chosen to examine how the assumptions and expectations of gender/sex differences are created, maintained, and or changed.

Constructing Gender/Sex in Communication

Although researchers have not found substantial or consistent sex differences in the ways people communicate, the fact is that cultural assumptions about differences persist, and those assumptions influence how one communicates and how one is assessed by others. Women are expected to be peacemakers, so if a woman is forthright, she may be judged rude. Men are expected to be forceful communicators, so if a man is conciliatory, he may be judged weak. Even if women and men do not really communicate differently, people expect them to. These expectations are real, and they have real consequences for people's identities and experiences.

In sum, society helps to construct gender/sex stereotypes in at least two ways:

1. Gender/sex conversational styles: Persons' communication follows (or violates) binary gender norms of feminine and masculine styles as prescribed by the predominant society.

2. Gender/sex perceptions: Social norms prescribing gender influence how persons perceive and assess themselves and others.

The second item makes clear that perceptions of oneself and others are influenced by the degree to which members of society have internalized gender/sex and other group expectations. People judge themselves and others according to how they define and feel about such gendered/sexed expectations. Although we necessarily discuss these two separately, they are inseparable in terms of how they actually influence social life. Finally, to address the questions of why such differences are constructed and what the impacts of these constructions are—such as who most benefits and who is most oppressed—one must reveal the links between seemingly innocent cultural constructions and the concept of hegemonic power relations.

Gendered Conversational Styles

One's communication or *conversational style* refers to the tendencies or patterns in the way one communicates (Norton, 1983; Tannen, 1984). The word *patterns* highlights that a person does not always behave in exactly the same way but develops recurrent elements of behavior that others use to describe that person. Communication researcher Robert Norton (1983) found that people do not rely on one style alone but on a repertoire of styles. Styles are defined by verbal and nonverbal qualities, such as rate of speech, vocal inflection, vocal pitch, pronunciation of words, volume, amount of talk and silence, and even topic preferences. A style becomes unique to a person when variances in each of these qualities are combined.

Gender is just one possible influence on a person's style. Cultural influences on conversational styles also have been studied in terms of race, ethnicity, social class, national origin, region of the country, and language (e.g., Carbaugh, 2002; Kikoski & Kikoski, 1999; Kochman, 1990). Consistent with the concept of intersectionality, each of these group identities influences a person's style as the identities interact.

Social expectations, gender identity, and related privileges and subordinations can affect the style one adopts and internalizes over time. For example, men's tendency to have larger bodies gives men larger vocal organs than women, and thus in general gives men deeper voices. However, some researchers say that body size differences are not enough to account for the divergent pitch used by many women and men. Some men tend to draw from the lower vocal range, and some women draw from the higher range (Knapp & Hall, 2002). This has been particularly documented in Japan, where women traditionally spoke in higher voices and were censured for failing to do so. More recent reports show that Japanese women's voices are deepening, perhaps because of their increasing social equality ("Japan's Feminine Falsetto," 1995). As this example illustrates, style differences cannot be explained solely by physiology. Women who speak in a higher pitch are more likely to be described as feminine. Men who speak in a lower pitch are more likely to be described as masculine. In a study comparing self-perceptions of gender roles and communication styles, women and men college students who identified with a communal feminine role preferred a selfless, caring style. Those who identified with an agentic masculine role preferred a goal-oriented, assertive style (Kirtley & Weaver, 1999). However, racial and ethnic identities were not taken into account.

Even as the existence of universal gender/sex differences is debunked by actual research, we believe it is useful to understand that cultural expectations are attached to the masculine/feminine binary and to learn where the lines of difference have been drawn. As you read about gendered communication styles here, remember that we present them to examine how speakers participate in communication to create and/or change gender/sex identity, not merely how speakers express gender/sex identity. Linguist Deborah Cameron (1996) hypothesizes that women and men alike tend to *construct differentiation* through discourse more than merely *expressing difference* in discourse. Not all the researchers cited here subscribe to the two-culture theory, but their research does help explain gender/sex assumptions in communication strategies. Conversational styles reveal one means by which cultural differences and inequalities are created and maintained on a micro (individual) and relational identity basis.

CHILDREN'S PLAY AND GENDERED STYLES

The two-culture theory of gender and communication discussed in Chapter 2 suggests that girls and boys are raised in gender/sex–segregated language user groups in which they develop opposing conversational styles. Researchers studying children's play find gendered interaction styles present, especially in same-sex groups (Sheldon, 1990; Thorne, 2003). However, much of this research is limited to the study of White, middle-class children. The girls studied tended to play in smaller groups, where talk has a central role. They negotiated who will play what roles, such as mother and child, what the situation will be, and so forth. Communication scholar Julia Wood (2007) summarizes girls' presumed play rules: (1) Use collaborative, cooperative talk to create and maintain relationships because "the process of communication, not its content, is the heart of relationships"; (2) avoid criticizing, outdoing, or putting others down; if criticism is necessary, make it gentle; never exclude others; and (3) pay attention to others and to relationships; interpret and respond to others' feelings with sensitivity (p. 125).

In contrast, boys studied tend to play in larger, less intimate groups, in which the focus is on an activity (not talk), competition, and asserting one's independence.

With preestablished games, such as sports, there is less need to talk to work out the rules and roles. Wood (2007) summarizes boys' presumed play rules this way: Use communication (1) to achieve something, to assert yourself and your ideas, (2) to attract and maintain an audience, and (3) to compete with others for the "talk stage" so that they don't gain more attention than you do; learn to get the focus off others and onto yourself (p. 124).

These rules may seem vaguely familiar to some, at least as cultural generalizations, but you may already be thinking of exceptions to them. Many of our women students tell us they played sports. The continued expansion of girls' participation in competitive sports likely is changing the way girls play. Also, the separate gender/sex rules of play just cited cannot explain shared play. Many African American boys and girls have a history of sharing the verbal games of *playin' the dozens,* or *signifying.* In these games of verbal competitive insult, one player places a topic or a person that matters to the other (such as the other's mother) in an implausible context. The competition tests wit, humor, sarcasm, and the ability to stay cool under verbal attack. Although boys have been observed playing these games more than girls, girls tend to have more serious penalties for players who violate the rules by attacking others with plausible contexts that are more hurtful, or by making derogatory statements behind others' backs (Morgan, 1999). The girls' play is more likely to lead to physical confrontation or extended ostracism than are the boys' verbal contests.

In another study of Mexican and Central American grade school students' playground activities near Los Angeles, sociologist Marjorie Goodwin (1999) found that the children did play in same-sex groups, but the girls playing hopscotch were highly competitive and quick to call others "out of the line." In a comparison of mainland Chinese and U.S. children's play, the U.S. boys were found to be more assertive than the girls in same-sex play, but the reverse was true of the Chinese children. In cross-sex conflict, both U.S. boys and Chinese girls used more direct responses, such as pushing or name calling (Kyratzis & Guo, 2001).

Linguist Penelope Eckert (2003) points out that the nature of play usually changes from childhood to adolescence. She suggests that this change is directly tied to gender and *heterosociability,* or the pressure to create a heterosexual identity, and that language plays a central role in this shift, particularly for girls. She observed that boys' playground activity changes from playing games to performing masculinity as athletes. Girls' playground activity changes from games to "standing, sitting, or walking around the periphery, watching the boys, heckling them, or talking intensely together." She argues that this behavior draws physical attention to those who do it and stands in stark contrast to other children's fast movements in active play: "This talk activity is a skill that girls consciously develop" (p. 385). This girls' talk is not only about their connection and collaboration but also about competition for male attention. These play tendencies clearly do not follow the guidelines outlined from the two-culture theory.

Yet, researchers using that theory claim that norms of sex-segregated children's play set the foundation for opposing adult feminine and masculine styles of conversation (Tannen, 1994a; Wood, 2007). You will find these clearly linked to stereotypic expectations for dichotomous feminine and masculine behavior. More recent British masculinity scholarship (Frosh, Phoenix, & Pattman, 2002) makes clear that different communication styles do not spring naturally from sex. Instead, as people develop their identities, the hegemonic power of gender/sex norms induce them to "draw on culturally available resources in their immediate social networks and in society as a whole." Because "these 'resources' are, generally speaking, strongly gendered," males and females receive different messages, are constrained differently, and have access to different codes (pp. 4–5).

FEMININE STYLE

Those who have a feminine style are perceived to view talk as an activity in itself rather than as a means of accomplishing a goal. Wood (2007) writes, "For feminine people, talk *is* the essence of relationships" (p. 126). Talk is seen as a primary means of negotiating and maintaining relationships. To build rapport, speakers use verbal and nonverbal cues that convey support to the other person, offering affirmations or questions that convey interest, and by seeking cooperation rather than competition (e.g., Coates, 1997; Johnson, 1996; Tannen, 1990). This is also called a *communal style*, which includes stereotypic nurturing, affection, helpfulness, and emotional expression (Lindsey & Zakahi, 2006).

The feminine-style speaker is perceived to use an indirect style of communicating, such as stating, "The coffeepot is empty," rather than directly requesting, "Please make some coffee." Indirectness is seen as less assertive or less confident (Lakoff, 1975). Persons who have lower social status may be more likely to use indirectness and politeness to gain compliance from others. People with higher status can afford to be more direct, making stronger public statements. This makes it difficult for persons who use a more feminine style of politeness to be effective in the public sphere. In New Zealand, linguist Janet Holmes (1995) gathered data from a wide variety of sources and found that the men she studied did not value or exhibit politeness as much as the women did. The women tended to give and receive more compliments than the men did, and the women tended to offer and receive more apologies than the men did.

However, indirectness is not used by all women or only by women, and for the most part, researchers do not know whether the participants studied viewed their behaviors as indirect. African American women's tendency toward a more direct style of communicating than that of White women in the United States is attributed to the former's struggle against slavery (Houston, 2000; Morgan, 1999). Indirectness is preferred by women *and* men in many collectivist cultures, such as Japanese, Korean, Chinese, and Native American groups. Indirectness can help promote a focus on group needs and identity rather than individual ones (Gao & Ting-Toomey, 1998; Gudykunst & Ting-Toomey, 1988). A classic study of the Malagasy culture found that the men use more indirect, polite speech, and the women use more direct speech (Keenan, 1974). The women of this culture tend to have more autonomy and sexual freedom, which might better explain the differing communication styles. Linguist Scott Kiesling (2005) finds that college fraternity brothers effectively use indirectness to express warmth and friendship toward each other in a heterosexist atmosphere. They bond through competitive sports, just being together, drinking together, joking, looking out for each other, and group membership rather than through direct expressions of affection.

Related to indirectness, feminine communication styles also tend to be seen as more polite because of the orientation toward other people's feelings and needs, showing respect for the other person's face or self-image. In reality, people in all cultures use forms of politeness depending on the situation. Politeness norms indicate what a society deems appropriate behavior. Politeness norms are a means of social control without force (Mills, 2003). In inequitable power relations, persons of lower social status tend to be more polite when conferring with a superior than persons of higher social status. The most commonly used example is from Japan, where women and men have traditionally spoken different gendered languages. The women's language is seen as "more polite, gentle, soft-spoken, nonassertive, and empathic" (Okamoto, 1995, p. 297). Japanese women have been observed to use different particles at the end of certain sentences, such as *wa, no* and *kashira*, which make a statement softer and more polite. Women and men are traditionally expected to use different words to refer to the same thing; in most cases, the masculine form is more direct, more abrasive, and considered of higher status. For example, "butt" in the feminine form is *oshiri*; in the masculine form, it is *ketsu*.

However, differences that once existed in Japan and elsewhere seem to be changing as gender roles change and inequalities lessen. Shoko Hayashi, a former student of ours, explains that "women using more polite speech" more accurately describes her mother's generation, in which the hierarchical relationship between women and men is more pronounced. Wives are supposed to treat their husbands as masters of the house. Recent research supports Hayashi's assessment. Linguist Yuki Mizokami (2003) analyzed data from previous studies of language styles in Japan and found that when the age of the participants was identified, gender/sex differences were much less for 20–30-year-olds than for middle-aged and older Japanese speakers. Polish women with paid employment and higher education also show dramatic changes in speech styles in recent years, moving away from traditional expectations of feminine politeness to a more direct style described as harsh, clipped, impatient, and rude (Baran & Syska, 2000, cited in Mills, 2003).

An interesting study of female phone-sex employees in San Francisco points to the complexity involved when style, power, sex, and sexuality meet. Linguistics scholar Kira Hall (1995) found that the activities of women who worked adult (900) fantasy lines challenged the notion that women's talk was powerless talk in this context. Hall makes clear that "sweet talk," which is typically a marker of women's powerlessness, can be quite powerful in a setting where the woman controls the conversation, furthering her own conversational and economic ends. Hall's goal is to make clear the subversive potential of employing powerless speech in cross-sex, heterosexual linguistic exchanges. She also found that regardless of race, age, class, or geography, the women working for adult message services would shift styles into "a definable conversational style that they all associate with 'women's language'" (p. 207).

The use of profanity contrasts with being sweet and polite. Slang and profanity have been viewed traditionally as rough, "manly" speech, inappropriate for ladies.

Females who use profanity are more likely to be criticized than men who use it (Spender, 1985). In a study of Australian working-class adolescents, the researcher found that as the boys grew closer to puberty, they decreased their use of culturally proper language, but as the girls grew closer to puberty, they increased it (Eisikovits, 1998). Consistent with this observation, in interviews the girls described coming of age as accepting their social responsibilities to conform, whereas the boys described coming of age as asserting their masculinity and individual rights. However, research on college students in New Zealand and the United States now indicates that women and men use expletives to convey power and group solidarity. There were sex differences in the types and severity of profanity used, and similarities in adapting its use to the context (Bayard & Krishnayya, 2001; Stapleton, 2003). Some women in positions of power swear. Former U.S. Secretary of State Madeleine Albright stated that she nearly gave then-Secretary of Defense Colin Powell an aneurysm with her bad language. In a media interview in which she watched a video of Cuban pilots celebrating the downing of a U.S. plane, Albright responded, "That's not cojones [balls], that's cowardice" (cited in Mills, 2003, p. 193).

Storytelling is another conversational device used to construct and display identities for others. Some researchers identify gendered ways of telling stories (Aries, 1996; Coates, 1996; Holmes, 1997). A primary feature of feminine storytelling is said to be that the process is more collaborative. One person's story becomes the group's story or an invitation for others in the group to share their stories (Coates, 1997). Simultaneous talk is seen less as interruption than as collaboration. Thus, the organization of the story may be less linear. The goal is to catch up on each others' lives (Holmes, 1997).

The above behaviors together illustrate how the so-called feminine conversational style is reflective of stereotypical White, heterosexual, upper-class femininity. The cultural expectations attached to this style construct femininity in opposition to masculinity and do not reflect the actual diversity of feminine styles.

MASCULINE STYLE

In Western culture, being a man is about not being a woman or not exhibiting any identity characteristics associated with women, such as effeminacy. Masculine style is constructed as distinct from feminine style. Those who subscribe more to a masculine style are said to use talk as a tool to accomplish a task, to solve a problem, to exert control, to assert themselves, or to gain independence and status (Cameron, 1997; Coates, 1997). In contrast to feminine style, masculine style avoids personal disclosure and vulnerability and is more direct and assertive. This also is called an *agentic* (agency) *focus*, with stereotypic behaviors such as dominating, leading, forcing, and showing ambition (Lindsey & Zakahi, 2006).

Masculine-style speakers may interrupt more than those using a feminine style and for a different reason. Whereas in a feminine style interruptions are said to be used more to build collaboration and support, in a masculine style interruptions are said to be used more to assert oneself when another person is speaking (Mulac, 1998; Mulac, Wiemann, Widenmann, & Gibson, 1988).

The masculine style also corresponds with unique ways of storytelling. Men studied tended to prefer to tell stories in ways that helped enhance their status and masculinity (Coates, 1997; Holmes, 1997). In an extensive study of 32 transcribed conversations among primarily White, middle-class, adult male friends in the United Kingdom, linguist Jennifer Coates (2003) identified more than 203 stories with the following unique features: First, the stories were about stereotypical masculine topics such as cars, sports, drinking, and technology; these topics helped detour the conversation away from personal self-disclosure and vulnerability. Second, the stories constructed a men's world; very few stories had female protagonists or characters. Third, the stories were detailed and long, allowing the men to hold the talk floor for a substantial period of time, making the conversation a series of monologues. Fourth, the speakers preferred one person speaking at a time rather than the simultaneous talk noted in the women's feminine storytelling episodes. Fifth, the organization of stories was more linear, with stories organized chronologically. Sixth, the men used profanity heavily. This was the most marked difference Coates found from women's conversations: "Swearing has historically been used by men in the company of other men as a sign of their toughness and manhood" (p. 46). Seventh, the men's stories stressed achievement or bragged. Eighth, the men engaged in competitive storytelling, seeing who could tell the bigger "fish story"; the storytelling became a competitive sport in a way Coates did not observe in the women's conversations. She argues that the men in her research were creating and maintaining their culture of masculinity through the way they constructed stories.

Although these descriptions about women and men, and feminine and masculine styles, infer that sex binaries directly lead to gender binaries, we have shown that there are actually wide variations in how people use what is labeled gendered conversational styles. However, there is some value in studying the two-culture conversational styles perspective. If one assumes that individual, relational, and group identities are negotiated through talk, then it makes sense that the talk is not random but occurs in patterned ways, such as through gender styles.

Styles are based on the cultural norms and hierarchies of speech communities. Thus, when studying talk, it is not enough to study isolated parts of conversation such as interruptions or amount of talk time. Rather, it is through the combination of such components that speakers make meaning. Style provides a framework for examining individual and group patterns and for examining how persons with differing styles negotiate their differences. Styles also make clear that these patterns are more likely learned over time and so are not always overt strategies but are used out of habit. Because of this implicit development over time, a risk in studying gender/sex from a styles perspective is forgetting that styles are not likely innate or innocent of cultural inequalities. Styles, like gender and identity, are created in a cultural political context, and stereotypical or not, they have real consequences for individuals and groups.

Cultural Perceptions of Gender/Sex Styles and Speakers

The second related way society constructs gender/sex stereotypes in talk is through the cultural values placed on the foregoing descriptions of gendered/sexed conversational styles. Not only are speakers gendered/sexed, but so are their listeners. Perceived differences in gender/sex communication style far exceed any actual ones (Kirtley & Weaver, 1999). Two prominent biases affect the reception of a message.

First, unlike the premise of the two-culture theory that people are raised in two different cultures, people are raised in a hegemonic patriarchal culture where stereotypical masculine, White, upper- and middle-class styles are highly preferred. This makes it more difficult for women and men who use other speech styles to be effective. Even when women and nonprivileged men use masculine style, it may not be as effective as when White men use it. Judith Baxter's (2002) ethnographic study of a 10th-grade speech class in England with primarily White students demonstrates this point. She found that the two qualities the male speakers used more than the female speakers yielded higher overall speech grades: humor and the greater reception of this humor by the teacher and students. Baxter explains that the results do not mean that the girls were deficient (some girls did use humor) but that the speaker–audience–gender/sex interaction provided a more positive reception of the boys' humor and thus gave them more opportunities to define themselves as effective speakers.

Second, people in privileged social groups do not realize they have a style. African Americans have a style, working-class people have a style, but White middle- and upper-class people consider their way of speaking neutral and normal (Nakayama & Krizek, 1999). One's conversational style becomes a perceptual lens for interpreting and evaluating others' ways of speaking. Conversational styles carry with them implicit values, whether the stereotypic expectation that a feminine style expresses the value of nurturing or the masculine style, the value of individual rights and leadership. People tend to prefer and value the styles they use, thus creating a less-than-objective means of assessing others' communication. People may consciously or unconsciously attempt to impose their communication style preferences on others and forget that they are interpreting others' behaviors through their own style expectations.

These two perceptual biases may at times contradict each other, trapping speakers such as men who prefer a feminine style or women who prefer a masculine style in no-win situations. This is most evident in the stereotypic labeling of women who express masculine styles as lesbians and men who express feminine styles as gays. Yet, lesbians and gays are no more likely to share consistent speaking styles than are heterosexual women and men (Livia & Hall, 1997).

People tend to expect one another to sound like a stereotype of the speaker's presumed group, and some groups' presumed styles are more socially preferred. A variety of evidence indicates that voice has been used to discriminate against some groups. Even though White women worked successfully in broadcasting during World War II, when White men came back from the war and needed jobs, the stereotype of women's voices as soft and high-pitched was pointed to as inadequate for broadcast (Kramarae, 1981). In a more recent laboratory study, predominantly White college students were asked to rate a series of voices on a continuum from masculine to feminine. The students preferred voices that were less expressive and lower pitched, and they rated these qualities as more masculine. They identified the less-preferred, higher-pitched voices as feminine (Lippa, 1998). Vocal profiling in telephone conversations also has been used by Whites to discriminate against Black-sounding people seeking jobs and housing opportunities (Johnson, 2002; Purnell, Idsardi, & Baugh, 1999; Wiehl, 2002).

[handwritten margin note: same w/ names on apps]

Another stereotypical gender/sex expectation that generates negative judgments is that women are better at giving emotional comfort, listening, and empathizing. To examine this, a research team led by Erina MacGeorge conducted a series of empirical tests on gender and supportive communication (MacGeorge, Graves, Feng, Gillihan, & Burleson, 2004). Unlike most, the research team asked participants to identify their genders, and the team looked for similarities in communication, not just differences. Participants were predominantly White, ranging in age from their twenties to their fifties, at a midwestern university. The researchers found that the men were just as responsive and supportive as the women when confronted with a distressed friend, and there were no sex differences in receiving support from others. There were gender differences in how participants offered support. People who identified as more feminine expressed sympathy and affirmed the other. People who identified as more masculine expressed sympathy by attempting to minimize the other's pain and offer help.

Style expectations and biases are not limited to gender/sex. Communication studies professor Marsha Houston (2004) points out that a history of racial distrust between African Americans and Whites has produced negative interpretations of each other's conversational styles. When Houston (2004) interviewed middle-class women about their own racial group's conversational style compared to that of the other group, the White women described their style as using "proper" English and distinct pronunciation. They viewed all African American women as speaking with a "black accent," being less "proper," and being pushy. The African American women viewed the White women's style as passive, friendly but phony, and weak. They viewed their own style as celebrating their sense of self, showing wisdom, fortitude, and caring (Houston, 2000).

These descriptions demonstrate that styles are not simply different but equal. Some carry more cultural prestige. Also, a given style does not serve all speakers equally. Some speakers are more socially privileged, and so are the styles they exhibit. Conversely, one can use the style of a more privileged group, but it may not be well received.

Power and Talk

As stated earlier in this chapter, hegemonic power relations construct gender/sex styles, stereotypical perceptions, and actual discourse. Baxter's (2003) feminist post-structuralist discourse analysis perspective defines *power* "not as a possession in somebody's hands, but as a net-like organisation [*sic*] which weaves itself discursively through social organisations, meanings, relations and the construction of speakers' subjectivities or identities" (p. 8). Because power is complex, we cannot assume that there is simply one discourse determining gender: there may be dominant discourses constructing stereotypical assumptions about masculinity, femininity and binary gender differences, but there may also be resistant or oppositional discourses advocating, for example, gender diversity, inclusion or separation. . . . Such discourses do not operate in discrete isolation from each other but are always intertextually linked, that is, each discourse is likely to be interconnected with and infused by traces of the others. (p. 8)

This intricate relationship and the multiple functions of conversational behaviors make it difficult to describe speakers' behaviors exclusively as attempts to gain, resist, or submit to power.

Yet, the consideration of power in gender relations and discourse is essential. As feminist linguist Mary Crawford (1995) writes,

To treat asymmetries of interaction as "style" differences ignores social realities. Speakers do not speak in a vacuum. They attempt to choose language that will "work" interactionally. Their use of language is situated and strategic. And, what "works" depends on the social status of the speaker and the power relations between speaker and listener. (p. 44)

Crawford invokes the concept of speech as strategic. Speakers are rational beings who behave in meaning-making ways. To do so, they may apply a number of different strategies to construct their conversations and intersectional identity.

Research on the speech patterns of gay, lesbian, bisexual, and transgender persons offers more observable examples of communication as strategic. When persons do not fit into the normative heterosexual culture, they must play with cultural norms of feminine and masculine conversational style if they want to construct an identity that is not heterosexual (Livia & Hall, 1997). Robin Queen (1997), in a study of lesbian comic-book characters such as Hothead Paisan, found the stereotypical straight feminine speech norms of overly polite forms and euphemisms combined with the stereotypical masculine norms of swearing and directness to create distinct styles. The contradictions of these behaviors make the style humorous, critical of cultural expectations, and unique.

In her work on first-wave women's rhetoric, Karlyn Kohrs Campbell (1989, Vol. 2) provides a rich collection of powerful women rhetors who strategically used cultural expectations of feminine speech style to gain effectiveness. Speakers such as Maria Miller Stewart, Sarah and Angelina Grimké, Susan B. Anthony, and Elizabeth Cady Stanton spoke despite social and sometimes legal prohibitions. Campbell argues that many of the first U.S. women to speak in public against slavery and for woman suffrage "strategically adopted what might be called a feminine style to cope with the conflicting demands of the podium. That style emerged out of their experiences as women and was adapted to the attitudes and experiences of female audiences" (Vol. 1, p. 12). Campbell argues that this feminine style was developed to push at sexist boundaries by using feminine gender expectations.

Not all early women rhetors were economically privileged Whites, nor did they all advocate woman suffrage. Labor activists provide interesting examples of diverse feminine styles. Emma Goldman was a working-class immigrant, Lucy Parsons was a working-class woman of color, and Voltairine de Cleyre was an educated, working-class White woman who eschewed marriage. Their speech styles necessarily differed (Horwitz, Kowal, & Palczewski, in press). British and U.S. suffrage advocates also used different styles. Donna Kowal (2000) argues that British speakers used greater militancy, invoking their working-class backgrounds and their affiliation with workers' movements. Rhetors advocating workers' rights, women's rights, and liberty make clear that a range of feminine styles exist and can be effective.

Furthermore, it is important to remember that even though many studies of feminine style have been of women, gender styles are open to all people. Particularly as the United States has become a more media-saturated society, feminine style has become more pervasive for women and men. No longer must a public speaker command an audience of thousands, standing in a town square, without the help of a microphone. Instead, when public officials speak to audiences, it is often through the medium of television, which brings them directly into the most personal places of people's homes. Political communication scholar Kathleen Hall Jamieson (1988) notes that when speeches were delivered in person to crowds of thousands, a highly personal style based on storytelling and one-on-one connections to an audience member was condemned as effeminate and ineloquent. However, "Television invites a personal, self-disclosing style that draws public discourse out of a private self and comfortably reduces the complex world to dramatic narratives" (p. 84), particularly when used by a president. Jamieson argues that President Ronald Reagan was thought of as "the great communicator" not because he was particularly eloquent but because he understood the medium of television, which was uniquely suited to the use of memorable narratives and visual "vignettes that capture his central claims" (p. 119). No one labeled his style effeminate, even though it was.

In the study of organizations, researchers have noted cultural shifts away from a more authoritative style of management to a more democratic style. Feminist critics (Fondas, 1997; May, 1997) note that descriptions of the two managerial styles are similar to stereotypical White masculine and feminine styles. The autocratic style is defined as controlling, with rigidly structured hierarchy. The democratic style is defined as collaborative and personable. Interestingly, the collaborative/feminine style of management has been found to be highly successful in team-based organizations, but no one seems to acknowledge the feminine elements of this style. Instead, it tends to be labeled collaborative, transformational, or interactive—not feminine. Women and men can use gender style strategies stereotypically associated with the other sex effectively. Many researchers have documented that the context of the interaction, such as job role and power and status goals, matters as much as, if not more than, the sex or gender of the participants in determining their styles and power assertions (Gordon, 1997; Yaeger-Dror, 1998).

Conclusion

Discourse is a primary way in which persons and groups continually negotiate gender/sex and other aspects of their identity. But contrary to popular assumptions, any presumed gender differences in conversation cannot be drawn along the single axis of sex. First, gender identity is constructed intersectionally with race, ethnicity, class, age, sexual orientation, and other identity ingredients, which together impact choices in behavior. Second, stereotypic cultural expectations and perceptions of gender/sex behavior strongly influence the construction of differences and related inequalities. Third, individuals make choices of behaviors according to unique situations. Fourth, it is impossible to establish simple causal links between gender and particular discourse strategies, such as interruptions or talk time. As British linguist Sara Mills (2003) concludes regarding the study of gender and politeness,

> Stereotypes of feminine and masculine behavior obviously play a role in the production of what participants see as appropriate or inappropriate speech. However, decisions about what is appropriate or not are decided upon strategically within the interaction rather than being decided upon by each individual once and for all. (p. 235)

Fifth, because the construction of choices, situations, and perceptions is cultural, it also is political. Understanding the power imbedded in discourse helps answer the question of *why* differences rather than similarities are culturally emphasized. After reviewing a large volume of research on gender in communication, researcher Kathryn Dindia (2006) notes that with all the pressure for people to conform to different gender/sex expectations in communicative styles, it is amazing how similar the sexes are in their communication. The similarities between women and men and the variances among women and men offer evidence that differences are not innate or universal.

Combining these five points, one understands that the process of gender/sex identity work in discourse is embedded in contradictions and personal and political tensions. Persons and groups must continually negotiate these contradictions and tensions to assert their identity and specific communication goals in diverse cultural contexts. The selective use of feminine and masculine styles in politics, management, and cultures should help make clear that patterns of communication often emerge as a particular way to respond to a particular situation. However, as situations, people, and cultures change, so, too, does the utility of the styles and their labels. Thus, rather than asking whether a person's speech is "feminine" or "masculine," perhaps people ought to ask what wide variety of ways of speaking allows each person to communicate more clearly, effectively, ethically, and humanely? Rather than asking how women and men communicate differently, researchers should explore how the range of gender options might be a resource for everyone, whether in interpersonal, group, or public settings. Condit's (1998) gender diversity approach, outlined at the end of Chapter 2, is one example of this.

Following Condit, we remind you that many people do not fit the neat binaries of male/female and masculine/feminine; they and others construct creative genderings and diverse gender/sex identities in talk.

Researchers on gender/sex and discourse now seem to agree that universal male/female differences in communication are not prominent. Persons are not prisoners of their gendered voices but *do gender* by consciously and unconsciously selecting communication strategies appropriate for different types of relationships and situations. Becoming conscious of the variety of strategies makes one a clearer, more effective, more ethical, and more humane communicator. More research is needed to help document the wide variety of ways people from diverse backgrounds perform their multiple social identities in unique daily interactions.

 **CHAPTER 4**

Gendered/Sexed Bodies

N othing is as intimately linked to one's sex/gender identity as how one feels and acts in one's body. This is perhaps why many assume that nonverbal communication is more biologically determined than verbal communication. Unless they are intentionally challenging gender/sex expectations, people tend to be less conscious of how they use their bodies to express gender and how their bodies use them to generate their identities. U.S. women usually do not think about whether or not to cross their legs, but they are more likely to think about the feminine taboo of sitting with their legs apart (especially in a skirt). Similarly, U.S. men usually do not think about sitting with their legs apart, but they are more likely to think about the masculinity taboo of sitting with their legs tightly crossed. Although biology influences gendered/sexed bodies, research shows that culture also influences not only bodily expressions but their frequency, contexts, and meaning. A person's body *does* gender; sex does not simply passively possess gender traits.

In this chapter, we do not focus on answering the question, do women and men nonverbally communicate differently? Instead, we explore the varied ways in which people sex and gender bodies and in which bodies sex and gender people. We examine how people use their bodies to communicate and how communication *shapes* people's bodies. We focus on how human beings perform identities as gendered, sexed, sexually oriented, raced, and classed persons.

Gender Embodiment: Why Nonverbals Matter

To provide a sense of gender as a body performance, we offer a classic example from psychologist Erwin Straus's research (1966). He examined a series of photographs of young girls and boys throwing baseballs and was struck by the differences in how they used space and motion:

The girl of five does not make any use of lateral space. She does not stretch her arm sideward; she does not twist her trunk; she does not move her legs, which remain side by side. All she does in preparation for throwing is to lift her right arm forward to the horizontal and to bend the forearm backward in a pronate position. . . . The ball is released without force, speed, or accurate aim. . . . A boy of the same age, when preparing to throw, stretches his right arm sideward and backward; supinates the forearm; twists, turns and bends his trunk; and moves his right foot backward. From this stance, he can support his throwing almost with the full strength of his total motorium. . . . The ball leaves the hand with considerable acceleration; it moves toward its goal in a long flat curve. (pp. 157–160)

Straus observed that the girls did not tend to bring their whole bodies into motion, but the boys did.

To explain these differences, Straus considered biological explanations, but he found that explanation lacking. The fact that women have breasts that might get in the way of throwing with full-body motion was irrelevant because the girls studied had not reached puberty. He also had to dismiss the idea that the girls were simply weaker, because a weaker person would likely throw the whole body into the movement to compensate. Instead, he concluded that the difference in style came from what he vaguely referred to as a "feminine attitude." He did not consider the possibility that the boys had been taught to throw and the girls had not. Nor did he consider that girls who throw "like a boy" often are ridiculed as unfeminine tomboys, and boys who throw like girls often are ridiculed as feminine and gay. Throwing has social implications for sex, gender, and sexual orientation.

Twenty-four years later, philosopher Iris Marion Young (1990) discussed Straus's observation in regard to what it means to "throw like a girl." Young demystifies the idea of a "feminine attitude," rejecting femininity and masculinity as biological; not all girls "throw like a girl" and not all boys "throw like a boy." Young compares the common gender/sex differences in throwing to other differences to make clear girls are *taught* to do these things, just as boys are *taught* to throw:

walking like a girl, tilting her head like a girl, standing and sitting like a girl, gesturing like a girl, and so on. The girl learns actively to hamper her movements. She is told that she must be careful not to get hurt, not to get dirty, not to tear her clothes, that the things she desires are dangerous for her. Thus she develops a bodily timidity that increases with age. (p. 154)

Girls and women experience their bodies in more guarded ways than boys and men because of how each person is *taught* to use and relate to her or his body.

Agreeing with Young's analysis, masculinities researcher Stephen Whitehead (2002) observes that most men do not experience their bodies in this guarded way. He acknowledges that there are always exceptions to these norms, but believes that "we should not allow the exceptions to deny the differing realities of the lived experiences of most women's and men's bodily existence" (p. 190). Social norms, repeated over and over in parental encouragement and warnings and in the bodies children see around them, make clear that children should perform the particular gender and sexual orientation that social norms dictate are appropriate to their particular bodies.

In contrast to guarded and feminine bodily experiences, Whitehead describes masculine bodily experiences: "The male/boy/man is expected to transcend space, or to place his body in aggressive motion within it, in so doing posturing to self and others the assuredness of his masculinity" (p. 189). Social norms of masculinity encourage boys and men to physically exert and be comfortable in their bodies. The influences of gender role socialization and social inequalities become clear: Women and men are encouraged to have different relationships with their bodies. One's relationship to one's body reveals whether one feels one has agency—control in life and over one's body.

Power, Not Sex Difference

Contrary to the prevalence of the two-culture theory as an explanation of gender in discourse (discussed in Chapter 3), the majority of researchers in nonverbal communication explain their findings as indicative of power relations (Knapp & Hall, 2002). Researchers studying gendered nonverbal communication tend not to conflate sex differences with gender differences but instead foreground sex differences understood as manifestations of sex privilege.

Nancy Henley (1977) was one of the first researchers in nonverbal communication to identify how power relations influence nonverbal interactions between sexes and races. In her studies of discrete behaviors called *nonverbal cues*, she finds that the absence of reciprocity in the behaviors transforms seemingly innocent intimacy cues into acts of dominance and submission. She compares nonparallel interactions between women and men to other unequal power relations, such as parent–child, customer–food service employee, and White–Black race relations. In each case, many nonverbal behaviors could be seen as expressions of intimacy, but it is unlikely that both parties equally use the same nonverbal cues. Nonreciprocal nonverbal forms and rejection of reciprocated behaviors indicate an unequal relationship. Henley calls this the "*micropolitics*" of nonverbal communication (p. 3), the subtle nonverbal ways in which unequal power relations are performed, negotiated, and expressed.

However, one should not assume that the power component of a nonverbal cue is overt or direct. For example, later research on smiling and status found that the rates of smiling were not different, but the reasons for smiling were. People in higher-status positions smiled to express pleasure; they had a choice. People in lower-status positions smiled more out of obligation (Hecht & LaFrance, 1998). Even if an individual cue, such as smiling, does not have a fixed gender identity, it is useful to examine such isolated cues to be able to more critically read the messages being sent about gender/sex, race, class, and other social identities.

Gender Performativity

Our approach to the study of gender/sex and the body is informed by philosopher Judith Butler's notion of gender performativity. Butler (2004) explains that even though "gender is a kind of doing, an incessant activity performed, in part, without one's knowing and without one's willing," that does not mean it is "automatic or mechanical" (p. 1). Instead, she describes gender as "a practice of improvisation within a scene of constraint" (p. 1). Gender is a command performance in which actors maintain minimal control over the content of the scene.

Butler emphasizes that performance is a habitual act that leaves little room for individual agency. Through the repetition of gendered behaviors over time, people continually construct their gender identities. The repetition is largely guided by social expectations and habit, not by free will. Although it makes sense that people do not get up each morning and consciously decide how they will perform their gender identity that day, the nonverbal behaviors of people who do not comply with gender/sex norms prove that overt resistance is possible. We review some examples of such persons later in this chapter.

Butler's insights make evident the inadequacies of traditional scientific laboratory studies of nonverbal communication. She moves beyond observing possible gender differences to ask why and how these behaviors occur. Similar to the social constructivist and post-structuralist approaches outlined in Chapter 2, Butler argues that even the physical body is largely culturally constructed and enacted through daily interactions. When humans (consciously and nonconsciously) behave in gendered ways, they construct, maintain, and change their own and others' notions of gender. Behaviors are at once personally, socially, and politically structured.

Although many studies isolate individual nonverbal cues, in reality all nonverbal communication works together to create a performance for an audience. Each person learns a script (or is socialized) about how to act, move, and communicate the gender appropriate for what others perceive her or his sex to be. Butler's performativity theory enables a more holistic look at the larger picture: What do all the nonverbal forms mean when combined in a body's performance?

Objectification Theory

Young, who re-analyzed "throwing like a girl," argues that gender-role socialization and inequalities are constructed in part through the objectification of females. Girls and women who do not use the full potential of their bodies do not have fully connected relationships with their bodies. Women and girls often are socialized to see themselves as objects, not subjects of behavior (Young, 1990, pp. 149–150). A girl or woman tends to see herself as acted upon (the object of motion), not as acting (the subject of motion). She reacts as an object receiving motion. This self-consciousness diverts her attention from making motion, leading to a disconnection from her body. Other researchers call this *objectification theory*.

You have probably heard the statement that mass media objectify women, but what does that mean? Objectification theory suggests that when a person is the

frequent receiver of a gaze that sees one solely as a sex object that exists for the
pleasure of the viewer rather than as a whole person, the person may internalize
the gazer's view of her or his body. Objectified people's perceived physical and sexual attractiveness may become more important to them than their morality, honor,
intellect, sense of humor, or kindness. Perfectionism can set in with unrealistic,
narrow standards of beauty, and negative self-images can contribute to low self-
esteem, depression, anxiety, and eating disorders (Fredrickson & Roberts, 1997;
Travis, Meginnis, & Bardari, 2000).

Men certainly experience objectification, but the sexual objectification of
women is more often physically threatening and used to express male heterosexuality (Fredrickson & Roberts, 1997). This does not mean that all men objectify
all women; however, sexual objectification creates a cultural norm that makes girls
and women more vulnerable to objectification and to measuring their self-esteem
through men's eyes.

Disconnection, as Young outlines, contributes to the negative effects of objectification. Women often are socialized to be more aware of their bodies than many
men, but at the same time, they may feel disconnected and powerless in relation to
their bodies. This contradiction also is evident for boys and men who feel they do
not meet society's expectations of physical masculinity. They may feel trapped in
bodies that are supposed to perform in a prescribed way but fail them.

African American men receive particularly contradictory messages about their
bodies. The predominant U.S. culture creates the contradiction of reverence for the
Black male body in sports and fear of it in crime (Whitehead, 2002). Cultural critic
Kobena Mercer (1994) described the contradictions surrounding Black bodies:

> Blacks are looked down upon and despised as worthless, ugly, and ultimately
> inhuman. But in the blink of an eye, whites look up to and revere black bodies,
> lost in awe and envy as the black subject is idealized as the embodiment of its
> aesthetic ideal. (p. 201)

Black men's bodies have been looked upon as violent, sexual, aggressive, and athletic (Jackson & Dangerfield, 2003). Their bodies are idealized and objectified
solely as superior athletes. Even in this act of reverence, the underlying assumption
is that athleticism comes more naturally to Black men, and therefore they are sub-
human (McKay, Messner, & Sabo, 2000). Accordingly, their athletic accomplishments may not count as much as Whites' athletic accomplishments because people
presume that Whites have to work harder.

Constructing a Critical Gender/Sex Lens

To understand the role of nonverbal communication in the gendering of bodies, it
is important to examine gender in the body from micro (individual nonverbal
behaviors) and macro (whole bodies performing within cultural contexts)
perspectives. As in Chapter 3, before we present research on gender in nonverbal

communication, we outline the limitations of the research to equip you to critically assess the material.

We find reason for caution toward traditional social science research on gender in nonverbal communication, which makes up the vast majority of published scholarship.

*First, **the meaning of any nonverbal (or verbal) cue is in the eye of the beholder**,* as that eye has been trained to see by the social order. One cue can have multiple (or even contradictory) meanings, and the link between the behavior and its function is not always apparent (LaFrance, 2002). Thus, although many researchers report only the predominant cultural meanings of nonverbal cues, these meanings may not reflect all persons' understandings.

*Second, **similar to research on discourse, most nonverbal research identifies people's behaviors according to biological sex, not gender, sexual orientation, race, class, or other identity.*** Research that generalizes to all women and men and that seeks to find the differences between the (presumed internally homogeneous) sexes is misleading. Furthermore, research on nonverbal communication largely assumes a heterosexual norm (Lovaas, 2003). Although gender, sex, and sexual orientation are deeply intertwined in perceptions of self and others, not all heterosexual women have feminine gender identities, not all heterosexual men have masculine gender identities, and not all bisexual persons have androgynous gender identities, and so forth.

*Third, **most of the research is conducted in artificial settings, and observers are shown only isolated parts of the face or head.*** Even research considered to have made major contributions to the field used only still photos showing isolated cues, such as a series of lips with degrees of smiles or a series of eyes with different expressions. Observers were asked to identify the meaning conveyed by each nonverbal cue (Ekman & Friesen, 1975). In real life, people express nonverbals, and observe others' nonverbals, in combination, not in isolation. People look at a whole face and the whole body accompanying the face, not just eyes or lips.

*Fourth, **most of the research on nonverbal cues and gender/sex is dated.*** We found few original studies published since the 1980s. Most of the publications from the 1990s to the present are meta-analyses, or summary reviews of earlier studies. Students of gender and communication might ask why researchers have stopped pursuing this line of research. It seems possible that this line of inquiry has been exhausted or is not as informative as once thought, possibly because of the limitations just noted. We would also like to think that rigid gendered norms in nonverbal expression are loosening.

As we noted in Chapter 3, even as differences are identified, they may begin to disappear. In the last 10 years, the meaning of crying in public has shifted for men. Former congressperson Patricia Schroeder (D-CO) was ridiculed for crying on television when she withdrew from the presidential race in 1987 (Schroeder, 1999). A *New York Post* columnist described Schroeder as "precisely what her supporters had sought to overcome—the stereotype of women as weepy wimps who don't belong in the business of serious affairs" (quoted in Witt, Paget, & Matthews, 1994,

p. 205). Yet, when President George H. W. Bush cried in public, media treated his tears differently.

> In the fall of 1994, *Time* magazine published a list of occasions on which George Bush shed tears while president. . . . The article is symptomatic in a number of ways of the politics of affect in contemporary American culture. First, it is clear that Bush's tears are "surprising" because sentimentality and the public display of emotion are conventionally seen as feminine characteristics. At the same time, however, the list demonstrates that there is space in American public life for sentimental men: big boys do cry, even when they become president. Finally, it is noteworthy that Bush's tears were deliberately publicized and that a major national magazine deemed them newsworthy. (Chapman & Hendler, 1999, p. 1)

In the wake of 9/11, male politicians have cried on a number of occasions. The interesting question is whether, if a woman presidential candidate again were to cry, it would be like Bush's crying, as proof of humanity? As a conscious display of emotion to heighten rhetorical affect? Or as an indication of her lack of emotional control?

Fifth, gender/sex stereotypes may contribute to self-fulfilling prophecies. For example, it is difficult to notice emotions and expressions in others or in oneself that are inconsistent with sex stereotypes. Hormones may contribute to different emotional experiences for women and for men, but there are vast individual differences among women and among men in emotional experiences (Fivush & Buckner, 2000). Stereotypes are maintained when people notice only emotions that are consistent with the stereotypes. These self-fulfilling prophecies can have real consequences as sex/gender stereotypes become the basis for socializing girls and boys. "Big boys don't cry" becomes a means of managing boys' emotions, making it difficult for men to express feelings of sadness or fear and for women and men to recognize when men are expressing such feelings.

Sixth, the relative power status of roles better explains the apparent differences. Emotion researcher Tracey Madden and her associates (2000) state, "Men and women may differ in the expression of emotion because they typically differ in level of power; women are likely to hold positions of lower power and status than men" (p. 282). The emotions of fear and sadness often are described as expressions of helplessness, and a person who has less power over her or his situation becomes more vulnerable to fear and sadness (Fischer, 1993). "In contrast, men express more anger than women, possibly because anger is associated with power and assertiveness" (Madden et al., 2000, p. 282). From this view, emotional expressions function as status markers in social interaction. Cognitive theorists believe that emotions are produced by a person's assessment of a given situation. Because many girls and women tend to have less social power and control, they more often may perceive themselves as helpless, sad, and anxious. This reaction would be a rational, rather than an irrational, response to an uncertain situation. Boys and men who perceive themselves as having more control over specific life situations would be less prone to such emotions (Madden et al., 2000).

Even with these limitations, this research helps one visualize how nonverbal cues contribute to the gendering of bodies. Communication scholars Barbara Bate and Judy Bowker (1997) argue that nonverbal behaviors are a primary way in which gender dichotomies are created and maintained. Unfortunately, identifying the masculine/feminine dichotomy does not necessarily point to a way out of it, nor does tracking the ways in which gender is performed tell us what gender *means* or why it is performed that way. Thus, after we describe the micropolitics of nonverbal communication research, we place it in a larger context of whole bodies, examining the political and personal implications.

Components of Nonverbal Communication

Proxemics

The term *proxemics* refers to the study of personal space, the invisible area around a person that is considered her or his territory. The size of personal space with which a person feels comfortable varies greatly by culture (Sommer, 1959). In U.S. culture, space is power. Persons of higher status tend to wield more personal space in their offices, seats, gestures, and homes. A review of proxemic research on gender concludes that "gender research all support[s] the theory that status is a powerful organizer of proxemic behavior" (Gillespie & Leffler, 1983, p. 141). Although this research was limited to the study of Whites in the United States, it consistently shows that the White women studied had smaller personal space, were more likely to have their personal space invaded by others, and were more likely to acquiesce to the invasion than were the White men studied.

The relative size of one's body influences the amount of personal space one is allocated. In U.S. culture, masculinity often is signaled by more muscular and taller bodies. This is perhaps most obvious in wedding photos of heterosexual couples. Short men often are placed on steps above the women, and tall women often are placed on lower steps or wear flat-heeled shoes. Taller men and men with more muscular bodies are perceived as more masculine; taller women and women with more muscular bodies tend to be perceived as more masculine, and thus their femininity or womanhood is questioned. Of course, there are limits to the power of larger-bodied persons. Society discriminates against persons who are considered overweight. Great variances in size among women and among men exist, but social expectations persist.

Haptics

The term *haptics* refers to touch. If unwelcome, touch can be the ultimate invasion of one's personal space; if welcome, it can be seen as a sign of intimacy and affection. If a touch is unwelcome, or if the touched person does not feel free to reciprocate the touch or feels pressured to do so, the touch is more likely a dominance behavior. Part of the reason such violations are difficult to determine is that they can be consciously or unconsciously cloaked in the garb of joking, friendship, warmth, or kindness. Sexual harassment and acquaintance rape are the most extreme examples of dominance related to haptics.

Sex-specific touching behaviors reflect and maintain gender socialization and inequalities. As discussed in Chapter 7, research shows that from infancy, boys and girls tend to be touched differently (Sandnabba & Ahlberg, 1999; Lytton & Romney, 1991). Girl babies and toddlers tend to be caressed more; boy babies and toddlers tend to be touched less, and when they are touched, they tend to be played with in a rougher fashion.

From adolescence to adulthood, women are found to exhibit more touch in the form of hugs or other cues of support, and men are found to exhibit touch with instrumental goals, such as asserting individual rights or sexual intent (Hall, 2006). A part of masculinity seems to be the act of invading others' personal space, particularly the space of women (LePoire, Burgoon, & Parrott, 1992). Yet, homophobia, the fear of being labeled homosexual or unmasculine, seems to keep many men from prolonged touching of other men (Kimmel, 2003). An exception is in sports, in which the competitive context makes male-to-male touch socially acceptable. In same-sex relationships, women are socially freer to touch than men. This seems to hold true with family members and friends. In established heterosexual relationships, both women and men are found to initiate touch, and the person who initiates tends to be viewed as exerting influence (Knapp & Hall, 2002).

Eye Contact

Eye contact can convey intimacy, power, or both. In research on superior/subordinate interaction, the subordinate is likely to maintain more eye contact when listening than the superior, regardless of the sex of the participants (Eakins & Eakins, 1988). If one is seeking approval, one is more likely to show attentiveness through eye contact. Looking away while speaking, so that one cannot monitor the other person's responses, can be a sign of power. Subordinates tend to illustrate attentive watching but avert their gazes when being stared at. In their review of research, Knapp and Hall (2002) report that men tend to use the gaze pattern typically associated with higher-status persons, whereas women tended to use the pattern associated with lower-status persons. Staring, on the other hand, tends to be seen as an invasion of personal space.

Cultural differences influence norms for eye contact. In many Asian cultures, women, children, students, and other lower-status subordinates traditionally avoid looking higher-status persons in the eye. In the Lua tribe of Kenya, sons-in-law are forbidden to look directly at mothers-in-law; in parts of Nigeria, inferiors cannot look at superiors (Klopf & McCroskey, 2007) because to do so is a sign of disrespect (Robinson, 2003). In these cultures, eye contact seems to be a tool to negotiate social status.

Body Movement

Body movement refers to demeanor, posture, and gestures. Judith Butler (1990a) aptly describes the relationship between gender and body movement: "Gender is the repeated stylization of the body, a set of repeated acts within a rigid regulatory frame which congeal over time to produce the appearance of substance—of a natural kind of being" (p. 33). The motions are repeated so frequently that they become at least unconscious if not involuntary.

Sociologist Nancy Henley refers to how one physically carries herself or himself as *demeanor* (1977). People tend to think of demeanor as something unique to an individual, but Henley points out that demeanor has strong social class and power attributions. Sociologist Erving Goffman (1963) found that demeanor is used to mark upper and lower status and that higher-status persons tend to have more latitude in their behavior. They can carry their bodies more loosely. Persons of lower status tend to be tighter, more attentive to their physical demeanor. When people are among peers, they tend to relax body tension (Mehrabian, 1972). In research on superior/subordinate interactions and gender/sex, the superiors, like many men, tend to display less concern about body posture compared to the subordinates, propping their feet up, leaning back, and so on (Eakins & Eakins, 1978, 1988; Henley, 1977). The subordinates, like many women, tend to be attentive to their body posture.

In a classic study, Goffman (1979) outlines how body posture is most explicitly choreographed in advertising. Although Goffman uses advertisements to explore how conventions arise regarding performances of gender, his point is that all people engage in these actions. Advertisements just provide one, very intentional location through which to understand these practices. The positioning of bodies in relation to one another provides clues to their "presumed *social* position relative to one another" (p. 26). In wedding pictures, men often are portrayed as standing (protectively) above women and children or sitting in the center with women behind them. Subordinates are shown lower or bowing. In advertisements, women often are shown recumbent, sprawled on beds, sofas, and even cars. Women often are posed with a "bashful knee bend" or with a canting (sideways tilting) posture (p. 45). Goffman describes these and other body practices as "ritual-like bits of behavior which portray an ideal conception of the two sexes and their structural relationship to each other" (p. 84). They are ritual-like because they are repeated so often that they become entrenched.

People also perform gender through immediacy cues, the ways in which they show interest in others through body movement. Research shows that women tend to use more immediacy behaviors than men (Eakins & Eakins, 1988). This seems consistent with feminine gender-role expectations to be more expressive, to focus on relationships, and to be supportive to others. The women studied leaned in more toward the other person, tilted their head toward the person, and nodded more than the men. The women also tended to use fewer and smaller gestures than the men. Superior/subordinate research shows similar patterns, with the subordinates showing more interest and attentiveness, but this likely varies with contexts, ethnicities, races, and age groups.

Nodding is commonly viewed as a submissive form of expression, and women are expected to nod more than men. However, a recent study of 189 students in a college classroom found that nodding frequency was situational. The men and women nodded equally often when the professor talked, but the men did not nod as much as the women when a student spoke. Both women and men students nodded more to the professor than to peers, thus attending to the status of the speaker rather than simply enacting gendered behaviors (Helweg-Larsen, Cunningham, Carrico, & Pergram, 2004).

Body Adornment

Body adornment includes dress, cosmetics, and tattooing. Art historian Ann Hollander (1978) posits that Western dress replicates the shape of the body through a more fitted style, and its primary function, beyond warmth and modesty, "is to contribute to the making of the self-conscious individual image" (p. xiv). People like to think that the way they reveal and adorn their bodies is solely an individualistic expression or practical decision, but it is intensely influenced by cultural norms, trends, gender, and social class. Furthermore, each person's dress influences that person; the dress one is socialized to wear influences one's interactions and self-image.

The relationship between dress and identity construction is apparent in the effects of gendered/sexed clothing on newborn children. An infant dressed in pink is commonly expected to be sweet, graceful, and pretty. An infant dressed in blue is expected to be strong, agile, and handsome. People respond to the infants accordingly, potentially creating a self-fulfilling prophecy (Rubinstein, 2001).

Sociologist Ruth Rubinstein (2001) argues that gendered clothing is a social tool to reinforce gender/sex differences in society and to "alert an approaching individual about suitability for sexual intercourse" (p. 103). Clothing that follows the contours of the body is most common in clothing designed for girls and women. Certainly, gendered clothing distinctions have decreased, even since the 1960s and 1970s, but it seems that as some distinctions disappear, others appear. In the United States, women's professional clothing restrictions have lessened. Politicians such as Senator Hillary Rodham Clinton wear pants instead of dresses, and men now sport earrings. Hats and gloves are no longer required for U.S. women in formal dress as they were until the 1960s. However, women's high-fashion shoes continue to be more restrictive and more harmful than men's (Harris, 2003); Western women's clothing is more revealing than in previous decades and lacks room, such as pockets, for practical things. This makes purses a necessity, again limiting ease of movement.

Women's bodies are treated as objects for adornment with jewelry, shoes, purses, cosmetics, dyed or treated hair, color-enhanced eyes, and color-coordinated clothing made from fine materials that require special care and limited activity. The message is that the natural body is sick or unacceptable. Men, too, are increasingly receiving critical messages about their bodies, inducing them to buy muscle-building products, steroids, tattoos, hair-enhancing products, and plastic surgery. Although their clothing generally is more comfortable than women's, they do not enjoy the wider spectrum of clothing types that women do, such as skirts.

Although Western men's clothing has not been studied as much as women's, in an exploratory study of 75 mostly White, 25-year-old men at a university in the United Kingdom, the researchers conclude that "our participants deliberately and strategically used clothing to manipulate their appearance to meet cultural ideals of masculinity. They vary the color, texture, pattern, fit, and size of garments to appear slimmer, taller, bigger, or more muscular than they believe their actual body shape to be" (Frith & Gleeson, 2004, p. 47). The researchers report that some of the men were reticent to admit they cared about their appearance, but when asked about their dressing and shopping habits, their concern was apparent.

The gender policing of one's dress is most apparent in responses to cross-dressing. People in the United States tend to be uncomfortable with cross-dressers because they do not conform to the norm. People commonly ridicule those who choose to wear clothing socially assigned to another sex. However, as noted in Chapter 2, such persons are more accepted in some other cultures. In reality, every-one engages in some degree of cross-dressing, as they adapt their dress to specific situations. During cold weather, women tend to wear pants, as do men. During hot weather, men tend to wear shorts, as do women. People who break gender norms by wearing androgynous clothing or clothing ascribed to another sex broaden dress options for everyone. Why is the vision of men in skirts laughable? There is no biological reason, and in many places men do wear skirts in the form of kilts, sarongs, caftans, or djellabas. The laughing response is just one indication of the disciplining power of clothing to dictate social norms for gender/sex and sexual orientation.

Some products have become common for women as well as men to use, such as tattoos, body piercing, and cosmetics, but if you look closely, you'll discover that tattoos and piercings are gendered masculine and feminine, and cosmetics are sex exclusive (even when all the ingredients are the same). These differences are further influenced by identity ingredients other than sex. In her history of modern tattoos, Margo DeMello (2000) studies how tattooing became the basis for com-munity maintained through magazines, shops, and conventions. She also explores the shifting class location of tattooing from the lower classes to all classes. However, even as tattoos have become acceptable for those outside the lower classes, the reasons that people tattoo are class based. Middle-class women and men both explain tattoos as a way of expressing individuality, spiritualism, per-sonal growth, and the sacredness of their bodies. In contrast, working- and middle-class women "are much more apt to explain their tattoos in terms of heal-ing, empowerment, or control" (p. 172). Women interviewed claim that the tattoos were a way for them to reclaim their bodies and to subvert the male gaze.

Facial Expressions

Facial expressions studies have focused on smiling (Eakins & Eakins, 1988; Hall, 2006; Henley, 1995). Although early studies found that women smile more than men, later studies found that subordinates smile more than superiors regardless of their sex. These conflicting research results raise the question of whether differences in smiling are due to sex, gender, or power. Actually, all three influence smiling, but none is a determinant. In experimental studies examining the effects of gender/sex and status, both affected smiling such that higher-status women and men smiled less than lower-status people, but in situations with clear gender norms, women smiled more than men (LaFrance & Hecht, 2000). Even when sex can be isolated as a variable, whether the sex difference is trivial or substantial is determined by one's "theoretical preference and methodological approach" (Hall, 2006, p. 60). Finally, just because a smiling variance is identified does not mean that one knows *why* the difference exists.

Nonverbal researchers Marianne LaFrance and Marvin Hecht (2000) propose the *demand expressivity theory* to explain sex differences in smiling. Gender roles create norms that people are expected to meet, and "norms governing facial display, particularly smiling, are different for females and males with females expected to show more smiling than males" (p. 120). This means that girls and women do not smile more than boys and men because they are happier but because social norms induce them to feel they must. Girls and women are socialized to be oriented toward pleasing others and to appear less threatening (Borisoff & Merill, 2003). Some women report that they expect negative reactions from others if they do not smile (LaFrance & Hecht, 2000). A review of 30 studies supports the theory; women tend to smile more than men in social interactions because of gender role expectations and inequalities rather than biology (Hall, Carter, & Horgan, 2000).

Another indication that smiling patterns are cultural is the fact that female and male infants smile equally, but by as early as age four, boys smile less. Judith Hall (1984) suggests that boys receive the message that they should be tough, and it is difficult to look tough if one is smiling; not smiling keeps others uncertain of one's emotions, thus allowing one to maintain the upper hand (Hall, Carter, & Horgan, 2000). In a meta-analysis of 150 studies, LaFrance and Hecht (2000) found gender differences to be strongest in the 18–23-year range, which is the maturation period during which pressure for sex differentiation is greater and when heterosexual attraction strategies are heightened. Differences begin to dissipate as people age (Hall, 2006).

In a classic qualitative study, sociologist Arlie Hochschild (1983) likens this feminine socialization to the emotional burden placed on service workers such as food servers and airline attendants. These employees typically are expected to hide their true feelings by smiling, no matter what the customer says or does. This kind of smiling is not an expression of genuine happiness but an automatic one that masks true emotions, is a burden to uphold, and makes it difficult for others to interpret one's true emotions. Conversely, in an ethnographic study of the more tradition-ally masculine profession of police officer, women on the Pittsburgh police force talked about learning "not to smile" as a way to reduce the risk that others would see them as incompetent or unprofessional (McElhinny, 1998). The women offi-cers felt compelled to manage their smiling behavior to comply with public expec-tations for officers (McElhinny, 1992).

Race, social class, and gender roles also interact with smiling patterns. Mothers of middle-class families tend to smile more than mothers in lower-class families. There are no significant differences between the fathers. The researchers suggest that the middle-class mothers in the study smiled more to fulfill middle-class expectations for "good" mothers—softer, warmer, and more compliant in public situations (Eakins & Eakins, 1988, p. 298). The fathers of both groups tended to smile less than the mothers, and yet their children interpreted their smiles as more friendly than the mothers', which suggests that the fathers' smiles were more appreciated and less expected. In research examining race and sex, the White U.S. women studied tended to smile more than the African American women (Halberstadt & Saitta, 1987), and the African American women studied did not smile more than African American men. It seems the African American women do not comply with White gender expectations here. However, when they do not meet these expectations, they may be perceived as hostile or unfriendly.

Nonverbal Sensitivity and Accuracy

Nonverbal sensitivity and accuracy is another area in which research has found some sex differences, with women tending to be more attentive than men to others' nonverbal cues (Friedman & Miller-Herringer, 1991; Hall, 2006). The women studied monitor other persons' behaviors more and are more responsive, showing empathy and attention. It follows that if women tend to be more attentive, they also may more accurately decode others' nonverbal cues. Several studies have indi-cated that women more accurately send and interpret others' nonverbal cues, espe-cially when focusing on facial cues (Ambady, Hallahan, & Rosenthal, 1995; Hall, 2006; Hall et al., 2000; McClure, 2000). These differences seem stronger for facial cues and weaker in terms of detecting deception, and some question exists as to whether the differences would hold true when judging the cues of an actual rela-tionship partner (Hall, 2006; Hall et al., 2000; McClure, 2000).

Researchers have suggested a number of explanations for these findings: (1) that brain differences and specializations are involved (Begley & Murr, 1995); (2) that the behavior is an example of social learning, wherein girls learn to be caretakers; and (3) that the behavior is a survival strategy of the less powerful, who need to be more attentive (Hall, Halberstadt, & O'Brien, 1997; Henley, 1995). Hall and asso-ciates (2000) argue that it is due to a combination of knowledge and effort. Women tend to decode nonverbals more accurately than men do because they have devel-oped better skills and because they consider the activity of accurate monitoring to be of greater value. Communication scholars Mark Knapp and Judith Hall (2002) suggest that this combination of skill and effort may help explain the belief in "female intuition" (p. 84). Because there do not seem to be consistent biological explanations for such behavior, the influences of social factors, such as roles, prohibit the making of any blanket claims about gender/sex proclivities in nonverbal sensitivity and accuracy.

Emotional Expression

Emotional expression occurs in the form of cries, frowns, hunched body, downcast eyes, pitch changes, and much more. All the ways one expresses gender are also ways one expresses emotion. Psychologist Stephanie Shields (2000) suggests that the daily practice of being an emotional person is congruous with the practice of being a gendered person. Researchers suggest that boys in many ethnic and racial groups are socialized from early childhood to hold in their emotions more than girls are (Vingerhoets & Scheirs, 2000).

When talking about emotion, one should distinguish the internal experience of emotion from the expression or communication of emotion. They are not necessarily the same, but because they are related, we discuss them together. The ability to experience and express emotion is universal for women and men and is not limited to humans (e.g., rhesus monkeys; see Suomi, 1997). However, the stereotype is that women are more emotional than men, suggesting that women both experience and express more emotion. The truth is that women and men experience emotions relatively equally, but women are *expected* to experience and express them more (LaFrance & Hecht, 2000; Madden et al., 2000).

These expectations parallel the stereotypes attached to masculinity and femininity. Femininity stereotypically has been associated with emotionality and masculinity with objectivity or rationality. Thus, when a person is labeled emotional, the inference is that the person is irrational, as if emotionality and rationality were opposed. For centuries, this stereotype has been used to justify women's limited public participation. As recently as 1996, when the U.S. Supreme Court ruled on a case concerning the Virginia Military Institute's (VMI) policy to admit only male students, typical arguments supporting VMI's policy claimed, "Compared with men, women are more emotional, less aggressive, suffer more from fear of failure, and cannot withstand stress as well," and, therefore, "Women are not capable of the ferocity requisite to make the program work" (Greenberger & Brake, 1996, p. A52). Fortunately, the Supreme Court rejected the argument based on this stereotype and opened VMI to women.

The fact that these gender/sex stereotypes are lodged in people's perceptions and are not accurate characterizations of people's actions was demonstrated in a recent laboratory study. Participants were asked to rate the intensity of anger and sadness expressed by a person in a photo in which hairstyle and clothing were altered to manipulate gender. The participants rated the intensity of emotions expressed by the feminine poser as stronger than those expressed by the masculine poser (Plant, Kling, & Smith, 2004). The persistence of such a gender/sex–dichotomous stereotype prevents observers (1) from recognizing men's emotionality and women's ratio-nality; (2) from valuing emotionality, because rationality is socially preferred in Western cultures; and (3) from realizing that the emotional and rational parts of people are interdependent.

Gender as Body Performance

This review of research on specific nonverbal cues reveals how gender/sex differences are perceived, created, maintained, and changed. However, given research limita-tions, drawing generalizations is problematic. Thus, we shift from the micropolitics of nonverbal communication to exploring the macropolitics of gendered bodies. We examine the politics of gendering bodies before turning to examples of how people adapt, resist, and change performances of embodied gender norms.

To understand gender as performance, it is helpful to study those who most expose and embrace gender's performative aspect: drag queens and kings. Just as Goffman's (1979) analysis exposes how ads magnify and choreograph gender by using visual resources to "transform otherwise opaque goings-on into easily read-able form" (p. 27), drag queens and kings make visible those things people typically do not see. People take note of a woman with slicked-back hair wearing pants, a button-down shirt, and a tie (unless she is part of the waitstaff at an upscale restau-rant). A man in a lovely silk skirt and twinset also would be remarkable.

The gender performances of transgender people expose the performative aspect of gender even as they remind one not to conflate sex, sexual orientation, and gen-der. A transgender person is not necessarily homosexual; many male cross-dressers are heterosexual (e.g., Drew Carey's brother on *The Drew Carey Show*). Additionally, transgender people challenge the idea of an "essential bond between masculinity and men" (Halberstam, 2005, p. 125). Men need not be masculine, and women can be, and there is not only one way to perform masculinity: "To king a role can involve a number of different modes of performance from earnest repetition to hyperbolic re-creation, and from quiet understatement to theatrical layering" (pp. 128–129). Similarly, drag queens' use of camp "mimics dominant forms of femininity to pro-duce and ratify alternative drag femininities that revel in irony, sarcasm, inversion, and insult" (p. 130). People's diverse performances of their sex's assigned gender can be recognized once one recognizes that gender is performative.

Overt gender performance is not reserved to those who practice drag. Sociologists Richard Majors and Janet Billson (1992) observe how African American street pimps reinvent racial stereotypes through the performance of a "cool pose." By posing, they present themselves as a spectacle of self-expression, detachment, and strength, instead of being victims of others' labeling. In the absence of other resources to indicate their masculinity, their flamboyant physical presence and expressiveness take on more importance. Consequently, Majors (2001) argues that many Black men have learned to use posing as a strategic tool to convey control and toughness.

When people internalize social expectations about gender/sex and the body, it becomes difficult for them to determine whether they construct their gender identities or whether gender/sex expectations begin to construct them. For more than 40 years, researchers have documented the negative effects of nonverbal cultural norms that objectify women and create prejudices against feminine men, such as low self-esteem, the glorification of male violence, sexual violence against girls and women, sexual harassment, domestic physical and emotional abuse, higher suicide rates for homosexual teens, and violence against LGBT people. These negative effects discipline bodies to perform gender in a particular way.

Attractiveness

Beauty can be a positive human aesthetic. However, cultural norms defining bodily beauty tend to have narrow, shifting boundaries that make them virtually unattainable, and attractiveness norms, such as gender/sex, have become binary concepts that differentiate women and men (Felski, 2006). Although physical attractiveness is valued for women *and* men (U.S. men are spending more on cosmetics, fashion, and bodybuilding), cultural pressures encourage women in particular to self-objectify and become preoccupied with physical appearances. Beauty's determination of the relative worth of a girl or woman is evidenced in the millions of dollars spent yearly on cosmetics and diets, the ubiquitous beauty literature advising them how to be attractive, and the growing popularity of plastic surgeries. Beauty costs.

Cultural ideals of beauty are difficult for all persons to attain because the norms are unrealistic. They are even more difficult to attain for persons with disabilities, persons with darker skin, persons of larger size, and older people (Gerschick & Miller, 2004; Kramer, 2005). An array of research shows that large-sized women face more difficulties with social mobility than large-sized men do. Body size, especially for women, tends to affect popularity, dating and marriage opportunities, educational and economic accomplishments, susceptibility to job discrimination, and work environments (Fredrickson & Roberts, 1997). Similarly, poor women and women who refuse to comply with social demands of beauty regularly experience humiliation, harassment, and discrimination. They are called lazy, mentally ill, unfeminine, and asexual (Travis et al., 2000).

Heterosexuality is inextricably linked to attractiveness, and both are culturally regulated. Some psychologists believe this conflation of beauty and sexuality has a heightened potential to oppress women because the culture regulates women's sexuality by regulating beauty. Cultural norms demand that women adorn themselves to be sexually attractive to men, and "This merger [of beauty and sexuality] moves sexuality into the public realm, making it concrete and external, and thereby amenable to inspection, definition, social monitoring, and control" (Travis et al., 2000, p. 239). Women's and men's sexuality is not private; it becomes public, social property.

Even though people speak of "natural beauties," beauty is anything but natural and unchanging. These changes are confined by aesthetic shifts but are influenced by social, economic, and political factors (Faludi, 1991; Travis et al., 2000). For example, in the 1910s and 1920s, when women entered the workforce in larger numbers and gained the right to vote, fashion became more revealing. Sexual appeal became about external appearance, with short flapper-style dresses. Pale white complexions, slender legs, narrow hips, and flat breasts were the ideal, causing many women to bind their breasts and to shave their legs and armpits.

In the 1940s and 1950s, after World War II ended and women were dismissed from factory work and relegated to their homes, advertisers told women and men that happiness was a beautiful wife who provided a clean home and cared for the children. Marilyn Monroe became a beauty icon and was the first woman to pose naked in *Playboy;* larger breasts and hips became sexy. Feminine self-worth was tied to making oneself attractive and to serving men and the home, a White middle-class ideal difficult for most women to attain.

Today, U.S. women are presumed to have the most gender/sex equality in history, yet the predominant notion of feminine beauty has become even more impossible to attain. Mass media images of models' bodies are perfected by airbrushing and computer alteration. Even women with the most perfect bodies are not perfect enough. Also, the ideal body type has become increasingly thinner. Marilyn Monroe's size 12 is considered large by today's beauty standards. Current *Playboy* centerfold models are 10% to 20% thinner than most women. According to advertising analyst Jean Kilbourne (1994), only 5% of today's women fit the preferred body type, which leaves 95% of women wondering what is wrong with their bodies. Because body size is not the only component of beauty, even fewer women attain the total beauty ideal. Author Naomi Wolf (1991) argues that, at most, 1 in 40,000 women fits the "beauty myth." It is not coincidental that the beauty industry benefits economically from this. Travis et al. (2000) conclude, "The economy virtually relies on women being obsessed with thinness and forever unsuccessfully attempting to achieve it" (p. 250).

When one compares current changes in cultural notions of masculine attractiveness to current changes in women's attractiveness, an interesting insight emerges: As women are encouraged to become smaller, men are encouraged to become bigger. The pop culture hero G.I. Joe went from the equivalent of a human man with biceps of 12.2 inches in circumference in 1964, to biceps of 26.8 inches in 1998. As a point of comparison, baseball power hitter Mark McGwire has biceps of only 20 inches, and he is 6 feet tall ("As G.I. Joe Bulks Up," 1999). The *New York Times* coverage of G.I. Joe's change was occasioned by the research of psychiatrists and psychologists who studied how men are beginning to face the same enormous pressures for body perfection that women have faced for centuries. According to the researchers, toys such as G.I. Joe are partly to blame for the creation of artificial and impossible images of male bodily perfection (Pope, Phillips, & Olivardia, 2000).

Notions of beauty vary by culture and race, which makes it clear that these notions are socially constructed. Race and beauty intersect; together they are culturally defined and prescribed (Cofer, 1997). Some Azawagh Arabs of Niger define ideal femininity as extreme fatness. Expansive thighs, belly rolls of fat, and stretch marks are seen as indicators of sexual desirability and upper-class status, for they render the women unable to work (Popenoe, 2004). Latino cultures tend to define feminine beauty as larger sized than White cultures do. African American cultures tend to define larger-sized women as strong physically and emotionally, not lazy or unfeminine as in the predominant White culture (Lovejoy, 2001). Traditional Asian Hmong culture values sturdy women who can work hard, which makes larger waists and hips attractive (Lynch, 1999). This creates conflict for some Hmong American girls and women who are becoming assimilated into the predominant White U.S. culture's standards of beauty.

The predominance of White Western notions of beauty among multiple ethnic groups in the United States as well as abroad is troubling. Some African American women internalize racism and think of their hair as a problem. Many spend substantial money and time to braid, straighten, or lighten their hair in attempts to "control" it or make it look more beautiful as defined by White hair standards (hooks, 1993). Other ethnic groups find their facial features to be a problem. Ethnographer Eugenia Kaw (1997) interviewed 11 Asian American women from middle-class backgrounds and a variety of Asian countries who had chosen to have eye surgery to make their eyes look more White European. They had internalized the notion that the White European face looked more energetic and assertive. They described their birth eyelid shape as looking "dull and passive," and they wanted to make a better impression in job interviews and other career moves (p. 62). If one examines women's magazines, self-help literature, and the beauty industry in countries like Japan and India, it becomes clear how White Western notions of beauty are sold to women who are unable to (and should not be induced to) attain those beauty standards. Beauty has become a tool to colonize women around the world (Hegde, 1995).

Despite the economic and cultural forces at play in the Western beauty industry, it is inaccurate to suggest that all women are passive victims of it. As Asian American women's choice of eye surgery for career enhancement demonstrates, persons tend to pick and choose what parts of the beauty myth they adopt, according to their unique needs. They often combine Western notions of beauty and fashion with their own cultural preferences. In a study of bride photos in Taiwan, ethnographer Bonnie Adrian (2003) found that engaged women and their families invest in elaborate photo shoots in White Western gowns, hairpieces, and makeup that render the bride unrecognizable. The women describe this act as a social status marker only and believe it has no implications for how they should look on a day-to-day basis. They know the beauty standards in the photos are artificial and do not think they affect their self-images.

Attractiveness and sexuality are not just individual experiences and identities but are constructed at the social and political macrolevel. Attractiveness norms most explicitly demonstrate that gender is a command performance. Even if you have an idea of how you want to look, you are bombarded by images telling you what you should look like, and others judge you not by your degree of self-determination but by how well you fit the cultural norm.

Eating Disorders

As our discussion of attractiveness indicates, self-esteem is strongly influenced by how one feels about one's body. Public messages communicated about ideal body size have consequences; turning an unrealistic mirror on oneself may induce shame, anxiety, depression, sexual dysfunction, and eating disorders. The rigid standard of feminine beauty as White, thin, and able bodied can become an ideal against which a person evaluates her own body (Kilbourne, 1994). The result is an efficient form of social control, a hegemonic notion of beauty and sexuality. No guns or physical force are needed. The desire for perfection, control, and self-hatred drive destructive cycles of eating disorders such as anorexia and bulimia. Starving and purging provide a temporary sense of control over one's body until the compulsion to starve and/or purge begin to control the person.

Although there are cultural differences in defining attractive body size, the most recent findings make clear that U.S. women across racial and ethnic groups tend to be dissatisfied with their bodies (Grabe & Hyde, 2006). Most previous research has focused on White women, which may partly explain why it was assumed that this group suffers most with body image issues. However, research on African, Asian, and Hispanic American women is now available. In a meta-analysis of 98 studies, Shelly Grabe and Janet Hyde (2006) found that all the groups of women studied reported significant dissatisfaction with their body images, with White, college-age women slightly more dissatisfied. Asian and Hispanic Americans are among the least studied groups, but previous research indicates that girls and women in these groups have lower body images like the White women studied (Grabe & Hyde, 2006; Lovejoy, 2001).

Negative body image is affecting men in increasing numbers, although researchers have been slow to document the effects (Olivardia, Pope, Borowiecki, & Cohane, 2004). Instead of thinness, masculine concerns tend to be about being underweight and lacking body muscularity. *Muscle dysmorphia* is the term for preoccupation with muscularity and the misperception of one's physique as small despite distinct muscularity (Pope, Gruber, Choi, Olivardia, & Phillips, 1997).

In one of the more comprehensive studies of the relationship between men's bodies, self-images, and health, psychiatric researchers administered a variety of tests to 154 college men, predominantly White Catholics aged 18–30. The researchers found that the men displayed substantial body dissatisfaction with their muscularity (Olivardia et al., 2004). The men's concerns were tied to competing with other men and gaining their respect, which demonstrates that for many men, body image is tied to constructing a masculine, predominantly heterosexual identity, which asserts gender hierarchy (e.g., Olivardia, 2001). The results also found a large—and likely unhealthy—gap between some men's ideal body images and their own body realities. This gap can lead to health problems related to excessive exercise, anabolic steroid use, and eating disorders. Problems such as these may go undiagnosed because heterosexual men, in particular, are reluctant to seek help for fear of appearing feminine or gay.

The men who have been identified as having the greatest tendencies toward eating disorders are gay men. Many gay cultures place a higher value on physical attractiveness than heterosexual men's cultures tend to, and some gay men report stresses similar to those on heterosexual women who work to make themselves attractive to men (Olivardia & Pope, 1997). It seems that for women and men, the more one's value is reduced to one's mere sexual attractiveness, the more one is likely to engage in self-destructive practices.

Refusing the Command Performance

As we summarize research on social norms' effects on bodies, remember that social norms continuously change. In the 1850s United States, one of the primary objections to the dress reform represented by the bloomer outfit was that it exposed the ankle, lending the outfit an erotic quality (Foote, 1989; Mattingly, 2002). For a middle-class woman, showing an ankle was shocking, even up until 1909 (Gordon, 2001). A cursory review of the *Sears Catalogue*, "the arbiter of fashion in small town America" (Olian, 1995, p. i), makes clear that women's dresses skirted to the floor were the norm in 1909, with barely a toe peeking out from underneath. Not until 1912 would ankles appear consistently as acceptable fashion. Now, women in the United States think nothing of exposing an ankle.

Even though social norms seem permanent, people push at them all the time. In many ways, the very people who are ostracized and ridiculed for being different in one era are the same people future generations thank for expanding gender and sex repertoires. In this spirit, literature professor Judith Halberstam wrote *Female Masculinity* (1998), about women who dress and act masculine. Such women illustrate that masculinity is not reducible to the male body and its effects. Halberstam explores how female masculinity, which is not simply an "imitation of maleness . . . affords us a glimpse of how masculinity is constructed as masculinity" (p. 1). Those who least fit the norms may be the people who most enhance understanding of how the norms are communicated, reiterated, and reinscribed.

People can understand their own and others' behaviors only by recognizing the interacting influences of gender *and* sex *and* communication. Women who decide not to color their gray hair, men who are balding and do not opt for implants, African American women who choose not to straighten their hair, Muslim women who wear hijabs—all broaden people's cultural assumptions about gender/sex and the body.

Even though nonverbal communication often is unconscious, when people decide to challenge social norms, they do so quite intentionally. If people's bodies are "performatively produced and compelled by the regulatory practices of gender coherence" (Butler, 1990a, p. 24), it makes sense that if people want to challenge gender norms, they need to identify locations where the performance becomes incoherent. No repetition is a perfect reproduction. As sex is reiterated through performance, the reiteration also creates "gaps and fissures," instabilities, and something "which escapes or exceeds the norms, as that which cannot be wholly defined or fixed by the repetitive labor of that norm" (p. 10).

If gender is understood as "the activity of managing situated conduct in light of normative conceptions of attitudes and activities appropriate for one's sex category" (West & Zimmerman, 1987, p. 127), people's activities can manage normative sex expectations in distinct ways. First, norms can be deployed against themselves to open space for change. Second, norms can be made visible so that their incoherence is highlighted. Third, norms can be overtly challenged. Finally, norms can be revalued, where that which is denigrated or invisible is valued and made present.

Using Norms Against Each Other

Earlier, we outlined how women's traditional role of mother creates social expectations about how women should act: listening, attending to others' needs, remaining in the private sphere. However, women have used the role of mother as their foundation for public advocacy. The Mothers of Plaza de Mayo formed in 1977 to protest the "disappearance" of their children under the repressive military regime that ruled Argentina from 1976 to 1983. Communication scholar Valeria Fabj (1993) explains how verbal argument was not an option, and a nonverbal form linked to women's traditional roles was necessary. A verbal response by men was not possible because the society was repressive, yet women as mothers were valued and could protest the state's murder of their grown children. Wearing their children's cloth diapers as headscarves (embroidered with the children's names and dates of disappearance) and carrying pictures of their disappeared children, the mothers marched around the plaza at a time when public protest was prohibited. Fabj argues it was the very "myth of motherhood," the social beliefs that attached to the women's bodies, that allowed them "to draw from their private experiences in order to gain a political voice, discover eloquent symbols, and yet remain relatively safe at a time when all political dissent was prohibited" (p. 2). Because they were fulfilling social expectations attached to devoted motherhood, they were able to violate social and legal norms that no one else could. A similar tactic was deployed from 1995 to 1999 in Istanbul, where mothers protested the disappearance of politically contentious individuals held in police custody (Baydar & Ivegen, 2006).

In much the same way as these mothers used their maternal bodies, women in Nigeria used the threat of their exposed bodies as a form of silent protest. From July 2002 to February 2003, thousands of Nigerian women ranging in age from 30 to 80 peacefully seized Chevron-Texaco's terminals, airstrip, docks, and stores, disrupting oil production (Agbese, 2003; Turner & Brownhill, 2004). The women demanded jobs for their sons, schools, scholarships, hospitals, water, electricity, and environmental protection. They wanted some of the wealth that was being pumped out of the ground to be pumped back into their communities. As part of the protests, one group of women threatened public nudity if their demands were not met. In the United States, public nudity is likely to be read as a sign that Mardi Gras or spring break is in progress, but in Nigeria women's public nudity is a traditional way of shaming men. The women explained: "Our nakedness is our weapon" (quoted in Wysham, 2002, n.p.).

The Nigerian and Argentinian women used social norms and prohibitions to pressure those in power to meet with them and to accede to their demands. The social norms demanding that women be good mothers can be used to violate other social norms if, by abiding by those other norms, women cannot fulfill the demands of motherhood. When social norms concerning how one should be in one's body contradict or conflict, the gaps and fissures that emerge can be productive places to explore new ways to be in one's body.

Making Norms Visible

The Guerrilla Girls, a New York–based group, formed to protest the exclusion of women from the art world. They employed the tactic of "zap actions," placing posters around New York City (Demo, 2000). Their first action was in 1985 and focused on the absence of women in the major museums and galleries in New York. "Using mass-media techniques and advertising world savvy" (Guerrilla Girls, 1995, p. 10), they quickly gained notoriety.

Their emblematic poster (see photo), which appeared in 1989 on buses in lower Manhattan, refigured Ingres's *Odalisque,* "a reclining figure whose sinuous nude back and hips have long stood for idealized female beauty. Rather than meeting the classical profile of Ingres' original, however, our eyes confront a large shaggy gorilla head, mouth open, teeth glistening. Twisted to meet us eye to eye, it challenges instead of seducing" (Guerrilla Girls, 1995, p. 7).

Challenging the objectification of women's bodies and positioning women as artists, the poster makes visible the naked body of a real woman, challenging the fetishized, artistically rendered bodies that seem to have exclusive presence in

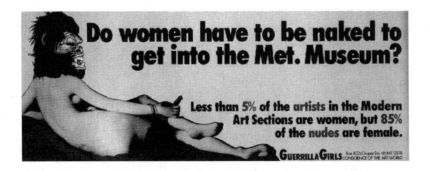

museums. It refigures what it means for women to be present, and it blocks the ability of museum defenders to claim that women are present as more than bodies on canvases. The poster makes visible the norm of women as objectified bodies even as the alternative of women bodies as artists is offered.

Overtly Challenging Norms

Communication scholar Bonnie Dow (2003) analyzes second-wave feminism's protest against the 1968 Miss American Pageant. In the second wave's first major public event, women challenged social norms of attractiveness. Women threw into trashcans bras as well as "girdles, high heels, cosmetics, eyelash curlers, wigs, issues of *Cosmopolitan, Playboy,* and *Ladies Home Journal*—what feminists termed 'instruments of torture' to women" (pp. 130–131). Although media coverage of the event referred to bra burning, *no bras were burned.* This event provides an interesting example of how those who challenge norms often are disciplined. Dow explains how the false claim of bra burning was used against the protestors: In a society obsessed with breasts, accusations of bra burning were a way of sexualizing and trivializing women's demands. For example, two years after the protests, Senator Jennings Randolph described feminists as "braless bubbleheads" in his response to the Women's Strike for Equality in 1970 (p. 130). In other words, even as people challenge norms, dominant social orders seek to reinforce them. Yet, more than 35 years after this initial protest, it is clear that many of the women's movements' challenges to attractiveness have taken hold (girdles, anyone?) even as new norms have replaced them (breast implants, anyone?).

Revaluing the Body

Bodies that have been denigrated or made invisible can be valued and made present. Communication scholar Kevin DeLuca (1999) explores how activist groups use the body as "not merely flags to attract attention for the argument but the site and substance of the argument itself" (p. 10). In U.S. society, homosexual bodies are marginalized because their sex, sexuality, and gender do not match up in the way dictated by heteronormativity. Thus, for such groups as ACT UP and Queer Nation, the presence of the body is the most powerful form of communication possible, "for it is the body that is at stake—its meanings, its possibilities, its care, and its freedoms. In their protest actions, the activists use their bodies to rewrite the homosexual body as already constructed by dominant mainstream discourses— diseased, contagious, deviant, invisible" (p. 17).

One also can rewrite the body by writing on the body with tattoos. Communication scholar Dan Brouwer (1998) studies the meaning of seropositive individuals who chose to tattoo themselves with symbols that would mark their HIV+ status. As DeLuca's analysis suggests, the tattoos are a way to make AIDS visible, a core goal of AIDS activist groups. However, Brouwer worries about this self-stigmatization: "The wearing of an HIV/AIDS tattoo is a precarious act, one that simultaneously disrupts expectations of the appearance of health and challenges norms of 'patient' behavior, yet one that also invites surveillance (which can be oppressive, punitive, or physically painful) and runs the risk of reducing the wearer's identity to 'disease carrier'" (pp. 115–116).

Conclusion

For every norming of people's bodies through expectations concerning nonverbal actions, locations of resistance arise. Yet, that resistance will face a response. Although the Mothers of Plaza de Mayo faced fewer reprisals than other activists did, the government punished many of them. Although the Guerrilla Girls have been active for more than 15 years, women continue to be underrepresented in major galleries and museums. Although dress standards have changed remarkably in the last 100 years, the range of individual expression in terms of dress really is quite limited (look around your classroom if you are unconvinced). Even as the most marginal of bodies are made visible, that does not mean they are accepted. Even if one recognizes that bodies' performances of gender are not natural, that does not mean it is easy to change the performance.

"Throwing like a girl" and "throwing like a boy" are far from natural behaviors. Social norms train people to throw, sit, walk, move, dress, smile, and be in ways appropriate to what a person's gender/sex is perceived to be. Cultures label particular movements of the body as gender/sex specific, and members of the culture then ridicule those who do not follow the prescribed behaviors. Over time, routinized movements of the body in gendered/sexed ways appear natural, which is why people perceive many elements of gender to be biologically determined and believe that biology is free from social influence.

Although the two-culture theory of gender communication links many of these practices to traditional gender roles and does not address the differences as indicators of inequality, most researchers argue that these roles and differences are not separate and equal but indicators of power differentials; they are separate and create inequality. The body, then, is an important location on which gender/sex identities are communicated, constructed, maintained, and challenged.

CHAPTER 5

Gendered/Sexed Language

anguage is more than a tool used to transmit information or a mirror to reflect reality. Language structures people's understanding of reality. Chapter 2 introduced you to symbolic interaction theory, which posits that meaning and identity are constructed through communication. This chapter approaches language from rhetorical and linguistic perspectives to explore the way discourses about gender/sex structure understandings of gender/sex, and hence structure gender/sex. People literally speak and perform their bodies and identities into being. Australian scholar Dale Spender (1985) describes language as "our means of ordering, classifying and manipulating the world. It is through language that we become members of a human community, that the world becomes comprehensible and meaningful, that we bring into existence the world in which we live" (p. 3).

The way in which language names a person as a sex and a gender determines how that person is perceived as a sex and a gender. For example, because the English language tends to recognize only two "opposite sexes"—female and male—it does not recognize the existence of intersex people. Quite simply, language has power—to oppress, deny, and subordinate. But language can also liberate, witness, and empower.

When studying communication, one studies not only how people communicate but what they communicate. The content of speech is as important as its form and style. For this reason, Jane Mills introduces her book *Womanwords* (1993) by noting, "Language is not solely a means of communication. . . . Language is at once the expression of culture and a part of it" (p. xiii).

Debate persists about whether language reflects or causes sexism. Actually, it does both. Language provides one way to trace the ideology of a culture, and language is also a way culture maintains itself. If people seek change, they cannot simply make that change by declaration. Rather, they need to articulate criticisms of how the culture maintains itself, offer visions of alternative worlds, and then share their ideas so that others' perspectives might shift.

To see the world in a different way, you must first understand how you see the world and recognize that what you see is in your control. Lexicographer Julia Penelope (1990) makes this clear: "What we say *is* who we are. Creating a universe of discourse that reflects a different way of perceiving the world requires understanding how the language we use indicates how we think and our awareness of the conceptual framework we've learned" (pp. 202–203).

Understanding how cultures teach gender and enforce sex, and how to challenge existing constructions of gender and sex, are communication issues. Thus, we focus on patterns of communication that speak to the ways in which sex and gender have been structured and in turn have structured the world. Sex is not a thing (even though the word is used to describe the human body), and gender cannot be held in your hands. Instead, when you study sex and gender, you study the trace evidence of them in communication.

Rhetorical scholar Kenneth Burke (1966) argues that human beings are symbol-using, symbol-making, and symbol-misusing creatures (p. 16). He does not stop at this description. Instead, he asks, "Do we simply use words, or do they not also use us?" (p. 6). Linguistics scholar Robin Lakoff (1975) answers this question: "Language uses us as much as we use language" (p. 3). Burke's question and Lakoff's answer direct students of language to consider the ways in which words influence people's interactions with each other and the world.

Burke (1966) describes how words operate together to constitute an ideology, and how that ideology induces people to act in certain ways: "An 'ideology' is like a spirit taking up its abode in a body: it makes that body hop around in certain ways; and that same body would have hopped around in different ways had a different ideology [or set of terms] happened to inhabit it" (p. 6). In relation to gender in communication, the language about sex and gender comes to inhabit human bodies, making them hop around, sit, stand, and throw in certain ways. Words about sex/gender form ideologies such as patriarchy, the gender binary, and heteronormativity. In this chapter, we identify some of the ways existing language practices and patterns make people "hop around" in one way rather than another. Whereas Chapter 3 discussed research about how people use language, this chapter analyzes how language uses people.

Theories Explaining the Power of Language

The struggle for speech has long dominated women's movements. From the 1300s through the 1700s, women struggled to gain access to education so their speech would be informed. First-wave feminists in the 1800s and early 1900s struggled for the right to speak both from the public lectern and through the ballot box. During the late 1900s, second-wave feminists struggled for a language with which to speak about their lives and grappled with language's power to shape, delimit, and interpret reality. Writing in 1963, Betty Friedan opened *The Feminine Mystique* with a chapter titled "The Problem That Has No Name." In it, she explains, "The problem lay buried, unspoken, for many years in the minds of American women" (p. 11). The problem was the general discontent of women caused by sexism.

The significance of women's demands for voice, as well as those of other marginalized groups, becomes clear after one examines theories explaining language's power. A number of theorists provide a rich vocabulary with which to understand why those concerned with gender and sex equality focus attention on language. Language orders the world, directing a person's attention in one way rather than another. Thus, this chapter is not about being politically correct but about being an ethical, conscious, and critical communicator. The following theories explain the significance of individual words, the power of symbol systems, and how particular symbols systems can dominate others. Words are never "only words."

Linguistic Relativity

The Sapir-Whorf hypothesis, also known as the *theory of linguistic relativity,* posits that language influences the way people perceive the world. In an oft-quoted passage, anthropologist Edward Sapir (1929/1958) explains,

> Human beings do not live in the objective world alone . . . but are very much at the mercy of the particular language which has become the medium of expression for their society. . . . The worlds in which different societies live are distinct worlds, not merely the same world with different labels attached. . . . We see and hear and otherwise experience very largely as we do because the language habits of our community predispose certain choices of interpretation. (p. 69)

Although people may know that things exist apart from language, they cannot know what those things mean or how they are to react to them, except through language.

This does not mean that people are incapable of thinking beyond the limits set by language. As Penelope points out, Sapir writes of the way "language is . . . a prepared road or groove" (quoted in Penelope, 1990, p. 203). A person's language creates paths of least resistance through which she or he can understand the world, and the more a person travels those paths, the deeper and more difficult it becomes to think outside the grooves, because "language focuses our attention on what we believe we know . . . and we neglect to glance aside at what borders the patriarchal grooves— the much larger, but apparently formless lands of all that we do not, but might know if we stepped outside the mainstream" (Penelope, 1990, p. 203). Language limits what you know, but it also provides the possibility of seeing beyond those limits.

Terministic Screens

An understanding of language's power comes not only from the science of linguistics but also from studies in the humanities. Burke focuses on the way in which a person's very essence as human is defined by the ability to use symbols. He defines human beings as the "symbol-using (symbol-making, symbol-misusing) animal" (Burke, 1966, p. 16) and argues that the ability to symbolize is the most unique attribute of humans, not the ability to reason, or to use money, or to deploy power. Burke is not alone in placing language at the center of human uniqueness. Okanagan Canadian author Jeanette Armstrong (1990) explains this from a Native American people's perspective: "We think about the things that formed us as thinking, human, walking people, different from the animal people. When we consider the spiritual place from which our thinking arises, the words become sacred things because they come from that place" (p. 28).

Words do not exist in isolation but combine to form *terministic screens* that direct people's attention away from some things and toward others. Burke's (1966) view of language highlights the "necessarily *suasive* nature of even the most unemotional scientific nomenclatures" (p. 45). All communication is persuasive because "even if any given terminology is a *reflection* of reality, by its very nature as a terminology it must be a *selection* of reality; and to this extent it must function also as a *deflection* of reality" (p. 45).

An example clarifies Burke's point. Reproductive freedom and abortion are rhetorically charged issues in the United States. Two main sides have long dominated the controversy: pro-life and pro-choice. People who are pro-life tend to refer to the "reality" as a *baby*, whereas those who are pro-choice tend to refer to the "reality" as a *fetus*. Each term selects, deflects, and reflects reality in a particular way and calls forth different clusters of terms that accompany it.

Baby accurately reflects reality insofar as some people often ask, "When is the baby due?" and some people perceive miscarriage as the loss of a baby. *Baby* also selects a particular aspect of reality to highlight; it focuses attention on how the reality is a fully formed human being separable from its gestational location. A person could leave a baby in a room unattended (but of course safely ensconced in a crib). However, when in the womb, it cannot be separated from its location. *Baby* also selects a particular type of relationship to other human beings; *babies* have mothers and fathers, not women and men. *Baby* also calls forth positive associations because U.S. culture is pro-natal; it celebrates the arrival of babies. People think of babies as innocent and pure. Once people think of the "reality" as a separate and distinct human being, to terminate its existence means that someone has committed murder.

In the process of selecting some parts of reality to highlight, *baby* also deflects part of reality. It deflects that the "reality" is located within a woman's body, and it deflects the possibility that women can be something other than mothers; if there is a baby, there is a mother. It also deflects the fact that people recognize stages in development in the human as it undergoes gestation, from zygote to embryo to fetus.

In the same way that *baby* reflects, deflects, and selects parts of reality, so does the term *fetus*. *Fetus* accurately reflects those very parts of reality that *baby* deflects. It reflects the reality that is described in medical and scientific terms, that gestational stages exist, and that a fetus cannot exist without a woman to carry it. In fact, *fetus* reverses the relationship: Babies *have* mothers, whereas women *carry* fetuses.

In selecting the medical reality, *fetus* highlights that the fetus is not a complete human being. Although people may fondly imagine cuddling a baby while sitting in a rocking chair, imagining cuddling a fetus is not quite the same. *Fetus* highlights the incompleteness of the human.

In the process of selecting, *fetus* also deflects attention away from the very things *baby* selects. *Fetus* deflects the emotional attachments people tend to have to small human forms, and it deflects the possibility that the fetus can be murdered. Fetuses are not murdered; instead, pregnancies are terminated.

Ultimately, words contain within them implicit exhortations to see the world in one way rather than another. Words "affect the nature of our observations." However, Burke (1966) goes even further, positing that "*many of the 'observations' are but implications of the particular terminology in terms of which the observations are made*" (p. 46). People see only that for which they have words.

Penelope (1990) extends this analysis from a gender/sex perspective to highlight how systems of sexism have influenced the words available:

> Language draws our attention to only some experiences in some ways, making it difficult to grasp and articulate those it doesn't provide labels or descriptions for. We can describe feelings and perceptions English doesn't provide words for, but finding an accurate description takes time and patience and some fluency with the language. Because English foregrounds only some aspects of experience as possibilities, we have a repertoire of specific gestures, sounds, words, sentence structures, metaphors, that focus our attention on just those activities named by patriarchy. (p. 204)

Examples of this lack of language will be discussed later when we describe semantic imbalance and semantic derogation.

Framing

The theory of framing, developed by cognitive linguist George Lakoff (2003), describes how metaphors influence thinking at a nonconscious level. For example, he explores how framing taxes as a *burden* influences people's understanding of them. People want to be relieved of their burdens, and anyone who interferes with another who is trying to relieve a burdened person is perceived as ill intentioned. This framing dominates the discussion of taxes in contemporary U.S. politics. But what happens if people think of taxes not as a burden from which to seek relief but as the dues citizens pay to be members of this great nation? What if taxes were not burdens you begrudgingly carry but your patriotic duty to the nation and to one another as citizens? Humans can reframe their understanding of a concept, act, or thing by creating an alternative conceptual metaphor.

Even terms that seem to have little to do with gender/sex can frame understandings of it. *Dependency*, as used in contemporary discussions of welfare, illustrates the power of framing. If one is not a taxpaying citizen, then one is considered to live in a state of dependency. Philosophy professor Nancy Fraser and history professor Linda Gordon (1994) analyze how the term *dependency* has evolved in relation to welfare and how that meaning represents a particular ideology. Given *dependency's* association with drug or alcohol abuse,

> Naming the problems of poor, solo-mother families as *dependency* tends to make them appear to be individual problems, as much moral or psychological as economic. The term carries strong emotive and visual associations and a powerful pejorative charge. In current debates, the expression *welfare dependency* evokes the image of "the welfare mother," often figured as a young, unmarried black woman (perhaps even a teenager) of uncontrolled sexuality. (p. 311)

This was not the term's earlier meaning: "In preindustrial English usage, the most common meaning of *dependency* was subordination" (p. 312), but it was a subordination that was normal, not deviant. A person who could live without laboring was independent; those who had to labor were dependent. *Dependency* denoted an inferior economic status, not a personal defect.

During the industrial era, the meaning of *dependency* shifted from referencing a social relation to referencing a sociological, political, or economic state; it designated a personal character trait. During the late 19th and early 20th centuries, as U.S. society moved into a post-industrial era, the term took on a distinctive meaning in relation to welfare. *Dependency* became a form of pathology considered avoidable and blameworthy. Those who relied on welfare were described as addicted to it. The association of welfare dependency with women was not accidental. During the 1950s, dependency had "very strong feminine associations" (p. 325).

Language as Power

Julia Penelope (1990) takes on George Lakoff's framing theory, arguing that a key step is missing because he does not ask "why some metaphorical concepts are more popular than others in patriarchal culture" (p. 30). Muted group theory provides one answer, the patriarchal universe of discourse (PUD) another.

Muted Group Theory

When Betty Friedan wrote about "the problem that has no name," she recognized that the English language does not serve all its users equally. Language is a social product. It is created, maintained, and changed by its users, but not all users have equal access to influencing the language. Those who belong to dominant groups within a culture have more influence over the language.

The history of dictionaries and the English language demonstrates this unequal power. English was developed predominantly by White male clerics and academics. Until modern times, educated White men who specialized in lexicography controlled the words chosen to be recorded in the dictionary and how they were defined. Their goal has generally been to "set forth a linguistic norm for a given community of speakers" (Kramarae & Treichler, 1992, p. 4), thus preserving the status quo and controlling the language, leaving those not in control of the language muted.

Social anthropologists Edwin Ardener and Shirley Ardener originally proposed muted group theory to explain why some people are unable to express themselves even when they have the physical ability to speak. The theory highlights how dominant and nondominant groups within a given culture have different cultural boundaries in their perceptions, as well as related language, and these are a way in which dominant groups can block others' power of actualization (E. Ardener, 1973).

Because of their muted positions in culture, persons in nondominant groups constantly must translate their ideas into forms that will be accepted by the dominant groups. They do not have the natural or easy access to communication possessed by those in the dominant groups. This affects not only their quantity of talk but also the content, timing, and mode of communication (S. Ardener, 2005). African Americans who speak Ebonics, or Black English, understand this. The pressure to speak dominant English is a pressure to "pass," to learn to speak White to be accepted or just to get by in dominant White culture. Even though in 1996 the Oakland, California, school board recognized Ebonics as a second language ("Oakland School Board," 1997, p. 12) and in 1997 the Linguistic Society of America recognized Black English as a legitimate language with its own grammar structures, semantics, and style ("LSA Resolution," 1997), it still is not accepted in dominant U.S. culture. Resistance to the creative expansion of language makes evident the politics of language.

Communication studies professor Cheris Kramarae (1981) extended the Ardeners' theory to explore the role of communication in processes of domination by focusing on how men as the dominant group block the actualization of women. She describes how muting occurs on two levels:

1. "Women (and members of other subordinate groups) are not as free or as able as men are to say what they wish, when and where they wish, because the words and the norms for their use have been formulated by the dominant group, men."

2. "Women's perceptions differ from those of men because women's subordination means they experience life differently. However, the words and norms for speaking are not generated from or fitted to women's experiences" (p. 1).

Intercultural communication scholar Mark P. Orbe (1998) further extends muted group theory with research on people of color, women, LGBT people, and those from lower socioeconomic classes to develop a theory of co-cultural communication. He identifies the factors that influence communication from nondominant group members to dominant group members:

Situated within a particular field of experience that governs their perceptions of the costs and rewards associated with, as well as their ability to perform, various communicative practices, co-cultural group members will strategically adopt a communication orientation—based on their preferred outcomes and communication approaches [e.g. assertive, nonassertive, aggressive]—to fit the circumstances of a specific situation. (p. 19)

These elements influence communication practices, such as emphasizing commonalities, self-censorship, avoiding controversy, bargaining, ridiculing self, confronting, and avoiding.

Muted group theory provides a way to understand that simply adding women's and other oppressed groups' voices will not create equality. Dominant groups mute through control of dominant discourse (S. Ardener, 2005). Those who resist must adapt or change the discourse.

Although nondominant groups may be at a disadvantage in language access, speakers are resilient. Orbe (1998) makes clear that "muted group status is not fixed; it is constantly reinforced, augmented, or challenged" through communication practices (p. 10). Oppressed and subordinated groups can speak to the problem of problems without names. Some women keep diaries or journals (Kramarae, 1981); in the United States in the 1960s, consciousness-raising groups were used by many White middle-class women to talk about subjects considered taboo, such as their sexuality (Campbell, 1973). Writers such as Gloria Anzaldúa use poetry, slang, multiple languages, unique forms, and profanity in academic writing (Palczewski, 1996). Sociolinguist Braj Kachru (1982) documents ways in which second-language speakers of English adapt the language to better reflect their worldviews, resulting in multiple world English*es*.

THE PATRIARCHAL UNIVERSE OF DISCOURSE (PUD)

Penelope (1990) focuses on the grammatical rules that govern language use, as well as the words. She argues that the English language is not neutral but supports patriarchy insofar as English creates a *patriarchal universe of discourse (PUD)*:

A 'universe of discourse' is a cultural model of reality that people use daily to decide how to act and what to say in specific contexts. . . . It is the same thing as 'consensus reality,' and those who accept its terms assume that it is an accurate description of reality. . . . In fact, people can be so attached to 'consensus reality' that its assumptions and predictions override contradictory evidence. (pp. 36–37)

When the model of reality is one in which a patriarchal system dominates, then that model tends to hide the exercise of male privilege.

The existence of a consensus reality explains why thinking critically about gender/sex can be so difficult. The language system pushes people to see things in a particular way. For example, according to the existing consensus reality, there are only two sexes, the sexes are opposite, and the words used to describe those sexes are not semantic equivalents. Penelope argues, "PUD divides the world into two, unequal, stereotypical spheres in well-defined, discrete areas of the English vocabulary that name people, their behaviors, attitudes, and activities in the world" (p. 38).

The interesting move in Penelope's analysis is that she makes clear that once people accept that language has power, then they need to start thinking about how those with power deploy language to maintain and extend power: by denying access to it (e.g., refusing education or public speaking forums), by stripping others of their languages (e.g., the forced suppression of Native American languages in Bureau of Indian Affairs schools beginning in the 1880s and continuing until passage of the Native American Languages Act of 1990), by generating rules of proper usage (e.g., proper English as a class and race marker), and by structuring the language in such a way that it masks power.

Language Can Be Used to Oppress and Subordinate

Thus far, we have described the general ways in which dominant groups structure reality through language. We now identify some specific examples of language-based gender/sex privilege. Of course, some of the examples may seem natural, unremarkable, or insignificant. This is part of the power of language. Linguist Deborah Cameron (1998) notes that "language is ideological. The same reality can be represented in any number of ways, and the power of linguistic conventions lies precisely in the selectiveness with which they represent the world, making one way of perceiving reality seem like the only natural way" (p. 161).

As we trace the locations of sexism in language, keep in mind that the examples are mostly derived from the United States. Our hope is that by learning to recognize the language patterns that reinforce sex and gender inequality, you will develop the critical faculties to think more politically about all language use, your own included. We happily admit that our discussion of language is *proscriptive*; part of our job description as communication scholars is to identify problems and offer solutions.

He/Man Language

The element of sexist language that has received the most attention is the use of sex-exclusive language such as the generic *he* or *man* used to refer to any person (female or male) or to all people (women and men). Research conclusively demonstrates that sex-exclusive language *does* influence the perception of those who read and hear it. Here is only a *partial* list of the studies that prove influence: Martyna, 1980a, 1980b, 1983; McConnell & Fazio, 1996; McConnell & Gavanski, 1994; Newman, 1992; Ng, 1990; Wilson & Ng, 1988. People do not read and hear *man* as a referent to all human beings, female and male, and people do not read and hear *he* as a referent for a woman. Every major style manual (APA, MLA, Chicago, Turabian, *New York Times*) requires sex-inclusive language that does not exclude half the population.

Most people forego sex-exclusive language in regular conversation. In a recent study of the actual use of the generic *he*, researchers Jeffrey L. Stringer and Robert

Hopper (1998) find that "[the] generic he occurs rarely, if at all, in spoken interaction" (p. 211). People no longer use the generic *he* in conversation, and style manuals discourage it in written communication. Thus, the debate over sex-inclusive language is resolved. Sex-exclusive language should not be used. Sex-inclusive language should be used.

Semantic Derogation

One way language has worn ruts into people's thinking is via semantic derogation (Schulz, 1975), in which two terms exist that ought to represent parallel concepts, but one term carries less positive connotations. One term is derogatory; the other is not. Penelope (1990) describes these terms as "semantically symmetrical (paired), but conceptually asymmetrical" (p. 48). Some scholars argue that derogation is sex based: "Because naming and defining is a prerogative of power, semantic shifts in vocabulary have been determined largely by the experience of men, not women" (Miller & Swift, 1993, p. ix).

Is this true? Consider the degree college students earn: the bachelor's degree. The parallel term is *spinster,* yet spinsters are thought of as dried-up old women who never married. However, the etymology of *spinster* indicates that positive meanings were once attached to it but have atrophied over time. Originally, *spinster* referred to women who spun fibers into thread and yarn. When men began to spin, the term referred to men, too. In the 17th century, the term began to refer to unmarried women (although some resisted this usage because *spinster* also was a colloquial term for "harlot"). In other words, the term became sexualized and derogated. Whereas *bachelor* referred to any unmarried man, a *spinster* was an unmarried women beyond the marriageable age, making clear that men are never too old to marry, but women can be. Other examples include *mistress/master; lady/lord; womanly/manly; tramp* (sexually active woman)*/tramp* (homeless man)*; to mother children/to father children; governor/governess;* and *sir/madam.*

An interesting pattern emerges in the derogation of nouns: Sexuality is used to derogate women. *Bachelor* and *spinster* ought to be equal, but *spinster* connotes someone who cannot get any sex. *Lord* and *lady* ought to be equal, but *lord* designates a ruler, whereas *lady* contains a prescription for how women should act. *Master* and *mistress* ought to be equal, but a *mistress* is a kept woman who gets sex by "stealing" it from another woman. *Governor* and *governess* ought to be equal, but again the masculine term connotes political power, whereas a *governess* is a person who takes care of others' children.

Semantic Imbalance

Semantic derogation refers to two terms that ought to be parallel but are not. *Semantic imbalance* refers to an overabundance of terms existing to describe something related to one group but few terms existing to describe the other. Think about this:

How many terms can you think of that describe a sexually promiscuous woman?

Now, how many can you think of that describe a sexually promiscuous man?

The number of terms available that negatively describe women swamps the list of terms that describe men. Only recently have terms like *player* come to carry negative connotations typically associated with *slut*.

Semantic imbalance is created not only when there are too many words but also when there are too few. Women often are referred to as *hysterical* (*hysteria*, derived from the Greek word for women's reproductive organs), yet men are not referred to as *testerical*. Similarly, men may be referred to as *womanizers*, but women are not *mannizers* (Penelope, 1990, p. 187).

Semantic Polarization and Polar Opposites

Semantic polarization occurs when two parallel concepts are treated as though they were opposed, like "opposite sexes." In case you had not noticed, we never use that phrase, primarily because it structures a perception of the world that we find problematic. The sexes are not opposite; all are human and may have more in common with those who are a different sex than with some who are the same sex. However, by framing the sexes as opposite, language re-entrenches the notion that there are two and only two sexes and that the characteristics of one cannot be possessed by the other. Communication scholar Barbara Bate (1988) explains, "If you see women and men as polar opposites, you are likely to believe that any features or quality of men should be absent from women, and vice versa" (p. 16).

Marked and Unmarked Terms

When one sex or race tends to dominate a category, people may sex or race-mark the category only when a nondominant person fills it. This creates the impression that a person is violating a norm. Because nursing as a profession is dominated by women, people tend to refer to "the nurse" when the nurse is a woman but refer to "the male nurse" when the nurse is a man. Similarly, you often see references to "female police officer" but not "male police officer," "male slut" but not "female slut," "Black professor" but not "White professor." In all of these examples, the race and sex of the person is incidental or irrelevant to the job she or he is performing. This construction is not as common as it once was, but it still is an interesting tendency to track. It reveals a great deal about cultural expectations and designated roles, which may explain why it is most persistent in university sports teams: The men's team is the "Bears," and the women's team is the "Lady Bears."

Trivialization

Another form of sexist language that is diminishing is trivialization, or the use of diminutives. Historically, Black men's masculinity was demeaned by the use of the term *boy*. Although *boy* does not initially seem like a derogatory term, when used by a White person (often younger) to refer to a Black man (often older), it exposes the power dynamic at play. No matter how old, wise, or respected, a Black man was forever diminished as an immature person, a boy. Women also often are referred to in ways that strip them of stature. Women are referred to as desserts: *honeybun, cupcake, sweetheart, tart*. Linguist Caitlin Hines (1999) argues that this is no accident, insofar as dessert metaphors refer to women not just as "objects, but sweet (that is compliant, smiling), and not just desserts, but *pieces* or *slices*" (p. 148).

To correct semantic imbalance and derogation, trivialization, and marked terms, it is not enough simply to erase them from our vocabularies. Cameron (1998) points out, "The crucial aspect of language is meaning: the point of non-sexist language is not to change the forms of words just for the sake of changing, but to change the repertoire of meanings a language conveys. It's about redefining rather than merely renaming the world" (p. 161). Therefore, attention to the vocabulary people have—or lack—becomes important.

Lack of Vocabulary

The foregoing examples point to problems in language use. However, as muted group theory clarifies, an equally challenging problem is a lack of language. Friedan's writing about problems without names highlights second-wave feminism's struggle to talk about sexism, sexual harassment, date rape, and marital rape. The second wave's attention to language makes sense. It is impossible to develop solutions to a problem when it has no name and hence is neither identifiable nor observable.

Spender (1985) argues, "Historically, women have been excluded from the production of cultural forms, and language is, after all, a cultural form—and a most important one" (p. 52). Its import stems from language's ability to "form the limits of our reality," because it is "our means of ordering, classifying and manipulating the world" and is how we "become members of a human community" (p. 3). However, because of women's exclusion from the "production of the legitimated language, they have been unable to give weight to their own symbolic meanings, they have been unable to pass on a tradition of women's meanings to the world" (p. 52). The fact that women have not had the same opportunity does not mean they have had no opportunity. One example of language development occurred during the debates over pornography that dominated women's movements in the 1980s.

Although men (as religious figures and political leaders) historically controlled the definition of *pornography*, they no longer monopolize its meaning. Historically, *pornography* possessed two meanings: (1) speech and (2) in the 1500s, images used as an assault on the church and state (Hunt, 1993). These interpretations dominated the word's meaning until the second wave of feminism began to challenge the way women's sexuality was defined. Andrea Dworkin and Catharine A. MacKinnon (1988) (among many others) focused on pornography's effect on women and redefined *pornography* as an act of sex discrimination, in the process rejecting a focus on pornography's effect on society's moral fiber (Palczewski, 2001). Although the ordinance they wrote did not survive judicial scrutiny in the United States, they influenced Canadian law regarding sexually explicit, violent, and sexist materials.

Developing a vocabulary enables you not only to name your experience but also to critically reflect upon it—an important component of coming to political agency. Influential African American feminist theorist bell hooks (1989) explains how "simply describing one's experience of exploitation or oppression is not to become politicized. It is not sufficient to know the personal but to know—to speak it in a different way. Knowing the personal might mean naming spaces of ignorance, gaps in knowledge, ones that render us unable to link the personal with the political" (p. 107). For hooks,

> Politicization necessarily combines this process (the naming of one's experience) with critical understanding of the concrete material reality that lays the groundwork for that personal experience. The work of understanding that groundwork and what must be done to transform it is quite different from the effort to raise one's consciousness about personal experience even as they are linked. (p. 108)

In other words, the development of a vocabulary with which to accurately describe one's experiences is an important process during which one needs to reflect on the political implications of that experience.

The Truncated Passive

Grammatical patterns as well as words provide evidence of sexism in language. Penelope (1990) argues that grammatical structures enable speakers to deny agency and perpetuate oppression. The prime culprit is the truncated passive, in which the use of a passive verb allows the agent of action to be deleted (or truncated) from the sentence. This example demonstrates the difference between when passives are and are not used:

No passive: That man raped that woman.

Passive without truncation: That woman was raped by that man.

Truncated passive: That woman was raped.

Each sentence is grammatically correct but operates very differently in its depiction of the event. Sentence constructions using the truncated passive enable blaming the victim because the victim is the only one present in the sentence.

Individuals who attempt to avoid explicit responsibility for the consequences of the power they exercise often use truncated passives. The result of "agent-deletion leaves us with only the objects of the acts described by the verbs. Passives without agents foreground the objects (victims) in our minds so that we tend to forget that some human agent is responsible for performing the action" (p. 146), as in the phrases "mistakes were made," "Hanoi was bombed" or "the toy got broken." Penelope explains, "Agentless passives conceal and deceive when it doesn't suit speakers' or writers' purposes to make agency explicit" (p. 149). As a result, "This makes it easy to suppress responsibility" and enables "protection of the guilty and denial of responsibility, . . . the pretense of objectivity, . . . and trivialization" (p. 149).

The Falsely Universal *We*

Political scientist Jane Mansbridge (1998) analyzes how the use of the collective *we* in political discourse can be used to represent a particular few by making invisible a distinct other. She explains, "'We' can easily represent a false universality, as 'mankind' used to" (p. 152). Thus, "the very capacity to identify with others can easily be manipulated to the disadvantage of" a subordinated group because "the transformation of 'I' into 'we' brought about through political deliberation can easily mask subtle forms of control" (p. 143).

One often hears politicians talk about how *we* need to do something or that *we* as a nation believe in particular values, when in reality they are referencing a particular segment of the population who they hope will vote for them. Granted, it is extremely easy to fall into using *we*, especially when a person wants to create a sense of identification and community. However, as Burke (1969) points out, any time identification is used, one must "confront the implications of *division*. . . . Identification is compensatory to division" (p. 22). When a group says, "we are alike," it also necessarily implies that others are *not* like them.

The De-Verbing of Woman

Just as many others have noted the semantic imbalance and derogation in nouns, imbalance and derogation also occur in verbs. The distinctions between the meanings of the verbs *to man* and *to woman*, which ought to be parallel, are intriguing. The *Compact Edition of the Oxford English Dictionary* (*OED*, 1971) lists the primary definition of the verb *man* as "To furnish (a fort, ship, etc.) with a force or company of men to serve or defend it" (p. 1711). Its definitions of the verb *woman* include "To become woman-like; with *it* to behave as a woman, be womanly . . . To make like a woman in weakness or subservience . . . To make 'a woman' of, deprive of virginity . . . To furnish or provide with women; to equip with a staff of women" (p. 3808). *Man* carries implications of acting, typically in battle and on ships. *Woman* carries implications of being acted upon. To *woman* is to become woman-like, to be made a woman, or to be deprived of virginity. Today, in contrast to the verb *man*, the word *woman* is seldom thought of as a verb at all.

The pattern described between *woman* and *man* also is present in other verb forms, such as *lord* and *lady*, *master* and *mistress*. *Lord*'s primary definition is "to exercise lordship, have dominion" (p. 1664). In contrast, the definition of the verb *lady* is "to make a lady of; to raise to the rank of lady . . . to play the lady or mistress" (p. 1559). To *lord*, one exercises lordship or has dominion. In contrast, *lady* means to be made a lady or merely to play at being a lady. Female verbs deny agency. Male verbs highlight it.

Master's primary verb form means "To get the better of, in any contest or struggle; to overcome defeat . . . to reduce to subjection, compel to obey; to break, tame (an animal)" (p. 1739). *Mistress* means "To provide with a mistress . . . to make a mistress or paramour of . . . to play the mistress, to have the upper hand . . . to dominate as a mistress" (p. 1820). Again, mastery involves agency, getting the better of, subjecting, compelling others to obey. *Mistress*, in contrast, is passive. A woman is provided for as a mistress; she does not mistress. Or she is made a paramour. Or she merely plays at being mistress. Or, if one focuses on the latter definitions in which agency is expressed, one realizes that it is often a false agency, for when a woman dominates as a mistress, she dominates (typically) "servants or attendants . . . household or family" (p. 1820). Agency is rarely involved; rarely is control possible and never over masters.

People, Places, and Topics of Silence

French philosopher Michel Foucault (1972) explores why speaking can be perilous. He hypothesizes that "in every society the production of discourse is at once controlled, selected, organized and redistributed according to a certain number of procedures, whose role is to avert its powers and its dangers, to cope with chance events, to evade its ponderous awesome materiality" (p. 216). Foucault outlines "rules of exclusion" that control the production of discourse: "We know perfectly well that we are not free to say just anything, that we cannot simply speak of anything, when we like or where we like; not just anyone, finally, may speak of just anything" (p. 216). Although Foucault proceeds to discuss principles of exclusion other than prohibited words, the focus of this section is on how to recognize silences attached to topics, people, and places.

Topics

Foucault notes that "we cannot simply speak on anything." Instead of saying that the control of topics defines those issues that *cannot* be talked about, it may be more accurate to say it controls those issues that cannot be talked about *without approval*. For example, during the Victorian Age, discussion of children's sexuality was forbidden simply because, at the time, children were not sexed. Currently, we might say that although U.S. citizens (who stress the importance of freedom of speech) *can* talk about anything they want, the gatekeeping function of the media determines what actually is discussed (Paulos, 1995). Although people may talk about anything, only a few topics are identified as worthy of extended public discussion.

We began this book with one example of a topic restriction: gender wars. Anyone who speaks about differences between the sexes receives extensive media coverage, but those who focus on the similarities receive little or no attention. One also can find this dynamic at play in classrooms: Given that a class is devoted to a particular topic, anything that is perceived as beyond that topic will generate discomfort. You know you are not free to talk about just anything.

Another example can be found in the intersection of popular culture and politics. People often condemn musicians for taking political stances; although musicians may sing about love and loss, political statements appear to be off limits. In 1973, country music icon Loretta Lynn celebrated the effect of the birth control pill on women's sexual autonomy. Her song "The Pill" chronicled a woman's ability to choose the number of children she would have, declaring: "You wined me and dined me/When I was your girl/Promised if I'd be your wife/You'd show me the world/But all I've seen of this old world/Is a bed and a doctor bill/I'm tearin' down your brooder house/'Cause now I've got the pill." Country music stations refused to play the song . . . until Lynn's female fans demanded to hear it (Craig, 2001). More recently, the Dixie Chicks have faced censure because of lead singer Natalie Maine's comment to a London audience on the eve of the 2003 Iraqi invasion that "we're ashamed the president of the United States is from Texas." In response, "the group received death threats and was banned by thousands of country music stations" (Tyrangiel, 2006, p. 62). Operating in a corporate consensus reality, audiences proclaim that they paid to be entertained, not to hear about politics. However, that consensus is never absolute, as the popularity of the Dixie Chicks' recent album, *Taking the Long Way*, demonstrates.

PEOPLE

A related prohibition concerns *who* may discuss certain issues: "Not just anyone . . . may speak of just anything." People either accept or reject the discourse of particular individuals. For example, women were absent from the public podium in the United States until 1831. In fact, for much of Western history, women were explicitly prohibited from speaking publicly by social mores and by law. Aristotle approvingly quotes Sophocles: "Silence is a woman's glory" (1 *Politics* 13:1230). Paul's letter to the Corinthians exhorts women to silence: "Let the women keep silent in the churches; for they are not permitted to speak . . . And if they desire to learn anything, let them ask their own husbands at home; for it is improper for a woman to speak in church" (1 Corinthians 14:34–35, New American Standard version). During the 1600s in colonial America, "the ducking stool held a place of honor near the Courthouse alongside the pillory and the stock" (Jamieson, 1988, p. 67). The stool's use? "Unquiet" women were tied to the stool and then dunked in water so they would be forced to choose between drowning and silence. During the 1700s, women who spoke too much were labeled "scolds," and literally "gagged and publicly exhibited before their own doors" (p. 68). Such prohibitions were not confined to ancient pasts. Into the 1900s, public outcry arose against women speaking to "promiscuous" audiences, meaning those audiences composed of both women and men (Zaeske, 1995). Examples of those who are not allowed to speak and write in the current episteme would include muted groups—members of socially subordinated or marginalized groups.

This rule of prohibition is not so much concerned with who may speak, however, as it is with who may speak *credibly* on an issue. As writings within women's studies demonstrate, women's voices typically are not accorded the same credibility as men's (Code, 1991). Similarly, hooks (1989) notes that when marginalized people speak as equals to authority figures, when they "talk back," their speech often is labeled "crazy talk, crazy speech" (p. 7).

Classrooms can reveal these power dynamics at work. For example, students rarely take notes when other students speak, nor do they direct their comments to other students but instead funnel them through the instructor. In the classroom, teachers are accorded power through the rituals of student–teacher interaction.

PLACES AND FORMS

The last discursive rule pertains to the accepted forms that concepts may assume, *how* or under what circumstances people can talk about certain issues: "We cannot simply speak of anything, when we like or where we like." Again, classrooms provide a microcosm wherein this rule may be discerned. Highly private information tends not to be discussed. Topics are chosen and placed in a particular order—a *when*. In addition, *where* delimits how people talk. Someone speaking from a podium is accorded more power than someone in the back of the room. When students do formal presentations, they often move to the podium. Students have been acculturated to the rules of discourse and recognize that the podium is a location of power.

An example of the power of location in public argument can be found in activist and author Andrea Dworkin's request that survivors of abuse allegedly caused by pornography speak from the same privileged location as the social scientists and experts during the Minneapolis City Council's Hearing concerning pornography (Palczewski, 1993). Given that Dworkin believed women's experiential evidence was more valid than artificial laboratory research, she demanded that women physically occupy the "where" of legitimacy; this demand was granted (MacKinnon & Dworkin, 1997).

Although these descriptions of the way in which power inheres in discursive rules may be discouraging, remember that resistance is an inherent part of any relationship of power. Foucault (1980) explains that the key to hierarchy lies in the fact that regardless of the current system of knowledge, resistance always is possible. Resistance, in this instance, is defined as a "centrifugal movement, an inverse energy, or discharge . . . [that is] omnipresent, dispersed, and productive" (p. 138).

The Dixie Chicks' continued popularity is one example of dispersed inverse energy. Women involved in the abolition movement are another. They resisted the rules of exclusion as they carved a space from which to speak in public, arguing that women's special benevolence legitimized their departure from the domestic sphere (Zaeske, 1995). With her addresses to Boston's African American abolitionist community between 1831 and 1833, Maria Miller Stewart was "the first U.S.-born woman and the first Black woman known to address mixed-sex and mixed-race audiences on political issues" (Sells, 1993, p. 339). Later, White Quaker sisters Sarah and Angelina Grimké spoke against slavery, arguing that the era's dictates on womanhood conflicted with their religious duty to speak out against the abomination of slavery. Historian Barbara Welter (1976) notes how, during this time period, women were expected to be pure, pious, domestic, and submissive. However, if a woman believed that slavery was an affront to piety, then she had to leave the domestic sphere to agitate against it. Ultimately, the rules governing the public sphere shifted. Slavery became a topic open to debate, women were slowly recognized as legitimate participants in this debate, and the evidence they brought from their own experiences began to count.

Unfortunately, even when marginalized groups have spoken and have been heard by their contemporaries, they may have been silenced in history. How many of the women referenced in the previous pages have you heard of? The danger of silencing a history is explained by poet and philosopher Adrienne Rich (1979):

> The entire history of women's struggle for self-determination has been muffled in silence over and over. One serious cultural obstacle encountered by any feminist writer is that each feminist work has tended to be received as if it emerged from nowhere; as if each of us had lived, thought, and worked without any historical past or contextual present. This is one of the ways in which women's work and thinking has been made to seem sporadic, errant, orphaned of any tradition of its own. (p. 11)

This is one reason why we cite so many authors and use so many block quotations. We recognize we are not the first to discover the insights outlined in this text. We want to honor others who have figured things out, and so we use their words instead of erasing them with our own.

Language as Violence

The previous sections focused on how specific parts of language (verbs, pronouns, and nouns) construct sex privilege through language. However, language in its most basic unit is not the only way in which oppression and subordination can be manifested. Language itself can be used as a form of violence. Critical race theorists examine the function of hate speech, recognizing the "relationships between naming and reality, knowledge and power" (Matsuda, Lawrence, Delgado, & Crenshaw, 1993, p. 5). They argue that hate speech (racist, homophobic, sexist, anti-Semitic speech) causes harm. Although the First Amendment has protected such speech, legal scholar Mari Matsuda (1993) argues that "an absolutist first amendment response to hate speech has the effect of perpetuating racism: Tolerance of hate speech is not tolerance borne by the community at large. Rather it is a psychic tax imposed on those least able to pay" (p. 18).

Although many of you have heard the saying, "Sticks and stones may break my bones, but words will never hurt me," the distinction between words and actions may not be as clear as once thought. Matsuda (1993) explains, "The deadly violence that accompanies the persistent verbal degradation of those subordinated because of gender or sexuality explodes the notion that there are clear lines between words and deeds" (p. 23). Although First Amendment absolutists argue that the appropriate response to "bad" speech is more speech, such an alternative is not always viable for those targeted by hate speech. Legal scholar Charles R. Lawrence III (1993) demonstrates a point we made earlier: Words are more than what they denote.

> Like the word "nigger" and unlike the word "liar," it is not sufficient to deny the truth of the word's application, to say "I am not a faggot." One must deny the truth of the word's meaning, a meaning shouted from the rooftops by the rest of the world a million times a day. The complex response "Yes, I am a member of the group you despise and the degraded meaning of the word you use is one that I reject" is not effective in a subway encounter. (p. 70)

Lawyer and legal scholar Catharine A. MacKinnon (1993) advocates the idea that words and images act, particularly on women's bodies: "Stopping pornography, and with it the sexualization of aggression and legitimized use of women from brothels to courtrooms, is women's only chance to gain, in or out of court, a voice that cannot be used against us" (p. 68). Although the anti-pornography law she and Dworkin developed was declared unconstitutional on First Amendment grounds, their rhetoric has influenced the way many think about sexually explicit images that degrade women.

Of course, just because one recognizes that language acts does not mean that one automatically accepts the need for legal redress. Debate about the appropriate response to pornography dominated the 1980s, and debate about hate speech dominated the 1990s. Those working against sexism, racism, religious intolerance, and homophobia disagree on the appropriateness of legal prohibitions against words that wound, noting the danger of collapsing a word into an action (Butler, 1997). However, all agree that we must respond to, answer, deny, reject, and condemn the use of language as a mechanism of violence.

Language as Resistance

If language has the power to create inequality and injustice, it also has the power to resist them. Through language, people can rename, re-envision, and re-imagine the world. Penelope (1990) explains, "Language is power, in ways more literal than most people think. When we speak, we exercise the power of language to transform reality" (p. 213). In this section, we highlight the theories that explain the emancipatory potential of language.

Before we proceed, we want to remind you that we operate from a gender diversity perspective and employ a multidetermined social context approach to gender/sex. Although as communication studies scholars we *focus* on language, we do not dismiss the importance of economics, politics, and law to social change. Our position is that language is a precursor to recognizing the need for and the possibility of change in these other areas. Penelope (1990) argues, "Changing our descriptions won't immediately change reality or eliminate white supremacy or male dominance, but it will change the way we perceive power imbalances and the conceptual structures that make them appear to make sense to us" (p. 214).

Talking Back

In *Talking Back* (1989), bell hooks outlines how simply speaking can function as an act of resistance. For those denied access to the public sphere or who have been named as people, places, or topics of silence, speaking rejects that naming. For any subordinated group, hooks explains, "True speaking is not solely an expression of creative power; it is an act of resistance, a political gesture that challenges politics of domination that would render us nameless and voiceless. . . . Moving from silence into speech is . . . a gesture of defiance that heals, that makes new life and new growth possible." "Talking back" is not talking for talk's sake, but "is the expression of our movement from object to subject—the liberated voice" (pp. 8–9).

As we talk about language in this chapter, we talk about not only the words themselves but also who is authorized to use them, on which subjects, from which social locations, and with what critical perspectives. For hooks, talking back is not simply the screaming of frustration, nor do all people speak as subjects and with a liberated voice every time they speak. She clarifies that "to speak as an act of resistance is quite different than ordinary talk, or the personal confession that has no relation to coming into political awareness, to developing critical consciousness" (p. 14). The distinction between ordinary talk and talking back is necessary for three reasons. First, it avoids trivializing or romanticizing the process of finding a voice; coming to voice is difficult political work. Second, it avoids privileging "acts of speaking over the content of the speech" (p. 14); when talking back, what is said matters. Third, it prevents the commodification of oppositional voices; when one recognizes the oppositional element of talking back, one can no longer treat it as mere spectacle. Talking back is not mere talk but talk with a political consciousness.

★Counterpublic Spheres

If disempowered peoples want to talk back, how do they develop languages that name their experiences and translate inchoate wants and needs into political demands? How are marginalized peoples able to experiment, inevitably making mistakes in the process, without fear that such mistakes might doom their political demands? Philosopher Nancy Fraser (1992) offers one way to think about how oppositional demands arise even in the face of a dominant public discourse that would seek to silence those who resist. Instead of thinking of the public as a single, unitary sphere, she argues that people ought to conceive of a multiplicity of publics, some of which exist in opposition to the dominant public. These oppositional locations she names *counterpublics*, "discursive arenas where members of subordinated social groups invent and circulate counterdiscourse to formulate oppositional interpretations of their identities, interests, and needs" (p. 123). They are not less than the dominant public but operate parallel to it.

Literary critic Rita Felski (1989) proposes that the women's movement and the civil rights movement have "inspired theorists to posit the growth of counter-public spheres, understood as critical oppositional forces within the society" (p. 166). We are attracted to counterpublic sphere theory because it draws attention to "the communicative networks, social institutions, and political and economic structures through which ideologies are produced and disseminated" (p. 9). Multiple determinants of power are examined, but communication is central. Counterpublics also allow one to conceptualize the interactions between communication and institutions because "the category of the feminist public sphere needs to be understood in terms of a series of cultural strategies which can be effective across a range of levels both outside and inside existing institutional structures" (p. 171).

Challenging ideologies of sex, race, class or nationality privilege is not simple; it requires attention to the various elements that influence the social order. For Felski, counterpublic spheres are one location from which a multilayered form of resistance can emerge because they employ "processes of discursive argumentation and critique which seek to contest the basis of existing norms and values by raising alternative validity claims" (p. 12) while also affirming "specificity in relation to gender, race, ethnicity, age, sexual preference, and so on" (p. 166).

The specificity of location allows one to develop alternative validity claims and new rules of argument. As discussed in Chapter 4, social norms are powerful. Philosopher Judith Butler's (2004) analysis of gender explains why "the capacity to develop a critical relation to these norms presupposes a distance from them, an ability to suspend or defer the need for them" (p. 3). Only then can an "alternative, minority version of sustaining norms or ideals" be articulated, often as a collective (p. 3). Thus, counterpublics provide the distance and solidarity needed to challenge norms.

Ultimately, the existence of counterpublics expands the space of argument by challenging assumptions as they respond "to exclusions within dominant publics . . . assumptions that were previously exempt from contestation will now have to be publicly argued out" (Fraser, 1992, p. 124). If one does not belong to the dominant public sphere, the articulation of needs becomes nearly impossible. Assuming a monolithic public sphere intensifies the subordination of marginal group needs. Fraser argues that in societies beset by inequality, theories that recognize multiple publics better promote the ideal of equality than does a single public sphere. Although absolute equality within a single public might be an ideal, it is not a reality, and pretending as though it is does more to maintain inequality than challenge it because "where societal inequality persists, deliberative processes in public spheres will tend to operate to the advantage of dominant groups and to the disadvantage of subordinates." When all peoples are required to discuss their needs in the dominant public sphere, "members of subordinated groups would have no arenas for deliberation among themselves about their needs, objectives, and strategies" and would always be "under the supervision of dominant groups. In this situation they would be less likely than otherwise to 'find the right voice or words to express their thoughts' and more likely than otherwise 'to keep their wants inchoate.'" The end result is that the marginalized group would be less able "to articulate and defend their interests in the comprehensive public sphere" (pp. 122–123). Multiple publics in the form of counterpublic spheres do not undermine public deliberation but enhance it.

Developing a New Language

A core function of counterpublics is to develop a way to make speakable those needs, interests, and identities that are inchoate. To do this, new terms may be developed. Philosopher Mary Daly (1987) explains, "New Words themselves are Mediums, carriers of messages" (p. 10).

Philosopher Sandra Harding (1995) outlines the power of naming for a marginalized group—in this case, women: "For women to name and describe their experiences in 'their own terms' is a crucial scientific and epistemological act. Members of marginalized groups must *struggle* to name their own experiences *for* themselves in order to claim the subjectivity, the possibility of historical agency, that is given to members of dominant groups at birth" (p. 128). In other words, in order to become agents, or people who act rather than people who are acted upon, a language on and of one's own terms is essential: "For marginalized people, naming their experience publicly is a cry for survival" (p. 129).

One example demonstrates the role of counterpublics in developing new language. Prior to the 1970s, *sexual harassment* as a term did not exist, even though the activity did: During slavery, African American women were sexually used and raped by their White masters; during industrialization, immigrant women were forced by economic necessity to acquiesce to the demands of their employers; and even during these contemporary times, women (primarily) are subjected to work environments where their sex is used as a basis of ridicule, often in the hopes of driving them from the workplace. When women experienced hostile, abusive, and violent workplaces, it was explained as having a "bad boss" or as further proof that women did not belong in the rough world of the workplace. With the burgeoning of the second wave of women's movements, women had both a physical and a discursive space in which they could come together to develop a language that made their interests articulable. The Women's Center at Cornell University held the first speak-out in 1975, where women around the country came together to name these experiences "sexual harassment" and articulate the harm as discrimination, whether in the form of hostile environments or as the quid pro quo demands of sex in order to keep a job. MacKinnon (2005) describes sexual harassment as "the first legal wrong to be defined by women," believing that "it took a women's movement to expose these experiences as systematic and harmful in the first place, a movement that took women's point of view on our own situation as significantly definitive of that situation" (p. 111). In 1986, the Supreme Court of the United States recognized sexual harassment as a violation of Title VII of the Civil Rights Act.

This example demonstrates the complex interrelations of levels of communication. Women experienced violence via a form of interpersonal communication.

Until they could name that violence, nothing could be done about it. By coming together in small groups and developing a vocabulary that could articulate their interests, women were able to take their demands from the counterpublic to the larger public, eventually effecting legal change, giving them grounds on which to contest illegal, not just inappropriate, forms of interpersonal communication.

Other examples of developing language abound. Feminist lexicographers have made efforts to create alternative dictionaries to reclaim the English language, using concepts and definitions that reveal and reflect the diverse experiences and oppressions of women, persons of color, working-class people, gays, lesbians, bisexuals, transgender people, and people with disabilities (e.g., Daly, 1987; Kramarae & Treichler, 1992; Mills, 1993). Going beyond the creation of new words, Suzette Haden Elgin (1984/2000, 1987/2002, 1993/2002) developed an entire language, Láadan, for her fictional *Native Tongue* trilogy ("Suzette Haden Elgin," 2004).

Women in other nations and in other times also have developed languages in which to come to voice. Communication scholar Lin-Lee Lee (2004) studies how, more than 1,000 years ago in China, women developed *Nüshu*, a female discourse used in "texts sung and chanted by rural woman over their needlework on pieces of red fabric, handkerchiefs, and fans" (p. 407). Chinese women were excluded from formal education in *Hanzi*, the official Chinese script that "was created by men for the use of men." *Nüshu* offered an alternative as "an oral phonetic transcription passed from generation to generation by women" (pp. 408–409). It developed in an area governed by patriarchal Confucian systems, in which men dominated women and subservience to superiors was morally required. *Nüshu* texts described the details of a woman's life and expressed feelings about "sexual inequality, low social status, and bad treatment" (p. 411). No one trained in ordinary Chinese can read *Nüshu*. Men who heard it could "understand it when performed, but they could not perform it, read it, or speak it themselves" (p. 409). This distinctive language "allowed women to have a voice, to create an individual and collective subjectivity that enabled them to confer value on and give importance to their lives" as it "transformed the hardships of women into tales that validated their lives and experiences" (p. 410).

Resignification

Even when a group of people has decided to speak, the group may not always have the language to do so. Language uses people by omission; if people lack a way to name, whatever they are talking about remains invisible. Other times, though, a word or words exist to denote the existence of a thing, and the connotation is disparaging. In such a case, creating another word may not be enough to displace the existing one. Instead, the linguistic tactic chosen is *resignification,* in which one rejects the existing meaning's normative power, exposes how the term's meaning is constructed, and attempts to change its connotation.

Scholars have written about the need to resignify or reclaim words. Randall Kennedy's *Nigger* (2002) explores the history of that term and its recent resurgence as an in-group way to name African Americans. Inga Muscio's *Cunt* (2002), as well as Eve Ensler's *The Vagina Monologues* (2000), reclaim *cunt*. Politicized sex workers resignify *whore*, as in Gail Pheterson's *A Vindication of the Rights of Whores* (1989). Elizabeth Wurtzel's *Bitch* (1998) praises difficult women, *Bitch* magazine offers a feminist response to pop culture, and Meredith Brooks's song "Bitch" proclaims "I'm a bitch/I'm a lover/I'm a child/I'm a mother/I'm a sinner/I'm a saint/ I do not feel ashamed . . . So take me as I am/This may mean/You'll have to be a stronger man."

Interestingly, when a word's history is researched, it almost always turns out that the word originally had a positive meaning and only recently came to carry negative connotations. When Muscio researched *cunt*, she found that its precursors originally were related to titles of respect for women or names of goddesses and that "the words 'bitch' and 'whore' have also shared a similar fate [to *cunt*] in our language. This seemed rather fishy to me. Three words which convey negative meanings about women, specifically, all happen to have once had totally positive associations about women" (p. 6). Urvashi Vaid (1995), in her analysis of LGBT rights, finds that *queer* originally was used as a form of self-naming by homosexuals. By the 1910s and 1920s, men who thought of themselves as different because of their homosexual attraction to other men rather than because of their feminine gender appearance called themselves *queer* (p. 42). *Queer* later developed the negative connotation still heard as an epithet in playgrounds and streets. This meaning did not develop overnight but, as Butler (1993) explains, "'Queer' derives its force precisely through the repeated invocation by which it has become linked to accusation, pathologization, insult" (p. 226).

This hints at the difficulty involved in resignifying a term. People cannot simply wish a term's connotation change. Butler's theory on the performativity of gender explains why this is the case: People tend to be "ventriloquists, iterating the gendered acts that have come before them" (Hall, 2000, p. 186). How does one get out of this repetitive loop? By resignification—the repeated invocation of a term that links it to praise, normalization, and celebration. Unfortunately, even when a term may be resignified within a group of people, that does not mean the new meaning carries beyond that group. Butler (1993) notes: "As much as it is necessary to . . . lay claim to the power to name oneself and determine the conditions under which the name is used, it is also impossible to sustain that kind of mastery over the trajectory of those categories within discourse" (p. 227). However, that may be one's only option.

Butler (1997) writes that people sometimes "cling to the terms that pain" them because they provide "some form of social and discursive existence" (p. 26). Guided by Althusser's theory of interpellation (whereby one becomes a subject because one is recognized by another), Butler posits, "The act of recognition becomes an act of constitution: the address animates the subject into existence" (p. 25). Thus, it is understandable that one might prefer being known as a *queer* or a *nigger* or a *bitch* to not being known at all. Additionally, even as dominant naming may disempower, it also creates locations for resistance, for "opening up of the foreclosed and the saying of the unspeakable." For Butler, "The resignification of speech requires opening new contexts, speaking in ways that have never been legitimated, and hence producing legitimation in new and future forms" (p. 41).

Even though resignification is difficult, it is not impossible. *Queer's* meaning has been altered (although not completely) with the emergence of queer theory and queer studies in the academy, as well as Queer Nation's chant "We're queer, we're here, deal with it." During the 18th century, *woman* was used in contrast to *lady*, the latter indicating refinement and the former connoting sexuality (Mills, 1993, p. 267). However, *woman* is now the preferred term because it connotes power and agency, whereas *lady* tends to connote prissiness. *Lady* prescribes that one should act in a restrained manner ("like a lady"), and it implies a class distinction (ladies are of a higher class). In an interesting twist, though, many women's sports teams still are called the Lady Cats, Lady Cavaliers, Lady Mocs, or Lady Tigers, perhaps implying they are not true athletes by linguistically marking them as female.

Strategic Essentialism and Rhetorics of Difference

Communication involves not only what people speak but who people speak as. As illustrated in Chapters 3 and 4, people perform identities. Often, those who are most marginalized are those most strongly denied a language with which to speak. Yet, when challenging oppressions, many people choose to speak from the very identity category that has been the basis of their oppression. When people speak as women, as people of color, as queer, as third-world women, as indigenous people, they thematize their identities as the legitimizing force of their rhetoric.

The relationship between identity categories and political action is a complex one. Although we are wary of claims of some innate or biological sense of identity, we also recognize that each person is categorized and that those categories have real effects. Even if there is no biological foundation to race, people who are categorized as Black, Hispanic, Arab, Asian, and so forth are subjected to stereotypes on the basis of that categorization. In terms of sex, even if the differences between women and men are infinitesimal, people treat men and women as different. Identity categories might be artificial, but they have real, material effects. Given that categories of identity difference do exist, how might they be challenged? One way is to be constantly vigilant about whether the perception of differences is warranted. Another way is to engage in what Gayatri Spivak (1996) has called *strategic essentialism* (pp. 159, 214).

Strategic essentialism has two important characteristics. First, the so-called essential attributes of the group are defined by the group members themselves. Second, even as the group members engage in essentialism, they recognize that it is always an artificial construct. When Fraser wrote about counterpublics, she referenced Spivak's work to explore how *subordinated social groups* create counterdiscourses that articulate *their* identities, interests, and needs. They do not deny they are a group but instead seek to control what it means to be part of that group. This reclaims agency. Jaqui Alexander and Chandra Talpade Mohanty (1997) explain, "Agency is . . . the conscious and ongoing reproduction of the terms of one's existence while taking responsibility for this process" (p. xxviii). The marginalized become actors instead of the acted upon.

For example, how are Black women's identities constituted by the dominant public sphere? Alexander and Mohanty posit that the taxpaying consumer is the model of citizenship in the United States. If you doubt this, think back to what U.S. citizens were asked to do in the wake of the 9/11 attacks; President George W. Bush, New York Mayor Giuliani, and Senators Daschle and Kerry all urged U.S. citizens to go shopping (Apple, 2001; Crenson & Ginsberg, 2002; Kowalczyk, 2001). In contrast to the consuming and taxpaying (White) citizens, much public discourse defines poor women of color as the "paradigmatic welfare recipients (when in fact, White women constitute the largest group on welfare) and the discourses of dependency, cultural deprivation, and psychological personality characteristics . . . used to discipline these women indicate that (Black) women on welfare are, by definition, neither consumers or taxpayers and, thus, are noncitizens" (p. xxxii). In response, Black women such as bell hooks, Ruby Duncan, Angela Davis, Patricia Hill Collins, and Lani Guinier and the Black women's welfare rights movement (Nadasen, 2005) have sought to redefine Black women's identities, interests and needs.

Even as scholars recognize that identities are fluid and contingent, and that clinging to them carries danger, scholars also understand "'identities' as relational and grounded in the historically produced social facts which constitute social locations" (Moya, 1997, p. 127). Identities matter insofar as they determine where a person fits within the social order as it presently exists. When one is positioned at the margin, this does not mean that one automatically articulates counterdiscourses but that such a person can provide a location from which a group oppositionally can "provide us with a critical perspective from which we can disclose the complicated workings of ideology and oppression" (p. 128). English professor Paula M. L. Moya (1997) argues that the external construction of identities influences experiences, and those experiences then inform what people know and how they know it. Moya urges everyone to remember that although "people are not *uniformly* determined by any *one* social fact, . . . social facts (such as gender and race)" *do* influence who we are (p. 132).

An excellent example of strategic essentialism is found in communication scholar Lisa Flores's (1996) study of Chicanas' development of a rhetorical homeland. Flores examines how Chicana feminists' creative works create a discursive space, distinct from the liminal borderlands in which they live—the space between the United States and Mexico that Chicana lesbian feminist Gloria Anzaldúa (1987) describes as where the "Third World grates against the first and bleeds" (p. 3). Flores explains that because Chicana feminists live between worlds—physically unwanted in the United States and not wanting to return to Mexico, emotionally seeking the safety of family while seeking respect as women—they must create their own homeland.

The development of a space of belonging, where they can assert agency in relation to their identity, cannot occur in the public sphere given their limited access to it, so Chicana feminists turn to what Flores calls private discourse, although counterpublic would be an apt description, too. Much as counterpublic theorists posit, Chicana feminists articulate their own identity, interests, and needs. Flores explains, "Through the rejection of the external and creation of the internal, marginalized groups establish themselves as different from stereotyped perceptions and different from dominant culture" (p. 145). Importantly, Chicana feminists do not remain an insular group. After they "carv[e] out a space within which they can find their own voice . . . they begin to turn it into a home where connections to those within their families are made strong" (p. 146). Once the counterpublic homeland is firmly established, "recognizing their still existing connections to various other groups, Chicana feminists construct bridges or pathways connecting them with others" (p. 146). Constructing a Chicano homeland is not limited to women. In a fascinating study of the effects of diaspora on Mario, a Chicano, B. Marie Calafell (2004) describes the way she is his "Chicano space" because she is the only other Chicana/o Mario knows (p. 188).

Across this discussion, we have tried to make clear that even as people strategically appeal to essential identities as locations from which to develop knowledge, create solidarity, and resist dominant definitions, the identities also are always critically examined. Sometimes, the identities are strongly embraced in order to create a sense of belonging. Other times, some identity ingredients are de-emphasized so that alliances can be built on the basis of other ingredients. Gloria Anzaldúa elegantly describes this multilayered process as creating bridges, drawbridges, sandbars, or islands (1990). Even as groups build bridges to others, sometimes moments of separation are needed, and the drawbridge is raised. For example, a moment of separation was recognized, and no attempt was made to force a bridge, when Native Canadian writers asked a White Canadian writer to move over.

Moving Over

Building alliances and creating solidarity across identity categories is a good thing. People ought to think about ways to build coalitions. However, whenever one seeks to represent others, one must be attentive to how one speaks for, with, about, or in solidarity with that other. The issue of who can speak for whom is a complex one. Those working in solidarity with marginalized groups have long grappled with it. English professors Judith Roof and Robyn Weigman edited a collection of essays that address this very issue: *Who Can Speak? Authority and Critical Identity* (1995). In it, scholars explore the problems presented by the act of speaking for others. When a White, U.S., college-educated, middle-class, Christian woman claims to speak for all women, she potentially erases them; this woman's concerns are probably not identical to those of a third-world, poor, Muslim woman of color. Members of a privileged group also may erase others when they seek economic advantage by passing themselves off as members of a marginal group. People need to be wary of instances of speaking for others, because it "is often born of a desire for mastery, to privilege oneself as the one who more correctly understands the truth about another's situation or as the one who can champion a just cause and thus achieve glory and praise. The effect of the practice of speaking for others is often, though not always, erasure and a reinscription of sexual, national, and other kinds of hierarchies" (Alcoff, 1995, p. 116).

However, this should not be taken as an excuse to not speak: "Even a complete retreat from speech is of course not neutral since it allows the continued dominance of current discourses and acts by omission to reinforce their dominance" (Alcoff, 1995, p. 108). Sometimes, when a group cannot speak for itself (due to political repression, lack of time or resources, etc.), then those with power have a responsibility to speak. Philosopher Linda Alcoff explains, "A retreat from speaking for will not result in an increase in receptive listening in all cases; it may result merely in a retreat into a narcissistic yuppie lifestyle in which a privileged person takes no responsibility whatsoever for her [or his] society" (p. 107).

One interesting case exists in which a race-privileged person stepped aside when asked by those for/as whom she was speaking. Anne Cameron, a well-known White Canadian author, wrote first-person accounts of the lives of Native Canadian women. Lee Maracle, a Native Canadian author of Salish and Cree ancestry and a member of the Sto:loh Nation, was sent as a spokesperson for a group of Native writers who met and decided to ask Cameron to "move over" at the 1988 International Feminist Book Fair in Montreal. When asked, Cameron did, indeed, move over (Maracle, 1989, p. 10).

The Native women's concern was that as long as Whites writing as Native women filled stores' bookshelves, no room was left for Native women. Maracle explains: "Anne is occupying the space that has no room for me. So few Canadians want to read about us that there is little room for Native books. There is little space for Native writers to trot their stuff. If Anne takes up that space there is no room for us at all" (p. 10). This example is fascinating because of the deep level of respect all the people involved had for each other. Maracle and the other Native Canadian women did not see Cameron as their enemy, and Cameron understood the basis of the request and honored it. The point is that sometimes material realities (monies for publishing, contracts, space on bookstore shelves) can inhibit the possibilities of the marginalized to be heard. People with privilege, whether race, class, sex, nationality, or religion, may need to step aside, move over, and make space when others wish to speak.

Verbal Play

Even though language matters and is a place of subordination as well as liberation, it also is a place of play, as demonstrated by Celeste Condit's (1992) playful reformulation of Burke's "Definition of Man." Instead of

the symbol-using (symbol making, symbol-misusing) animal inventor of the negative (or moralized by the negative) separated from his natural condition by instruments of his own making goaded by a spirit of hierarchy (or moved by the sense of order) and rotten with perfection (Burke, 1966, p. 16).

Condit believes people should think of themselves as

People [who] are players with symbols inventors of the negative and the possibility of morality grown from their natural condition by tools of their collective making trapped between hierarchy and equality (moved constantly to reorder) neither rotten nor perfect, but now and again lunging down both paths. (p. 352)

So, how do we play with examples of language as subordination? Taking the example of the de-verbing of *woman*, we now play with *woman, mistress,* and *lady* as verbs.

We could integrate new vocabulary into our repertoire that recognizes *woman, lady,* and *mistress* as active. If a woman is "an individual human being whose life is her own concern" (Cicily Hamilton, quoted in Kramarae & Treichler, 1992, p. 490), then *woman* as a verb can mean "to populate a place with courageous, self-identified people." *To woman* is not to populate a place for military battle, nor is it to prepare for a show of deference to hierarchy, but instead it is the creation of a critical mass of souls who are willing to do what needs to be done to maintain and create life-giving forces. For example, "We need to woman the world with crones, hags, spinsters, harpies, and viragos."

An additional, special use of *to woman* exists with language as its object. For example, if one *womans* the language, then one raises gender/sex questions about language, not so much to occupy it as to open it to inspection. For example, when *history* is womanned to *herstory* (even though *history* is not etymologically sexed), gender/sex questions are raised that heretofore have been unasked, in part because history was not open to inspection.

Accepting conventional meanings of *mistress* as someone who controls, someone who teaches, and someone who is sexual, we can brew up an interesting verb form. *To mistress,* then, means to determine one's own sexuality, or to teach your body to be sexual in the way you want it to be and not the way society demands; here, control is not an issue of restraint but one of self-determination. For example, "I have mistressed the lusty powers of my body; they are mine and no one else's."

Lady derives from an Old English term meaning both *loaf* and *knead* (Mills, 1993, p. 133). Accepting those roots, *to lady* means to knead an idea and then to let it set and rise; *to lady* an idea allows it time to grow. Unlike *lord, lady* is not an indication of control but denotes active involvement (kneading) and recognition of another's need for space and time in which to develop. For example, we ladied this chapter through its many stages, occasionally kneading ideas and at other times letting them alone to mature.

In addition to offering *woman/mistress/lady* as counters to *man/master/lord*, we also can explore language for sexings of its verbs by playing with inclusive or generic verb forms. Although *people* already is a verb form, meaning "to furnish or fill with people or inhabitants; to populate" (*OED*, 1971, p. 662), perhaps we also need to expand our language so that we are able to *human* and *person* things as well. Gender- and sex-inclusive terms must develop, as well as womanned terms, to counter the phallocentrism inherent in male action verbs.

Conclusion

Language is fun, fascinating, and of real consequence. Learning to speak clearly, vividly, passionately, and with joy is not drudgery. Work is work, but work also can be play. However, even as we play, we still must recognize that rules exist. Almost everyone is familiar with Robert Fulghum's book *All I Really Need to Know I Learned in Kindergarten* (2004) and its list of rules. The first few are "Share everything. Play fair. Don't hit people. Put things back where you found them. Clean up your own mess. Don't take things that aren't yours. Say you're sorry when you hurt somebody" (p. 2). Although most people may have learned these rules in kindergarten, translating them into language rules may not happen until later (college, maybe?).

Here is our playful reinterpretation of the rules. Like Anne Cameron, share, even if it means moving over. Be fair in the way you describe the world, giving all people recognition of their existence by avoiding the falsely universal *we* and sexist language. Do not use violent language. When you use words borrowed from another, make sure you make clear where you found them. If your language is messy, imprecise, or causes messes because it is violent or uses truncated passives, clean up your language. If a term has a specific meaning as part of a co-culture or counterpublic, do not use it unless granted permission. And, should you ever hurt someone with your language, apologize. Sticks and stones may break bones, and words may break spirits.

Understanding the power of language requires all language users to be more conscious of the words they use and the worlds they construct. Native Canadian author Jeanette Armstrong (1990) outlines a powerful language ethic held by her people:

> When you speak, . . . you not only have to assume responsibility for speaking those words, but you are responsible for the effect of those words on the person you are addressing *and* the thousands of years of tribal memory packed into your understanding of those words. So, when you speak, you need to know what you are speaking about. You need to perceive or imagine the impact of your words on the listener and understand the responsibility that goes with *being* a speaker. (pp. 27–28)

Even though she describes her nation's ethic, Armstrong believes responsibility is shared by all who use language:

> We are all responsible in that way. We are all thinking people. We all have that ability and we all have that responsibility. We may not want to have that responsibility or we may feel unworthy of that responsibility, but every time we speak we have that responsibility. Everything we say affects someone, someone is hearing it, someone is understanding it, someone is going to take it and it becomes memory. We are all powerful, each one of us individually. We are able to make things change, to make things happen differently. We are all able to heal. (p. 29)

This call to a language ethic may seem strange, given that we have noted the permeability of language. Sometimes, a person may use a term and not recognize that its meaning may have moved on. Mistakes do happen, but as Alcoff (1995) is quick to remind, "a *partial* loss of control does not entail a *complete* loss of accountability" (p. 105).

So, speak, speak out, speak loudly, speak softly, speak kindly, speak kindness, play with what you speak, speak playfully, speak in solidarity with others, speak with power, speak truth to power, speak back to power, talk back, talk.

PART II

Institutions

CHAPTER 6

An Introduction to Gender in Social Institutions

nstitutions, like individuals, communicate gender and are gendered through communication. In this chapter, we argue that gender is much more than a personality trait and is itself a social institution. To develop a complete picture of gender in communication, one must study how a culture's predominant social institutions influence an individual's life, and how individuals can affect the policies, procedures, and practices of social institutions. Analysis of institutions' communicative practices is essential to developing one's critical gendered lens. Sociology professor Kathleen Gerson (2004) explains that because "private choices are rooted in social arrangements over which individual women and men have only limited control, a gender lens reminds researchers to shift the focus from passing judgment on individuals to understanding the larger social contexts in which personal choices and strategies are crafted" (p. 164). Accordingly, not only should communication that occurs within institutional structures be studied, but so, too, should communication about and from institutions.

In this book, we embrace an analytical approach that constantly interrogates the interrelations between micro (interpersonal) and macro (institutional) practices of gender. Our discussion of prejudice in Chapter 1 illustrates this. We referenced philosopher Sandra Harding's (1995) insight that prejudice in the form of individuals' false or bad beliefs does not *cause* sexual and racial inequalities. Harding emphasizes, and we concur, that discrimination is maintained through complex sets of social institutions that interact with, structure, and influence individual beliefs, beliefs that often are prejudiced. Although persons may possess prejudices, to think of sexism or racism as exclusively lodged within individuals is to misdirect attention. As Harding reminds readers, thinking of prejudice "as the *cause* of racial (or gender, class, or sexual) inequality tends to lodge responsibility for racism on already economically disadvantaged whites" (p. 122), because people often think of them as the group that most overtly expresses racist and sexist attitudes.

Obviously, individual prejudice contributes to the maintenance of systems of discrimination. Ultimately, though, the most powerful engines that drive and sustain racism, sexism, and heterosexism (and hence construct race, gender, and sexuality) are embedded in a society's institutions. Harding argues that one should view inequality as "fundamentally a political relationship," as a strategy that "privileges some groups over others" (p. 122). Because discrimination is made normal and unconscious through institutionalization, to end discrimination people must identify the ways in which it operates on an institutional level via its institutional communicative practices. Attention must turn to the institutions that structure people's relationships to themselves, to each other, and to society.

You probably have heard the phrases *institutionalized racism* and *institutionalized sexism*, but what do they mean? Sexism, racism, homophobia, classism, and other inequalities are not institutions in and of themselves, but they become so embedded in institutional communicative practices and norms that it becomes almost impossible to identify them as forms of discrimination; they seem to be just the way the world is. Unlike intentional expressions of prejudice, institutional sexism and racism often are unconscious. When someone hurls a sexist or racist epithet at another human being, it is easy to point to and identify the presence of prejudicial attitudes. However, when one looks at systemic inequalities, it is difficult to identify who is responsible (because no one single person is), and impossible to locate the intent to discriminate (because no single person is behind the discrimination).

Studying gender/sex in communication is complex because gender/sex is constructed and communicated on the personal and interpersonal microlevels and the public and social macrolevels simultaneously. One can talk about the macro- and microlevels as theoretically distinct, but they are interdependent in practice. This means the relationships between the levels and influences are difficult to outline in a clear, cause-and-effect fashion. The ways in which people experience gender on the personal, interpersonal, and social levels are complex and may create internal tensions as different institutions' gender expectations contradict one another.

When we introduced *contradiction* in Chapter 1, we noted that it can be internal (within a person), external, and most likely both. The way in which one experiences and enacts gender in communication at a personal level may not fit others' expectations of how one should act and may be inconsistent with the demands some institutions place on one even as one fulfills the gender demands of other institutions. For example, at work a manager who is a woman might have to be directive, confident, and in control; but at worship she is a follower, is humble, and gives over control to a higher power; and at home she is a facilitator, an empathizer, and a partner.

Institutions are complex intersections of people, practices, beliefs, and organizational structures. The practices of institutions can result in inequality. Just because one cannot directly identify and locate intent does not mean that no discrimination occurs. Communication analyses of institutional practices and norms can reveal possible contributors to inequality. For example, political communication scholars could study whether U.S. citizens define citizenship in a way that is raced and sexed, in order to explain why so few women are in the U.S. Congress or why there has never been a female and/or Asian, Hispanic, or African American president of the United States. Communication education scholars could study whether gendered communication expectations explain why so few men are in the elementary teaching profession. Media scholars could study whether news reporting on crime contributes to the overrepresentation of African American men in U.S. prisons. Rhetoric scholars could study representations of women's bodies as objects to understand why women's credibility as public speakers is lower than men's. Organizational communication scholars could study whether the corporate culture of law firms contributes to the lower presence of women of color, particularly African American women.

Our point is that to be able to identify the communicative practices that maintain gender and sex norms, norms that often dictate different and unequal treatment, one must examine how institutions maintain and perpetuate gender.

What Is an Institution?

Institutions seem amorphous because they are not reducible to specific organizations or groups but are composed of the practices and beliefs that link groups and organizations together. Communication researchers have found helpful work by sociologists that explains how organizations, people, and institutions interact. Sociologist Margaret Andersen (2006) defines *institutions* as "established patterns of behavior with a particular and recognized purpose; institutions include specific participants who share expectations and act in specific roles, with rights and duties attached to them" (pp. 30–31). This definition foregrounds the facts that people compose institutions and that institutionally sanctioned patterns of behavior determine who counts as a person insofar as "institutions define reality for us" (p. 31). In addition to understanding the internal dynamics that define institutions, one also should be aware of three external characteristics.

First, like identities, institutions are complex and intersecting. No institution operates in isolation from others. Education systems can influence gender/sex–stereotypic or –nonstereotypic career choices. Religious marriage rituals inform people's gendered understanding of family. Media are used by all institutions to communicate worldviews. Although we examine different institutions in the following chapters, none can be separated from the influence of other institutions.

Second, all institutions influence and are influenced by the institution of gender. Sociologist Joan Acker (1992) explains how "a whole institution is patterned on specific gendered relationships. That is, gender is present in the processes, practices, images, and ideologies, and distributions of power in the various sectors of social life" (p. 567). One cannot understand the subtle dynamics at play in the institutions of family, education, work, religion, or media without a gendered lens.

Third, "institutions are often intertwined with the state" (Martin, 2004, p. 1258). When researchers refer to "the state," they are referring to the government. They study how it plays a role in perpetuating and maintaining other institutions' power. A government can codify particular institutional practices in law and then enforce the practices through "the police, the military, the courts, and—more informally, although by no means less importantly—rhetoric and framing of national concerns and ideology" (pp. 1258–1259). For example, recent debates over same-sex marriage and the move by many states to prohibit it foreground the roles of religion and the state in determining which romantic unions are legitimate and which are not.

Institutions play powerful roles in culture and personal life. We next explore in a general way how that power is wielded through communicative practices.

Institutional Control and Hegemony

Although we have mostly talked about the ways institutions serve to perpetuate and normalize discrimination and violence, institutions and the interlocking systems they create also serve useful functions. They organize daily life, in the form of the school day or workday; advance the development of people, as in business trade and educational systems; protect people, as in traffic laws and health care systems; address social evils, as in foster care programs for neglected or abused children; and give meaning to life, as in religions and gendered/sexed cultural identities.

As institutions fulfill these functions, they wield a great deal of power via social control. Social institutions distribute cultural resources, constrain and facilitate actions, allocate power, and assign rights and responsibilities (Lorber, 1994; Vannoy, 2001). Martin (2004) adds that social institutions have a legitimating quality about them "that proclaims the rightness and necessity of their arrangements, practices, and social relations" (p. 1257). For example, the ideology of gender differences is widely believed and accepted as a truism; how many times have you heard or said, "Men and women are just different." Our point is that the differences that are noted, viewed as significant, and praised are those that are highlighted by the institution of gender and are normalized by their integration throughout other institutions. The functions institutions serve are not value free, apolitical, or universally positive.

Social institutions are largely created and maintained by the predominant groups within particular historical, cultural, and political environments. As such, the institutions help to maintain the values, ideology, and worldview of the predominant groups. The discussion in Chapter 5 of sexism and racism in language demonstrates this. Social institutions, communicating through the dominant language, sustain and create *cultural hegemony*, defined in Chapter 1 as "the process through which the interests of a dominant group become dominant by establishing their beliefs as common sense."

Institutions' power comes not from a single act of enforcement that everyone immediately identifies as an exercise of social control. Instead, institutions exercise control through subtle forms that many people do not perceive as acting upon them. Or, if they are perceived, people believe their conformity is voluntary.

One principal tool of social institutions that is least obvious is cultural ideology, introduced in Chapter 1. *Cultural ideology* refers to the ideas, values, beliefs, perceptions, and understandings that are known to members of a society and that guide their behaviors. Communication scholars have found useful Italian political theorist Antonio Gramsci's concept of *hegemonic or ruling ideology* (Zompetti, 1997). Gramsci argues that social control is accomplished primarily through the control of ideas. People are encouraged to see an idea as common sense, even if it conflicts with their own experiences. By following the cultural norms that guide behaviors, members uphold the ideology. Another way to look at this is to see social institutions as tools of cultural ideology. Either way, institutions and ideology support each other. By recognizing gender as a social institution and examining how it intersects with other primary social institutions, one is better able to recognize the falsehood of such commonsense assumptions and instead realize the diversity of gender/sex experiences (Buzzanell, Sterk, & Turner, 2004).

Gender Is a Social Institution

Sociologist Patricia Yancey Martin (2004) offers a comprehensive definition of social institutions that explains why gender itself is a social institution. She outlines 12 characteristics of social institutions. Institutions (1) are social, (2) persist across time and space, (3) have distinct social practices that are repeated, (4) constrain and facilitate behavior, (5) designate social positions characterized by expectations and norms, (6) are constituted by people, (7) are internalized as part of people's identities, (8) have a legitimating ideology, (9) are contradictory, (10) continually change, (11) are organized and permeated by power, and (12) are not separable into micro and macro phenomena (pp. 1256–1258). Gender possesses all these characteristics. Gender expectations span times and geographies, generate recurring practices, and are incorporated and regenerated by individuals who often interpret their genders not as externally influenced/internally embraced power relations but instead as parts of their personalities. An institutional approach to gender highlights gender as much more than a personality type.

Gender is a cultural ideology and a social institution. Gender is not just something that individuals express but is also "the property of collectivities, institutions, and historical processes" (Connell, 1987, p. 139). Gender organizes social life. The workings of social ideology and institutions can be identified in people's use of gender/sex to designate divisions of labor, organize public and private life, distribute resources, create status structures, and so forth.

Approaching gender as an institution encourages one to think of gender as more than the roles individuals internalize. Gender's importance is not reducible to people's personalities, because "gender refers to the complex social, political, economic, and psychological relations between women and men in society. Gender is part of the social structure—in other words, it is institutionalized in society. . . . Our understanding of gender in society cannot be reduced to roles and learned expectations alone" (Andersen, 2006, p. 32). One does not refer to individuals' race or class roles; why, then, assume there are gender roles? To explain social group identities as merely individuals' learned roles masks privileges and inequalities and puts the blame for these solely on individuals. One cannot really understand gender without examining its intersections with other institutions, because

> gender is systematically structured in social institutions, meaning that it is deeply embedded in the social structure of society. Gender is created not just within families or interpersonal relationships (although these are important arenas of gender relations), but also within the structure of all major social institutions, including schools, religion, economy, and the state. . . . These institutions shape and mold the experiences of us all. (Andersen, 2006, p. 31)

Accordingly, because gender is not solely located within individuals, social change is not just a matter of individual will or effort. The transformation of gender and other social inequalities requires change at both micro- *and* macrolevels. Thus, recognizing gender as cultural ideology embedded across institutions, and as a social institution, affects how one studies it. It requires macro- and microlevels of analysis, recognizing multiple types of influence, issues of power, and how all these are related. Examining gendered/sexed violence from institutional and personal perspectives provides an example.

Institutionalized Gendered/Sexed Violence

Institutions enforce and sustain gender expectations. Enforcement mechanisms can appear noncoercive for those who abide by socially sanctioned gender roles. But for those who violate role expectations, the coercive power of institutions becomes overt. When biological men exhibit femininity, they are disciplined, sometimes through overt violence, as was army private Barry Winchell, who was murdered by two other soldiers because of his relationship with a preoperative male-to-female transsexual. When biological women exhibit masculinity, they, too, face violence, as is made clear by the murder of Brandon Teena, a story cinematically told in *Boys Don't Cry*. Challenges to gender norms usually do not pass unremarked and unnoticed by dominant institutions.

Not only are gender/sex norms violently enforced, but gendered/sexed violence is institutionalized, normalizing gendered violence across institutions. The prevalence of violence against women is an outgrowth of socially imposed gender norms. The gendered/sexed nature of rape becomes clear when one recognizes that it is predominantly men who commit sexual violence predominantly against women and children. Rape not only informs what it means to be a woman but also exposes what it means to be a man within present institutional structures. The Centers for Disease Control and Prevention (CDC) (2005b) report that in the United States, between 20% and 25% of college women report experiencing rape or attempted rape and that 1 in 6 women (17%) and 1 in 33 men (3%) report experiencing a rape or attempted rape during their lifetimes. Victims of rape appear to be at an increased risk of being raped again, and sexual violence perpetrators are at an increased risk of raping again.

Women are not the only people involved in a rape. Across all these statistics, men commit most acts of sexual violence, whether against men or women. Among acts of sexual violence committed against women who are over the age of 18, 100% of rapes, 92% of physical assaults, and 97% of stalking acts were perpetrated by men. Among acts of sexual violence committed against men, 70% of rapes, 86% of physical assaults, and 65% of stalking acts were perpetrated by men (CDC, 2005b).

Further evidence that sexual violence is a systemic rather than only a personal problem is that sexual violence is recognized internationally as both a public health and human rights issue. On October 2, 2002, the World Health Organization (WHO) released the first "Global Report on Violence and Health." In this report, WHO recognizes the way in which domestic violence disproportionately affects women. Worldwide, "almost half the women who die due to homicide are killed by their current or former husbands or boyfriends, while in some countries it can be as high as 70%" (para. 6). In September 1995, at the United Nations Fourth World Conference on Women in Beijing, the governments attending endorsed a Platform for Action that declared, "Violence against women is an obstacle to the achievement of the objectives of equality, development and peace. Violence against women both violates and impairs or nullifies the enjoyment by women of their human rights and fundamental freedoms" (United Nations, 1995, §D1.112).

Even if a woman has never been raped, she is affected by the possibility that she could be raped. At some point, almost every woman thinks about how to avoid rape by choosing to travel with others or stay home, choosing well-lit streets rather than more direct but darker routes, and so on. For this reason, feminist activists Barbara Mehrhof and Pamela Kearon (1971/1973) identify rape as an act of terror, explaining, "It is not an arbitrary act of violence by one individual on another; it is a political act of *oppression* . . . exercised by members of a powerful class on members of the powerless class" (p. 233).

Even if a man never rapes, he is taught a type of masculinity that makes rape possible. Sociologist R.W. Connell introduced the concept of *hegemonic masculinity* to name the "pattern of practices . . . that allowed men's dominance over women to continue" (Connell & Messerschmidt, 2005, p. 832). Although Connell recognizes that a plurality of masculinities exists, he focuses on the form of masculinity that is normative, the type that has been the most honored way to be a man, even if it is not the type that is most prevalent. Hegemonic masculinity does not require all men to engage in overt toxic practices, but it does encourage men to remain silent to protect their own masculinity when others commit such practices. In doing so, they become complicit in the violence (Katz, 2003).

Social norms maintained by institutions enable the sexing and gendering of violence. Media representations can eroticize and personalize violence. Legal norms can blame those raped rather than the perpetrators of violence. Educational settings can foster the prevalence of sexual violence, particularly at the collegiate level. Conceptions of family can make marital rape impossible to recognize. Recognizing how violence is institutionalized makes clear that violence cannot be prevented only by jailing the perpetrators. Far too many instances of male violence against women occur for it to be due simply to individual pathology. Cultural changes are required because men who perpetrate this violence are not acting independently of cultural influences.

When men are violent toward women or other men, they are not acting as abnormal men but as men who have internalized the social expectations of masculinity. Men's studies scholar Harry Brod (1987) explains,

Whether learned in gangs, sports, the military, at the hands (often literally) of older males, or in simple acceptance that "boys will be boys" when they fight, attitudes are conveyed to young males ranging from tolerance to approval of violence as an appropriate vehicle for conflict resolution, perhaps even the most manly means of conflict negation. From this perspective, violent men are not deviants or *non*conformists; they are *over*conformists, men who have responded all too fully to a particular aspect of male socialization. (p. 51)

The goal, then, is not to force society's mores onto these men, but to encourage them to distance themselves from this male socialization. Brod (1987) notes that the question one should ask is not "What is wrong with these men?" but "How can we strengthen the mechanisms of resistance by which nonviolent men have avoided acting on society's prescriptions for male violence, and how can we eliminate such prescriptions?" (pp. 52–53).

The truth of Brod's description is borne out in statistics. Men's studies scholar Michael Kimmel (2004) reports that "in several surveys, many men indicated that they would consider [rape] provided the conditions were 'right' and they knew they would not get caught. In a survey of American college men, more than 1/4 (28%) indicted they would likely commit rape and use force to get sex, 6% said they would be likely to commit rape but not use force, and 30% said they might use force but not commit rape, 40% (less than half) said they would do neither" (p. 280). According to Kimmel, violence is not an act of masculinity but an effort to *attain* masculinity. Men and boys who feel they must prove themselves to others are the primary perpetrators of violent acts. In relation to sexual violence, Kimmel argues that the desire to rape comes not from feelings of power*ful*ness but from feelings of power*less*ness: "Rape is less a problem of a small number of sick individuals and more a problem of social expectations of male behavior, expectations that stem from gender inequality (disrespect and contempt for women) and may push men toward sexual predation" (p. 281).

Rape is not about being sexual but about proving one's sexuality. Sociologist Diana Scully (1990), who interviewed convicted rapists, reports that rapists view rape as more about violence than about sex because the crime "makes sex the weapon in an act of violence. It's less a crime of passion than a crime of power, less about love or lust than about conquest and contempt, less an expression of longing than an expression of entitlement" (cited in Kimmel, 2004, pp. 280–281). Masculinity tends to socialize men to believe they should be entitled to power; if they do not find that power in their work or their socioeconomic standing, they may take it from their personal relations.

In the United States, gendered/sexed violence and violent thinking are part of hegemonic masculinity. Masculine violence has become normalized as a form of communication. Michael Kimmel (2004) believes, "Men learn that violence is an accepted form of communication between men, and between women and men. It's so commonplace, so deeply woven into the fabric of daily life that we accept violence as a matter of course—within families, between friends, between lovers" (p. 278).

Does this mean that all men are rapists? No. Yet, because masculine men need not devote time and energy to thinking about how to avoid violence, all masculine men benefit from the institution of gender that normalizes violence against women and feminine men. Does this mean that all women are victims? No. Yet, all women potentially can be victimized by rape.

The institutionalization of violence has effects beyond the microlevel of interpersonal relations. The fear of sexual violence affects women's participation in civic institutions. Political scientist Amy Caiazza (2005) analyzed factors affecting men's and women's levels of civic participation. She asked, "Do perceived levels of safety from crime or violence influence men's and women's decisions to become involved in their communities?" (p. 1607). Because many activities involved with civic participation occur at night, when women feel most vulnerable to attack, it is important to start thinking about the way systemic, institutionalized forms of sexism might influence women's full civic participation.

Caiazza studied women's levels of participation and correlated them to women's fear of potential violence. She found that "for women as a group, a sense of perceived safety is strongly related to involvement in the community, while a lack of perceived safety is linked to disengagement. In contrast, among men as a group, safety plays a relatively insignificant role in encouraging or discouraging engagement" (p. 1608). Of course, this conclusion is moderated when one recognizes that safety is not equally experienced by all women; poor women tend to be less safe, and so their participation is not influenced by the perceived loss of safety (which they normally lack anyway) but by other factors. Caiazza's research makes clear that "gender-based violence is an issue relevant to political and civic participation" (p. 1627). Some women participate less than men in politics, city councils, and legislatures not because they are disinterested in politics but because their fear of violence functions as a deterrent to participation.

When sexual violence is examined in this way, antiviolence measures are no longer just a way to decrease crime or maintain law and order but are also "a way to strengthen U.S. democracy and women's access to it" (p. 1627). This exposes how gender/sex affects something as taken-for-granted as citizenship. Although every person is equal under the law of the land, the reality is that gender as an institution, and the institutionalization of gender/sex violence, make women's ability to participate unequal to men's.

The preceding discussion has focused on an acute act of violence: rape. However, violence is committed not only in the form of overt acts of physical aggression. Because it is systemic, it also occurs in subtle, pervasive ways. Poverty, famine, environmental destruction, lack of adequate water, lack of adequate health care, and lack of adequate education also can be understood as forms of systemic violence (Tickner, 1992); and with their chronic status, they kill just as effectively as, if not more than, acute acts of violence such as war (Reardon, 1985). For example, philosopher Chris Cuomo (1996) documents less obvious, yet pervasive, violence done by the military. She urges people to consider the effects of militarism on the environment and women, explaining that "military institutions probably present the most dramatic threat to ecological well-being on the planet" (p. 41). Why might this claim be true? Because the military is the largest generator of hazardous waste in the United States, a massive consumer of fossil fuels; 9% of all the iron and steel used by humans is consumed by the global military. Where did Cuomo find her information? In a book by William Thomas (1995), a U.S. Navy veteran. Poverty, too, does violence to a person's body. Journalist Barbara Ehrenreich (2001) attempted to live for one year on the wages possible for a U.S. woman without higher education credentials or personal connections. She found out quickly that one cannot live on the minimum wage; her nutrition suffered, her safety was placed at risk in lower-income housing, she was more often the victim of verbal abuse by strangers, and she was sleep deprived.

Understanding the complex ways in which violence is normalized by communication practices across social institutions should make one better able to identify sources of gender oppression and social control for women and girls and for men and boys (Miedzian, 1993). You can begin to trace the links between predominant cultural ideology and its tools of control. These are the necessary first steps toward ending violence. Communication scholar Julia Wood (2005) writes, "Widespread violence exists only if a society allows or endorses it. In other words, the epidemic of gendered violence reflects cultural values and social definitions of femininity, masculinity, and relationships between women and men" (pp. 258–259). Wood names violence an *epidemic* to make clear the intensity of the problem. Renaming is needed for one to begin to realize the functions violence serves in social institutions. By examining violence as gendered, one can begin to identify the ways in which it is socialized into such things as raising children, work, education, religion, media, and even interactions with the environment.

One can also begin to understand how institutions contribute to and are related to a continuum of violence around the world, from gender intimidation to verbal and psychological abuse, to sexual coercion, to physical abuse and murder (Kramarae, 1992; Wood, 2005). The subtler forms create a context in which even the more explicit forms of violence become normalized. Wherever violence happens, the incidents are not isolated but systemically related. In the chapters to follow, we hope to help you identify the links between gender, violence, social institutions, and communication.

Part Preview

Every major social institution in a culture affects the construction of gender/sex, and gender/sex as an institution influences the functioning of every other institution. Martin (2003) points out, "Gendered practices are learned and enacted in childhood and in every major site of social behavior over the life course, including in schools, intimate relationships, families, workplaces, houses of worship, and social movements" (p. 352). Connected to this dominant role of gender is an institutionalization of gendered violence. Unfortunately, we cannot dedicate a separate chapter to every institution. Instead, we chose institutions that seem most central to culture, are major sites of oppression/subordination and resistance, and ones where the links to communication are clearest. This latter criterion is sometimes difficult as communication scholars have much work yet to do on gender and social institutions. As a consequence, we include some institutional information that may not seem directly tied to communication, but that assuredly affect communication. For example, when we discuss gender/sex in work in Chapter 9, we must necessarily include information regarding the passage of laws to better assure fairness in hiring, statistics on unequal pay scales, and sick-leave and promotion policies that may contribute to institutionalized racism, sexism, heterosexism, etc. All of these contribute to a communication climate that is gendered, raced, and sexed.

We begin our discussion of specific social institutions by examining the one that is perhaps most immediately experienced by each person: family. Family communication is heavily influenced by gendered/sexed cultural expectations of family and these, in turn, affect the gender identity development and communication of individuals. Education is the next institution that affects persons from childhood on. Communicative interactions within school walls are filled with learning, but also with sexual harassment, bullying, and physical violence. Following this, we consider work as a social institution, including the gendering of paid and unpaid labor, organizational cultures or climates, and gendered/sexed barriers such as sexual harassment. We turn next to a social institution not previously included in gender in communication texts: religion. Few other social institutions can rival the power of religious doctrine, culture, and practice in establishing and controlling one's deep-seated identities and values. We end with a discussion of media, a communication institution in its own right, but also one that functions as an amplifier for other institutions.

Family

M(ost people experience family at a deeply personal level; many of one's most intense interpersonal exchanges occur within one's family.) However, family is not just the location of interpersonal relationships. It also is (a social institution that genders its members and is organized along gendered lines by other social forces.) One cannot study gender in communication without studying communication in and about family. The construction and performance of gender/sex happen in public discourse about family and in individual families.

(Public communication *about* family influences understandings of gender and family. The institution of family is "not a natural, universal, or permanent institution" (Cloud, 1998, p. 393). The way people communicate about family influences the institution's structure and how the institution structures its members) Public figures proclaim the state of the family to be an indicator of the state of society (Ruane & Cerulo, 2004). Media representations in television shows, movies, and advertisements idealize the nuclear family, depicting an ideal few families actually achieve (Taylor, 1991). Scholars even examine ways in which the nuclear family is used to structure political discourse (Lakoff, 2002).

(Communication that occurs *in* family settings influences a person's understandings of gender and family) Family communicates norms governing gender/sex, sexual orientation, and other identity ingredients. Quite simply, "Families and gender are so intertwined that it is impossible to understand one without reference to the other. (Families are not merely influenced by gender; rather, families are *organized* by gender) (Haddock, Zimmerman, & Lyness, 2003, p. 304). (This organization is apparent in the prescribed roles played in many families: mother, father, daughter, son, sister, brother, grandmother, grandfather, aunt, uncle. These roles are sex marked and designate responsibilities, expectations, and power hierarchies.) The presence of these roles also is used to indicate when a group constitutes a family. For example, many think that a female mother, a male father, and children must be present for a group to qualify as a family.

Family is usually the first source of information about gender and one of the most influential. It is the primary place where many people are taught that women and men are essentially different and hence should have different and/or unequal roles (Risman, 1998). The term *gender roles* is commonly used to refer to feminine and masculine social expectations in a family based on a person's sex. Females are traditionally expected to take on the role of caretaker, and males are traditionally expected to take on the role of leader.

Gender role socialization largely takes place within families, particularly via parental modeling and parent–child interaction (Turner & West, 2006b). When mothers and fathers have gender/sex divisions of labor in the home, they tend to pass on those same divisions to their children; when women tend to work in the kitchen and men tend to gather in front of the television at family functions, traditional gender socialization is entrenched. Sociologists, psychologists, and communication researchers agree: Family communication practices construct gender.

Scholars point out how traditional gender roles reflect and reinforce stereotypical gender/sex differences and ignore the diverse ways in which persons across cultures, races, ethnicities, personalities, birth order, sexual orientations, and generations actually develop and perform gender in families (Galvin, 2006; Turner & West, 2006b). Persons developing gender identities through family interactions are not limited to the two stereotypes. However, even though persons' lived experiences stretch well beyond these two choices, predominant ideology tied to the institution of family continually imposes the stereotypes upon persons.

By focusing on family as an institution, we make clear how practices that at first glance appear to be innocent, idiosyncratic family traditions are actually contributors to the institutionalization of gender/sex discrimination. Micropractices (who cleans the toilet?) are maintained by individual socialization (who is typically assigned the chore of cleaning the toilet?) as well as macrostructures of discourse (how often is toilet bowl cleaner advertised during the World Series versus weekday television soap operas?) and law (what is a fair wage for those who clean toilets versus those who mow lawns?).

You may be reading this and thinking, "These gender stereotypes aren't true today . . . at least not in my family." They are not as present in our own families, either. The persistence of stereotypes—despite examples to the contrary—is evidence of the ideological power of this social institution. Even though people may not want to or may not be able to live up to gender/sex roles, they still are judged against the norms attached to the roles. This demand to abide by a role is what sociologists Virginia Rutter and Pepper Schwartz (2000) call a *gendered social script*: "[Gendered social scripts] are the rules that people carry around in their heads about what they ought to be like as men or women (straight, gay, lesbian, bisexual, transgendered, or intersexed) and what others ought to be like as men or women. . . . What makes the study of gender and intimate relationships so interesting and personal is that everyone is subject to gendered social scripts, but no one ever lives up to those expectations" (p. 62).

Most people also like to think of themselves as the exception to the norm. If you like to cook, being the primary food preparer does not seem like a sex role demand (or burden). But this leaves unanswered the question, why are more women than men socialized to like cooking and expected to be skilled at it? Why are more men than women socialized to like making household repairs and expected to be skilled at it?

In this chapter, we explore cultural expectations and gendered/sexed ideals that are constructed and maintained through the institution of family. First, we outline how family constructs gender through communication that occurs within family's institutional constraints and through communication about family that reinforces nuclear family ideology. Next, we outline the limitations of existing research to help you develop a critical gendered lens for examining research. Specifically, we expose how the myth of the nuclear family influences the institution of family and the personal gender/sex experience of family. We then address distinct relationships that construct gender in families and identify communication norms that sustain cultural violence. Finally, we examine the ways in which family can be more liberating for everyone.

Family as a Social Institution

In this chapter, we avoid using the phrase *the family* to refer to this institution except when referring to the nuclear family ideal that has gained hegemonic status within the institution. *The family* suggests that only one model of family exists, when in fact a wide variety of family structures exist within and across cultures. The highly respected academic journal previously named *Journal of Marriage and the Family* changed its name in 2001 to the *Journal of Marriage and Family* to better recognize the diversity of actual families (inside cover).

Despite the diversity of family forms, gender role expectations are delimited by the ideal of the traditional *nuclear family* (also called the *family of procreation* [Turner & West, 2006b]), which is composed of two parents (one male and one female) and biological children, with the male as the primary wage earner and the female as the primary homemaker. This ideal of the nuclear family exposes how family is an institution as it influences social interactions, creates ideology that persists across time, develops distinct social practices, and constrains and facilitates what is considered appropriate behavior (Martin, 2004). Each person is part of a family, and family, in turn, becomes a central part of a person's identity. Most important for the purposes of understanding family as an institution, however, is recognition of how nuclear family ideology is used to organize people within a family and to organize families in relation to one another as better or worse.

Although many people assume that their family structure will mirror the nuclear family ideal, the reality of what is normal (meaning what is most common) is quite different and decidedly *not* the nuclear family. Recent U.S. surveys show

*recent
Stats?*

that 38% of marriages end in divorce, about 75% of divorced persons remarry with a 60% chance of divorce, 50% of marriages occurring this year are expected to end in divorce, close to 30% of homes are headed by a single adult, 52% of families have no children under 18, and 30% of children will live in blended families at some point (CDC, 2005a; The International Stepfamily Foundation, 2006). In 2000, 73% of women with children worked outside the home. In most two-parent homes, both parents work outside the home (Hochschild, 2003).

Although many refer to the nuclear family as if everyone knows what it is, sociologist Stephanie Coontz (1992, 2006) describes the nuclear family as the *elusive* traditional family because historians cannot point to one specific time when this family structure actually predominated. In fact, "it has never been a form in which all families did, or could, participate" (Cloud, 1998, p. 393). These historical facts remind one that family, like gender, is socially constructed at macro- and micro-levels of communication.

As noted in Chapter 1, stereotypical notions of masculinity and femininity emerged during the Industrial Revolution of the 1800s. So did the nuclear family concept (Cancian & Oliker, 2000). In preindustrial, pre–mass production times before the 1700s, families were work units, and all members (including children, boarders, and hired hands) worked to contribute to a family's economic livelihood. Work was shared across sexes and age groups, an extended family lived under one roof, and single-parent households were common because of early mortality. The extended family of parent(s), children, and other blood relatives, although never as dominant in the United States as in other countries, remained popular even during the Industrial Revolution (Ruane & Cerulo, 2004). The traditional nuclear family is neither as old nor as common as is popularly suggested, yet its ideology became dominant, prescribing well-defined and exclusive gender roles.

As the Industrial Revolution progressed, manliness was established by a man's ability to support his family with his income alone. Women were told that the public sphere of business belonged to men exclusively, despite the fact that not all families could afford to live on the man's wages alone, nor did all families have men. Only middle- and upper-class White British and U.S. women were able to focus exclusively on the family's social activities and household needs, and they did so by hiring less fortunate women and children for minimal pay.

Even though not all women could afford to stay at home, domesticity became the norm for judging all women's worth. Victorian *true womanhood* was defined as pure, pious, domestic, and submissive (Welter, 1976). Such an idealized conception of womanhood was achievable only by middle- and upper-class White women; women of color and poor women could not attain the ideal of true womanhood, because of their race and class (Mohanty, 2003). Despite this, the ideal still held power over them; dominant society used it to declare them bad women. Nor did this norm reflect the reality of all middle- and upper-class women. The antislavery and suffrage activists described in this book violated true womanhood's demands of domesticity and submissiveness, declaring that in order to live by their religious convictions, they had to violate domesticity by publicly speaking out against injustice (Campbell, 1989).

The nuclear family and its rigid gender roles became firmly institutionalized during the 1950s. Rapid economic growth and popular media representations enabled and normalized the male wage earner. Television was widely available, promoting family life in such shows as *Father Knows Best* (1954–1962), *Ozzie and Harriet* (1952–1966), and *Leave It to Beaver* (1957–1963), which portrayed the modern true woman exemplified by June Cleaver. In each show, the family was a White, middle-class, heterosexual, married, middle-aged couple with children, living in a suburban environment. The father was the sole wage earner, and the home was his haven against the cold business world. The mother did not work outside the home and was the nurturer who had milk and cookies ready when the children arrived home from school, and drinks and dinner ready when the father arrived home from work.

Advertisements, in the form of commercials accompanying these shows and print ads in women's magazines, promoted domestic technology to make women's housework easier. In actuality, the marketing messages increased women's workload because they raised standards of cleanliness. Many women actually spent more, rather than fewer, hours laboring in the home (Oakley, 1981). At the same time, increasing consumer demands induced 2 million more middle-class White women to work outside the home than in pre–World War II times, leading to concerns about how women would juggle the demands of work and home (Ruane & Cerulo, 2004). Of course, many poorer White, African American, and Hispanic American women never left the workforce and have always had to juggle work and family demands.

The narrow nuclear definition of family directly or indirectly affects everyone; either one is in a family and is encouraged to live up to the ideal, or one is not in a traditional family and is condemned or pitied for not living up to the ideal. Despite the diversity of actual family forms, the traditional nuclear family persists as the normative ideal. Even in non-U.S. cultures, the ideal of the nuclear family is growing more pervasive, increasingly influencing more cultures (Ingoldsby & Smith, 2006). To be perfectly clear: We are not criticizing individual families who fit the nuclear family model. Instead, we are criticizing the predominant cultural ideology that suggests there is *only* one type of *normal* family. We question why this narrow, unrealistic concept of family became and remains so pervasive.

Interlocking Institutions

To understand how and why the nuclear family became institutionalized, it is necessary to study how family interlocks with other institutions. Family studies researcher Alexis Walker (1999) explains that "families can only be understood in relation to the broader social context or what is considered to be the public domain" (p. 439) because the "broader social systems and structures impinge on everyday family life, reproducing inside families the divisions that exist outside of them" (p. 449). If gender/sex divisions appear in the workplace, they likely will appear in families and vice versa. Part of the nuclear family myth is that it is self-sufficient (Ruane & Cerulo, 2004), but in reality extended family, work, religion, schools, social services, media, and law influence it (Turner & West, 2006a).

Politics and law constitute and legitimate the ideology of the nuclear family. U.S. politicians and clergy repeatedly use the slogan *family values,* in which *family* means nuclear family (Cloud, 1998). The slogan, popularized in the early 1990s, referred to a heterosexual married couple and multiple children living together in a home guided by conservative Christian principles. Presidential candidate Pat Buchanan used this phrase in the 1992 presidential election to advance a "cultural war . . . for the soul of America" (para. 37).

U.S. congresspeople also used the rhetoric of the nuclear family in debates over welfare reform, positioning the nuclear family as the ideal to which other family structures are compared negatively. In congressional hearings held during the 1990s, lawmakers let an outmoded view of family direct legislation that President Clinton eventually signed into law (Gring-Pemble, 2003). Legislators argued that welfare programs that provided funds to mothers encouraged women to leave their husbands and that intact nuclear families were almost always better for children than single-parent ones. This argument ignored the testimony to the contrary from women of color and poor women who did not have nuclear families on which to rely.

Family also intersects with the institution of work. The issue of domestic labor recurs in discussions of gender/sex in family communication because it not only produces household goods and services, it also produces gender (Coltrane, 1989; Hochschild, 2003; Shelton & John, 1996). Imbalanced housework distribution between men and women is one the clearest indicators of the continuing influence of the nuclear family norm and its inequitable gender roles. Research consistently demonstrates that "there is no better predictor of the division of household labor than gender[/sex]. Regardless of one's attitude about 'gender' roles, the resources one brings to the relationship, and the time one has available, there is nothing that predicts who does what and how much one does in families than whether one is a woman or a man" (Allen & Walker, 2000, p. 7).

Surveys show that although the number of hours men spend doing housework has increased, both wives and husbands in heterosexual couples still estimate that wives spend from 5 to 13.2 more hours a week doing housework than husbands (Lee & Waite, 2005; Shelton & John, 1996). Arlie Hochschild (2003) labels this housework imbalance the *second shift:* "Just as there is a wage gap between men and women in the workplace, there is a 'leisure gap' between them at home. Most women work one shift at the office or factory and a 'second shift' at home" (p. 4).

How do individual relationships maintain these unequal work expectations? Psychologist Francine Deutsch (2004) examined heterosexual couples' interactions and found that the men in her research used five communication strategies to resist sharing household labor duties: (1) passive resistance or ignoring requests to help; (2) feigning incompetence (e.g., ruining the laundry); (3) praising the spouse for her skills; (4) applying lower standards when doing the work, whereby the person who cares more about the standards takes over the task; and (5) denial by exaggerating their own relative contributions, particularly as compared to past generations of men. These strategies enabled the men, and the women they live with, to maintain the status quo. Expectations matter. Numerous other studies show that the mothers' expectations about the fathers' involvement in child care have more influence on fathers' degree of involvement than even their own expectations (Doherty & Beaton, 2004). Thus, mothers do tend to have some say about how involved fathers are likely to be in the labor of child care.

Evidence from alternative family structures further demonstrates how gender/sex roles are constructed through domestic labor. Contrary to the assumption that same-sex couples mimic wife–husband roles, research shows that most same-sex couples reject a gendered division of labor (Peplau & Beals, 2004). Instead, they divide labor based on flexibility, not earnings or gender (although earnings seem to influence relative power in gay couples). Gay couples studied tend to divide tasks by ability and interest, and lesbian couples tend to share tasks. In a study of 66 lesbian mothers with children ages 4–9, both partners consistently agreed that household labor and decision making should be shared equally (Patterson, 1995). Although the birth mother tended to do more child care, the differences were drastically lower than for the heterosexual couples in other studies. Less is known about gay fathers, but research finds that gay couples who adopt or use surrogate mothers are particularly dedicated to being parents and tend to more actively share household labor and child care (Peplau & Beals, 2004).

Finally, the nuclear family and its institutionalization of prescribed gender/sex roles interlocks with the institution of *compulsory heterosexuality*, the assumption that only one legitimate way of loving and one legitimate form of family is possible (Rich, 1986). The nuclear family not only excludes persons who are homosexual, bisexual, or transgendered, but it also risks alienating persons who are widowed, child free, single, or living in extended families.

The assumption that heterosexual romantic love should be the basis of a marriage is a core U.S. value, but it, too, is not universally shared and was not always the basis of marriage, even in the United States. Into the 1800s, marriage was based on financial need, control of reproduction, political concerns, and family arrangements, not love (Cancian, 1987). These factors still play a role in many marriages, particularly outside the United States. Passionate love is just one form of love between sexual partners, and it does not tend to be the most enduring form. It may be that unrealistic expectations for passionate love may be partly responsible for the high divorce rate in the United States (Ruane & Cerulo, 2004).

Family Constructs (and Constrains) Gender

From an institutional perspective, it becomes clear how communication both *in* and *about* family constructs gender. However, much of the research examining communication within families does not explore ways in which institutional norms influence how one communicates in family settings. Thus, we do not provide an exhaustive summary of all research on family communication. Instead, we review studies of intrafamily communication that clarify the fact that those relationships do not arise anew in each family but are influenced by previous family experiences and larger social forces. To make clear how much family communication research ignores institutional considerations, we first outline the limits of traditional research that does not question the nuclear family norm.

Research Focuses on the Nuclear Family

Researchers are not immune from the ideological influences of the nuclear family. For years, Talcott Parsons and Robert Bales's (1955) functionalist view of family prevailed. They argued that social order was dependent upon what they believed was a natural sexual division of labor in the family. Thus, research took for granted wives' and husbands' gendered roles and primarily focused on White, U.S., middle-class, heterosexual couples. Relatively little research on family focused on the ways in which a wide variety of families construct, maintain, and change gender roles, cultural identities, and inequalities (Walker, 1999). Even scarcer is communication research that critically analyzes family as a social institution and the construction of gender/sex identities through family interaction.

In the 1970s, family studies researchers began to challenge the assumption of dichotomous, (supposedly) complementary gender/sex roles, in which women were expected to be *natural* caretakers of the home and family and men to be *natural* monetary providers and leaders of family (Peterson, Bodman, Bush, & Madden-Derdich, 2000). Sociologist Jessie Bernard (1972) questioned the nuclear family as a model measure of family health or success. She identified "his vs. her marriage," in which men tend to benefit more from the culturally constructed roles. Bernard provided the stimulus for other researchers to begin to unmask the ways in which the predominant family myth contributed to narrow gender roles and inequalities.

The research we present in the following sections does not presume the correctness of the nuclear family. Instead, it highlights how gender role and sexual orientation expectations influence interpersonal communication and in the process reinforce the construction of inequitable gender identities. Families are composed of multiple distinct but interrelated relationships. We focus our review on the relationships most often studied—parent–child relationships and couples—and how each of these contributes to the construction of gender identities.

Parent–Child Communication

One primary function of the family is to teach and maintain cultural norms, including gender norms and roles. We discussed several theories about this in Chapter 2. In this section, we explore a few in more depth.

SOCIAL LEARNING AND MODELING

Parents provide a model for children's gendered identities because children are closest to parents physically and emotionally and for a longer period of time. Through often unconscious social learning, children observe and internalize particular types of behaviors. They are most likely to model these behaviors if they admire the person(s) they are observing and are rewarded for following the behaviors.

The sexual division of household labor serves as an example of social learning. Research shows that heterosexual couples' perceptions of what is fair tend to be sex biased. The women and men studied tended to expect women to do more of the housework, in part because the men were expected to do more paid labor. Furthermore, much household labor, especially that which involves communication activities such as emotional support and communication to other family members, often is not recognized as work; therefore, some of the possible inequality is not even counted (Shelton & John, 1996). Even if parents tell their children that work should be equitably shared, when women do more domestic labor than men, children tend to learn the gendered lesson they *observe*, not what they are *told*.

Conversely, if children grow up in homes where the division of household labor is not sexed or rewarded in traditionally gendered/sexed ways, they may model a different gendered identity. Our students from the rural Midwest often tell us that growing up on a farm can provide more gender-inclusive models of work; girls and boys both work in the fields and care for farm animals. However, the work inside the home seems to remain more clearly "women's work." This latter point is consistent with research suggesting that gender roles for boys, particularly in White families, are more rigid than for girls (Kimmel, 2000). Girls may bale hay, milk cows, and take out the trash, but boys still tend not to vacuum, prepare meals, or do the laundry.

A substantial amount of research has examined whether having gay or lesbian parents negatively affects children's gender identity development. In a review of this research, Letitia Peplau and Kristin Beals (2004) report: "There is no evidence that the children of gay and lesbian parents differ systematically from children of heterosexual parents. . . . No significant differences have been found in psychological well-being, self-esteem, behavioral problems, intelligence, cognitive abilities, or peer relations. . . . There is no evidence that the children of gay or lesbian parents are confused or uncertain about their gender identity" (p. 242). Less research is available tracking the sexual orientation of children and their parents, but what does exist shows that the majority of children from lesbian and gay parents grow up to identify as heterosexual, just like children from heterosexual parents (Patterson, 2000).

Gender/Sex Interaction: Parents' Influence

Children learn gender/sex identities not only by watching their parents but also by interacting with them. Most research assumes that parents teach gender norms through nonconscious, routine forms of interaction. For example, some primarily White, middle-class parents have been found to habitually interact with children based on their sex, rewarding behaviors that are gender/sex appropriate and discouraging those that are not (Lytton & Romney, 1991; Sandnabba & Ahlberg, 1999). Mothers and fathers alike have been found to habitually reward daughters for demonstrating interpersonal skills and politeness, and to reward sons for demonstrating physical or verbal aggression (Leaper, Anderson, & Sanders, 1998).

However, a recent qualitative study points out how this gender teaching actually may be quite conscious. Sociologist Emily Kane (2006) interviewed 42 women and men parents in Maine with an average age of 35, from diverse family, social, and ethnic backgrounds. She found that women and men, lesbian and gay and straight, White and African American and Asian American, dual and single parents, actively encouraged their preschool-aged daughters' interests and behaviors considered typical of boys. These parents reported "enjoying dressing their daughters in sports themed clothing, as well as buying them toy cars, trucks, trains, and building toys. Some described their efforts to encourage, and pleased reactions to, what they considered traditionally male activities such as t-ball, football, fishing, and learning to use tools" (pp. 156–157). Fathers especially wanted their daughters to be athletic. In contrast, although many parents did tolerate some gender flexibility for sons, such as playing with dolls or learning to cook, it was to a much lesser extent. For example, boys' desire to own or play with Barbie was particularly troublesome to most, especially heterosexual fathers. Even mothers who said they personally were more open to such behaviors expressed concern that their sons would be teased for being homosexual. One heterosexual couple whose son wanted a Barbie felt they had compromised by giving him a NASCAR Barbie. As a group, the parents *consciously* selected activities, toys, clothing, and decor for boys' rooms that would encourage masculine identity construction.

Even though the sample is small, it provides rich insights. The study indicates that parents believe their choices will help steer their children in the gendered and sexually oriented ways the parents prefer, and that gender is not simply a matter of allowing some natural identity to emerge. One also can infer that the parents realize that girls who adopt traditional masculine behaviors will raise their social status, but boys who adopt feminine behaviors risks losing social status.

Other research supports these conclusions, finding that African American and White fathers tend to teach traditional gender expectations more than mothers, particularly to sons (Hill, 2002; Maccoby, 1998). In one study, a White, middle-class, heterosexual man said of his son, "If [he] were to be gay, it would not make me happy at all. I would probably see that as a failure as a dad . . . because I'm raising him to be a boy, a man" (quoted in Kane, 2006, p. 163). Sociolinguists Sarah Fenstermaker and Candace West (2002) call this the influence of *social accountability*. As people construct their own and others' gendered identities, they make a conscious effort to do so in ways that make them more socially acceptable.

Gender and sexuality expectations affect parent–child interaction from the day of birth. Some parents studied tended to hold girl babies closer and for longer periods of time and engaged boys in more activity; this was especially true of fathers. Parents studied tended to describe their infants in a gendered fashion: Boys tended to be described as better coordinated, stronger, and more alert, whereas girls tended to be described as dainty, quiet, and beautiful (Bornstein, 1995).

In an experimental study of 33 European American middle- and upper-class children and parents, child development scholars Eric Lindsey and Jacquelyn Mize (2001) found that children and parents seemed to understand certain contexts as demanding particular gendered behaviors. When parent–child interaction is in the form of pretense play (imaginary play using verbal relabeling of roles and objects), mothers and daughters engaged more often; when parent–child interaction is in the form of physical play (running, tickling, playing with bat and ball), fathers engaged less with daughters, but mothers did not vary their play amount according to the sex of the child. The researchers suggest that because physical play is more common in the father–son dyads, and pretense play is more common in the mother–daughter dyads, the children likely come to associate these forms with particular gendered interactions, internalizing them in their gender schema for socially appropriate behavior. Conversely, when the female *and* male parents engaged in more imaginary play, children engaged in more imaginary play with their peers regardless of their sex. When female *and* male parents engaged in more physical play, children engaged in more physical play with peers. Thus, parents played an active role in gendering their children's development and interaction. Contrary to the gender differences perspective, there was no simple parent–child gender influence determined by the sex of the parent or of the child.

Even though both parents influence children's gender development, a substantial amount of research has focused on father–son relationships. Researchers find that this relationship affects sons' attitudes and behaviors relating to sexuality, women, and physical and emotional violence directed toward women (Dick, 2004; Floyd & Morman, 2003). Communication scholars Kory Floyd and Mark Morman (2003) report that fathers today are generally more affectionate with sons than fathers in previous generations and that both parties value physical affection in the relationship. They also report that fathers tend to be less affectionate with sons as the sons reach adolescence, suggesting cultural taboos against male affection are taught in family interactions.

The intersection between race and gender/sex is an important influence on parenting style. Black feminist scholar Patricia Hill Collins (1994) describes an alternative form of motherhood evident among those who must prepare children to face discrimination. Although many (mostly upper-class Whites) might think of mother as the gentle soul who provides unconditional love and protective nurturing, others (many working-class people and African Americans) might think of mothers as the people who gave them the strength and the ability to handle life's hard knocks.

This *militant motherhood* appears in families, and in the public sphere when women rhetors assume the persona of mother. Communication scholar Mari Boor Tonn (1996), in her study of labor activist Mary Harris "Mother" Jones, describes how militant motherhood uses "assertive, even aggressive, modes of presentation. Militant mothers not only confront their children's enemy, but must also train their children to do likewise if the threat they face is ongoing and systematic" (p. 5). Quite simply, militant motherhood is not sweet and gentle but uses "bawdy, rowdy, and irreverent personal expression. . . . Such mothers also may bait, tease, and otherwise provoke children in order to acclimate them to attack, to provide practice at fighting back, and to sharpen their emotional control" (p. 6).

GENDER/SEX INTERACTION: CHILDREN'S INFLUENCE

Although most research tends to focus on parents' role in socialization, children, too, play an active role in constructing their gender. An example of how adolescent and teen children may actively select gendered interactions with parents comes from research on sons' and mothers' communication. A review of this research reports that sons studied were more likely to be withdrawn in conversations with their mothers than were daughters, were more likely to interrupt their mothers, and accepted fewer directives from their mothers (Morman & Floyd, 2006).

According to gender schema theory (discussed in Chapter 2), children acquire a gender identity between ages 2 and 3. From then on, they may use that identity to selectively choose stimuli that seem consistent with this identity. Therefore, not only do parents tend to give children gender-specific toys, but children tend to choose gender-specific toys once they have been socialized to desire them. Further research is needed to document and explore this. Research also is needed on how siblings influence each other's gender identities. Socialization is a negotiated, two-way process, and gender, race, and other cultural expectations matter (Hill, 2002; Peterson, Bodman, Bush, & Madden-Derdich, 2000).

Adult Friends and Lovers

The "socially approved economic and sexual union" represented by romance and marriage between heterosexual couples are the cornerstones of the traditional nuclear family (Ruane & Cerulo, 2004, p. 175). As discussed in Chapter 1, the assumption that men and women communicate differently is reinforced by stereotypes attached to the social expectations for heterosexual romantic relationships. Hegemonic masculinity, subordinate femininity, and heterosexual romance reinforce the normative power of the nuclear family.

U.S. culture treats heterosexual marriage culminating in the nuclear family as the ultimate form of romantic expression; the cultural assumption that everyone is heterosexual and wants to be married is named *heteronormativity*. From early on, children are pressured to have boyfriends and girlfriends; to learn to flirt with the other sex; to devalue, distrust, and compete in platonic same-sex friendships; and to see marriage as a life accomplishment. In the best-known fairy tales, the strong young man saves and then marries the beautiful young woman, and they live happily ever after. Such fairy tales contribute to unrealistic romantic expectations and enforce the notion that women are weak and need to be saved by men and that men are strong and never need to be saved. Some African American women point out that these fairy-tale expectations are particularly harmful for them because there is no Prince Charming coming for them (DeFrancisco & Chatham-Carpenter, 2000). Due to racism and classism, Black men face unique barriers to becoming knights in shining armor.

Regardless of race, class, or sexual orientation, people are socialized to want marriage. Children, particularly girls, play bride and groom, and the wedding industry induces people to spend more than $40 billion a year on weddings in the United States alone. Related rituals reinforce the marriage desire. The Debutante Ball from African American culture and *Quince* from Latin American culture are coming-out parties families throw for their daughters when they turn 15 or 16. Girls wear fancy white gowns, and the family invites everyone they know to a dinner dance. The event marks a girl's transition into womanhood, but it is a particular type of womanhood—a virginal, upper-class, heterosexual one (Vida, 1999).

Sociologist Chrys Ingraham (1999) argues that this popular cultural obsession with "white weddings" is fed by U.S. soap operas, television sitcoms, popular movies, women's magazines, and dress shops. This fantasy day is so seductive that many parents and couples end up spending well beyond their means (the average cost of a wedding is $20,000). Ingraham believes that the romanticized white wedding (and we would add the Debutante Ball and *Quince*) are primary cultural tools for institutionalizing heterosexuality as the norm, as "the standard for legitimate and expected social and sexual relations" (p. 11). The predominant socialization toward heterosexual romance and family literally marries women and men into intimate legal bonds. Marriage (especially if it results in children) remains a primary way in which women, White women in particular, can raise their socioeconomic status.

Another indication of the ideological power of heterosexual romance is how other relationships, such as friendships, are devalued. Although researchers and laypeople alike realize that a romantic partner alone cannot meet all of one's interpersonal needs, friendships receive no legal, political, religious, or other institutional support. Friendships, particularly cross-sex friendships, often are seen as a threat to dating and marital relationships. In reality, many persons report enjoying cross-sex platonic friendships, and the taboos of doing so seem to be lessening with each generation (Monsour, 2006).

Same-sex platonic friendship is more socially acceptable, but it, too, pales in social significance to heterosexual dating and marriage. Existing research on friendship tends to reinforce heteronomativity; it primarily studies heterosexual persons in same-sex friendships, and it studies such friendships not to explore friendship dynamics but to determine sex differences in expressions of intimacy. The two-culture, gender/sex differences approach described in Chapters 1–3 is apparent here. The research presumes that women's interaction style is more nurturing and men's style more task oriented, and then infers that women define intimacy through self-disclosure and men through shared activity (Wright, 1982). By suggesting that women and men cannot be friends because of presumed innate sexual tensions, and that same-sex friends share universal expressions of intimacy, the heterosexual romantic bond is maintained as the only way women and men can connect.

The privileging of heterosexual romantic relationships is one of the mechanisms that sustain the ideology of heterosexual romantic marriage and the nuclear family. We now outline specific ways in which adult romantic and platonic relationships contribute to the creation and maintenance of the institution of family, particularly stereotypical gendered/sexed notions of families. Whether or not you personally aspire to the normative ideal, the ideology affects you. One certainly has the right to want the ideal of marriage; our intent is simply to assure that the dreams are based on informed choices.

DATING RELATIONSHIPS

The heterosexual dating relationship is the most studied type of nonmarital relationship—a fact that indicates the social privilege attached to it. Relatively little research examines the role of gender in dating relations for same-sex partners, transgendered persons, non-White couples, or non-Western couples. What is known is that even though dating patterns have changed tremendously in the United States (more hooking up instead of dating, more couples cohabitating, and more persons delaying marriage or choosing not to marry), the ideological normativity of heterosexual intimacy persists.

This ideology of intimacy is manifested primarily through romance expectations. Images of heterosexual relationships in movies demonstrate this. The most desired romance is young, between a masculine man and feminine woman, usually of the same race or ethnic group (those that are not are considered erotic and exotic), and it hinges around *passionate* sexual attraction. (The fact that many of the expressions of passion would be considered stalking should they happen in the real, rather than the celluloid, world is happily ignored.)

Every day, many women expend a great deal of time and energy to make themselves sexually attractive to men. Their choice to focus on their attractiveness to men is one indication that they value heterosexual romance above everything else, including friendships, career, and even family. Anthropologists Dorothy Holland and Margaret Eisenhart's (1990) classic ethnographic study of 23 Black and White women at two southern universities found that the women believed they "could not gain prestige from academic successes, organized extracurricular activities, participation in political causes, or relationships with other women" (p. 90). Instead, the only way these women were able to raise their self-esteem and social prestige was through romantic relations with men. Their focus on heterosexual romance undermined their education and same-sex friendships. Research on women's friendships consistently demonstrates that compulsory heterosexuality encourages many girls and young women to see each other as competition for male attention.

In a review of the literature, communication scholar Sandra Metts (2006) identifies general patterns in the gender role scripts of dating relationships, noting that "both gender and dating are social constructions enacted through communication" (p. 25). Regardless of sexual orientation, the men studied placed priority on physical attractiveness, and the women emphasized personality (Peplau & Spalding, 2000). The scripts also include men more often taking the lead in sexual relations. Metts comments, "Perhaps no other aspect of dating escalation reflects gender scripts as fully as first sexual involvement, particularly sexual intercourse" (p. 31).

In terms of heterosexual dating norms, the predominant expectation is still that men will initiate dates and physical intimacy and that women will take primary responsibility for relationship maintenance (Laner & Ventrone, 2000). Because intimacy tends to be associated with the feminine domain, heterosexual men who show sensitivity and caring often are labeled unusual or special men. When one views intimacy in this gendered/sexed way, women are held responsible for relationship maintenance, and men are seen as less competent in expressing intimacy (Cancian,

1987). Both popular and scholarly literature describe this particular script in terms of how women show affection by talking and men by doing.

However, researchers have begun to question whether significant gender differences in expressions of intimacy actually exist. First, women as well as men demonstrate intimacy in a variety of shared activities and levels of self-disclosure. Men's studies scholar Scott Swain (1989) suggests that men tend to use covert forms of intimacy that may not be recognized as intimacy, such as joking with, telling stories about, and playfully punching each other. Second, both women and men appreciate partners who do tasks, such as domestic favors, as an expression of intimacy (Cancian & Oliker, 2000). Third, in the closest friendships and romantic relationships, men self-disclose more and women do more favors for each other than is common among less intimate relationships. Paul Wright (2006) reports that sex/gender differences in friendship disappear when one studies close, rather than casual, friendships. Finally, communication scholar Michael Monsour (2006) argues that the continued battle over which sex/gender has the most intimate same-sex friendships is condescending to both friendship types. It reinforces stereotypic two-culture notions of gender/sex, again ignoring diverse experiences due to race, age, and class and reinforcing the cultural emphasis on heterosexual romantic relationships.

Marital Communication

Just as heterosexual dating is the most studied type of nonmarital relationship, heterosexual marriage is very likely *the* most studied type of interpersonal relationship. Much of this research focuses on marital conflict. This is not surprising, given that people are socialized to have unrealistic marital expectations, that marriage requires intense interdependence, that marriage holds great social import, and that statistics indicate 50% of marriages will end in divorce—all of which threatens this institutional icon.

One has only to scan the local bookstore's popular psychology section to know that gendered/sexed communication problems in marriage are expected. These expectations are largely based on assumptions of stereotypical gender differences. The book title that most reflects the stereotype is *Men Are from Mars, Women Are from Venus*. The publisher has sold more than 7 million copies in 40 languages, and the book was on the *New York Times* best-seller list for 339 weeks. By suggesting that women and men are not even from the same planet, popular writers such as John Gray (1992) offer unrealistic and unhealthy communication advice, reinforcing gender stereotypes and inequalities (DeFrancisco & O'Connor, 1995). When family therapists reviewed Gray's advice, they found that it directly contradicted findings of marriage and family research, feminist theory, and principles underlying the "best practices" of the counseling field (Zimmerman, Haddock, & McGeorge, 2001, p. 55).

For example, Gray asserts that innate sex differences exist, endorses the presumption that domestic labor and relationship work is women's work, and claims that men are not good listeners and cannot do or value talk as much as women do. Based on Gray's analysis of the problem, the most partners can hope to do is try to understand and accept these differences and resign themselves to inherent inequalities.

In contrast, family therapists and marriage counselors call for shared partnership, equitable relational power, and ongoing metatalk about one's relationship. Psychologist John Gottman (1994) has studied marital communication for more than 30 years and is able to predict with 94% accuracy which marriages will fail, based on negative interaction and communication patterns. Gottman argues that behavioral change is necessary to create more mutually satisfying interaction patterns. He and psychologist Nan Silver (1999) state, "When a man is not willing to share power with his partner, there is an 81 percent chance that his marriage will self-destruct" (p. 100).

Gottman (1994) and other researchers have focused on a particularly ineffective pattern of marital conflict called the *demand/withdrawal pattern*, in which the partner who most wants change demands, and the one who resists change withdraws, resulting in a failure to resolve the conflict. Substantial research shows that wives tend to approach husbands to demand that some need be met, and the husbands withdraw, refusing to engage.

Two different interpretations of this pattern have been offered. First, a two-culture theory approach suggests that the woman is demanding because her relationship orientation is toward talk and that the man withdraws because he is socialized to value unilateral problem solving; men prefer to fix problems alone, and if a problem cannot be repaired, men will not see value in discussion (Tannen, 1990).

In contrast, family studies scholar Alexis Walker (1999) interprets this pattern from a power perspective. In her review of research on families from 1989–1999, she found that the demand/withdrawal pattern of wife–husband conflict occurs *only* when discussing something the wife wants. She argues that because marriage as a social institution is already structured to men's advantage (as with the uneven distribution of domestic labor, income inequalities, etc.), it is usually women who need to demand change. To avoid change sought by wives, husbands withdraw. The power of the one least interested in participating in change controls the dynamic.

Additional evidence makes clear that the pattern is not attributable simply to gender/sex differences in communication styles. Walker found that this conflict pattern reverses in abusive relationships: "Indeed, a communication pattern of husband demanding and wife withdrawing . . . is related to both husbands' physical violence and psychological abuse" (p. 443). In a review of this research, communication scholars Kristin Anderson, Debra Umberson, and Sinikka Elliott (2004) find, "Husbands in abusive relationships may be more demanding than other husbands because they are often concerned with controlling and regulating the behavior of their wives or partners" (p. 633). The husband-demand pattern is most common in more severe physically abusive heterosexual relationships. Furthermore, higher levels of verbal aggression and violence by both wives and husbands occur in relationships where the husbands feel less powerful (Sagrestano, Heavey, & Christensen, 2006). Here, the wives' demanding is perceived by the husbands as an indicator of her power, which prompts violence. Thus, demand/withdrawal patterns are not simply due to gender/sex differences; they shift according to power dynamics.

Similarly, communication scholar Loreen Olson (2002; Olson & Lloyd, 2005) reports that when couples are violently aggressive, a partner's reciprocity of aggression depends on shared relational power. If there is a power imbalance in the relationship, reciprocity is less likely, regardless of the sex/gender of the partners. However, Olson notes that power inequalities in heterosexual relationships are usually sex related, meaning that women are less likely overall to reciprocate aggression.

Although relational conflict is inevitable, not all conflict is harmful to relationships, not all conflicts involve abuse, and not all conflicts end in violence. However, verbal abuse is usually a precursor to psychological and physical abuse, and much of this is gendered and sexed (Evans, 1992).

Domestic Violence

As we discuss interpersonal violence that occurs in families and other affective relationships, we want to make clear that a focus on individual persons or relationships is insufficient to understand domestic violence. Family and other institutions sustain systemic forms of gender and sex inequality and violence, making the family one of the United States' most violent social institutions and women and children the most common victims.

Not all domestic violence is the same. What is called *common couple violence* (CCV) is more likely the result of a couple's inability to resolve their conflicts in an effective way (Olson, 2002, p. 104). CCV is more likely to be symmetrical in partner initiation and reciprocity of aggression, and the violence is less likely to escalate or become frequent over time. The remainder of this section focuses not on CCV but on the type of domestic violence tied to patriarchal institutional norms and inequalities that is most likely to escalate to bodily harm.

Family is supposed to provide safe haven for members. Although families do this for many people, they also are the location where serious levels of violence occur. Despite the emotional ties many feel toward their families, it is important to remember the facts:

- Every day in the United States, four children die as a result of child abuse and neglect that occurs in a family.
- Every day in the United States, four women are murdered by their husbands or boyfriends.
- Women are ten times more likely than men to be victims of domestic violence.
- Yearly in the United States, more than 4 million children are abused or neglected by family members; 27% of women and 16% of men report having been victimized as children.
- One in four women reports having been raped or physically assaulted by an intimate partner. This statistic is true both for the United States and globally.

SOURCE: National Clearinghouse on Child Abuse and Neglect Information, 2004; National Organization for Women, 2006; Family Violence Prevention Fund, 2006; U.S. Department of Health and Human Services, 2005; World Health Organization, 2005a.

These statistics explain why Dr. Lee Jong-wook, director-general of the World Health Organization, states that the first global study on domestic violence "shows that women are more at risk from violence at home than in the street and this has serious repercussions for women's health" (WHO, 2005b). The same appears to be true for children (International Society for Prevention of Child Abuse and Neglect, 2004).

In a discussion of the domestic production of masculinity in the United States, Michele Adams and Scott Coltrane (2005) highlight the linkage between masculinity and violence: "We expect and encourage boys to pursue our cultural ideals of masculinity. From early in their youth, we teach them (through for instance toys and sports) to symbolically correlate competition, violence, power, and domination with masculinity" (p. 237). As children, boys are socialized to relate to family in a particular way. By encouraging boys in this way, "we are . . . defining boys and men away from the family" (p. 237).

Contrary to common belief, men who abuse intimate others are not just those who are psychologically imbalanced. Researchers and clinicians report that abusive men test as "normal on measures of mental stability, social adjustment, and other standard clinical criteria"; concomitantly, "women who remain in violent relationships also are not demonstrably atypical of women in general" (Wood, 2001, p. 241). Domestic violence, particularly the abuse of women by men in the domestic setting, should not be understood as an aberration in an otherwise-functioning gendered family institution. Instead, gendered violence ought to be seen as an expected component of the heteronormative family form.

Communication scholar Julia Wood (2001) interviewed 20 heterosexual women (12 White, 5 Black, 1 Native American, 2 "mixed ethnicity," and most working- or middle-class) who had been in abusive romantic relationships while 14–32 years of age. Wood found that the women were strongly invested in predominant heterosexual gender expectations and fairy-tale notions of romance. Many spoke of failing in their responsibilities as women to care for their partners, or they insisted the abuse was out of character for the Prince Charming who had originally swept them off their feet. The women felt it was their job to protect their partners by hiding the inappropriate behaviors. One of the women insightfully noted that by hiding the abuse, she enabled herself to continue believing in the fairy-tale romance. Others subscribed to a darker romance narrative in which they expected abuse from romantic partners, believing that "it is normal for relationships to be hurtful to women" (p. 253). They would not leave the relationships because they needed men to feel complete. Similarly, communication scholar Karen Rosen (1996) found that the 22 young, predominantly White women she spoke to who had survived abusive heterosexual romantic relationships described being seduced into the relationships in part through the desire to fulfill the specific fairy tales of *Cinderella* and *Beauty and the Beast.*

The institution of family further enables violence because it hides and denies that violence occurs there. Because U.S. cultural ideology promotes the belief that the primary function of family is to create a *home* (a welcoming, protective, loving, intimate environment), when violence occurs in the home, the first reaction of family members and communities is to deny its existence. For this reason, anthropologist Joshua Price (2002) urges, "That notion of home needs to be shaken off in order to see that violence against women is abetted, enabled, by the normative ideal" (pp. 40–41).

Sex differences exist in terms of who in the home is most likely to be victimized by violence and who is most likely to commit violence. Although women and men are both capable of and do violence to each other and to children, researchers and clinicians continue to find that women are far more likely to be the victims of men's domestic abuse than to be the perpetrators of violence against family members. In 2000, 1,246 women and 440 men were killed by intimate partners (Rennison, 2003). As the CDC statistics in Chapter 6 make clear, most of the violence was done by men.

The motivation for violence also breaks along sex lines. Women's violence toward men is more often committed in self-defense than is men's toward women. Sociologist Donileen Loseke and women's studies professor Demie Kurz (2005) suggest the following:

> Men's violence toward women and women's violence toward men are not the same, because these acts occur within the historical, cultural, political, economic and psychological contexts of gender. . . . This gendered context includes the history of tolerance of men's violence toward women that continues to be taught and reinforced in social institutions such as sports and fraternities. It includes the normalization of violence against women in heterosexual romantic relationships. (pp. 84–85)

The statistical differences described earlier are not the result of inherent sex differences but are the result of socialization practices that tend to train men into a form of masculinity that sees violence as a solution to problems.

Another indicator of how domestic violence is gendered/sexed is found in the data concerning children's abuse of parents. While not as common as partner abuse, mothers in particular incur various degrees of violence from male sons (Jackson, 2003). In a U.S. survey regarding parental abuse, mothers describe this violence as a feature of mothering they have come to accept. Of the 220 children studied, ages 6–12, the more the children believed in the inherent superiority and privilege of men in the family, the more they and/or their fathers abused their mothers (Graham-Bermann & Brescoll, 2000).

Many people do not live the ideal of the nurturing nuclear family, and as long as people cling to the ideal and fail to recognize the pervasiveness of violence in U.S. families, real pain is denied, and productive solutions are ignored. Safe and healthy families require effort on the part of the individuals in them and the society in which they are situated. Alternative family structures exist, and it is to these emancipatory forms we now turn.

Emancipatory Families

No family is perfect, and we do not advocate the replacement of one monolithic model of family with another. Instead, we explore non-nuclear family structures to offer a range of possible models. A variety of family forms can provide a safe haven where the members feel loved, accepted, and are able to grow to their fullest potential. This is what we mean by *emancipatory families.*

We already have identified several factors that contribute to healthy family dynamics, including letting go of a monolithic notion of family and recognizing the wide variety of ways persons already constitute families. We examined the predominant assumptions of stereotypical gender/sex roles in the family using a critical gendered lens to make the potentially destructive nature of these cultural myths visible.

Family studies professor Kyle Kostelecky believes that "we spend more time as parents trying to create clear gender roles which are actually destructive" (personal correspondence, fall 2005) than trying to create more flexible gender roles that are liberatory and responsive to each person's individuality and lived experience. "Clear gender roles" often are narrow and prescriptive, creating ideals few can attain and thus harming those who cannot. As an alternative, Kostelecky says, "Just as we teach racial tolerance, we need to teach gender tolerance." Families are one important place where this tolerance can be taught and lived. More flexible gender roles and teaching gender tolerance can help families be more adaptable to cultural *and* individual needs.

An example of more flexible gender roles in family is engaged fatherhood. If the norm has been for fathers to play more emotionally distant, wage-earning roles, then an alternative is for fathers to play more active, interpersonal roles in the day-to-day care-taking of their children and other family members (such as elderly parents or ill siblings).

Wide variances in fathering have always existed, and researchers continue to find more evidence of fathers playing central roles in child rearing (Dienhart, 1998), but like the myth of the nuclear family, the myth of the distant, wage-earning father persists. Thus, not only do more men need to be involved fathers, but the predominant cultural discourse about fatherhood as removed and detached must change. One location of this need for change is popular culture, such as films. When men do portray caring and nurturing, they still are described as unusual or special (e.g., *Boyz N the Hood*, *Crash*). When women exhibit the same behaviors, they are just doing what they should do as women (e.g., *Stepmom*). These portrayals sustain the norms rather than challenge them (Dienhart, 1998).

The reality is that men *are* primary caregivers. A 2005 U.S. Census Bureau report shows that 2 million men report being single fathers, up from 393,000 in 1970. Single fathers account for one sixth of the nation's single parents, and 98,000 men are stay-at-home dads whose wives work outside the home (U.S. Bureau of the Census, 2006). A growing body of research documents primarily heterosexual middle-class men's efforts at engaged parenting (Dowd, 2000). In a review of research on single fathers, Barbara Risman (1998) reports that the results are highly consistent: "Homemaking does not appear to be a problem for single fathers—few recruit female kin or paid help to perform the 'female' tasks of housekeeping" (p. 49).

Fathers can do housework and nurture children, even when they are not single parents. Family studies professor Anna Dienhart (1998) studies how some White heterosexual couples negotiate shared parenting. The couples in their thirties found it necessary to deliberately co-create alternatives to traditional parenting roles. Some used a tag-team parenting approach, in which they traded responsibilities back and forth according to the needs of their hectic lives. In some cases, the man was a stay-at-home parent, in some the woman was, and in others they both worked outside the home. More important than who did what was a shared commitment to equal responsibility for parenting.

From this exploratory study, one can see that for change to happen, both parents must work together and have the support of the community. Dienhart concludes that "women and men do not create their visions of fatherhood and motherhood in isolation from each other, nor in a cultural vacuum" (p. 16). Parenting and family are defined by more than the particular people involved in a specific family. Social and cultural expectations inform the way each person *does* family and parenthood. Dienhart also concludes that mothers must let go of the desire to privilege their relationships with their children over the fathers'. Similarly, she found that the men in the study were aware that, unlike mothers, society gave them the *option* to be involved with parenting. They realized they needed to give up the privilege of noninvolvement. The changes toward shared parenting worked because these couples were resourceful and found the changes rewarding. They recognized they were capable of re-envisioning family and parenting in a way that was healthy and equitable.

The benefits of engaged fathers are many, not only for children and mothers but also for fathers. In a review of research, communication scholars William Doherty and John Beaton (2004) found a positive relationship between involved parenting and a father's psychological well-being, confidence, and self-esteem.

One indicator of the cultural bias against involved fathers is the serious lack of research on any aspect of fathering until the late 1990s (Dienhart, 1998; Dowd, 2000). By ignoring the role of fathers, the field of family studies reinforced predominant notions of parenting as women's natural and expected responsibility. Although fathering research is now being conducted, much of it, like the research on mothers, has focused on White, middle-class fathers who are primarily secondary caretakers and playmates for their children. Research on divorced fathers, regardless of ethnic background, has shown an even more limited nurturing role. The reality is that noncustodial parents do have difficulty being involved parents. Compounding negative portrayals of fathers of color is the stereotype of Black fathers as irresponsible (which ignores the economic and educational disadvantages faced by many who are trying to provide for families) and the machismo, dictatorial image of Asian and Hispanic men (which makes it difficult for them to be seen as nurturing in the home).

Law professor Nancy Dowd (2000) argues that when we examine the roles fathers play, we must examine social expectations for White men, Black men, Hispanic men, gay men, and so forth. Fatherhood must be understood from an intersectional perspective:

> Men's identities as fathers do not exist in isolation from their identities as men. Indeed, that broader masculine identity arguably poses the most difficult challenge to a redefined and differently lived fatherhood. . . . As long as masculinity is defined in opposition to femininity, and requires devaluing and stigmatizing things labeled feminine, men will be blocked from or conflicted by learning from female role models. The learning and valuing of nurture [*sic*] is blocked by misogyny and homophobia. . . . It is also challenged by the embrace of violence as a part of masculinity, a value or trait antithetical to nurture and care. (pp. 181–182)

This passage establishes the relationship between hegemonic masculinity and domestic violence, as discussed earlier. Dowd further points out that because being economic providers is a main way in which men prove their masculinity, "Black men are denied the means to be men in traditional terms" (p. 75). Thus, noninvolvement of fathers may be tied to social class. Poor men, regardless of race, ethnicity, or sexual orientation, have a more difficult time being involved in parenting. As long as men are expected to be the primary wage earners in the home, their ability to share parenting will be limited. Thus, if we want to seriously reconsider fatherhood, we also must reconsider motherhood and work outside the home (Dowd, 2000).

Performing fatherhood presents even greater social stigmas for gay men. Psychologist Charlotte Patterson (1995) says, "The central heterosexist assumption that everyone is or ought to be heterosexual is nowhere more prevalent than in the area of parent-child relationships" (p. 255). Despite the increasing numbers of gay men parenting, social recognition of their ability to parent is limited. In fact, the public debates over so-called family values in the 1980s–1990s posited homosexual and other non-nuclear families as a primary threat to family values. In reality, today's gay families are more likely to have a stay-at-home parent than heterosexual families are.

Conclusion

In this chapter, we traced some ways in which family as a social institution, and the predominant cultural ideology of the traditional nuclear family, construct and maintain gendered/sexed identities of difference and inequality. The importance of the family becomes especially vivid when we examine the prevalence of gendered/sexed violence and norms that contribute to it. As future research better documents the diverse ways in which individuals construct families across cultures, families may be better able to create the good homes they are expected to provide.

CHAPTER 8

Education

In this chapter, we examine the ways in which communication in and about education plays a central role in creating and maintaining gender/sex identities, relationships, and inequalities. Joan Swann (2003), a British professor in education and language studies, explains the relationship between gender and education:

> Insofar as gender is "done" in educational settings it is done, to a large extent, through language. And insofar as language is gendered in educational settings, this will affect girls' and boys' development as "schooled subjects," in their experiences of education, and what they get out of it. (p. 624)

Education profoundly affects persons' lives, and the gendered nature of education can positively and negatively influence those lives.

Like family, formal education is a social institution. The general characteristics of institutions discussed in Chapter 6 are present in formal education, particularly in how it legitimates ideologies, such as particular types of knowledge and learning, and how it persists as an institution over time (Martin, 2004). Whether one is referring to elementary, middle, or high schools, public or private schools, colleges, community colleges, trade schools, universities, or graduate and professional schools, they all share the explicit objective of learning and seek to promote the values associated with this process. Because of the lofty, seemingly unselfish ideals of educating people, it often is difficult to think of the so-called ivory tower of intellectual enrichment as a place of stereotypes and oppressions such as racism, sexism, classism, and heterosexism.

How learning and teaching occur is heavily influenced by the predominant values and norms of the larger society. Culture influences the way knowledge is constructed, curricular and extracurricular opportunities, teacher education, teaching and learning strategies, classroom structures and norms, administrative structures, disciplinary procedures and policies, the content of textbooks, and options and relative values in career paths.

Education is political. Knowledge is not value free, nor is the process of acquiring it. Researchers, teachers, and students do not check their values and beliefs at the laboratory or classroom door. Rather, their values, beliefs, and cultural expectations influence what they bring into the classroom or laboratory, as well as the interactions that happen in the education process. When those values include essentialist views regarding gender/sex, race, and class, a contradiction emerges in the heart of education's ideals. Education can oppress people instead of equipping them with the tools necessary for personal and community decision making and growth.

Education as a Social Institution

The institution of education has a long history of teaching gender/sex identity. During the early 1800s, British public schools taught boys how to be ruling-class men, preparing them for leadership in the armed services and business. This British model became the basis for schools in formerly colonized countries such as Australia, New Zealand, Canada, India, South Africa, and the United States (Kimmel, 2004; Swain, 2005). U.S. public education originally was intended exclusively for White, upper-class boys. Not until the early 1900s did poor people and racial/ethnic minority persons obtain education, particularly past the eighth grade. Public education as we know it today—education for all—did not become the norm until the mid-1900s.

Only White women from wealthy families could obtain higher education before the 1900s, and even they were discouraged from taking courses in what were considered the masculine domains of business, science, and mathematics. College for women consisted of courses consistent with women's domain, focusing on domestic skills. Training in mathematics and the sciences was virtually nonexistent.

The opponents of education for women during the Victorian era believed that women could not withstand the rigors of higher education. One common argument against coeducation posited that females' and males' minds were radically different and that coeducation would be harmful to both:

> Some worried that educating women and men together would "emasculate" the collegiate curriculum, watering it down by forcing the inclusion of subjects and temperaments better omitted, slowing down the pace, or otherwise reducing standards that would allow women to keep up. (Kimmel, 2004, p. 160)

Psychologists from that era believed that coeducation would "harm girls by assimilating them to boys' ways and work . . . robbing them of their sense of feminine character," and harm boys by "feminizing them when they need to be working off their brute animal element" (G. Stanley Hall as cited in Kimmel, 2004, p. 160). In yet another example of the conflation of sex, gender, and sexuality, opponents of coeducation also believed it would lead to homosexuality.

This overt teaching of gender/sex in formal education may seem surprising by today's standards, but assumptions concerning sex-based brain differences are behind the current demand for single-sex education, and assumptions about gender/sex are still part of the curriculum today, even if less overt, in the form of the hidden curriculum: educational practices that implicitly assume a White, male, middle-class standard for both the knower and that which needs to be known. Examples of this bias in education include history texts that do not adequately acknowledge the contributions of women and racial and ethnic minorities in social movements, wartime efforts, or local politics (Loewen, 1995); children's story-books that portray stereotypical gendered/sexed careers for women and men (Gooden & Gooden, 2001); teachers' tendencies to learn boys' names better and more quickly than girls' names or to give boys more of their time and attention (Sadker & Sadker, 1994); teachers who discourage boys from taking home economics or girls from taking math and science courses (AAUW, 1992); educational contexts in which it is considered a normal childhood prank to bully children who are labeled effeminate (AAUW, 1993); the fact that most elementary teachers are still female and underpaid compared to similar professional positions; and the fact that most principals, particularly in high schools, are men (NEA Research, 2003). Such omissions help to maintain stereotypes, inequalities, and privileges tied to gender/sex, race, sexual orientation, ethnicity, social class, and physical ability.

Interlocking Institutions

Like family, the institution of education has an extended influence on individuals' identity construction. Once children enter the first grade in the United States, they usually spend an average of seven hours a day, five days a week in a formal education institution. Children who graduate from high school have a minimum of 12 years of formal educational influence during their most formative psychological, physical, moral, and intellectual developmental period. It is not surprising that education's influence extends beyond the classroom and educational material taught.

The institution of education influences work, government, family, and media, and is influenced by each of these. For example, U.S. employment options are influenced by the educational opportunities students are afforded. Differences in educational opportunities often determine which job opportunities are open to a person. The stereotype that males tend to have better aptitudes for technology creates a cycle in which they are encouraged to study in this area, are better received in the business market after graduation, and command more of the higher-paying jobs (Kramer, 2005). Even today, when women now account for more than 50% of college students nationwide, many majors continue to be dominated by one sex. Men students dominate the computer and information sciences (72% compared to 28% women), women dominate education (77% compared to 23% men), men dominate engineering (80% compared to 20% women), and women dominate foreign languages (71% compared to 29% men) (U.S. Department of Education, National Center for Educational Statistics, 2003).

Governmental funding priorities influence education. Title IX of the 1972 Educational Amendment Act makes it illegal for federally funded schools to discriminate on the basis of sex. Under this law, these schools (from kindergarten to graduate school) are required to offer comparable opportunities for females and males in curricular and extracurricular activities. While most schools have not fully closed the gender gap, the legal monitoring of educational institutions' actions has made a difference. Title IX has increased the number of females participating in sports, equitable funding across extracurricular programs, and efforts to counter discrimination by encouraging more girls and racial minority students to excel in mathematics and science.

It's Not About Sex Difference

When we describe education as a gendered institution that profoundly influences the way people think, we make clear that a critical gender analysis of education must go further than simply comparing individual women and men for possible differences in educational experiences. A critical gender analysis of communication in and about education explores the very way societies conceive of and pursue truth and knowledge.

The institution of education is a creator and keeper of socially sanctioned and respected knowledge. This is perhaps the most pervasive influence of the institution. It legitimizes what is recognized as knowledge. Predominant social constructions of identities, such as gender stereotypes, are examples of how some knowledge about identity is recognized more than others and how some are viewed more positively than others. Hegemonic power is at play in the very construction of truth, reality, and wisdom: that is, knowledge construction. The philosophical study of knowledge, *epistemology,* asks a communication question: How do humans know what they claim to know? This area of study recognizes more than one way of knowing and that there are fewer absolute truths than the institution of education and the predominant culture recognize. The process by which a belief comes to be labeled as "the truth" is a rhetorical process. Being an educated person employing a critical gendered lens means understanding that knowledge is perceptual. In other words, before accepting information, the receiver should be aware of the sources of knowledge and the processes used to construct that knowledge.

Even as education maintains and transmits predominant social beliefs, it also can challenge cultural stereotypes such as the binary view of gender/sex. Feminist theorists employ this capacity to challenge when they critique the theories and research methods used by traditional academic disciplines to produce biased knowledge (Alcoff & Potter, 1993; Bannerji, Carty, Dehli, Heald, & McKenna, 1991; Code, 1991; Harding & Hintikka, 1983/2003). Much of what is given the status of knowledge in the United States is the product of White, Western, capitalist, masculine viewpoints. This does not mean that women and men, people of color and Whites, or people from Eastern and Western countries have opposite ways of thinking. Instead, this insight is meant to highlight that knowledge is constructed through myriad means, including intuition, experience, and emotions in addition to the scientific method. However, the predominant Western cultural ideology of rationality, scientific objectivity, and statistics has dominated what are accepted as appropriate research methods and what is determined to be worthy of the label *knowledge.*

Because of this, to most fully investigate the interaction of gender and education, we deconstruct the nature of knowledge itself and the limited ways in which knowledge is considered legitimately constructed. What society comes to recognize as legitimate knowledge and useful information are reflections of their makers' views of the world, silencing other ways of knowing. This was part of the original rationale for creating women's studies programs in U.S. colleges and universities during the 1960s:

> The purpose of Women's Studies was to enable women to become authorities on their own lives; to construct their own knowledge about women according to their own criteria as women; to empower themselves through knowledge making. . . . Central to the practices of Women's Studies scholarship was the principle that the knowledges which were forged in its name should be subjected to rigorous scrutiny to ensure that the interests of women were being served and that a contribution was being made to the development of a better world. (Kramarae & Spender, 1992, p. 3)

Moving beyond the dominant White, Western, masculine way of knowing, feminist scholars challenge linear cause–effect models of constructing knowledge and recognize the multiple truths possible when one considers the unique contexts of race, class, and gender.

Feminist epistemology involves a number of practices. It rejects rigid disciplinary boundaries in research (which is why, when we talk about gender/sex in communication, we talk about philosophy, sociology, psychology, and other fields). It recognizes that insider views may not be the same as outside researcher views, and that *insider* does not mean biased, and *outsider* does not mean bias free. It embraces collaborative rather than hierarchical control of learning. And it includes researchers' values and perspectives as part of the research instead of pretending that researchers are all-knowing and objective. The result of feminist research is a *knowledge explosion* (Kramarae & Spender, 1992) that continues today as feminist methodology is mainstreamed into many research theories and methods across disciplines, making major contributions to the natural sciences, social sciences, humanities, and more.

The field of cognitive developmental psychology provides a well-known example of what happens when women's gendered/sexed experiences are included in researchers' investigations. Mary Field Belenky, Blythe McVicker Clinchy,

Nancy Rule Goldberger, and Jill Mattuck Tarule (1986) studied women and the process of knowledge construction. Their research intentionally paralleled the work of William Perry (1970), who interviewed primarily male students each spring as they progressed through Harvard University. From his analysis, Perry concluded that developmental thinking skills move from a simplistic either–or view of knowledge, to recognizing multiple perspectives and the social construction of knowledge, and culminate in choosing between multiple perspectives and committing to a perspective as a means of developing a strong sense of personal identity. Although this approach is consistent with some of the feminist views of epistemology outlined above, Perry's model of learning suggests a hierarchal process in which one moves toward increasing independence in thought, as if independent thought were the ultimate measure of moral intelligence. His findings were primarily drawn from the study of men, yet his conclusions claimed to describe all educated persons.

Belenky and associates (1986) used comparable interview methods over a 5-year period but interviewed 135 women learners from diverse class and ethnic backgrounds and school contexts. They found similarities to the intellectual development process identified in Perry's study, but they also found important distinctions. In Perry's study, an adversarial doubt seemed to be a primary motivator for the men's intellectual journey. For the women in Belenky et al.'s study, the seeking of confirmation for one's ideas seemed to be a primary motivator. Belenky et al. suggest that gendered socialization may induce some women to start the learning process with an interest in relational support rather than argumentative doubt. (However, some men are motivated by confirmation, and some women are motivated by doubt.) The women in the study also talked about their intellectual development in a distinctly personal way; they described it as gaining "voice." Styles of learning progressed through various stages: (1) silence, (2) received or passive ways of knowing, (3) subjective ways of knowing, (4) procedural knowing, or seeking knowledge through so-called objective or subjective processes, and (5) constructed knowing, or realizing that knowledge is constructed and requires a degree of personal commitment and the ability to critically debate perspectives. The women who exhibited a constructed approach to knowledge were flexible, open to multiple ways of knowing and incorporating the other approaches in their learning efforts. However, as the researchers point out, they cannot conclude that these types of learning are a hierarchical process as Perry's study of elite Harvard men suggests.

A serious limitation of the study by Belenky et al. is that it suggests absolute differences in women's and men's ways of knowing and that the differences are universal (Barnett & Rivers, 2004). If one truly wants to question knowledge construction, it is important that one not assume that any single set of participants can speak for all persons across genders, sexes, races, classes, sexual orientations, nationalities, and ethnicities. We report the study here because it illustrates how knowledge and education can be gendered/sexed and classed communication processes and that learning can be oppressive (as in silenced or passive learning) or empowering (as in constructed knowing).

Education Constructs (and Constrains) Gender

In this section, we explore the construction of gender/sex differences and inequalities through a variety of institutional components: teacher and administrator interactions, sports, educational materials and curricula, higher education, so-called gender gaps, single-sex education, peer pressure, bullying and sexual harassment, and violence on college campuses.

Teacher and Administrator Interactions

No other social institution promotes the notion that girls and boys are different as constantly as education. If you visit a grade school, you will likely see common practices such as these: boys and girls are told to stand in separate lines as the class progresses to the cafeteria or playground; children are sex segregated to eat lunch; teachers divide the class by sex during educational and extracurricular activities; sports teams, physical education classes, and playground activities are regularly sex segregated.

Whether meaning to or not, teachers and administrators tend to make sex distinctions a central part of children's identities. When children attempt to cross sex lines, they may be reprimanded and told they do not belong there. If it is not acceptable to intentionally segregate children by race, why is it acceptable to segregate by sex? Although (one hopes) teachers would never ask all the students of color to stand in a line against one wall and the White students to stand against another, many may not think twice about segregating girls and boys this way. Nor would teachers punish all members of a racial group just because a few misbehaved; unfortunately, it is not uncommon for all the boys or all the girls to be punished because of the behaviors of a few (Kramer, 2005).

Adults often assume that children have same-sex preferences for friends, whether they do or not, and plan activities accordingly (Frawley, 2005). Competitions are commonly organized as girls against boys. The practice is cultural; it is not based on sound pedagogical learning practices. No evidence proves that segregated gender/sex competition in school activities, such as spelling bees and math quizzes, yields any positive educational, social, or psychological results. Such practices encourage girls and boys to see each other not only as different but as opponents (Sadker & Zittleman, 2005).

Men's studies scholar Jon Swain (2005) points out that even teaching styles can enforce gender lessons for children. The common emphasis on competition, constant testing, strict discipline, and hierarchy emulated by many women and men teachers reflects traditional masculine qualities and teaches these qualities particularly to boys (p. 216). Earlier classroom observation studies found that the female and male teachers studied tended to call on boys more frequently, to ask boys more thought-provoking questions, and to give boys more time to answer (Sadker & Sadker, 1994). In such cases, the lessons taught seem to be about difference and inequality.

With these practices, educators instill the notion of difference, encouraging girls and boys to view each other as the *other*. Linguistically, many teachers reinforce the notion of difference by referring to their class as *girls and boys*, rather than *students*. These practices also reinforce the assumption that one is only a boy or only a girl. In this school environment, where does the transgender or intersex child stand?

Sports

Sex segregation of games and sports begins at an early age. The increased popularity of coeducational soccer teams in the United States in the last few decades has helped provide a sex-inclusive activity for many grade-school children, but sports has traditionally been a masculine domain. As discussed in Chapter 4, boys literally act their bodies into masculinity, and sport is one location in which they do so. Swain (2005) notes that in addition to teaching styles, athletics is a primary place where boys learn (and exhibit) masculinity:

> For much of the time, boys define their masculinity through action, and . . . the most esteemed and prevalent resources that boys draw on to establish status are physicality and athleticism, which are inextricably linked to the body in the form of strength, toughness, power, skill, fitness, and speed. (p. 224)

Since the passage of Title IX, girls' and women's athletics have received a huge boost in financial and other support. As girls' participation in sports proves their toughness and athletic abilities, it also builds character, confidence, competence, comfort with their bodies, and social acceptance or popularity. Girls who participate in sports also tend to do well academically (Kramer, 2005). Unfortunately, sports remain a threatening place for gays, bisexuals, and transgender persons (Kramer, 2005). Women of color who participate in sports, particularly at predominantly White colleges and universities, find a place to take pride in their racial identity that they likely would not have otherwise (Stratta, 2003). Although sports provide opportunities for African American athletes to excel in a racist culture, rhetorically that excellence often is framed as proof of stereotypes about innate abilities rather than as the result of hard work and earned accomplishments.

Finally, the predominant cultural identity of an athlete is confounded with gender stereotypes. The better the male athletes are, the more masculine they are perceived to be. The better the female athletes are, the more they feel compelled to wear makeup, do their hair, or paint their nails to retain their femininity. High school girls' teams often demonstrate this, styling each other's hair before a game. One could see such behavior as a celebration of the ability to look feminine and be an athlete at the same time, but it also could be proof of the pressure to maintain some semblance of heterosexual femininity.

Educational Materials and Curricula

Not too long ago, children's literature and educational textbooks were overwhelmingly filled with gender/sex stereotypes and, in many cases, completely omitted the positive contributions of women and other marginalized groups. A 1974 study sponsored by the U.S. Department of Health, Education, and Welfare reported that out of 135 texts and readers surveyed from 16 publishers, boy-centered stories outnumbered girl-centered stories by a 5 to 2 ratio, 3 times as many adult male characters as adult female characters appeared, and 6 times as many biographies of men as women were included (as cited in Kimmel, 2004). One consequence of Title IX was an effort to eliminate, or at least greatly reduce, gender bias in educational materials. This led to multiple investigations of textbooks, literature, and other educational materials for gender/sex bias and resulted in many improvements.

Even in the 21st century, children's picture books continue to exhibit gender stereotypes. Female characters are much more likely than male characters to be seen caring for children or doing household chores, but male characters are portrayed in a wider variety of roles and careers (Gooden & Gooden, 2001). Male characters are significantly more likely than female characters to be portrayed as possessing traditional masculine traits, such as argumentativeness (Evans & Davies, 2000). On the positive side, contemporary children's picture books are more likely to depict girls and women as main characters, in active rather than passive roles, and with more expansive career options. Yet, while women may pursue diverse careers, portrayals of boys and men remain rigid, omitting them from nurturing roles (Kimmel, 2004).

Improvements appear slowly in textbooks. In a review of public elementary school textbooks, instructional communication researchers Cheri Simonds and Pamela Cooper (2001) report that male characters, references to male authors, and male depictions still greatly exceed those for females, and Whites still are portrayed in texts more than other racial and ethnic groups. In a study of five high school English literature anthologies (an area traditionally considered a feminine domain), Mary Harmon (2000) found that the number of women authors still was limited, and the number of pages accorded to individual male authors was significantly higher. Even the descriptions of the authors were sexist. Men's accomplishments were highlighted, whereas women's family relations were highlighted. Perhaps most amazingly given that the subject is language, the textbook editors did not use sex-inclusive language.

Much of the research on sexism in educational materials has focused on images of girls and women. Complementing this work, sociologists Lorraine Evans and Kimberly Davies (2000) studied masculinity in first-, third- and fifth-grade literature textbooks published in 1997. They found that despite the publisher's nonsexist guidelines and the mandates of Title IX, two publishers of educational series virtually mirrored each other in presenting males in stereotypically masculine ways, as aggressive, argumentative, and competitive. Male characters exhibited these qualities more than the female characters, who were more likely to be described as affectionate, emotionally expressive, passive, or tender.

Textbook representations may be more balanced at the college level. Karen Yanowitz and Kevin Weathers (2004) examined 15 educational psychology textbooks used to train future teachers and found no gender/sex stereotypes in portrayals, with one exception. The books contained more negative portrayals of boy students as troublemakers in the classroom.

Curriculum, too, is gendered and contributes to the gendering of knowledge. Some of this is obvious: Home economics traditionally is seen as a feminine domain, whereas shop and auto mechanics are seen as masculine domains. Less obviously, literature and language arts classes are associated with femininity. Girls have tended to perform reading and writing skills better than boys, and as men's studies scholar R. W. Connell (2000) points out, emotional expression and relationships, commonly associated with femininity, are prevalent in those subject areas. In contrast, Connell notes that math and science are seen as masculine, not just because boys have tended to perform better in these areas but because they are more directly linked to the stereotypic masculine public domain of production, technology, and commerce.

Curriculum's history of gender/sex typing alone cannot explain girls' and boys' gravitation toward these subjects and tendencies to excel in those consistent with traditional gender expectations, nor can it explain why many children do not follow these patterns. Other explanations are needed, such as students' own contributions to their identities and the influences of teachers, administrators, parents, and society. For example, when the first talking Barbie was marketed in 1992, the words she uttered included: "Math is hard!" Fortunately, nearly 800 million consumers objected, and subsequent talking Barbies did not make that comment. The message, however, was evidence of the common belief that girls can't do math, and the unspoken message was that boys can.

Some teachers have been found to differ greatly in their expectations for boys and girls (Spender, 1989), encouraging boys in mathematics and science and girls in reading and writing (AAUW, 1992). We know that differences in these areas are not biologically determined, because once the disparities were pointed out and teachers adapted their teaching strategies, skills began to equalize. The gender/sex gap in math and science is closing, and thousands of girls have benefited from the educational and extracurricular attention (AAUW, 1998).

Today, teachers' gender/sex expectations in courses are less blatant, but adults can implicitly encourage gendered/sexed learning in other, more subtle ways, such as in extracurricular activities, interpersonal interactions, and career advising. As recently as the 1960s, career options for women with college educations were primarily in nursing or teaching. Much has changed since then; despite this, relatively fewer women work in higher education administration, and fewer men teach young children. Male primary school teachers face questions about their masculinity and the public's fear that they may be pedophiles (Kramer, 2005).

Higher Education

Many studies document discrimination experienced by women in higher education (Fox, 2001; Sandler, Silverberg, & Hall, 1996; Statham, Richardson, & Cook, 1991). This discrimination is not just relevant to students. The university professorship traditionally has been considered a male position, and men continue to dominate this profession (Fox, 2001). Women and minority faculty continue to have a much more difficult time getting hired, being evaluated positively by students and administrators, and getting promoted, particularly at the more elite schools or in male-dominated academic fields (Haag, 2005; Kerber, 2005). Women and minority faculty may be evaluated more harshly than White men faculty. They tend to be more closely observed and evaluated, and they are more likely to have to prove their competence to receive a positive evaluation, whereas men are likely to be perceived competent at the outset and may only have to demonstrate incompetence before receiving negative evaluations (Haag, 2005). Women are more likely to be judged by actual accomplishments, although men are more likely to be judged on their promise (Wilson, 2004). Students, too, tend to more harshly evaluate female faculty, particularly African American women faculty. They are more often challenged and viewed negatively, regardless of their teaching performance (Turner, 2003).

Michael Messner (2004) points out that being a professor (as opposed to being a teacher) continues to be gendered masculine. Therefore, if a male teacher acts masculine, he becomes a better professor; however, if a female teacher acts feminine, she may have a more difficult time being seen as a good professor. Messner found that women faculty are judged first on how well they perform femininity, then on their teaching—which creates contradictory expectations that are difficult to fulfill. This has negative consequences for women and men faculty who are perceived as feminine.

Gender/Sex Gaps

When one adds together the common practice of pitting boys against girls in school, sexist educational materials and curricula, and gender/sex barriers in higher education, it is not surprising that attitudes of resentment and distrust follow. Communication that occurs *in* educational settings interacts with communication *about* educational settings. Descriptions of the ostensible gender gap in education deserve analysis. A critical gender/sex lens can be used to examine communication about education from popular culture, academics, and government.

In the last 16 years, many educators and popular authors have fed the widespread belief that there are gender gaps, or gender wars, in education. The current "war" seems to date back to the early 1990s, when the American Association of University Women (AAUW, 1992), an organization committed to promoting education and equality for girls and women, published a national U.S. survey, the results of which indicated that many girls received less attention from their teachers than boys did and that the self-esteem of many girls suffered as a consequence. Several other studies and popular books reaffirmed this claim (Orenstein, 1994; Pipher, 1994; Sadker & Sadker, 1994).

Soon thereafter, claims of how education was failing boys appeared: "The overrepresentation of males in special education classes and in virtually every other category of emotional, behavioral, or neurological impairment is undisputed" (Kleinfeld, 1998, p. 8). Girls read more and read and write better than boys, particularly in the earlier grades. Girls tend to get better grades in middle and high school. Boys get suspended from school more and get involved in crime, alcohol, and drugs more. Finally, more young women than young men now go on to college (Gurian & Stevens, 2005; Sommers, 2000). The "gender wars" in education were declared.

Christina Hoff Sommers (2000) is best known for criticizing the suggestion that girls are shortchanged in education. She argues that boys, not girls, are shortchanged, particularly in reading and writing skills and the attainment of college degrees. The title of her book, *The War Against Boys: How Misguided Feminism Is Harming Our Young Men*, reveals the assumption underlying her criticisms: that educational equity is an either–or struggle between the sexes. She declares that the claim that girls are being shortchanged is a myth, a calculated distortion of the facts to gain media attention. She also argues that much of boys' problems are innate:

Boys need far more discipline, structure, and authority in their lives than do girls. . . . Boys must be actively constrained by a whole phalanx of adults who come into contact with them—parents, teachers, neighbors, policemen, passers-by in the streets—before they can be expected to control their asocial, egoistic impulses. (pp. 180–181)

Surprisingly, Sommers seems to blame boys for their problems, as if they were animals that must be tamed. She repeats the "boys will be boys" excuse for inappropriate masculine behavior (Spender, 1989) and ignores all the boys and men who do not behave this way. Other popular authors make similar claims about boys, highlighting differences in brain makeup (Gurian & Stevens, 2005). This does not explain why White boys tend to do better in school than African American boys.

Current research shows that, regardless of a child's sex, the more impoverished the school a child attends, the less likely the child is to receive an adequate education. Currently, African American boys lag the farthest behind in U.S. education. White teachers and administrators more readily characterize them as chronic bad boys than they do other students with the same types of behaviors (Ferguson, 2000). Psychologist Judith Kleinfeld (1998) points out that African American boys, as a group, score lowest on virtually all educational measures, and African American girls far exceed them in graduation rates and professional degrees.

James Earl Davis (2001), a professor in educational leadership, explains that the problem for many boys is racism and classism, not some innate biological boyness. He also argues that many young African American boys and men contribute to educational underperformance because of the way they construct their masculinity: as a masculinity that challenges a school climate that excludes and labels them as having academic problems. They may perform a hypermasculinity to protest and defy authorities. This rigid definition of masculinity often is imposed on peers to encourage masculinity compliance, and thus it becomes self-defeating.

The best explanation may be that the gender gap in education exists for *both* girls and boys, but because they tend to be socialized in different ways and because observers have gendered expectations, the gender gaps tend to be manifested in different ways (Sadker & Zittleman, 2005). For girls, it may be lack of attention from teachers, and for boys, particularly racial and ethnic minority boys, it may be much harsher punishments than girls receive for misconduct. Both are gendered (and likely raced and classed) treatments that may have negative consequences.

As we discussed in Chapter 1, a problem with the gender wars image is that it diverts attention from underlying social injustices. In this chapter, we find that girls and boys alike face gender struggles in education. Our intent is not to pick sides in the gender battle but instead to point out that by framing this as a gender battle, girls as well as boys are being short-changed, particularly minority ones. To claim that boys as well as girls get left behind is not to ignore the overt forms of sexism that do exist. Based on survey data, the prevalent view among children is that it is still better to be a boy than to be a girl (Reay, 2001; Sadker, 2002).

Single-Sex Education

In an attempt to address the concern about girls and boys being left behind academically, many educational programs have turned to single-sex education. The belief is that it will help counter a multitude of social problems, including underachievement, low self-esteem, drugs, teen pregnancy, and gang violence. Education programs have turned to segregating boys and girls in classes, grades, and even buildings. This movement is relevant to our study of gender in communication because several of its underlying assumptions reflect stereotypes about gender/sex differences addressed in this text. Furthermore, the movement may reinforce such stereotypes and maintain gender/sex norms in communication.

A major proponent of single-sex education is Dr. Leonard Sax, executive director of the National Association for Single Sex Public Education (NASSPE). One of the assumptions Sax and the Association hold is that universal gender/sex differences appear in the learning styles students prefer. Proponents argue these are tied to physiological differences, such as differences in hearing abilities and brain functioning. In some studies, girls have been found to be able to hear softer sounds than boys. What is Sax's solution? "The simplest way to accommodate these differences in a coed classroom is to put all the boys in the front and the girls in the back" (NASSPE, 2006b, para. 3). He also suggests that lower, more masculine voices are needed for boys to learn better. Another learning style discussed is tied to assumed gendered personalities. Girls are said to be more critical of their performances and so do better in school when they are encouraged, regardless of how good their grades are. Boys are said to inflate their abilities and so put forth less effort. The advice is to use stricter, more formal lecture methods with boys and more collaborative learning methods with girls.

The NASSPE (2006a) assumes that females and males have differently wired brains, which calls for teaching math separately: "In girls, navigational tasks are assigned to the cerebral cortex, the same general section of the brain which is responsible for language. In boys, the same tasks are handled by the hippocampus, an *ancient* nucleus buried deep in the brain, with few direct connections to the cortex" ("Teaching Math"). With girls, the wiring calls for more applied examples; with boys, teaching should focus on the numbers and less on the context.

The NASSPE website cites impressive cases of improved grade performance for students in single-sex education programs around the United States and abroad. However, these examples have limitations. One is that sex-segregated education is based on sex, not gender and/or sexual orientation. It assumes, once again, that sex equals gender. The NASSPE assumes that all females think and behave femininely and that all males think and behave masculinely. In reality, boys with highly feminine gender identities and girls with highly masculine gender identities might do better in coeducational schools than in single-sex schools. The debate over single-sex education is yet another location for essentializing gender/sex and fueling the gender wars metaphor.

Second, the truth is that any improved performance is probably due to a combination of improved teaching strategies, not just to sex segregation. In our own community, Liz Crowley, the principal of a predominantly Black grade school with a highly successful single-sex program, makes this point: "I don't think you can just put kids in a gender-specific classroom and see results" (quoted in Campbell, 2006, p. 3A). Her school has adopted uniforms, has formed tighter learning communities with the same students and teachers together for a year or more, has initiated year-round schooling, has intensified busing, and has used home visits from the teachers *in addition to* single-sex classes. Other factors that improve learning in same-sex programs are smaller class sizes, improved self-esteem from the opportunity to excel in a wider variety of activities, and ways to assess one's gender identity beyond being attractive to the other sex (Sadker & Zittleman, 2005).

Third, single-sex education will not address the problem of essentializing gender/sex and related inequalities. As we have explained, the structure of formal education has traditionally followed a masculine model. Single-sex educational programs could still be teaching male privilege. In early research on boys-only education in England, researcher Dale Spender (1989) found that boys replaced a gender/sex hierarchy with a gender hierarchy, bullying effeminate boys.

Same-sex schools likely will reinforce false essentialist notions about gender/sex and perhaps about class and race. Social pressures to perform gender/sex do not happen only in multisex contexts. In fact, some of the most abusive sides of femininity and masculinity are exhibited in same-sex groups, such as in college fraternity houses where members may compete to have sex with many women, or in sororities and girls' cliques where they may label each other sluts and snobs.

Education scholars Valerie Lee, Robert Croninger, Eleanor Linn, and Xiangiei Chen (1996) compared coed high schools with all-boy and all-girl independent high schools. They noted sexism in all the schools, but it was most severe in the all-boys schools: "The findings suggest that without daily interactions between genders[sexes] to contradict the messages being sent by the media, boys have little chance to learn nonsexist behaviors" (p. 243). In fact, if a goal is to improve gender relations, students need opportunities to build their communication skills, trust, and respect by working together.

Peer Pressure

If a battle is being waged, it is not between girls and boys but among them. By the third grade, students have been found to migrate to same-sex groups and to chastise those who do not. In a groundbreaking study, sociologist Barrie Thorne (1993) observed playground and classroom behaviors of children in the fourth and fifth grades at working-class schools with some racial and ethnic diversity. She found a tendency for girls and boys to self-select, playing in groups based not only on sex but also on race and class. Boys' play, with a few girls included, was characterized by more physical aggression in larger groups, controlling larger spaces of the playground. Girls' play was characterized by smaller groups and less physical activity, such as talking or waiting in line to jump rope. Girls and boys most often played together in games such as kickball, foursquare, chase, or tag, but when teams were chosen, they were chosen by sex. The brave few students who risked crossing sex borders were subject to ridicule from other students and the scrutiny of their teachers. Thorne concludes that children play an active role in sex segregation at school, and those who braved crossing sex lines may also play an active role in broadening views of friendship across gender/sex lines.

Peer groups provide girls and boys with collective meanings and influence what it means to be a girl or boy. Although each group develops its own unique meanings tied to other social factors such as race, ethnicity, social class, and popular culture symbols, gender identity is a strong part of the message taught. Boys tend to impose notions of masculinity on other boys, and girls tend to impose notions of femininity on other girls. Those who do not conform become the oppressed. For boys, the subordinated are labeled effeminate or gay; for girls, the subordinated are called wallflowers or unattractive.

Adolescents tend to experience intense peer pressure to conform to the group's norms in order to be a part of the group (Swain, 2005). At this point, peer groups have more influence on children's gender identities than do parents or the adolescents themselves. Thus, one's gender identity construction is more a collective process than an individual one, which is why boys may be more socially polite when encountered singly than when they are in groups (Connell, 2000). A sort of gang behavior can take over. Boys who conform too much to school expectations instead of group expectations get labeled *goody boy, brown-noser, teacher's pet, wimp, sissy, girly girl,* or *fag.* Researchers suggest that the word *gay* is the most common word of abuse used among schoolboys. Homosexuality is seen as a threat to masculinity, and so the person using the term against others is attempting to distance himself from it (Connell, 2000; Swain, 2005).

As children enter middle school and high school, having a girlfriend or boyfriend of the other sex becomes a means to gain status. Jon Swain (2005) points out that "having" a girlfriend is simply a continuation of efforts to declare one's heterosexuality (p. 223). A key point here is that attitudes toward school and students' identities tied to sexuality and gender/sex become conflated. This may explain why the academic performance of many girls, especially Whites and Hispanics, declines in middle and high school and why eating disorders are especially prevalent among them (AAUW, 1992, 2001). Getting good grades is not considered "cool." Researchers point out that this is also true for boys. Masculinity has traditionally been defined as brawn, not brain, and education is seen as a passive, feminine activity (Connell, 2000; Francis & Skelton, 2005).

Bullying and Sexual Harassment

Since the 1999 shooting of students at Columbine High School in Colorado, students' mistreatment of each other has received greater public attention. Many public schools have adopted a zero-tolerance policy on violence. What used to be considered bad behavior is now recognized as a criminal act. The male students at Columbine who murdered their peers were retaliating against others' bullying. Sadly, bullying is so widespread that communities attempting to create laws and school policies against bullying struggle to define it. One suggestion is that *bullying* is "physical, psychological, and/or verbal intimidation or attack that is meant to cause distress and/or harm to an intended victim" (Christie-Mizell, 2003, p. 237). Bullying is usually done by older children against younger or physically smaller children and by boys against girls and effeminate boys. The estimated number of students who experience bullying in a given school year ranges from 20% to 30%. Among students surveyed, 75% report being bullied at some time in their elementary and junior high school years. Bullies tend to be male, aggressive, tough, impulsive, and lacking empathy. They often come from families with high conflict, authoritarian parenting styles, and economic stress (Christie-Mizell, 2003). In a survey of 1,059 Italian elementary and middle-school children, both boys and girls who witnessed physical violence between their parents were more likely to bully other children. This was particularly true of boys (Baldry, 2003).

Today, several states have passed or are considering passing anti-bullying laws, but more work is needed to examine why bullying occurs and what its consequences are. R. W. Connell (2000) addresses the first of these questions:

> Groups of boys engage in these practices, not because they are driven to it by raging hormones, but in order to acquire or defend prestige, to mark difference and to gain pleasure. Rule-breaking becomes central to the making of masculinity when boys lack other resources for gaining these ends. (pp. 162–163)

If bullying is not corrected, it can become training for more serious forms of intimidation and abuse. Nan Stein (2005), senior research scientist at the Center for Research on Women at Wellesley College, suggests that bullying creates a cultural context in which sexual harassment is common.

The AAUW (1993, 2001, 2006) was at the forefront of raising national awareness about sexual harassment in schools. Their initial survey included 1,632 students from diverse backgrounds, Grades 8–11, from 79 schools around the United States and defined *sexual harassment* as "unwanted and unwelcome sexual behavior which interferes with your life" (AAUW, 1993, p. 6). The results revealed an astounding 4 out of 5 students (81% of all students, or 85% of girls and 75% of boys) identified themselves as having been the target of some form of sexual harassment during their school lives. Girls experienced sexual harassment more often than boys, and African American boys experienced it more than White boys.

Harassment tends to increase during middle school years. Many of the students surveyed acknowledged harassing others (66% of boys, 52% of girls). The greater portion of this harassment took the form of nonphysical contact (making sexual comments, spreading sexual rumors, and sexual jokes, gestures, looks). The scary thing is that most students reported doing the harassment simply because it was a part of the school culture, saying, "It was no big deal" (p. 11). However, those who were harassed reported skipping school to avoid the harassment, cutting classes, not participating in classes, struggling with concentration in class, making lower grades, feeling less confident, and feeling self-conscious.

In 2001, the AAUW repeated the study with 2,064 students. Students' knowledge of what sexual harassment is and the schools' sexual harassment policy had improved. Even though more boys reported being victims of sexual harassment than in the previous study, the girls were still more likely than the boys to experience sexual harassment. Across a variety of research reviewed, students overwhelmingly acknowledge the existence of bullying and sexual harassment in schools, but they are not likely to report it because they see it as normal and/or they are afraid to come forward (Hand & Sanchez, 2000; Stein, 2003, 2005).

Nan Stein (2003, 2005) specializes in investigating sexual harassment in kindergarten through the 12th grade. She reports that very little research has been done on the harassment of gays, lesbians, bisexual, and transgender students in schools, but given estimates of more than 2 million sexual minority students in public schools, these students likely face a high risk of abuse, particularly by peers. Stein also argues that because bullying and other forms of harassment are seen as normal, schools become training grounds for domestic violence.

As this research suggests, boys are not the only ones who bully or harass. Girls do it, too. Researchers find that female forms of harassment tend be less physical, relying more on mean-spirited words and actions of exclusion. Journalist Leora Tanenbaum (2000) wrote about her own experience of being labeled a slut in school and interviewed 50 other girls and women from around the country who had been targeted as sluts during junior or senior high school. The participants had nothing in common in their backgrounds except that they all had been sexually stigmatized by male and female peers. The reasons for the abuse were multiple: being a social outcast, developing breasts earlier than one's peers, or being the target of revenge. Tanenbaum found that such verbal abuse ruins social reputations, hurts self-concept, affects academic performance, leads to sexual promiscuity and experimenting with drugs, and sets one up to be a target of rape. Girls' and women's participation in this name-calling should not be surprising. Just as boys and men are pressured to prove their masculinity and heterosexuality, girls are pressured to view each other as competition for male attention, leading to insider cliques and bullying.

In 2006, the AAUW examined sexual harassment at the college level. Again, this was a nationally representative survey of women and men students from diverse racial and ethnic backgrounds and sexual orientations who attended community colleges, four-year colleges, and universities, private and public institutions, in big cities and in small towns. Results show that 62% of all college students report being harassed in some way, including having sexual rumors spread about them, being forced into unwanted physical contact (from ostensibly accidental touching to rape), enduring sexual comments, and being spied on. Female and male students were nearly equally likely to be sexually harassed on campus. Females were more likely to be the target of sexual jokes, comments, gestures, and looks. Males were more likely to be called gay or a homophobic name.

Many men and even more women said the harassment was emotionally disturbing and damaged their educations and college experiences. The female students said they were likely to change their behavior as a result of the harassment; for example, avoiding a particular location on campus. They also found it harder to concentrate on their studies and harder to sleep at night. Lesbian, gay, bisexual, and transgender students were more likely to experience harassment than heterosexual students, and were more troubled by it. Female as well as male students were more likely to be harassed by men than by women. The students said the harassment happens everywhere: in classrooms, in residence halls, at parties and bars, and from peers and university staff.

Fewer than 10% of those harassed reported the harassment. The number one reason they gave was similar to that given in the study of early grades: It is considered commonplace. The majority of those who admitted harassing others said they thought it was funny. The reality is that it is not funny. The communicative behaviors of bullying and harassment create an environment that is not conducive to learning.

Sexual Violence on College Campuses

College campuses are unique communities in which students face challenges in academic and social realms. College is a time of experimentation in relationships and with sexuality, alcohol, values, and personal and group identities. Two landmark studies have revealed that institutions of higher education are not free of the social injustices that exist outside them but may actually be contexts in which individuals, particularly women, are at risk.

In 2000, the National Institute of Justice (NIJ) published *The Sexual Victimization of College Women* (Fisher, Cullen, & Turner, 2000), which summarizes a national study based on 4,446 randomly selected women students from college campuses across the country. The authors report that 2.8% of the women had experienced attempted or completed rape during a period of almost 7 months (27.7 rapes per 1,000 women students). Projecting these statistics over the length of an average college career (about 5 years), Fisher et al. predict that between 1/5 and 1/4 of college women will be the victims of an attempted or completed sexual assault. These assaults occur in contexts that often are complex and involve individuals who know each other, who may have been drinking, and who engage in sexual activity out of fear of harm or abandonment (Abbey, Ross, McDuffie, & McAuslan, 1996). In comparison, incidences of sexual assault by strangers are relatively rare.

Among the women surveyed, 13.1% were stalked during a year's time, with each incident lasting an average of 60 days. *Stalking* is a form of sexual violence that has not traditionally been recognized. The NIJ survey (Fisher, Cullen, & Turner 2000) also included verbal and visual victimization and found a range of behaviors that make women students feel threatened. Verbal victimization seems commonplace. About half the respondents were subjected to sexist remarks, catcalls, and whistles with sexual overtones. One in five women received obscene phone calls and was asked intrusive questions about her sex or romantic life. Of those surveyed, 2.4% were observed naked without their consent. Fewer than 5% of those who said they had been victimized reported the sexual victimization to law enforcement officials.

Part of the problem of sexual violence in college contexts is the pervasive abuse of alcohol. Leading researchers on alcohol and sexual assault report at least half of all violent crimes involve alcohol consumption by the perpetrator, the victim, or both (Abbey, Zawacki, Buck, Clinton, & McAuslan, 2001). Predators commonly use alcohol as a means to reduce perceived responsibility for their aggressive acts and to increase the blame placed on those they victimize.

What encourages sexually violent behaviors? Communication studies scholar Sean Gilmore (1995) studied college men at a large midwestern university to examine how they talked about casual sex with women. He interviewed more than 100 men living in fraternities and residence halls and found that they used a variety of commonly known phrases to characterize casual heterosexual relations as a "game" and women as "the conquest." In a film documenting sample interviews, the men referred to women who "needed to be dick-slapped," referred to sex as "he did it to her" or "he did her until she bled," and spoke of "going around the world," a competition of having sex with women from as many different hair colors, or races, or parts of the world as possible (Gilmore & Terek, 1990). The men were quick to qualify that such portrayals were not used to describe loving romantic relationships, and they did not know if the men actually performed all the sexually demeaning games they described, but the language and the competitive sex stories were clearly a part of masculine university culture.

Because college campuses house large numbers of young women and men living in a concentrated area who tend to be exploring their sexual identities, certain members are at risk for sexual violence. Jackson Katz (1999), a national gender violence educator who works with U.S. college campuses and military groups, argues that the predominant culture's definition of masculinity as aggressive, virile, and dominant perpetuates violence against women, LGBT persons, and other men.

This review of how education genders/sexes persons should make clear that constructions of differences become constructions of inequalities and contribute to a continuum of forms of violence. Diverse influences from gendered curricula, norms of behavior, and abuse interrelate to create a powerful gendered/sexed institution that is not able to reach its potential of liberating persons through education.

Emancipatory Education

Bias in education, particularly bias tied to gender/sex, race, ethnicity, sexual orientation, and class, must be eliminated. Bias can limit students' ambitions and accomplishments, affecting them throughout life. Specifically addressing the bias tied to gender/sex, educator Timothy Frawley (2005) notes that "polarized approaches to education fail to recognize a middle ground for children who are not strongly gender-typed as masculine or feminine. The aim should be to not only stop labeling children as such, but to also accept and encourage androgynous behavior for both" (p. 222). Similarly, education researcher Jane Rolland Martin (1991) calls for "a gender-sensitive model of an educated person" that does not fall into the simplistic trap of biological determinism and false dichotomies (p. 10).

What is a gender-sensitive model? It is more than focusing on individual learning styles and needs. Although an individual focus sounds good in theory, it does not address the underlying structural barriers in education that are tied to racism, sexism, classism, and homophobia. Instead, the individualized approach could help mask these problems by failing to recognize them (Francis & Skelton, 2005). Despite this, attention to learning styles is important, but one should not assume that teaching strategies that work for some girls will not work for some boys. Children should be exposed to a variety of teaching strategies.

A gender-sensitive model also is more than single-sex education, which is at best a temporary response to a larger cultural misconception. Even advocates of single-sex education acknowledge that at some point boys and girls need to learn to work together. If children can learn to appreciate each other in the classroom, it can make a difference in their lives, and the lives of others, outside the classroom.

Gender/sex–sensitive education can be achieved only if one addresses the entire learning environment. Educators must pay attention to what is on the shelves and walls of schools, making sure they send inclusive, nonstereotypical messages. Schools also must provide opportunities for girls and boys to play together safely at recess. The gender-sensitive in-class techniques proposed by educator Tamara Grogan (2003) focus on practical ways teachers can create more inclusive classrooms. For example, rather than letting students gravitate to race, class, and single-sex groups, teachers can have students line up or group according to birthdates, favorite foods, or interests.

This does not mean that girls can never be grouped together to work on math, or boys to read, or that teachers must police same-sex friendships. There is value in same-sex learning and interacting, but creating a community that includes gender/sex, race, class, and sexual-orientation diversity enhances education. Strict gender/sex divisions are oppressive and harmful to all children.

So, how does one know when attention to gender liberates rather than constrains? A distinction between *gender-specific* and *gender-relevant* educational programs is helpful (Connell, 2000). Most of the existing changes in education and curriculum have embraced a gender-specific model that targets only one sex. In contrast, a gender-relevant model includes girls and boys, and it attempts to make the gendered dimension of social life and education a part of the discussion. Educators directly address stereotypical assumptions as a part of the lesson, be it reading, writing, math, or science. Connell describes the benefits of a gender-relevant approach:

> The symbolic gendering of knowledge, the distinction between "boys' subjects" and "girls' subjects" and the unbalancing of curriculum that follows, require a gender-relevant not gender-specific response—a broad re-design of curriculum, timetable, division of labour among teachers, etc. The definition of masculinities in peer group life, and the creation of hierarchies of masculinity, is a process that involves girls as well as boys. It can hardly be addressed with one of these groups in isolation from the other. (pp. 168–169)

Connell argues for coeducational programs in which the construction of students' critical gendered lenses is a part of the educational curriculum.

Another approach to gender-sensitive and gender-relevant education focuses on teaching styles. Teaching methods themselves contribute to liberatory or oppressive educational experiences. Brazilian educator Paulo Freire (1972) argues that the traditional lecture-based instruction style can be oppressive, particularly to groups already marginalized and silenced. He describes the lecture model as a "banking" model of teaching, in which the teacher's role is to "fill" students' brains with information, and the students' role is simply to "store the deposits" (p. 63).

The alternative is *connected teaching* (hooks, 1994), which suggests that learning is more accessible when topics are concretely related to learners' individual life experiences rather than taught in abstract ways, isolated from context. Connected teaching requires teachers to provide examples to which students can relate, to share the ways in which they themselves connect to the material, to be more flexible with their teaching styles, and to be less controlling. It also requires teachers to share control over the learning process by being willing to engage in the learning moment with students rather than simply using the classroom as a place to report what one knows. Author and educator bell hooks (1994) explains that it requires the instructor to make herself or himself vulnerable in the classroom and to make uncertainly and diversity of opinions acceptable parts of the learning process, and it requires students and instructors to explain or defend their ideas. The instructor works together with the students to construct knowledge through interaction. The ultimate goal is to learn how to learn, which requires recognizing the complexity of class members' identities.

The final alternative emerges from global educational programs that focus on girl children. The United Nations (UN) and many nongovernmental organizations (NGOs) have long recognized the intersecting, systemic influences of gender/sex oppressions in education, family, poverty, health, and other social factors that contribute to human rights and livable lives. When persons are illiterate, they are more likely to be poor and uneducated, to have poor health and limited access to paid work, to be more susceptible to violence from others, and to have a shorter life expectancy. In the last several decades, these international organizations have focused on the plight of women and children, particularly in poor regions of the world, as represented by the UN Platform for Action, adopted at the 1995 Fourth World Conference on Women in Beijing.

Countries in South Asia, for example, "account for the largest numbers of poor people in the world and have the highest number of children who do not attend school—46 million, more than half of whom are girls" (Subrahmanian, 2005, p. vii). Because of economic limitations and cultural traditions, girls usually are the last to be placed in schools and the first to be removed. South Asian girls' barriers to education include cultural biases such as son preference; cultural beliefs about women's appropriate roles that keep girls working at home; lack of gender/sex–sensitive infrastructure, such as latrines; unfriendly school environments; lack of community involvement to ensure girls' safety at school; lack of positive role models for girls; practices relating to early marriage, such as dowries; weak legal frameworks that do not implement free primary education or enforce child labor legislation; and labor market discrimination, which offers low returns on women's education (Subrahmanian, 2005).

In such contexts, focusing on girls' education is important because females are the caretakers and educators of children; when organizations invest in girls' and women's literacy and education, they invest in entire families and communities. Consequently, the UN has targeted girls' and women's education for improvement. The New Millennium Development Goals' third goal is to "promote gender equality and empower women" and to "eliminate gender disparity in primary and secondary education, preferably by 2005, and in all levels of education no later than 2015" (Millenium Campaign, 2004).

This recognition of the unique oppressions of girls and women in education worldwide provides a fuller picture of the challenges regarding gender/sex and education. It reminds us that the strategies and solutions developed in the United States should be informed by what is happening elsewhere and should be held globally accountable. Instead of focusing on gender wars in education, the U.S. institution of education needs to better invest in all students.

Conclusion

Education is composed of communicative practices—lectures, books, activities—that teach students to perform gender. Detailed analysis of educational practice demonstrates the gendered/sexed elements of education, including who is educating whom, about what, in what way, and for what purpose. Educators and those being educated have an opportunity and responsibility to think about how the classroom can be a microcosm for multiple social inequalities *and* for social change.

CHAPTER 9

Work

The understanding that women and men are never only women and men, that each person possesses an intersectional identity, was first developed in relation to the institution of work. As you might recall from Chapter 1, legal scholar Kimberlé Crenshaw first used the word *intersectionality* in a 1989 law review article that examined Title VII of the 1964 U.S. Civil Rights Act that made employment discrimination on the basis of race, color, religion, sex, or national origin illegal. Crenshaw explores how the law, meant to prevent discrimination, was failing Black women because it did not recognize the intersecting ways in which they faced discrimination. If a Black woman sought redress under the law, employers would demonstrate that they were not racist because they treated Black men fairly, and that they were not sexist because they treated White women fairly. This meant that unique forms of discrimination faced by Black women were erased, such as the stereotypes of mammy, matriarch, superwoman, castrator, and sapphire created during slavery and persisting into contemporary times (Parker, 2003). For this reason, Crenshaw (1989) concludes that "the intersectional experience is greater than the sum of racism and sexism" and, thus, attention to intersectionality is essential to explain "the particular manner in which Black Women are subordinated" (p. 59). Therefore, to study gender/sex in the workplace, one needs to be attentive not only to gender and sex but also to race, class, nationality, and other identities.

Crenshaw's point from almost two decades ago is still apt. Work is one of the institutions in which discriminatory gender constructions based on sex *and* race are most manifest. Crenshaw has influenced emerging scholarship studying the way in which work functions as a social institution that is gendered, raced, and classed and which itself genders, races, and classes. Although research is beginning to examine the way in which work as an institution maintains the interlocking systems of sexism and racism, little organizational communication research examines race, sex, and class as interdependent processes (Parker, 2003). In this chapter, we rely on the emerging scholarship that does explore the intersecting ways in which people participate in the "saying and doing" of gender in the workplace (Martin, 2003, p. 342).

In this chapter, we also explore the ways in which communication in and about work is gendered and genders. Studying work as a social institution makes clear that gender/sex, and the inequitable treatment of people because of their gender/sex, are much more than individual problems. A critical gendered lens is particularly appropriate when analyzing the institution of work and the way it intersects with other institutions such as the family, because such a lens focuses on how "private choices are rooted in social arrangements over which individual women and men have only limited control" and thus redirects researchers away from blaming individuals and toward "understanding the larger social contexts in which personal choices and strategies are crafted" (Gerson, 2004, p. 164). One must study communication about work, not just communication in workplaces, to understand the complex relationships between work and gender.

An example of communication about work makes clear the need for a wide-angle lens when analyzing work and gender. Since 2003, the U.S. and British popular presses have coined the term *off-ramping* to describe an "opt-out revolution" in which an increasing number of professional women supposedly are leaving their careers temporarily to be stay-at-home moms (Belkin, 2003; O'Kelly, 2004; Reed, 2004; Story 2005a; Wallis, 2004). This public communication about work is problematic. First, the claim that unprecedented numbers of women are off-ramping is simply factually incorrect, given that "economic data provides *no* evidence to support these anecdotal accounts" (Boushey, 2005, p. 1). Second, the stories depict women as making an independent choice to stay home. Being a full-time parent is certainly a valid life choice, but factors other than personal preference influence these seemingly individual choices. Such factors include the following:

1. Economics: The late 1990s affected women's employment options differently from earlier recessions.

2. Work structure: Organizational practices that are family unfriendly create pressures in response to which parents (mostly mothers) feel they must choose between work and family.

3. Family structure: Many women have partners who are unable or unwilling to off-ramp.

4. Difficulty on-ramping: Those who off-ramp face nearly insurmountable barriers to reemployment when they seek to on-ramp.

Finally, the off-ramp choice is not viable for all women. Black women have a history of greater likelihood of becoming single parents, of earning more than their husbands, and of needing to help support extended family; additionally, "for generations black women have viewed work as a means for elevating not only their own status as women, but also as a crucial force in elevating their family, extended family and their entire race" (Clemetson, 2006, p. G1). Whether women choose to on- or off-ramp, their choices are constrained and defined by institutional structures.

It is impossible to cover all of the intricacies of work and gender here. Thus, we intentionally limit our discussion to research that explores (1) the communicative practices through which work constructs gender and (2) the communication about gender that constructs work. The examples we offer are neither exhaustive nor definitive, but they should introduce you to analyses of communication at and about work enabled by a critical gendered lens.

Work as a Social Institution

The meaning of work is not universal. From culture to culture and from time to time, the meaning and significance of work shifts. At the present time in the United States, if someone were asked to define work, she or he would most likely define it as paid work *outside* the home. "Working mothers" are those women with young children who also work outside the home for a wage. Of course, if you were to ask a mother who does not have a wage-paying job that requires her to leave the home, "Do you work?" the answer ought to be a resounding "Yes!" Child rearing is work, but because it is not paid, people do not tend to think of it as work (Daniels, 1987). Revealingly, a phrase exists to name *working mother,* but the phrase *working father* sounds odd. It is expected that men continue to work at wage labor after the births of their children. "Stay-at-home dads" seem to be anomalous, although their numbers are growing. Of the 26.5 million men who are part of a heterosexual married couple, 98,000 are stay-at-home fathers (which is less than .3%) (U.S. Bureau of the Census, 2006). The number is higher among non-nuclear family forms. Among male same-sex couples, 26% include one stay-at-home parent, which is 1% higher than the percentage of stay-at-home parents from heterosexual married couples and 4% higher than for female couples (Bellafante, 2004).

The notion that work is something that occurs outside the home is a Western bias, part of White U.S. cultural beliefs that the public (the realm of work and politics) is distinct from the private (the realm of the family). In many countries, work for pay is conducted in the home (Curran, 2000).

In the United States, the Puritan inculcation of a "work ethic" creates the expectation that all people ought to *want* to work hard, even if they do not like their jobs, because work itself is considered a good thing. The almost unquestioned belief that work is good and the demonization of those on welfare demonstrates the way rhetorical constructions of work maintain its function as a social institution (Schram, 1995). An "ideal worker" ethic exists, and is repeated through public discourse, that "equates work commitment with uninterrupted employment and very long workweeks" (Gerson, 2004, p. 166).

It is important to note, though, that work expectations are not consistent across sexes. Work is not a gender- or sex-neutral institution. Sociologist Dana M. Britton

(1999) argues that to portray "organizations as 'gendered' is needlessly generic; organizations, per se, are 'masculinized'" (p. 469). Thus, as we describe the way in which work is an institution, many of the characteristics also will make clear how it is a *masculine* institution.

The reason work is best understood as a masculine institution becomes clear when one explores work's institutional characteristics. In the United States, work is *social* insofar as it is considered a characteristic of what makes Americans American—they are dedicated to work. In some ways, a man is not a real man unless he is gainfully employed (Connell & Messerschmidt, 2005); the job a man does is "a major basis of identity and what it means to be a man" (Messerschmidt, 1996, p. 33). Every (male) U.S. citizen (women with small children are exempt from this expectation, unless they are on welfare) is expected to work, to become a "taxpaying citizen" (Pateman, 1989).

Work persists across time, although its exact form has shifted in the United States from an agrarian economy, to an industrial economy, and now to a service economy. Work is composed of distinct social practices that recur. Work demonstrates this characteristic with its ever-repeating schedule: 9 to 5, Monday through Friday, or in the case of shift work, midnight to 8, 4 days on, 3 days off (a schedule approximately 25% of the North American population experiences). Perhaps more interesting for this chapter is the way in which sex segregation in jobs (men tend to be firefighters, and women tend to be nurses) is "an amazingly persistent pattern" insofar as "the gender/[sex] identity of jobs and occupations is repeatedly reproduced, often in new forms" (Acker, 1990, p. 145).

Predominantly male occupations possess more social value, as indicated by more pay, prestige, authority, and opportunities for advancement. Numerous studies have demonstrated that if an occupation is female dominated, it tends to carry less prestige, authority, and autonomy. However, even if two occupations' pay and power are equal, if an occupation is populated by more men than women, both men and women value that occupation more highly (Britton, 1999). This conclusion comes from a study of correctional officers, one of the few professions in which pay, prestige, authority, and autonomy are the same, yet the percentage of female and male officers differs according to whether the prison is for women or men; both women and men prefer to work in the male prisons simply because they are *male* prisons. Britton found that the gendering of organizations is maintained through communicative practices such as "organizational structure, ideology, interactions among workers, and in the construction and maintenance of individual identities" (p. 456).

Power permeates work in complex ways—horizontal as well as vertical (Mumby, 2001). Bosses exercise power over workers, but power can also be exercised between workers as a result of sex or race privilege. As the persistence of sexual harassment demonstrates, workers can exercise power over one another.

Work as an institution both constrains and facilitates actions by individuals. Think about the K–12 school year. Classes tend to run from 8 a.m. to 3:30 p.m. with three months off in the summer. Although this schedule worked well when most children were the offspring of farmers and were needed to assist during summer harvests, it makes less sense when U.S. parents work a year-round 9-to-5 schedule and tend to have few or no guaranteed vacation days (Gerson, 2004). Yet, flextime, which allows people to schedule work hours outside the 9-to-5 workday, is slow in coming.

Work as a legitimating ideology also is evident in recent debates over welfare reform. Although many women and men who are mothers and fathers choose to work and so place their children in day care, the women tend to be the only ones criticized for not being good mothers. Whereas women who work outside the home are criticized for placing their children in day care, poor women who have had to rely on welfare while they remain home to care for young children are considered bad mothers because they do not work: "The only women for whom wage work is an unambivalently assigned social responsibility are welfare mothers" (Mink, 1995, pp. 180–181).

This contradiction and irony are hallmarks of institutions (Trethewey & Ashcraft, 2004). Is work good? It depends on whether you are a middle-class woman with small children or a poor woman. Is work valued? It depends on whether or not you are independently wealthy. These contradictions, as well as changes in the economy, may breed changes in work as an institution.

Scholars study work at the macrolevel when they examine shifts in late or post-industrial capitalist society. They also examine work at the microlevel when they study interactions between workers. In communication studies, the analysis of the intersections between work's micro- and macrolevels has taken the form of *critical organizational communication perspectives*, which examine organizations as "intersubjective structures of meaning" in which identity and power relationships are produced, maintained, transformed, and reproduced "through the ongoing communicative activities of [their] members" (Mumby, 2001, p. 585; Parker, 2003, p. 259).

Interlocking Institutions

The intersections between U.S. institutions become visible when work as it is presently structured comes into conflict with family. The public/private division described earlier portrays work and family as opposite social institutions, each with different demands, values, and goals. As a result, the institutions of work and family generate tensions in people, causing many to feel they must choose one over the other. These choices are gendered, raced, and classed.

The conflict between work and family in the United States was made evident by sociologist Arlie Hochschild (1997). Her study found that the rapidly increasing time stress in U.S. culture induces more persons to choose work over family because of the rewards work promises. These pressures could be recalibrated. Work and home *could* be structured to mutually support each other. For example, in Nordic countries, work pay tends to continue even during parental leave; benefits provided at the birth of a child are reduced if both parents do not take time off work; and parental leave is nontransferable, thus prompting both parents to take time off. Lawmakers in Nordic countries have structured work benefits to challenge the pattern whereby women tend to carry disproportionate responsibility in child rearing (Moss & Deven, 1999). Unfortunately, U.S. family leave is not structured this way, meaning that the tensions between work and family persist.

Many of the tensions are different for women and for men. Most workers also are parents, but work structures do not treat male and female parents equitably. Childbirth and parenting affect men and women differentially. Women birth children, and the childbirth process is called labor for a reason; should breast-feeding be chosen, only women can breast-feed. However, neither of these facts automatically means that women must be or should be the primary caregivers to small children. In fact, as of 2000, 51% of U.S. mothers with children under the age of one year were employed.

This reality contributed to the passage of the Pregnancy Discrimination Act of 1978 and the Family Medical Leave Act of 1993 (which allows up to 12 weeks of unpaid leave for pregnancy, personal, or family reasons). These U.S. laws are meant to create conditions whereby people affected by pregnancy and caregiving are not penalized and are able to return to their jobs after a leave. Although both of these laws are necessary and significant, they demonstrate that legal change alone is not sufficient to create equality; a change in the communication about an issue also is necessary. Communication studies scholar Celeste Condit (1990) explains that "the process of convincing requires not only that a given policy be accepted but also that a given vocabulary (or set of understandings) be integrated into the public repertoire" (p. 6).

In the case of work and family, a vocabulary that recognizes the complex ways in which women experience parenthood has not yet been developed. Lori West Peterson and Terrance L. Albrecht (1999) found that in discussions of work and women's childbearing processes, maternity leave was interpreted as a *benefit* (something that would be a bonus or a business's choice and not a guaranteed right), and pregnancy was interpreted as a *disability* (a condition belonging to one person, which also renders the other parent, usually a father, absent). This limited vocabulary repertoire meant that even with legal protections and leave policies in place, work's male-centered structure continues to present challenges to women who are about to be parents. A study done by organizational communication scholars Patrice M. Buzzanell and Meina Liu (2005) confirms that the work–family culture and supervisory relationships played a key role in determining the degree to which women were satisfied with a company's leave policy and hence were able and willing to return to work after childbirth.

A critical gendered lens directed at organizational communication focuses attention on work–family dilemmas not as individual problems but as located in institutions. The alternative is to blame women for the tensions created by social institutions: "Without a framework that acknowledges the gendered nature of these [work–family] dilemmas, individual women can be left bearing the lion's share of responsibility for 'solving' socially constructed problems, including the time squeezes that have become so widespread" (Gerson, 2004, p. 165). Our foregrounding of institutions as gendered should expose the way in which discrimination is subtle and systemic. A system of institutional norms maintained through both micro- and macrolevels of communication impedes gender/sex equality.

Work and education also interlock to reproduce power differentials. Studies of African American women and work make clear that their experiences of subordination in the institution of work begin in school, when counselors and teachers tend to steer them away from particular work aspirations (Parker, 2003). The problems African American women face are intensified at the time of job entry, and then exacerbated with job advancement (or the lack thereof). Summarizing the research, communication scholar Patricia S. Parker (2003) concludes that "research on African American women's work experiences reveals the persistent structuring of organizational divisions along race, gender[/sex], and class lines that occurs through power-based communicative practices, such as the enactment of ordinary, daily procedures and decisions" (p. 268). How African American women are talked to and talked about influences the types of work they and others consider suitable for African American women.

As we note in other chapters, however, a description of institutions solely as locations of subordination is incomplete. They also are locations of resistance. Despite institutionalized forms of control, many African American women identify locations of resistance and seek empowerment in work. In balancing the work–family dilemma, they develop communities of "*othermothers* and *fictive kin* to help each other with balancing work and family" (Parker, 2003, p. 268). They also find ways to develop resilience through their spirituality, as we explore in Chapter 10 (Collins, 1998).

Our attention to the ways in which institutional structures of work affect African American women differently from White American women should make clear that a critical gendered lens applied to the institution of work does not generate a simple list of different experiences for women and men. One should be attentive to the differences among women and men as well as to the similarities between women and men.

It's Not About Sex Difference

Many books have identified ostensible differences between women and men's communication strategies in the workplace (e.g., Tannen, 1994b). However, many of the verbal and nonverbal activities in the workplace that are characterized as feminine actually tend to be practiced by men as much as, if not more than, by women. Differences emerge not in the actual practice of communication but in others' interpretation of it. This is perhaps most notable in the area of emotions and organizations. For the most part, the expression of emotion at work is considered inappropriate. Men (and women) are expected not to cry or to show fear, sadness, or joy; it is more appropriate, however, for men to show anger. Ultimately, though, it is impossible to compare and contrast women's and men's emotions because they are specific to the social context (Hearn, 1993), meaning that emotions considered organizationally appropriate when expressed by a man are perceived as inappropriate when expressed by a woman.

Despite the stereotype that women are more emotional than men, the reality is that men express emotion at work, too; however, their expressions often are not coded as emotional. This points out how emotions themselves are "social discursive constructions": "Men, masculinities, organizations and emotions do not exist in some unmediated form. They are all socially and discursively mediated, partly through each other; ... other concepts and other men, masculinities, organizations and emotions" (Hearn, 1993, pp. 148–149). What others count as an emotional expression depends on the expresser's sex/gender (Parkin, 1993).

If one studies activities rather than emotionalities, it appears that men engage in practices that are stereotypically attributed to women more than to men, such as "wasting time talking to coworkers, pretending to like people they dislike, making decisions based on affect rather than 'objective' evidence, and ignoring rules in favor of particularistic sentiments. ... When women coworkers socialize, they waste time; when men coworkers socialize, they advance their careers" (Martin, 2003, p. 358). The one distinction is that men tend to do some communicative behaviors differently from women. "Peacocking" and other self-promoting behaviors, in particular, were directed only at other men: "The audience(s) to whom/that [sic] men hold themselves accountable at work relative to gender[/sex] is ... primarily other men" (p. 358). In other words, the differences claimed by some to exist do not exist, and the differences that do exist tend not to be coded as distinctive masculine behavior because the work institution is gendered masculine, and so the behavior appears neutral. Martin (2003) concludes her empirical study by explaining, "Men's desire for other men's attention, company, and approval is relatively ignored in the organizational literature, leaving the homoemotional, even flirtatious (and some say homoerotic) character of men's relations with each other at work unacknowledged" (p. 360).

These subtle practices highlight how mechanisms of exclusion and discrimination are not always readily apparent, even if they are demonstrably present. As Martin (2003) explains, "Men need not invent schemes for excluding women from daily work processes in order for women to experience exclusion. As men engage in gendering practices consistent with institutionalized norms and stereotypes of masculinity, they nonetheless create social closure and oppression" (p. 360). For this reason, the insights offered by communication studies become important. Not only can careful analysis of public discourse about work and welfare show the ways both are gendered, but close analysis of organizational communication dynamics can enable one to trace the gendered norms of interaction in work settings.

Work Constructs (and Constrains) Gender

Social inequalities are manifested and maintained through work. The interrelation of economies enabled by expansions in technological capabilities, as well as the ability for communication technologies to "shrink" the world, has been labeled *globalization* (Held & McGrew, 2000; Sassen, 1998), which itself interacts with gender. Shelves of books explore the meaning of globalization and its gendered implications (e.g., Aguilar & Lacsamana, 2004; Parrenas, 2001). Hundreds of law review articles explore the success of legal remedies for employment discrimination. Entire books have been devoted to the feminization of poverty (Goldberg & Kremen, 1990), and the pathologizing of women of color as "welfare queens" is a recurring subject of study (Asen, 2003; Hancock, 2004; Mink, 1995). Scholars have studied the differences between white-collar, blue-collar, and pink-collar work both in the United States and abroad (Mastracci, 2004; Ogasawara, 1998). Also of interest are the reasons for and meaning of the wage disparities between women and men (and people of color and White Americans), and the interrelation between work, education, family, and society (Buzzanell, Sterk, & Turner, 2004).

Evidence of inequality based on sex (and exacerbated by race, nationality, and relation to the globalizing economy) is undeniable. Globally, according to research conducted for the United Nations Development Fund for Women, a "[sex] gap in earnings exists across almost all employment categories" (Chen, Vanek, Lund, & Heintz, 2005, p. 3). Contributing to this imbalance is the fact that women tend to bear responsibility for unpaid household work and thus often are restricted to home-based employment, further limiting their earnings (Chen et al., 2005).

Structural inequalities in earnings are found in the United States as well. In 2003, although women's wages in relation to men's had steadily been improving, U.S. census data indicated that for the first time, women's earnings declined in relation to men's, down from the 2002 high of 76.6% (Longley, 2004). Women tend to earn only about 75.5% of men's wages, even when hours and job prestige are held constant (Blau & Kahn, 2000). At the top corporate levels, women earn 8% to 25% less than their male counterparts (Bell, 2005). A recent report by the U.S. General Accounting Office (2002) found that "women managers continue to lag behind their male counterparts in both advancement and pay" and, in fact, are worse off by comparison in 2000 than they were in 1995 (p. 1). The GAO report also found that in only five of the ten industries studied did women hold a number of management jobs proportionate to their representation in the workforce. However, income inequity and job segregation are not the only ways the gendering/sexing of work manifests itself.

The fact that work institutions maintain and are sites of inequality is well established. However, this leaves unanswered the question as to *how* work produces these inequalities. It is easy to recognize that the outcome of work as an institution creates systemic forms of discrimination. More difficult to identify are daily practices, which often appear insignificant when viewed as isolated instances, that accumulate to create discriminatory outcomes. Fortunately, many scholars of organizational communication have studied the micropractices of work in order to identify how work organizations are gendered masculine.

Sociologist Joan Acker pioneered the study of the way in which work is gendered, particularly through its organizational structure. Her research and theorizing makes clear that "organizational structure is not gender neutral" (Acker, 1990, p. 139). She calls for a systematic theory of gender and organizations (although most of her comments focus more on sex in terms of unequal treatment of women and men). Her five reasons for attention to gender and organizations are (1) the sex segregation of work, including which work is paid and which is unpaid; (2) income and status inequality between women and men and how this is created through organizational structure; (3) how organizations invent and reproduce cultural images of sex and gender; (4) the way in which gender, particularly masculinity, is the product of organizational processes; and (5) the need to make organizations more democratic and more supportive of humane goals. These five are also intersecting processes that make issues of power, control, and dominance gendered.

Acker's pioneering work has influenced organizational communication studies to the point that Dennis Mumby (2001), a renowned critical organizational theorist, has definitively declared, "It is impossible to study and theorize adequately about organizational power without addressing its gendered character" (p. 609). Mumby's work, as well as work done by others (Ashcraft & Mumby, 2004; Buzzanell, 2000; Calás & Smircich, 2001; Trethewey, 2001), has begun to correct one of the "great blind spots, and errors" of organizational theory: the assumption that organizations are gender neutral (Rothschild & Davies, 1994, p. 583).

In the 1970s, scholars began to recognize the way in which the structure of organizations, rather than the individual characteristics of women and men, generated gender differences (Kanter, 1977). The outgrowth of attention to gender and work organizations makes evident that

> advantage and disadvantage, exploitation and control, action and emotion, meaning and identity, are patterned through and in terms of a distinction between male and female, masculine and feminine. Gender is not an addition to ongoing processes, conceived as gender neutral. Rather, it is an integral part of those processes, which cannot be properly understood without an analysis of gender. (Acker, 1990, p. 146)

Despite the clear evidence of gender and related inequalities in work organizations, a vision of the abstract worker persists—a bodiless, sexless, emotionless worker who does not procreate. This sex- and gender-neutral worker is not actually neutral but instead is a man. Acker (1990) explains, "It is the man's body, its sexuality, minimal responsibility in procreation, and conventional control of emotions that pervades work and organizational processes." In contrast, "women's bodies are ruled out of order, or sexualized and objectified, in work organizations" (p. 152). Martin (2003) confirms that the way in which gender is done in organizational work settings continues to constrain women insofar as the way in which men and women socially construct each other at work affects their work experiences, and this tends to impair women workers' identities and confidence (p. 343). In stating this, Martin is careful to note that "multiple masculinities and femininities exist, and people practice, and are held accountable to, specific kinds depending on their bodies (health, attractiveness), class, race/ethnicity, religion, sexual orientation, age, nation, and other social statuses" (p. 355).

Race, Gender, and Work: Black Women in Work Contexts

Patricia S. Parker (2003) has provided an exhaustive review of the literature on African American women and the way in which they experience control (and exercise resistance and create empowerment) in raced, gendered, and classed work contexts. Parker highlights the way in which race, gender/sex, and class "structure communicative practices in everyday organizational life—such as hiring and recruitment rituals, interaction patterns, and symbolic processes—that contribute to African American women's continued subordination and oppression in the U.S. labor market" (p. 258). What is important to note is that African American women face this subordination not just from White men but also from White women (Parker, 2003, p. 271; for research on Hispanic women, see Calás, 1992; for research on working class women, see Gregg, 1993).

The work practices that maintain and create subordination are not always overt, like quid pro quo sexual harassment, but can be more subtle, located in "ordinary, daily procedures and decisions . . . the hidden microprocesses and micropractices that produce and reproduce unequal, and persistent, sex-, race-, and class-based patterns in work situations" (Parker, 2003, pp. 264, 261), such as who is asked to do which type of tasks. Consistent with the point made in Chapter 1 and revisited in Chapter 6, racism and sexism are not located in individuals' prejudices but in political practices. Accordingly, Parker reviews literature on and calls for additional research into (1) organizational divisions of labor between women and men, along with allowed behaviors and work spaces; (2) symbolic constructions of women and men, femininity and masculinity; and (3) workplace interactions between women and men. Each of these three areas is fertile ground for study, theorizing, and activism in communication studies.

Consistent with the spirit of this book, Parker also identifies forms of resistance and empowerment that individuals, in this case African American women, can employ. Institutionalized forms of discrimination, although powerful, are not monolithic. Brenda J. Allen (1996) explores the way African Americans seek empowerment (see also Allen, 1995, 1998). Parker's review of Allen's work highlights how Allen's view of empowerment recognizes that it is "an ongoing process of resistance and transformation through individual agency *and* collective action" (Parker, 2003, p. 279, emphasis added). A single instance in which one confronts a racist or sexist comment does not determine whether one is empowered; empowerment is not solely an individual endeavor. Thus, Parker (2003) identifies five themes concerning African American women's resistance: "a) developing and using voice, b) being self-defined, c) being self-determined, d) connecting to and building community, and e) seeking spirituality and regeneration" (p. 280).

Class, Race, Gender/Sex, and Work: Care Work

Historically, women have tended to be the primary caregivers to small children, and women of color have often been hired by White women to be caregivers. Job segregation not only occurs across sex lines but also across race lines within sex.

Again, an intersectional approach enables one to see ways in which systemic inequalities manifest themselves. As a paradigmatic example, "Black women's initial overrepresentation in domestic service reflects the intersections of race, gender, and class—the idea that Blacks are best suited for servitude, that women belong in the private sphere of the home, and that work done in the home does not deserve significant economic reward" (Harvey, 2005, p. 791). With the globalization of the economy, this dynamic has been extended to cover not only Black women but also Filipina women in Canada (Welsh, Carr, MacQuarrie, & Huntley, 2006) and Latina immigrants in the United States (Hondagneu-Sotelo & Avila, 1997).

Sociologist Mignon Duffy (2005) speaks directly to this issue in an essay analyzing how care work is segregated along race, class, and sex lines; we would add age, with young and old women being valued less, paid less, and more often hired as care workers. Duffy analyzes jobs that would be considered part of reproductive labor, such as domestic service, health care, child care, teaching, food preparation, and cleaning and building services. Her analysis was situated within broader research that establishes that the U.S. labor market is "stratified, segmented into various sectors that provide workers with grossly unequal wage levels and access to opportunities for advancement" (p. 71). This stratification is neither race nor sex neutral, because "interlocking systems of gender and racial oppression act to concentrate women and people of color in those occupations that are lower paying and lower status" (p. 71). Even within care labor, stratification can be found in which White women assume the public face of care work, populating those jobs that call for the most interaction with others, that are most professionalized, and that pay more. In contrast, "women of color are disproportionately represented in the 'dirty, back-room' jobs such as maids and kitchen workers" (p. 72).

Even as the differences between women are highlighted, one also should remember that care work is not solely the responsibility of women, even though they may be most represented in its ranks. Also, the work performed by paid care workers benefits men, other family members, and society as a whole (Duffy, 2005).

Violence, Gender/Sex, and Work: Sexual Harassment

Perhaps the issue that makes most evident the power relations present in work is the issue of sexual harassment. As we indicated in Chapter 6, we pay special attention to institutionalized violence—how violence becomes normalized through institutional processes. In the workplace, the normalization of violence most clearly takes the form of sexual harassment (for broad considerations of violence and organizations, see Hearn, 1994).

In Chapter 5, sexual harassment was discussed as an example of the power of naming, along with ways for counterpublics to develop a vocabulary that articulates subordinated groups' interests and needs. The naming of sexual harassment and the creation of legal redress for those who experience it have done much to counter gendered/sexed violence in the workplace. However, even with the evolutions in law and the raising of public consciousness about harassment as a result of the Anita

Hill–Clarence Thomas hearings (The Black Scholar, 1992; Morrison, 1992), sexual harassment persists. The U.S. Equal Opportunity Employment Commission (2005) reports that, in 2004, women filed 84.9% of the 13,136 charges of sexual harassment. However, many instances of sexual harassment are never reported to the EEOC. Most studies indicate that 40% to 70% of women and 10% to 20% of men have experienced sexual harassment in the workplace. Although some examples exist of women harassing men, men harassing men, and women harassing women, by far the most predominant form of harassment is men harassing women.

Interestingly, there is a disjuncture in how men and women generally interpret sexual harassment. Quid pro quo sexual harassment appears easily identifiable, but sexual harassment in the form of the *hostile work environment* has not developed a consensus definition, at least not a consensus between masculine-identified men and nonmasculine-identified women. Women tend to define more acts as constituting harassment and are more likely to perceive coercion in a particular situation, whereas masculine men are more likely to blame the person harassed instead of empathizing with that person (Quinn, 2002). For this reason, some feminist jurisprudential scholars have advocated that the courts use a reasonable woman standard rather than a reasonable man (or person) standard when adjudicating legal complaints (Kerns, 2001).

In a study of the meaning of "girl watching," sociologist Beth A. Quinn (2002) identifies some of the reasons for this disjuncture. To understand what sexual harassment *means*, Quinn asked sexual harassers and those harassed what it meant to them. Quinn studied a form of harassment that tends to be labeled as such by women but defined as play by men who engage in it. It also is an activity of which the woman being watched may be unaware, although other women may not be. Thus, it seems that the target of the action may not be the particular person being watched but in fact may be other men and, indirectly, other women in the organization. Quinn found that girl watching functions as a form of gendered play among the men studied, as "both a source of fun and a mechanism by which gendered identities, group boundaries, and power relations are (re)produced" (p. 393). It is a form of play that bolsters masculinity by being premised on "a studied lack of empathy with the feminine other" (p. 391). In fact, the play targets the watched woman as a game piece, an object, rather than another player; she is not the intended audience. Quinn outlines the complex dynamics of femininity, masculinity, sexuality, and competence implicated in girl watching:

> The gaze demonstrates their right, as men, to sexually evaluate women. Through the gaze, the targeted woman is reduced to a sexual object, contradicting her other identities, such as that of a competent worker or leader. This employment of the discourse of asymmetrical heterosexuality (i.e. the double standard) may trump a woman's formal organizational power, claims to professionalism, and organizational discourses of rationality. . . . Calling attention to a woman's gendered sexuality can function to exclude recognition of her competence, rationality, trustworthiness, and even humanity. In contrast,

the overt recognition of a man's heterosexuality is normally compatible with other aspects of his identity; indeed, it is often required . . . because being seen as sexual has different consequences for women and men. (p. 392)

Quinn demonstrates that sexual joking and girl watching is "a common way for heterosexual men to establish intimacy among themselves" (p. 394). Of course, this begs the question, why do some men base their bonding on the sexual objectification of women?

In a culture of hegemonic masculinity, men become men by performing their virility in front of other men. When asked what "being a man" entailed, the people Quinn interviewed indicated that it involves "notions of strength (if not in muscle, then in character and job performance), dominance, and a marked sexuality, overflowing and uncontrollable to some degree and natural to the male 'species'" (p. 394). One way for men to perform uncontrollable sexuality is through girl watching.

Most interesting in Quinn's study is that when pushed to look at girl watching from a woman's perspective, the men who claimed not to see the act as constituting a hostile work environment *did* understand the harm of these supposedly innocuous acts. Thus, Quinn concludes that differences between men and women "in interpreting sexual harassment stem not so much from men's not getting it . . . but from a . . . lack of motivation to identify with women's experiences" (p. 397). Men who have learned to perform masculinity *correctly* must not demonstrate empathy; thus, they fail to see harassing behaviors from the perspective of the other. This means that sexual harassment is an example not only of one man exerting power over one woman but of how masculinity itself is premised on a relation of dominance of men over women. This, of course, has important implications for training programs about sexual harassment. It is not enough simply to inform people about actions that constitute sexual harassment. It also is necessary to challenge prevailing notions of masculinity that discourage empathy in men.

Absent from these general statistics about harassment is the way race influences interpretations of sexual harassment. Again, intersectional analysis is expanding the understanding of how the communicative practice of harassment functions. In a study of Canadian women, researchers sought to determine how diverse women understood harassment (Welsh et al., 2006). They conducted focus group research with Black women; Filipinas working as part of the Live-In Caregiver Program; White women in unionized, male-dominated manufacturing settings; and mixed-race women employed by the federal government. They found that race and citizenship played a significant role in how women defined harassment; White women's definitions were most similar to the legal definition. In contrast, the Black women and Filipinas tended to not label harassing behaviors *sexual* harassment, in part because the behaviors could not be distinguished from harassment on account of race and/or citizenship status. One explanation offered was that the White women interviewed faced some of the most violent and severest forms of harassment, the type most easily redressed through legal means. The Black women described themselves as individually able to handle the harassment without needing to seek legal redress. In addition, when harassing behaviors are perpetrated by Black men, Black women do not label it sexual harassment but instead view it as a form of sexism that has been normalized in the Black community.

Finally, it is important to turn the reflective lens of analysis on sexual harassment laws themselves. They, too, construct gender in a particular way, one that actually limits the effectiveness of the law in addressing all forms of harassment. Judith Butler (2004) argues that legal scholar Catharine MacKinnon's formulation of sexual harassment law is premised on the belief that gender is the "concealed effect of sexualized subordination within heterosexuality" (p. 54). Because MacKinnon (1987) examines gender as "a matter of dominance, not difference" (p. 51), for her, men's harassment of women genders women feminine. This viewpoint inextricably assumes that one's gender is determined by one's sex and therefore examines gender only through the framework of heterosexuality. Limiting harassment codes to harassment because of sex, wherein men harass women, presents two problems. First, it limits the power of recognizing sexual harassment as sex discrimination. Second, it makes the law blind to cases of same-sex gender harassment, wherein people are harassed because their gender does not match the expectations attached to their sex.

Law professor Katherine Franke (1997) argues that viewing sexual harassment as something men do to women "is both descriptively underinclusive and theoretically short-sighted" (p. 771). It does not adequately articulate the wrong of sexual harassment in the workplace but instead presents it as the wrong acts of one person against another. Her argument is that we need to be clearer that sexual harassment is "a tool or instrument of gender regulation . . . undertaken in the service of hetero-patriarchal norms. These norms, regulatory, constitutive, and punitive in nature, produce gendered subjects: feminine women as sex objects and masculine men as sex subjects. On this account, sexual harassment is sex discrimination precisely because its use and effect police hetero-patriarchal gender norms in the workplace" (p. 772). In this conception, sexual harassment is not something men do to women because they are women but something that people do to other people to maintain strict gender/sex binary norms and inequalities.

Conceiving of sexual harassment as an attempt to maintain gender norms enables one to recognize the harassment of masculine women and feminine men by women and men. Law professor Francisco Valdes (1995) explores this very issue, commenting on how the conflation of sex and gender (for example, in the belief that gender discrimination is a woman's issue only) makes the law blind to the fact that women could harass men for being feminine. Similarly, because gender and sexual orientation are conflated, many assume that feminine men are gay and hence harass them on the basis of a falsely attributed sexuality. This makes it difficult for straight, feminine men to receive redress, because their harassers will say they harassed not because of sex but because of sexual orientation—and limited protections exist for harassment based on orientation. Thus, straight, feminine men receive little protection. The complexity of the issue of sexual harassment makes clear why it is important to understand the complexity of gender. It also provides a

fascinating example to explore how the discourse of law structures social understandings of sex, gender, and orientation.

Work as Liberation and Locations of Empowerment in Work

Even as power dynamics in the institution of work constrain people's options,
locations of resistance open up. In the case of African American women, many seek
ways to empower themselves and others in work settings. In the case of Latina
immigrants, many redefine *mother* to mean "wage earner," as they leave their own
children in order to earn money caring for others' children (Hondagneu-Sotelo &
Avila, 1997). In the case of White women in the United States, some have codified
forms of legal redress to use against sexual harassers. The reality is that even as
work can constrain, it also "provides women with the same rewards that it has historically offered men, including a degree of economic independence and enhanced
self-esteem" (Gerson, 2004, p. 166). Work can be liberating, and working at jobs
that violate gender expectations can transform the way in which work is gendered.

A society's understandings of gender/sex, race, and class are not static. In the
process of repetition, the weaknesses in the norms can be worked—sometimes
quite subtly or even unintentionally and sometimes quite overtly and very intentionally. The way in which gender is institutionalized across other institutions
makes clear that this practice finds its persistence and stability in its institutionalization. However, gender also is "dynamic, emergent, local, variable, and shifting"
(Martin, 2003, p. 351).

One example of the shift can be found in how "children of the gender revolution" of the 1970s conceive of the ideal family–work relationship. In interviews of
adults 18–32 years old, Kathleen Gerson (2004) identified a tendency to favor a
form of family in which both the mother and father work outside the home, even
if the person had been reared in a family in which the mother was the primary
caregiver and did not work outside the home. The people raised in traditional
family structures felt their mothers would have been "happier, more satisfied, and
less reliant on others" had they worked outside the home as well. Perhaps more
importantly, though, the work conditions of the parents were as important as having a job, and the family processes were more important than the family form. As
Gerson (2004) explains, "Children feel better about their parents' situations when
mothers and fathers alike can count on secure jobs that offer personal gratification
but do not drain them of needed time and energy for family life" (p. 171).

Conclusion

Sociologists, lawyers, economists, political scientists, anthropologists, and communication studies scholars study work. Work is something in which virtually every

person engages, whether it is paid or unpaid (such as housework), and if one does not work, that in itself is a basis for judgment. Work can be extremely rewarding, can be considered more an avocation than a vocation, and people can consider their jobs a core part of their identities. However, work also can be extremely dehumanizing, something done only as a means to the end of earning money to pay for the necessities of life.

The way a culture's economy is structured exposes much about what is valued in that culture; capitalist economies tend to value consumption instead of intergenerational preservation. However, the nature of work is changing. Late capitalist societies' economies have shifted from agrarian, to industrial, and now to service oriented and information based. The economies of countries referred to as developing have been extremely decentralized, and many individuals engage in subsistence farming. However, colonialism and resource exploitation have always meant that the economies of nonindustrialized countries were inextricably linked to so-called developed countries.

Work as an institution both genders and is gendered. The jobs people do, people's interactions with others at work, law and discourse—all influence the performance of gender/sex. In turn, gender/sex influences how people understand work and its relation to family, identity, and culture. The tensions and intersections that exist between work and family, work and leisure, work and law can only be improved if one overtly considers gender as part of that mix.

CHAPTER 10

Religion

B ecause a person's religion is based on faith, a belief in a higher, infallible power, the idea that it should be analyzed as an institution might cause discomfort. For example, although Judeo-Christians tend to label the Lakota creation story a myth, Judeo-Christians tend not to label the book of Genesis a myth. However, religion can be analyzed as one of many institutions of cultural influence, and religions' messages inform how people are sexed and gendered. Influential postcolonialist theorist Gayatri Spivak (2004) explains, "Religion in this sense is the ritual markers of how we worship and how we inscribe ourselves in sexual difference" (p. 104). Religion informs not only people's personal relationships with their god(s) but also people's relationships with their bodies.

Religion also influences the definition of family, the value of education, and the importance and division of work. Religion, like all social institutions, constructs gender/sex, is constructed by gendered/sexed people, and is a location of both subordination and empowerment. This complexity highlights the need to understand the relationship between spiritual equality and social equality.

Religion is one location in which people find validated their intrinsic worth as human beings. Most religions declare spiritual equality before their supreme deity. For example, in Christianity many cite Paul: "There is neither Jew nor Greek, there is neither slave nor free person, there is not male and female; for you are all one in Christ Jesus" (Galatians 3:28, New American Standard Version). In Islam, it is believed that both women and men are capable of knowledge, and "seeking knowledge is an obligation for every Muslim man and woman" ("Understanding Islam," n.d., question 11). In the Qur'an, men and women's requirements and responsibilities are described as equal and parallel:

Surely the men who submit and the women who submit, and the believing men and the believing women, and the obeying men and the obeying women, and the truthful men and the truthful women, and the patient men and the patient women, and the humble men and the humble women, and the almsgiving men and the almsgiving women, and the fasting men and the fasting women, and the men who guard their private parts and the women who guard, and the men who remember Allah much and the women who remember—Allah has prepared for them forgiveness and a mighty reward. (Qur'an, Shakir, 033.035)

These passages raise the question of how spiritual equality before God's eyes intersects with social equality. How do people reconcile the spiritual equality of all people with the institutional and social inequality of some people?

Even though many religions proclaim spiritual equality, religious texts often are used to justify social inequality. Our argument is *not* that religion is uniquely sexist; it is not. Instead, we seek to explore the ways in which religion and gender/sex intersect in ways that are discriminatory *and* liberatory. Ultimately, social change comes about not by rejecting social institutions wholesale but, as Judith Butler (1993) points out, by "*working the weakness in the norm*" (p. 237), finding those locations within institutions' norms wherein the potential for productive social change resides.

Religion as a Social Institution

When we refer to religion as an institution, we want to make clear that we are referencing the institutions that mediate people's relations with a higher power or divinity, not a person's personal relationship with that power, which is typically referred to as *spirituality* (Klassen, 2003). Clearly, spirituality and religion are intertwined insofar as religion influences a person's spirituality. However, one can be spiritual without participating in an institutionalized religion.

We also want to note that this distinction between spirituality and religion is a Western artifact and makes little sense when discussing South and East Asian religious practices. In many Asian cultures, one is not religious because one belongs to a particular church, temple, or shrine but because one lives in the culture. In China, Confucianism influences understandings of morality; in Japan, people practice ancestor worship (Dorman, 2006); and in Taiwan, the prevailing religion does not have a specific name but is composed of "beliefs, rituals and organizations that deeply permeate the secular life of the individual and society" (Yang, Thornton, & Fricke, 2000, p. 121). Spirituality is infused throughout the culture in every daily practice and is not split off into a formal religion (Narayanan, 2003).

Thus, when we describe religion as an institution, we are speaking from a Western perspective and about religious institutions that rely on the Old Testament (Judaism, Christianity, and Islam). Our examples presume that religion can be distinguished from the broader culture, even as we recognize that religion influences the broader culture. Our point in noting this bias is not to discredit our insights into how religion functions but to point out why a more extensive discussion of the religious practices of South and East Asia is missing and to make clear that many of our points would not explain those practices.

Religions function as institutions. Those who belong to a religion share common memories, references, practices, beliefs, and rituals (Eid, 2003). Religions are social because they are constituted by collectivities of people who, through interaction, create and maintain the religion; most religions involve collective worship. Religions persist across time and space, spanning generations as they are passed from parent to child, elder to neophyte, even when groups are geographically dispersed. Religions are composed of rituals and practices that recur with every Sabbath, holy day, or celebration.

Religions both constrain and enable behavior. They constrain insofar as they impose rules of morality, and they enable insofar as they provide people with a moral center from which to act. Religion is structured around social positions that help people make sense of where they fit (e.g., layperson, priest, imam, rabbi, acolyte). Religions are composed of embodied agents insofar as religions are practiced by actual people. Religion is internalized by those who identify with it, in that being religious becomes part of who that person is, as in "I am Catholic," "I am Muslim," or "I am Jewish."

Religion is structured around a legitimating ideology, often an ideology that positions itself as the only legitimate, and hence legitimating, one; religions present themselves as outlining the one true and right relationship to (their) God. For example, *catholic* means "including or concerning all humankind" or "universal," so naming the Roman Catholic Church *Catholic* is meant to signal its universality as the one true religion. Religions, like all institutions, are rife with conflict, whether it be the Baptist schism in 2000 in the United States over the new statement of faith, or Muslims' divisions into Shia and Sunni, or Western scholars' differentiation between Theravada/Hinayana and Mahayana Buddhism (although one should remember that the different strands of Buddhism developed with little physical conflict, which may say something about how that religion institutionalizes nonviolence as part of its creed).

Because of internal tensions, religions change. However, change does not come easily, because religions are organized in accord with and permeated by power, as the hierarchical structure of most religious organizations makes clear. Finally, religious people and religions mutually constitute each other; individuals constantly constitute religions, and religions constantly constitute individuals' identities.

In 2004, the Pew Forum on Religion and Public Life, one of the most respected U.S. polling groups, conducted a survey to examine the intersection of politics and religion in the United States. As part of the survey, it outlined the general breakdown of people into religions: 84% of people describe themselves as belonging to an organized religion, 26.3% describe themselves as Evangelical Protestant, 16% as Mainline Protestant, 17.5% as Roman Catholic, 2.7% as other Christian faiths, 2.7% as other faiths, and 1.9% as Jewish, leaving 16% unaffiliated. Globally, 33% practice Christianity; 21% practice Islam; 14% practice Hinduism; 6% each practice indigenous religions, Chinese traditional religions, and Buddhism; 0.36% practice Sikhism; 0.22% practice Judaism; and 16% consider themselves nonreligious (Adherents.com, 2005).

Religious institutions participate in the construction of sex, gender, and sexuality. Regardless of whether one is examining the general functioning of religion or a specific religious tradition, using a critical gendered lens enables one to understand more about how gender influences religious identity and how religion influences the construction of gender. Especially given the energy religion expends on delimiting acceptable forms of sexuality (virtually every religion views human sexuality as a source of sin), the study of religion is central to understanding the construction of and intersections between sex, gender, and sexuality.

One can argue that religious institutions are gendered/sexed insofar as they tend to assign relatively rigid gender roles according to one's sex; men serve in official positions of power. For example, in Roman Catholic and Eastern Orthodox churches, women cannot be ordained as priests, and the Southern Baptist Convention in 2000 announced that only men could serve as pastors. In Islam, women cannot serve as imams. Even in the more mainline and liberal Christian churches in which women can be ordained, they tend to serve as assistant or associate pastors, not senior pastors. When a woman does ascend to a position of power, it can spark controversy, as demonstrated by the 2006 election of Bishop Katherine Jefferts Schori to lead the U.S. church in the Anglican Communion. Yet, even in those religious traditions with the most stringent restrictions on women's role, challenges arise. In 2003, 7 women in Europe were excommunicated for violating the Catholic ban on ordination, and now 15 U.S. women face excommunication for participating in ordination rituals in 2006. Dr. Amina Wadud faced death threats when she became the first Muslim woman to lead Islam's Jum'ah prayer before a mixed congregation on March 18, 2005, in New York City.

One also should note the struggles of faith communities over the inclusion of homosexuals. As religions structure understandings of sex and gender, they also grapple with understandings of sexuality, of what is and is not acceptable. Many people's condemnation of homosexuality is informed by religious beliefs. Despite many religious traditions' rejection of homosexuality, people of faith struggle to find ways to reconcile their faith and their sexuality. DignityUSA works toward respect and justice for all LGBT persons in the Catholic Church (www.dignityusa.org). Queer Jihad (www.well.com/user/queerjhd/) and Al Fatiha (www.al-fatiha.org) provide locations for lesbian, gay, and queer Muslims to work through issues of homosexuality in Islam. The documentary *Trembling Before G-d* (DuBowski, 2003) portrays the stories of lesbian and gay Hasidic and Orthodox Jews who seek to reconcile their love of faith with their homosexuality.

Even when religious institutions dictate rigid sexualities and gender roles, individuals still find empowerment and fulfillment in their religious traditions. We take seriously the fact that people, particularly people of color, see religion as creatively productive in their lives and as a site of resistance to broader social injustices. Although the institution of religion is important in structuring people's understanding of who they are and where they fit in the universe, religion (perhaps more than any other institution) also highlights how "institutions are constituted and reconstituted by embodied agents" (Martin, 2004, p. 1257). Religion is as much about people's daily practices of religion as it is about scripture and belief systems.

Just as global feminism challenged assumptions about how to study gender/sex, recognition of global religions has challenged the way religion is studied. Intersectionality is now at the center of religion studies. Religion scholar Nancy Frankenberry (1994) highlights how religion is so intertwined with gender and other axes of oppression "that it is no longer possible for philosophers of religion to presume that religion exists as some common universal underlying all particular religions; only particular, culturally variable religions exist, and even the very concept of religion itself needs to be recognized as a modern and Western concept" (para. 9). Just as global understandings make clear that a range of genderings exists, so, too, does a range of religious practices.

To explore these diverse expressions of religion, one can study communication about and of religion in the form of "religious experiences, texts, transcriptions of interviews, personal accounts, rituals, or religious communities," as well as images of divinity and the documents declared definitive by church leaders (Thie, 1994, p. 232). When expansive forms of religious communication are studied, it becomes clear that "religions and divinities are more than a source of violence . . . religions are also a source of resistance, hope, and struggle" (p. 232). Thus, in this chapter we discuss the official documents and creeds of religions as well as the daily practices of religious people.

Interlocking Institutions

Those who hold privilege often are not aware of the way their identities *are* identities. Dominant codes privilege particular races, sexes, and even religions. Chapter 1 outlined the strategic rhetoric of Whiteness whereby, in the United States, those who are White do not think of it as a race or culture (hence the use of the term *White* instead of *Euramerican*), although Whites code Black (African American), (Brown) Mexican American, and (Yellow) Asian American as races and cultures. Much as Whiteness functions as a strategic rhetoric, so can Christianity. In the United States, the holidays celebrated often are Christian; Christmas and Easter are prime examples. Although most Christian students would react extremely negatively if their school decided to hold classes on Christmas Day, they tend to not recognize when classes are scheduled on the high holy days of other religions, such as Yom Kippur and Ramadan. In many ways, Christianity has been institutionalized as the dominant religion in the United States. Given this dominance, it also influences other institutions' constructions of gender.

The dominance of Christianity has been woven into U.S. institutions. From the founding fathers to contemporary presidents, the notion that the United States exists in a special covenant with God has predominated. The founding fathers believed that the new republic was a special experiment watched over by a higher power. In an influential essay, political scientist Robert Bellah (1967) notes that in every major speech by a U.S. president, God is invoked. However, he asks, given the separation of church and state enshrined in the U.S. Constitution, "how is a president justified in using the word *God* at all?" (p. 3). His answer is that church–state separation has not excluded religion from the political sphere. Even though religion is intensely personal, and worship is private, "there are . . . certain common elements of religious orientation that the great majority of Americans share. These have played a crucial role in the development of American institutions and still provide a religious dimension for the whole fabric of American life, including the political sphere" (pp. 3–4). Religion influences U.S. governance and citizenship. Accordingly, even though U.S. citizens often think of themselves as belonging to a secular (as opposed to a religiously fundamentalist) state, the reality is that religious elements infuse U.S. national symbolism and understandings of citizenship.

The way in which religion, gender/sex, and civic identity are interwoven is evident in the reaction of the United States to polygamy. During the 1850s, numerous novels appeared about the dangers of the Mormon practice. However, the public outcry was not just about regulating a religion's practice; it also was about reinforcing the nation's boundaries. In these novels and news stories, the description of Mormon practices "racializes polygamy and its practitioners as not fully white, Christian, or civilized" (Burgett, 2005, p. 90). Religion became intertwined with race because the argument was that those who practice polygamy could not really be White. Criticisms of religious practices expose not only how a society thinks about religion, but also how it understands race, sex, and citizenship.

In contemporary times, the notion that the United States is a special beacon of God-fearing freedom has been invoked to justify a variety of foreign policies (for example, the greatest opprobrium hurled at the leaders of the then-Soviet Union was that they were "godless communists"). Communication scholar John Murphy (2003) outlines the ways in which President George W. Bush's rhetoric concerning the 9/11 attacks incorporated religious forms, references, and passages. Murphy argues that the president's rhetoric presented "[an] interpretation of 9/11 as God's test of his chosen people" and "imbued the struggle against al-Qaeda and for America's soul with religious, even apocalyptic, significance" (p. 625).

Another example of religion intersecting with citizenship is the fight over woman suffrage. Interestingly, women both supported and opposed women's voting rights, and complex arguments concerning gender, sexuality, religion, nationality, and citizenship circulated throughout the controversy. Catholics tended to be antisuffrage and highlighted how the vote would violate the religious admonition that woman's place was in the home. Protestant supporters of suffrage appealed to anti-Catholic sentiments fed by the fear that Catholics as a voting block would overtake Protestants, hence more Protestant women needed suffrage. Finally, Protestant opponents of woman suffrage argued that if the vote was extended to women, Catholics' power as a voting block would be increased, and they deployed the stereotype of Catholicism as effeminate to intensify the feminizing effect of the vote (Palczewski, 2005). For antisuffragists,

> of special concern was the alleged nightmarish march of a female Catholic army descending upon the polls under orders of their priests and bishops. "Cathedrals and ignorance" awaited the future of America. Alarmed by the rise of urban political machines, which, in turn, were fueled by the votes of Irish, Polish, and Italian men, antis feared that the country would suffer greater harm at the hands of "Bridget," "Natacha," or "Maria." (Jablonsky, 1994, p. 45)

The debate about woman suffrage was about more than just whether women as a sex deserved the vote. It also implicated issues of religion, citizenship, culture, immigrant status, and gender, which, perhaps, explains why woman suffrage took so long to be realized.

It's Not About Sex Difference

As with other assessments of gender and sex, many people operate under the fallacious assumption that women and men experience religion differently. In fact, most studies of sex/gender and religion start from the assumption that women are "more religious" than men (Preston, 2003). Like most assumptions about difference, this one does not survive close scrutiny. Leslie J. Francis (1997), a psychology of religion expert, offers an exhaustive review of the English-language literature addressing the supposed differences between women's and men's expression and levels of religiousness.

Nearly every essay about religiosity repeats the stereotype that women are more religious than men, linking religious activity to sex and not to gender identity. The statistical evidence comparing women's and men's religious activity is compelling— but the numbers alone do not explain what the numbers mean. Francis concludes that research that simply assumes a correlation between sex and gender is not persuasive. One's gender orientation is *the* variable that most determines one's level of religiousness. It is more determinative than one's conception of the sex of one's god(s), stereotypical gender role socialization, one's social location, or one's relative comfort with risk taking. Women who tend toward more masculine gender orientations tend to be less religious, and men who are more feminine in their orientations tend to be more religious. Obviously, because of social pressures for women to be feminine, it makes sense that a correlation between sex and religiosity might appear, but one must remember that the intervening variable of gender orientation, not sex, is *the* influential factor. Assuming that differences in religiosity are explained solely by sex would be wrong. A more complex understanding of gender is required, one that explores not just how gender influences religiosity but also how religion structures gender/sex.

Religion Constructs (and Constrains) Gender

Every religion constructs gender in one way or another. Religions speak to the relationships between men and women, and to how to be a good man and a good woman, and rarely are the ways to goodness the same, even though most major religions speak to spiritual equality. The institutional structures of the major religions of the world (Islam, Judaism, Christianity, Buddhism, Taoism, and Confucianism) all have outlined a particular role for women.

For example, on July 31, 2004, the Roman Catholic Church released the "Letter to the Bishops of the Catholic Church on the Collaboration of Men and Women in the Church and in the World" (Ratzinger, 2004). The letter was written by Cardinal Joseph Ratzinger, who on April 19, 2005, would become Pope Benedict XVI. The letter was offered as a definitive statement of men's and women's roles in the Church and the world. The introduction explains that the letter was written because "[the] Church is called today to address certain currents of thought which are often at variance with the authentic advancements of women" (sec. 1), currents that tend to emphasize "conditions of subordination in order to give rise to antagonism" and to deny differences between the sexes (sec. 2).

Sister Joan Chittister, O.S.B. (2004) notes in her response how the letter both empowers and constrains. The letter is progressive in its call for recognition that the institution of work needs to be altered to recognize the demands working mothers face and in its celebration of values traditionally associated with women, values that embrace an orientation toward others. Finally, the letter recognizes that those values can be found in women as well as men.

The letter also constrains. First, it embraces a theory of sex and gender that is most like the biological theories outlined in Chapter 2 and thus adopts a binary understanding of sex. Second, the text posits feminism as an adversary and in the process tends to treat feminism and its theories as a monolithic whole, which the diversity of theories in this text ought to make clear is not an accurate description. Third, the letter conflates sex and gender to the extent that it sees women as the sole repository of feminine values, even as it recognizes that men might be able to participate in those values. Fourth, it circumscribes women's role, consigning it to two sexual locations: a woman is either a mother or a virgin. Finally, even though the letter encourages a form of active collaboration between women and men and seeks to move away from a metaphor of battle as descriptive of the relationship between the sexes, the letter almost exclusively focuses on what women should do and spends little to no time on what men should do. Theology professor Edward Collins Vacek (2005) explains that the letter is "not really about collaboration," for it "scarcely mentions the myriad ways men and women collaborate" (p. 159).

Perhaps the best way to understand the way in which the institutionalized forms of religion have delimited gender roles is to explore two of the dominant religions, Christianity and Islam. The history of antipathy between these two religions (as embodied in the Roman Catholic Crusades to capture the Holy Land from Muslims from the 11th through the 13th centuries) might make one think that they have little in common. However, religious scholars have noted the ways in which these two religions share much when it comes to understanding women's and men's roles.

Finnish religion scholar Elina Vuola (2002) analyzes how Christian and Islamic fundamentalisms share much. She explains that the rise of both forms has been "accompanied by a vigorous promotion and enforcement of gender roles whose explicit intent entails the subordination of women" (p. 175). In particular, she notes how Western Christianity (as represented by the Vatican) and Islam (as represented by some Muslim states) have begun to cooperate on a wide range of issues concerning women's political and social rights, reproductive freedoms, and women's roles in their religious traditions. She finds that "Judaism, Christianity and Islam have more in common in their image of women (and sexuality) than they have differences" (p. 183). Thus, the Vatican and Islamic states have worked together against progressive changes to protect women's human rights on the international and national levels. At the international level, the Vatican has aligned with Muslim nations to attempt to block progressive language on reproductive and sexual rights in the Beijing Platform for Action (Petchesky, 1997).

However, for Vuola, this is not an argument for forsaking religion. Instead, it is an argument for understanding how religion constructs gender and for women and men to play a more conscious role in thinking through religion and how it influences people's understandings of themselves. Religion informs many people's identities. Thus, "women are not going to—nor do they have to—give up their cultural, political and religious traditions simply because they are used against them." (p. 191). Thus, we now explore the ways in which men and women have reappropriated and reinterpreted religions and ethical traditions through their communication practices.

Rereading the History of Women Religious

One of the ways people have attempted to reappropriate religion is to reread its history. In most religions, men have held institutionalized power and hence have been the ones with the authority to interpret key religious texts. However, women have long sought to make clear the central role played by women in religion. Religious communication scholar Helen Sterk (1989) examines the ways women are represented in the Bible. She argues that most (male) religious authorities typically focus on women's limited roles as wives, slaves, or mothers of important men. However, this particular understanding of women's role in the Christian tradition is not an accurate representation of what is in the Bible. In part, translations have created artificial limits for women's roles. For example, *anthropos* was long translated as *man*, rather than as *humanity*, which is more accurate. Additionally, numerous stories in which women play important roles, such as the stories of Rahab, Jael, Deborah, Esther, Mary Magdalene, Martha, Joanna, and Susanna, could be highlighted. However, these more expansive readings of women's roles have been constrained in Christian religious traditions. In turn, these religious traditions then inform the secular roles allowed to women and men.

Sterk's point is *not* that the Bible is sexist but that society's sexism has led to interpretations of the Bible that are sexist insofar as they ignore women's presence. Using a gendered/sexed lens, Sterk argues that women's centrality to the Christian tradition is easy to find in scripture. It also is easy to find in practice.

Within Catholicism, women played a significant role, writing on issues of morality and doctrine. In medieval times, a life in service to the Church was the only option for women who wanted to live a life of the mind. Hildegard of Bingen (1098–1179), a 12th-century German nun, spoke to the life of women in *Scivias,* her major religious work. In the 13th century, Hadewijch, a Flemish mystic, joined the Beguines, a group of devout women who lived "a life of apostolic poverty and contemplation without taking vows as nuns" (Hart in Hadewijch, 1980, p. 3). Catherine of Sienna (1347–1380), an Italian nun of the Dominican order, was one of two women to be granted the title of Doctor of the Roman Catholic Church. Julian of Norwich (1342–1423), an English nun, wrote about the spiritual problems encountered between the soul and God.

Later, Sor Juana Inés de la Cruz (1651–1695), a Mexican nun, was a poet and theological writer. Following the distribution of one of her essays, a bishop chastised her. Her response, *La Respuesta* (1987), is a defense of women's rights to education and culture, presaging the demands of the U.S. first-wave women's movement by almost a century. The writings of these women all demonstrate that despite constraints, women were drawn to religious traditions and found locations of resistance within them.

Religion Constructs Masculinity: Muscular Christianity

As the examples presented thus far illustrate, religion influences how one performs and understands sex, race, gender, and sexuality. Religion circumscribes roles for women, sanctions particular sexualities and sexual practices, and is intertwined with understandings of race. We next emphasize how masculinity and religion are inextricably intertwined.

During the Victorian era, women were to live up to the standard of the "angel in the house," with the "preeminent Angel in the house" being the Virgin Mary (Krueger, 2000, p. 179). The angel ideology was premised on the notion that women's domestic duties were essentially a spiritual calling. In other words, religion was a central component of women's identity as women.

While Christian religions defined women as the angel in the house, they defined men as the strength of the public realm. Scholars who have focused on how gender, sex, and religion intersect have found that "there were distinctive patterns of men's spiritual experience" (Bradstock, Gill, Hogan, & Morgan, 2000, p. 2). This research into *muscular Christianity* explores the way in which Christian religions gendered men with particular forms of masculinity. Muscular Christianity was "defined simply as a Christian commitment to health and manliness" (Putney, 2001, p. 11) premised on the belief that an association existed between "physical strength, religious certainty, and the ability to shape and control the world around oneself"

(Hall, 1994, p. 7). Although its roots go back to the Bible, muscular Christianity did not emerge as a dominant theme until the 1850s, when it appeared as a phrase describing a popular novel of the day, Charles Kingsley's *Two Years Ago* (1857). The concept would emerge in England and quickly travel to the United States.

The push for more muscular forms of religion emerged as a response to the insecurities and fears many men faced during an age in which change overwhelmed them. The United States had just survived the Civil War, women in increasing numbers were working, and the nation was industrializing. As Donald E. Hall (1994) explains in his book on muscular Christianity, "The broad strokes in the discourse of the muscular Christians were reactions to threats posed by a world growing ever more confusing and fragmented.... Muscular Christianity was an attempt to assert control over a world that had seemingly gone mad" (p. 9).

Muscular Christianity not only gendered White, Protestant, native, male U.S. citizens, it also functioned as a location to discipline, through caricature, the bodies of lower-class, Irish, and non-European men. The struggle was not only over how particular male bodies would act in the world but also over "social, national, and religious bodies," for which the particular male body functioned as a metaphor (Hall, 1994, p. 8). Like the female body, the male body is a site for struggle, because it serves "as a paradigm and metaphor for male-dominated culture and society" (p. 6).

The rise of muscular Christianity also can be read as a battle over the gender of the Protestant Church. The muscular Christianity movement sought to make the Church masculine but faced resistance from evangelical Protestant churches who at that point were particularly enamored of feminine iconography such that by the 1850s, they were "channeling much of their energy into praising such stereotypically 'female' traits as nurturance, refinement, and sensitivity" (Putney, 2001, p. 24). Such a focus clashed with the muscular Christians' glorification of such "stereotypically 'male' traits as strength, courage, and endurance" (p. 24).

Muscular Christianity also faced resistance because the Puritan tradition viewed sport as a "sinful diversion" because "exercising one's muscles for no particular end except health struck many Protestants in the mid-nineteenth century as an immoral waste of time" (Putney, 2001, pp. 20, 24). One found salvation through work, and sport was viewed as play. Thus, for U.S. Protestants during the antebellum period, organized sports were anathema. In fact, in his book exploring the rise of muscular Christianity in the United States, Clifford Putney (2001) cites Washington Gladden, who grew up in the 1840s thinking that "if I became a Christian it would be wrong for me to play ball" (p. 20).

Muscular Christianity would find acceptance in the post–Civil War era. During the 1880s and through the 1920s in the United States, a number of factors influenced the willingness to accept muscular Christianity. First, Protestant church leaders as well as secular reformers were worried about the church becoming feminized as women came to outnumber men in church attendance and also began to assume more leadership positions. Second, depopulation of the rural areas and the increasingly urbanized population meant that men could not be assured of physical activity doing farm work. Third, the influx of Catholic immigrants began to threaten the dominance of Protestantism. America's Protestant establishment "entertained fears of well-bred but overeducated weaklings succumbing before muscular immigrant hordes" (Putney, 2001, p. 31). Finally, the emergence of the modern (meaning working) woman worried male church leaders. From 1900 to 1920, the number of women working in white-collar jobs increased threefold (Putney, 2001). (Note: the facts that poor, mostly immigrant women faced sweat-shop conditions and that African American women had been forced to work as slaves seemed not to bother those in power; instead, it was the increasing frequency of *their* women working that seemed to induce panic.) Of course, this period also saw the eventual achievement of woman suffrage. Those who criticized these trends believed that "if gender rules could not be straightened out, and if substitutes (moral and physical), could not be found for life on the farm, chaos loomed. Some spoke of imminent 'race suicide' caused by cessation of marriage by people of the 'right sort'" (Putney, 2001, p. 32). Eventually, progressive-minded Protestant clergy began to embrace the ideal of muscular Christianity, creating bowling leagues in their basements and declaring Sunday sports allowable (Ladd & Mathisen, 1999).

Given this history, it becomes clear that the centrality of sports to the hegemonic U.S. male identity is tied to religion. Muscular Christianity and its secular counter-part of the strenuous life (as advocated by Theodore Roosevelt) would dominate social life at the turn of the 19th century and into the 20th. Even though its promi-nence waned in the years after World War I (1914–1918) because many thought that muscular Christianity had fanned the flames of war, its effects persisted. Even as the movement lost some of its intellectual influence, "paeans to health and manliness continued to emanate both from the mainline churches and from best-selling authors" (Putney, 2001, p. 200). The recent resurgence of muscular Christianity among the Promise Keepers and the Fellowship of Christian Athletes indicates that the connection between religion and masculine identity is not a thing of the past.

Religion as Liberation and Locations of Empowerment in Religion

Although religious appeals have been used to outline strict gender roles, and scriptural grounds have been used to justify women's and minorities' social inequality (see Gaffney, 1990), religion also has long played a significant role in people's liberation. Maria Miller Stewart (1803–1879), the African American woman who was the first woman to speak to mixed-sex audiences, argued that she had been called by God to speak against the evil of slavery. Even though she knew she would face extreme opposition to speaking in public—and she did—she cited her faith in God and her belief that she was doing God's work as authorization for her entry into the public sphere (Sells, 1993).

Spirituality and religion play a central role in much African American women's rhetoric (Pennington, 2003); Sojourner Truth (1797?–1883), Harriet Tubman (1820–1913), and Fannie Lou Hamer (1917–1977) provide archetypal examples.

All of them cited their spirituality as enabling and motivating them to take incredible risks as social activists—respectively, as an abolitionist, a conductor on the underground railroad, and a voting rights activist. Sociologist Patricia Hill Collins (1998) finds, "Spirituality, especially that organized through and sanctioned by Black Christian churches, provides one important way that many African-American women are moved to struggle for justice" (p. 244). For them, the institution of their church provides a location for the development of a powerful spirituality, a spirituality that is "not merely a system of religious beliefs similar to logical systems of ideas" but rather "comprises articles of faith that provide a conceptual framework for living everyday life" (p. 245).

Not only does religion function as a powerful motivating force for individuals, it also functions to create a sense of group worth and community. In the antebellum United States, slaves' singing of spirituals constituted an act of resistance for all slaves, male and female, insofar as the songs "constituted themselves as members of a valued community, as fully human in their desire and ability to create, as chosen for special notice by God, and as capable of acting on their own behalf" (Sanger, 1995, p. 190). During the civil rights movement (1955–1965), the Christian churches attended by African Americans played a vital role in their struggle for employment and voting rights, not only organizationally but also philosophically (Chappell, 2004).

Even as religion motivated those who struggled for civil rights, gender continued to define the roles played by women and men, consigning women to serve "invisible" (though essential) leadership roles in the movement at the grassroots level, where they were a vital bridge between the movement and potential constituents (McNair Barnett, 1993; Robnett, 1996).

In pointing out the role religion played for African Americans, one should not infer that it played no role for Whites. In fact, White women who became involved in the civil rights movement seemed to do so not as a result of direct experiences of oppression (such as those inflicted on African Americans) but because of feelings of empathy informed by their religious beliefs (Irons, 1998).

Ultimately, those who have studied the role of religion in the civil rights movement have concluded that "one cannot understand Black women's ability to cope, or their activity to ensure liberation and empowerment, without addressing their religious and spiritual heritages, beliefs, and practices" (Klassen, 2003, para. 11). Thus, when studying the public rhetoric, organizational relations, and interpersonal expressions of African American women activists, it is important to identify those places in which religion offers a motivation and basis from which to resist social injustice.

Given religion's central role as a cultural influence, it is important to explore the role religion plays in maintaining cultural identity in the face of colonization. With the example of slavery, the Christianity of their captors was forced on the slaves, but they were able to weave their own traditions into it and use it as a force for cultural cohesion. However, not only can one adapt to an imposed religion, one also can resist its imposition.

In Chapter 4, we briefly referenced Islamic veiling practices as a form of nonverbal resistance. We now expand upon the example, highlighting the complex religious and secular significance of the veil, the fact that the veil is used by men and women as well as by Christians and Muslims, and how the veil has been misread by the West. We end this chapter with a discussion of the veil because it provides an excellent example of how religion is a site of resistance and emancipation but also can be used as a justification for subordination.

Veiling practices provide a paradigmatic example of a nonverbal form: artifacts. Fadwa El Guindi (1999), an anthropologist who revolutionized the study of covering practices, explains that "veiling is . . . a language that communicates social and cultural messages" (p. xii). A critical gendered lens, attentive to issues of intersectionality and colonialism, embraces the role of the world traveler (rather than the arrogant perceiver) and can avoid the error of many Western critics who view the veil as "a sign of women's backwardness, subordination, and oppression" (p. 3). World travelers recognize (1) the complexity of cultural practices, (2) the way in which their own cultures veil (or impose a dress code), and (3) that many Islamic women wear the veil as a form of empowerment.

First, a world traveler should note how the term *veil* is problematic. It is the lone word English-speaking peoples use to describe a vast range of clothing options. El Guindi (1999) explains that Arabic has no single linguistic referent for the veil. Because the practice differs between groups, cultures, and times, multiple words exist: "*burqu', 'abayah, tarhah, burnus, jilbab, jellabah, hayik, milayah, gallabiyyah, dishdasha, gargush, gina', mungub, lithma, yashmik, habarah, izer*" (p. 7). Each type can be differentiated by whether it is a face cover, a head cover, or a body cover. This linguistic subtlety contrasts to the "indiscriminate, monolithic, and ambiguous" Western term *veil* (p. 7). El Guindi reminds analysts that each form of covering reveals, conceals, and communicates differently.

Within Arabic, the multiple terms distinguish between these subtle differences, whereas in English the single term obscures the complexity of body-covering practices. In Afghanistan, women (were forced to under the Taliban, but now might choose to) cover their bodies and faces with the *burqu'*; in Iran women (choose to, but are sometimes forced to) wear the *chador*, which covers the body but leaves the face free; and women from Indonesia choose to wear the *hijab* (which covers the hair and neck but leaves the face revealed) even when living in the United States because it is part of their identities. Despite this complexity, those in the West obsessively critique the harem (another misunderstood concept), polygamy, and the veil, all of which have been held to be "synonymous with female weakness and oppression" (p. 10).

What might explain the West's misreading of the veil? In reality, the veil has a longer history in Christian traditions (where it is associated with living secluded from worldly life and sex) than in Islam. Most images of the Virgin Mary show her wearing a headscarf much like a *hijab*, and Catholic women were required to wear head coverings to church until the 1960s. The narrow interpretation of Islamic covering practices may be more informed by Christianity's interpretation of the practice than by the meaning of the Islamic practice.

Although the practice of veiling has religious connections, the links are not unique to Islam (many Christians veil their faces during wedding ceremonies), and not all practices have religious foundations. At the time of Islam's rise in the 7th century, veiling was already practiced by many different cultures in the Eastern Mediterranean and the Middle East (Cichocki, 2004). Even though the *burqu'*, due to media coverage of the Taliban in Afghanistan, is perceived to be an expression of Islam, it actually is part of a secular tradition (El Guindi, 2005a, p. 262). It was imposed not as part of religious expression (given that face coverings are prohibited by Islam in the most sacred spaces of worship and during pilgrimages to Mecca) but as part of a culture in a particular country at a particular time.

Additionally, body covering practices are embraced by women and men. The contemporary dress code for Muslim men and women is to "wear full-length gallabiyyas (jilbab in standard Arabic), loose fitting to conceal body contours, in solid austere colors made of opaque fabric. They lower their gaze in cross-sex public interaction and refrain from body or dress decoration or colors that draw attention to their bodies" (El Guindi, 2005b, "The Dress," para. 1). Researchers who examine only women's clothing practices fail to notice that the standards of dress expected of women *and* men call for a de-emphasis of the body. It would be unfair to read dress standards calling for head and body coverings as evidence of women's oppression. This becomes even more evident when women's political uses of the veil are recognized.

Veiling did not take on its overt political dimensions until the 19th century, "when European powers justified the colonial project by claiming to rescue Muslim women from the oppression of savage faith, most readily visible in the practices of veiling and seclusion" (Cichoki, 2004, p. 51). Interestingly, at the same time that colonial powers were seeking to save Muslim women, no one was calling for the rescue of Catholic nuns, who also wore veils (in the form of the habit) and lived in the seclusion of their convents. As colonized nations began to fight against colonial powers, veils became a form of resistance. Women donned the veil to protest Westernization and modernization's pressure on women to adopt revealing clothing.

In 1936, Iran's Shah Reza Pahlavi's embrace of Westernization included banning women from wearing the *chador*. His impetus for this move was his belief that women served best as decorative accessories to men. In response, even women who considered themselves modern began wearing the *chador* to protest the Shah's regime. When the Shah's son was eventually overthrown in 1979, the Ayotollah Khomeini then required women to wear the *chador,* causing many women who had worn it as a form of resistance now to protest against it. The garment is not the problem; the mandate to wear it or not to wear it is the problem. The veil is "a complex symbol: female emancipation can be denoted by either wearing it or removing it; the veil can acquire both secular and religious meaning in that it either denotes resistance to colonization, or ties with the Islamic tradition" (Cichoki, 2004, p. 49).

Egypt presents a similar pattern. In mid-1970s Cairo, young, urban, female college students began veiling themselves from head to toe in contrast to the more Western forms of dress favored by their parents. As Islamic movements have grown, "dress has played a pivotal symbolic, ritual and political role in this dynamic phenomenon. The new vocabulary and dress style embodies a moral/behavioral code. Islam has struggled to position itself vis-a-vis the Islamic veil" (El Guindi, 2005b, "The veil," para. 2). Quite simply, the "Islamizing of life politics and resistance" as represented by young women's wearing of veils "is directly related to the colonial/imperial assault on Arabs and Muslims" (para. 2). Women veiled as a way to renew traditional cultural beliefs in reserve and restraint and as a response to pressures from Western materialism, consumerism, and commercialism. Even though the Egyptian government tried to resist women's move to veil (universities banned veils), courts eventually threw out the prohibitions.

Given the empowering role religion has played for women of color and third-world women, it makes sense that "those who most understand religion and spirituality as relevant to feminist scholarship tend to be women of color and those engaged in postcolonial studies" (Klassen, 2003, para. 13). Our point in providing so much detail on veiling practices is to make clear how the practices of non-Western cultures often are misread. El Guindi (2005b) highlights the missteps those interested in gender, sex, and religion should avoid. When Christian people filter their understanding of a non-Christian culture through their own religious tradition, "efforts to understand the Middle East have resulted in distorted perspectives about Islamic constructions of gender, space, and sexuality" ("Two Notions of Gender," para. 1). Western European society's understanding of the relationship between the domestic (private) and the public is distinct from Arab and Islamic society's understanding. The West's understanding of piety as separate from worldliness and sexuality results in a focus on seclusion and virginity, missing the nuances of Islamic conceptions of space and privacy as they pertain to veiling.

In case you think misreadings of the veil have no effect, we end with a discussion of how Western misinterpretations of non-Western traditions have real effects. Understanding the complex ways in which gender/sex and religion intersect is important. Communication studies scholars Kevin Ayotte and Mary Husain (2005) demonstrate why it is even more important to make sure that the presuppositions of one religious tradition are not imposed on other traditions' practices. They analyze how the *burqu'* was used in portrayals of Afghan women to present them as slaves in need of rescue by the West. They track how "the image of the Afghan woman shrouded in the burqa has played a leading role in various public arguments seeking to justify U.S. military intervention in Afghanistan following the 9/11 attacks" (p. 113). Prior to September 11, President Bush never commented on the repressive conditions under which Afghan women lived. However, after September 11, the administration "launched a new initiative to publicize the brutal treatment of Afghan women and girls by the Taliban regime. Events include meetings with women leaders, a Saturday radio address by First Lady Laura Bush, and release of a U.S. State Department report on gender apartheid by Secretary of State Colin

Powell" ("Bush Administration," 2001). Two official statements were made by Bush, including his December 12, 2001, remarks on signing the Afghan Women and Children Relief Act of 2001. In 2002, Bush included longer commentary about Afghan women in four separate statements (G. Bush, 2001–2002).

Administration comments and media coverage provided a justification for military intervention in Afghanistan. Ayotte and Husain explain that "collapsing differences among Muslim women through the use of the burqa as a generalized symbol of female oppression performs a colonizing function" and hence justifies a military engagement in Afghanistan (p. 118). Unfortunately, such a justification may have resulted in an engagement that did more harm to those it was meant to help. First, demonization of the *burqu'* diverts attention from the fact that the garment was mandated. The issue is not the *burqu'*, but the lack of freedom of choice. Second, the demonization of the *burqu'* denies the possibility that women might choose to wear it. The result is that many U.S. citizens now believe that because Afghan women are unveiled, they are free. This ignores how Afghan women continue to face enormous structural and physical violence.

Conclusion

Religious institutions construct the gender of their own members through doctrinal declarations, historical narratives, and intersections with other dominant institutions. Religion informs how people understand *man* and *woman*, delimits acceptable sexual practices, and is inextricably linked with race and nationality. Religion also informs people's understandings of the gender of those of other faiths through misreadings of verbal and nonverbal practices such as veiling. A gendered lens attentive to issues of intersectionality and informed by a world traveler ethic can offer a nuanced understanding of religious communication.

Even as religion constructs, and in the process constrains expression of, people's sex, gender, and sexuality, it also provides a location from which people can engage in resistance. Religion is not solely an institution of constraint; it empowers. In religion's celebration of grace and the inherent worth of humanity, it reassures those whose humanity has been denied by others that they are blessed. The complexity of religion makes clear why continued scholarship on the intersections of religion, sex, gender, sexuality, race, and nationality are warranted.

CHAPTER 11

Media

Media are ubiquitous in contemporary U.S. society: prints, paintings, television, movies, radio, newspapers, comics, comix, novels, zines, magazines, CDs, podcasting, and the Internet, to name just a few. Note that our list of media includes forms that fall outside the scope of commercial mass media and popular culture. Also note that we talk about plural *media* and avoid the phrase *the media*. Media are not a monolith; no such thing as "the media" operates as a single, unified, controlling entity. Instead, media compose a complex set of production and consumption practices. Thus, the gender representations found in one medium can respond to gender representations in another. For example, the Guerrilla Girls zap actions discussed in Chapter 4 use the pop-art medium of posters to criticize the absence of women from the high culture medium of major New York art museums and galleries (Demo, 2000).

We intentionally use an expansive understanding of media to counter a class bias. Until Herbert J. Gans's landmark *Popular Culture and High Culture* (rev. ed. 1999) was published in 1974, mass media and popular culture products were not treated as possessing significance and seriousness equal to that of high culture. Gans's book established that the distinction between mass culture and high culture was itself a cultural production. Yet, the distinction between media (as low or popular culture) and art (as high and "real" culture) persists. This distinction is embedded in a class bias based on the distinctions between high art typically accessible only to the wealthy (e.g., Renaissance paintings and literary novels) and pop art (e.g., pinup posters and Harlequin romances). We mention all forms of media because *all* media communicate understandings of gender, and gender influences all forms of mediated communication.

Although media contain conflicting discourses, it is useful to recognize the existence of *culture industries* (Horkheimer & Adorno, 1972) to draw attention to the way popular culture mirrors industrial factory processes, creating standardized goods for consumption. The media outlets that produce, sponsor, display, and distribute cultural goods and services are most recently typified by increasing commercialization and concentration of ownership (Brooker, 2003). Although no singular message is produced by culture industries, it is possible to identify dominant messages as well as ways in which culture industries co-opt and tame the oppositional messages of such noncommercial media as zines, indie music, slam poetry, and performance art.

As exciting as media studies are, they also present difficulties for textbook writers. We want to explicitly address these difficulties. First, it is particularly difficult to keep examples fresh; media products are ephemeral. Shows, actors, and musicians that are popular one year are not the next. Many books written in the early 2000s focus on Britney Spears, whose record-breaking sales and pop icon status made her worthy of study. Now, she is more often the butt of jokes. Accordingly, we recognize that many of our examples may be obsolete by the time you read this book. We will try to be as current as possible, knowing, as Heidi Klum explains to contestants on Bravo's *Project Runway,* "You're either in or you're out."

Second, for every example that illustrates a point, you are likely to think of a counterexample—demonstrating one of the interesting features that exists across media and within a particular medium: Popular culture and its media of transmission present "inescapable levels of *contradiction*" (Gauntlett, 2002, p. 255). This is unsurprising given that contradiction is one of the characteristics of institutions (Martin, 2004). It is these contradictions that temper the power of media to exert absolute control over gender identities. Like other institutions, even as media reiterate norms concerning gender, media also enable people to work the weaknesses in the norms and challenge common assumptions. English professor Sherrie A. Inness (2004) notes that "action chick" characters—such as Lara Croft of *Lara Croft, Tomb Raider;* Buffy of *Buffy the Vampire Slayer;* Xena of *Xena: Warrior Princess;* Aeryn Sun of *Farscape;* and (we would add) Zoe Washburne of *Firefly*— "can be rooted in stereotyped female roles but can simultaneously challenge such images" (p. 6). Despite these contradictions within and across media forms, dominant messages do emerge that support hegemonic constructions of gender.

Finally, like every institution, media are far too complex to cover adequately in a single chapter. A variety of forms and content exists, as well as different economic types, including mass advertising communication and specialized communication that may be noncommercial or subsidized (Budd, Entman, & Steinman, 1990). An impressive range of scholarship exists on gender across the variety of mediated texts. This chapter provides a mere taste of this scholarship.

Why all this scholarship, particularly on visual media? Mitchell Stephens (1998), in *The Rise of the Image, the Fall of the Word,* argues that the most recent shift in communication form, particularly in more economically privileged countries, is from the word to the image, such that "most of the world's inhabitants are now devoting about half their leisure time to an activity that did not exist two generations ago"—watching television (p. 7). By the late 1980s, 98% of homes in the United States had at least one television. This "video revolution" is the "third major communications revolution, and the disruptions occasioned by the first two—writing and print—are surprisingly similar to those we are experiencing now" (p. 11). The ubiquity of mediated images from television, movies, and music videos "are perhaps the most powerful familiarizing influences shaping our contemporary society" (Westerfelhaus & Brookey, 2004, p. 305). Media scholars believe that just as religion, and then science, outlined how people should behave and should be, "mass entertainment now performs a similar normative role in our media-saturated society" by providing myths, or recurrent story structures, through which human beings understand who they are and where they fit in a social order (p. 305). Given the explosion of visual media, this chapter primarily focuses on television, movies, and magazines.

Initially, we explore theories explaining media's institutional power and identify a middle ground between the undue pessimism of controlling media effects and the undue optimism of absolute individual agency. Once we've provided an understanding of media as an institution, we highlight some of the ways media intersect with other institutions, as well as ways in which studies of media and gender make clear the inadequacy of sex differences as an explanation. We then examine how media construct gender through content and audience positioning. We end with an examination of the simultaneously liberatory and constraining nature of media presentations.

Media as a Social Institution

It might seem odd to approach media as an institution: How can television signals, movie projections, or radio waves be an institution? In part, people's reluctance to consider media an institution is because of its relative youth, especially electronic media's. Although most institutions have long histories, "the mass media institution is a recent creation" (Martin, 2004, p. 1258). We approach media as an institution to make clear that to focus on a particular broadcast or single medium is inadequate. Media share conventions regarding construction of content and construction of audience. Additionally, media are one of the primary mechanisms that reiterate gender while also providing locations in which resistance can occur, in both construction and reception. However, even as we discuss the possibility of oppositional readings of media messages, we emphasize that such readings are not equally available to all audiences and that when they are available, they are not readily transformed into counterhegemonic politics. One reason is the economics of media.

Media Economics

Studying media as an institution directs attention to the economics of media production and programming. Media messages are not simply artifacts created for art's sake; economic processes and institutional patterns govern them. Television provides the clearest example with which to understand the relationship between economics and content. With every commercial break and overt product placement, one is reminded that "commercial television is first an economic medium" (Budd et al., 1990, p. 172). Its very structure makes this clear: "Ads that sell commodities . . . *to* audiences are part of a system in which media corporations sell audiences *as* commodities to advertisers" (p. 172).

Once one recognizes the role of economics, it becomes clear that "television programming's ideological role is not incidental to its status as a commodity but, rather, is thoroughly implicated in it" (Dow, 1996, p. xix). Because shows are crafted to appeal to a particular market—one that can spend money—"mass mediated texts might be viewed . . . not as giving the populace what they want but as compromises that give the relatively well-to-do more of what they want" (Condit, 1989, p. 110). Class matters. *The OC, One Tree Hill, Everwood,* and *Smallville* all portray well-to-do families in which the teens have ample spending money. *America's Next Top Model* and *Project Runway* submerge viewers in a fashion industry that dictates that style must change from season to season and year to year, even when there is no reason for change except the economic need to maintain and increase consumer demand for clothes. Even *TV Guide* now includes a multipage section, "Radar: Stuff We Can't Live Without," which tells viewers where they can buy items seen on TV.

Media and Power

Given that the United States is a consumer culture, understanding media is one way to understand how power, an element of media as an institution, manifests itself. As Martin (2004) notes, "Institutions are organized in accord with and permeated by power," insofar as they both constrain and facilitate behavior by members of a society in which the institution exists (p. 1258). Media exert power over how people do gender. Although it is true that a movie is a movie and an advertisement is an advertisement, neither is ever *just* a movie, or *just* an advertisement. These media forms also always influence social norms concerning gender, race, class, nationality, and all the other ingredients that constitute identity, for they provide models of what it is to be feminine or masculine, and encourage people to buy products that will make them more so.

Female beauty is one example of media power over gender. Beauty norms change, and a driving force in that change is media representations of beauty, from Renaissance paintings to computer-generated images of the perfect thigh in Christian Dior's advertisements for cellulite control (Bordo, 1997) or the perfect woman in the digitally idealized Lara Croft (Herbst, 2004). Although "many audiences in the United States resist the idea that images have an ideological intent" (hooks, 1992, p. 5), the idea that media are about more than just entertainment, information transmission, or making money is an accepted foundation of media research. Communication scholar Bonnie Dow's (1996) insight about television is true of all media forms; they are "simultaneously, a commodity, an art form, and an important ideological forum for public discourse about social issues and social change" (p. xi).

Rigorous academic analysis of media's ideological function might seem to condemn or destroy the pleasure one feels when watching a movie or reading a lifestyle magazine. That is not our goal. Instead, it is to encourage you to develop critical consciousness about media even as you take pleasure from it, and to use that critical consciousness as the basis for political action. Philosophy professor Susan Bordo (1997) points out, "Cultural criticism clears a space in which we can stand back and survey a scene that we are normally engaged in living in, not thinking about" (p. 14). Media criticism is not about dismissing people's personal choices and pleasures; it is about "preserving consciousness of the larger context in which our personal choices occur, so that we will be better informed about their potential consequences, for ourselves as well as for others" (p. 16). As noted in the chapters on work and family, if people continually attribute power differentials between people to simple individual choice, they lose the ability to analyze, challenge, and change institutionalized power.

Media and Hegemony

The concept of *hegemony* introduced in Chapter 1 is particularly useful when discussing media power. Media, as an institution of civil society, shape the cognitive structures through which people perceive and evaluate social reality (Dow, 1996). However, this hegemonic system is not all powerful. It must be maintained, repeated, reinforced, and modified in order to respond to and overcome the forms that oppose it. Thus, "Hegemony, rather than assuming an all powerful, closed text, presumes the possibility of resistance and opposition" (p. 14). Media, as a central institution of civil society, maintain hegemonic understandings of gender even as they create gaps and fissures in representations of gender. For instance, although a few noteworthy examples of masculine women appear in popular TV shows (e.g., ambitious, callous, self-centered Cristina Yang on *Grey's Anatomy*) and feminine men (e.g., *Grey's* gentle, empathetic, kind George O'Malley), the vast majority of characters tend to abide by traditional gender/sex expectations. Note also, in these examples, that although the women may *act* masculine, they still meet feminine standards of attractiveness, and although the men may *act* feminine, they still meet masculine standards of attractiveness. Standards of attractiveness tend to be violated only when a character is *bad;* their physical ugliness is used to match their ugliness of character, whether it is in the form of the witches in fairy tales or Jason in the *Friday the 13th* movies.

Most of the debate about media is about the precise scope of their power. One side, represented by the work of Theodor Adorno (1991) and the Frankfurt School, argues that mass media have considerable power (or a hegemonic hold) over people as they "churn out products which keep the audience blandly entertained, but passive, helping to maintain the status quo by encouraging conformity and diminishing the scope of resistance" (Gauntlett, 2002, p. 41). Media create false consciousness, making people believe they exert control over what they view (and what they think about what they view) when in reality they have little or no control. The other side, represented by the work of John Fiske (1987) and cultural studies, argues that people do not consume media offerings mindlessly but instead actively and creatively engage with them, "using 'guerilla' tactics to reinterpret media texts to suit their own purposes" (Gauntlett, 2002, p. 41). These varied purposes are possible because, Fiske believes, media message are *polysemous,* or open to a range of different interpretations at different times. Meaning is not determined by the media providers but created individually by each person.

The best explanation of media power lies somewhere between these two extremes. Clearly, pervasive media messages have an effect, particularly in the consumerist society in the United States. However, it also is clear that people can resist media influence—or even turn it around—if they are critical media consumers. Thus, it would be counterproductive for us to side exclusively with the media hegemony side of the debate if we want to enable you to be creative and productive contributors to the public discourse in which media participate. Like British media scholar David Gauntlett, we believe that "it seems preferable to assume that people are thoughtful and creative beings, in control of their own lives—not least of all because that is how most people surely see themselves" (p. 111). However, it also is true that people's level of thoughtfulness and creativity is influenced by their education (formal and otherwise). Thus, one should (1) examine how powerful or effective oppositional responses are, compared to the power of hegemonic messages; (2) try to discern the roles media play in facilitating oppositional readings (Dow, 1996); and (3) explore what we, as textbook authors, and you, as students, can do to facilitate critical abilities.

Media Polyvalence and Oppositional Readings

Fiske may be correct that textual polysemy exists, but the range and richness of the possible meanings depend on the ability of audiences to produce them. Additionally, media texts cannot be all things to all people, because media foreground some interpretations as preferred. Accordingly, Celeste Condit (1989) argues that instead of the concept of polysemy (having a multitude of meanings), researchers should use *polyvalence* (having a multitude of valuations): "Polyvalence occurs when audience members share understandings of the denotations of a text but disagree about the valuation of these denotations to such a degree that they produce notably different interpretations" (p. 106).

Oppositional interpretations of mainstream media texts should be understood in their social contexts, and some contexts provide more opportunities and training in resistant readings. Different people at any given time also have different resources available for resistance and must expend more or less effort to construct resistant readings. It is easy to "acquire the codes necessary for preferred readings"; however, "the acquisition of codes for negotiated or oppositional readings is more difficult and less common" (Dow, 1996, p. 13), and transforming those readings into political action is the most difficult and least common of all. Because the acquisition of such codes requires work, one consequence is "the tendency of such burdens to silence viewers" (Condit, 1989, p. 109).

Our goal is to make clear the rhetorical context of mediated messages. Condit (1989) explains that "mass media research should replace totalized theories of polysemy and audience power with interactive theories that assess audience reactions as part of the full communication process occurring in particular rhetorical configurations" (p. 104). Mediated messages do not occur in a vacuum but in a particular place, at a particular time, and to particular audiences. A rhetorical approach reminds us that "audiences are not free to make meanings at will from mass mediated texts" because "the ability of audiences to shape their own readings . . . is constrained by a variety of factors in any given rhetorical situation," including "access to oppositional codes . . . the repertoire of available texts," and the historical context (pp. 103–104). Critical tools, such as a gendered lens, must be provided if audiences are to create oppositional readings. This speaks to one of the criticisms of many cultural studies approaches. Some critics who celebrate the ability of audiences to create oppositional readings often forget that if an audience lacks a critical framework, a critical reading is less likely (Budd et al., 1990). Although Gauntlett is correct that people are thoughtful and creative, it also is true that not all people "are equally skilled in responding to persuasive messages with countermessages" (Condit, 1989, p. 111). Even though people *could* view media in different ways, they tend to produce similar readings, and these similarities reveal things about identity, gender identity included.

Interlocking Institutions

Of all the institutions that intersect, media may be the most interconnected. Not only are media an example of an institution, but they also are the mechanisms by which other institutions are represented and constructed, insofar as television participates in "interpreting social change and managing cultural beliefs" (Dow, 1996, p. xv). For example, representations of family distributed by media inform each person's understanding of the meaning and behavior of family, whether the representations are in the form of "family values" sound bites from politicians (Cloud, 1998; Smith, 1995) or in the form of the idealized family life of the Camdens on WB's *7th Heaven* or the McNamaras' dysfunctional family life on FX's *Nip/Tuck*.

Media interact with the institution of gender as they provide mechanisms through which representations of work, family, education, and religion are communicated. However, these representations are not necessarily straightforward. Because "media messages are diverse, diffuse and contradictory," they do not enter unfiltered into people's worldviews; instead, they are "*resources* which individuals use to think through their sense of self and modes of expression" (Gauntlett, 2002, p. 256). As resources, media messages of gender both constrain and enable, modeling for people often-unobtainable ideals of attractiveness while also expanding people's limited understandings of their locations in the world. Perceptions of masculinity and femininity change across time, and records of those changes are found in media representations that both push and resist those changes.

It's Not About Sex Difference

Although much criticism of media has focused on their creation of an unattainable standard of beauty for women, this beauty norm does not affect all women identically, and men are beginning to grapple with similar pressures for the ideal body.

Differences Among Women

Even though many commentators focus on media representations of femininity as the primary place in which women are socialized to body image ideals, "the degree to which this message is internalized varies depending on factors such as race, nationality, and sexual orientation" (Harvey, 2005, p. 796). Differences in reception to media messages exist across races and within sexes. However, even though images may be understood as unobtainable and hence are less powerful, they still influence self-perception (Spurgas, 2005). Although much has been made of the lower incidence of anorexia in communities of color, its incidence is on the rise, in part because mediated images of beauty submerge racial and ethnic differences between bodies such that all women are held to a single standard attainable not only by very few women but perhaps not by anyone, considering the degree of airbrushing used in magazine images (Bordo, 1997).

Although all women may be held to beauty standards, the standard is not the same for all women. Intercultural media researchers Katherine Frith, Ping Shaw, and Hong Cheng (2005) examine how beauty is constructed in magazine advertising. Using cross-cultural analysis, they compared advertisements in magazines published in Singapore, Taiwan, and the United States. Overall, magazines in Taiwan and Singapore were dominated by ads for facial beauty products, and U.S. ads focused on clothing. They also found that women and their bodies were more sexualized in the U.S. advertisements than in the Asian advertisements. They concluded that the charge that advertising presents women as sex objects is not a universal phenomenon. Interestingly, though, when an advertisement appearing in an Asian magazine did sexualize a woman, the model usually appeared Caucasian.

Similarities Between Women and Men

Body image pressure does not come from people of another sex and the media they peruse but from the media targeted at people of that sex. As noted in Chapter 4, women tend to overestimate the degree of thinness men find attractive. Why? One explanation is that the ideal of extreme thinness is most prominent in magazines targeting women, not in men's magazines. Similarly, men tend to overestimate the degree of muscularity attractive to women. Why? Same dynamic:

"The ideal male body marketed to men is more muscular than the ideal male body marketed to women" (Frederick, Fessler, & Haselton, 2005, p. 81).

Men are increasingly influenced by body image aspirations; like women's, men's body norms have changed across time (Bordo, 1999). As Gauntlett (2002) demonstrates in his analysis of magazines targeted at men, "There is general agreement . . . that this is not a particularly stable time for the 'male identity'" (p. 9). Even though male identity may be in flux, this does not mean that a hegemonic masculinity does not exist.

Media representations are one location where hegemonic masculinity is identifiable, particularly in relation to sports coverage. In his analysis of baseball star Nolan Ryan, Nick Trujillo (1991) explores five characteristics of a *U.S. hegemonic masculinity* (a masculinity we would argue is actually a White U.S. hegemonic masculinity) contained in mediated communication: (1) It defines power in terms of physical force and control; (2) it is defined through occupational achievement; (3) it is represented in terms of familial patriarchy, in which the man is the breadwinner; (4) it is symbolized by the frontiersman and the outdoorsman; and (5) it is heterosexually defined. But remember that although this masculinity may be hegemonic, it does not deny the existence of nonhegemomic forms. For example, hip-hop offers forms of Black masculinity to which even some Whites aspire (H. Gray, 1995; Smith, 2002), and some critics argue that contemporary media represent masculinity as part of ornamental culture once reserved for femininity (Faludi, 1999).

Media representations of model men are important because they present an image to which other men can aspire. In relation to men and media, media scholar Robert Hanke (1998) explains that "hegemonic masculinity is won not only through coercion but through consent, even though there is never complete consensus" (p. 190). People *want* to participate in the socially sanctioned and idealized notions of masculinity and femininity. During Michael Jordan's heyday as a professional athlete, men *wanted* to "be like Mike." Now, they want to be like Brad, Tiger, Jude, and Sean.

Media Construct (and Constrain) Gender

In this section, we first consider media content and effects analysis, examining the relative visibility of sexes and races in media programming, and review studies exploring the effect of exposure to media images of sex, sexuality, violence, and gender. We then turn to ways in which media not only construct gender representations but also construct audiences' genders.

Media Content and Media Effects

The bulk of research on media has focused on the product: the content of media. Media content analysis attempts to quantify what is in mediated products. This research may count the relative number of women and men visible in television programming, the amount of violence in children's programming, or the increasing number of sexually explicit acts in prime time. Media effects studies attempt to quantify the effects of these numbers: whether the relative absence of women influences perceptions of women's credibility, whether violence in cartoons leads to violent acts by children, or whether sexually explicit materials increase the proclivity of some men to rape. Such research is incomplete. It often is premised on the assumption that the audience is monolithic and plays a passive receiver role. However, this research still is worthy of consideration because such analyses are politically powerful. Identification of various problematic media representations is one way to start the conversation about the role of media in contemporary society.

WOMEN, MEN, AND VIOLENCE IN MEDIA

Women and minorities (and especially women of color) are underrepresented in U.S. media. In the news arena, on Sunday morning public affairs shows, women represent only 14% of the guests. At the major TV networks (ABC, NBC, CBS) women reported just 25% of the stories in 2004. In the entertainment arena, during the 2004–2005 prime-time season, 39% of the characters were women, and 61% were men (a drop of 2% for women from the previous year). The women tended to be younger than the men, and 77% of them appeared White (Everitt, 2005; Gibbons, 2005). The situation is not any better globally (Shivdas, 2000).

Others have explored the way women are portrayed when they are present. The Media Education Foundation's video *Dreamworlds II* (Jhally, 1995) educates viewers about sexual imagery in music videos, and the video *Killing Us Softly 3* (Kilbourne & Jhally, 2000) focuses on advertising's images of women. Women's and minorities' absence in media, and presentations of women as sex objects, may create the perception that they are not agents of action, capable of commenting on and acting in the world.

Violence in children's programming also is a significant concern. The National Cable Television Association funded the $3.5-million, three-year National Television Violence Study to assess the nature (not just the number) of violent scenes in children's programming (Shifrin, 1998). The Parents Television Council (Fyee, 2006) studies and condemns the prevalence of violence in children's programming, noting an average of 7.86 violence incidents per hour (as compared to 4.71 instances per hour found in adult-targeted prime-time programming). Such research presumes that watching violence can lead individuals to behave in violent ways. Although the PTC study notes that other research has demonstrated the possibility of such a link, their study does not provide evidence of such a link in the programs reviewed.

Media content analyses imply that because media has a particular content, a particular effect follows. Media effects research does not take this for granted but instead seeks to demonstrate the cause–effect relationship. Most effects research focuses on the effects of media violence, sexual content, and minority stereotyping (Hendriks, 2002). More than 1,000 studies have established a relationship between television violence and aggressive behavior in children (Shifrin, 1998). Communication research demonstrates that exposure to violent media is directly related to violent and risky behavior and that those who identify as more masculine like violent movies more than those who identify as more feminine (Greene & Krcmar, 2005). Social scientists Neil M. Malamuth and Edward Donnerstein (1984) research the effects of viewing pornography on men's willingness to commit rape.

More recently, health communication researcher Alexandra Hendriks (2002) has called for a broadening of media effects research to study the effects of media on body image. Although much has been written assuming a connection between media images of women's bodies and women's body images, media effects research has not been conducted explicitly to prove or disprove a connection. L. Monique Ward (2005) similarly has called for increased attention to media's influence on children's and adolescents' beliefs about gender, race, sexuality, and themselves. Quite simply, the medium of television constructs gender as it provides young people with ideas about what is normative and expected (Ward & Rivadeneyra, 1999). The effect of this norming deserves further exploration.

All these studies, even though they come from different political and methodological backgrounds, share a few things. First, they suggest that media are best understood through a study of their representations and hence tend to ignore (to varying degrees) the process of production and the role of the audience. Second, they tend to treat the audience as passive and universal; they assume that all audiences respond to images similarly and are not capable of counterhegemonic readings of media images. Third, they assume that one can distinguish between good and bad representations; they tend not to recognize that representations are contradictory (e.g., an image can be sexually liberating and sexually objectifying at the same time).

Although the explanation of media function is incomplete in this approach, the advocates who ascribe to it are correct about one thing. Media *do* influence people's beliefs and behaviors. Media representations of violence are *one* of the ways gendered violence is normalized in U.S. culture; media images of hegemonic masculinity present violence as the answer to problems: If someone kills a man's family, his solution is to kill them even more violently, as in *Mad Max* (1979), *The Patriot* (2000), or *The Punisher* (2004). Media representations are *one* of the influences on body image; the incredible shrinking celebrities Nicole Richie, Lindsey Lohan, and Hillary Duff are but one manifestation. Although early content and effects analysis tended to simplify the relationship, more recent work analyzing media content attends to the interactions of social context, economics, and audiences.

MEDIA DEPICTIONS OF RAPE

To understand the subtle and often difficult-to-trace effects of media constructions of gender/sex, we offer a summary of some exemplary research on media representations of rape. Such representations not only provide insight into how women are gendered and raced as deserving or undeserving victims but also into how men are gendered and raced as perpetrators or saviors. The studies recognize that media representations interact with broader social contexts, which leaves open the possibility that different audiences will interact with these media representations in different ways.

Communication studies scholar Lisa Cuklanz (1996) explores the way in which media representations interact with broader social activism concerning rape. After analyzing news coverage of two prominent rape cases, she finds that media coverage tends to offer only a fragmented understanding of rape law reform. In contrast, she found that movies did a better job of presenting rape victims and survivors sympathetically. Cuklanz (1998) also analyzes how television series portrayed rape at the height of social activism against it, from 1976–1978. She found that virtually every prime-time representation of rape turned it into a story more about the male protagonist who was seeking to avenge the rape than about the woman who had experienced the rape. This reaffirmed the traditional understanding of rape as taking something from a man rather than doing violence to a woman. Additionally, most of the rapes presented were stranger rapes, not the more common acquaintance rape or marital rape. Because the male protagonist became the primary nurturer of the rape victim, Cuklanz argues that "masculinity emerges here as the solution rather than the cause of the victimization of women through rape" (p. 444). Given the relationship between sexual violence and hegemonic masculinity, such portrayals misdirect attention.

Working in a similar vein, media scholar Sujata Moorti (2002) analyzes news and prime-time television to determine if and how rape is raced. Moorti highlights the diverse ways different media approach rape. Whereas daytime talk shows and some prime-time television shows provide viewers with a "multiplicity of approaches" to understand sexual violence, news tends to re-entrench the patriarchal view of rape (p. 213). Despite this diversity, however, Moorti argues that little in the way of new insights are offered concerning the continued prevalence of rape. Instead, media images of rape depict either how it affects White women or how it is a consequence of Black masculinity.

This binary is confirmed by media coverage of Freaknik, a weekend of pre–final exam street parties held in Atlanta throughout the 1980s and 1990s. Originally started as a picnic for students from historically Black Spelman and Morehouse colleges, the event grew so large that in the mid-1990s it attracted up to 200,000 primarily African American student and nonstudent participants from across the country. In addition to the traffic congestion and property crimes that seemed to go along with the event, local hospital emergency rooms reported a 400% increase (from 4 to 20) in rapes treated, from the weekend before Freaknik to the weekend of the event. Media researcher Marian Meyers (2004) asked, how were African American women represented in media stories about Freaknik? Meyers asked this because of the lack of attention to intersectionality in most media studies. Either depictions of women as victims are analyzed without attention to race, or depictions of Black men as perpetrators are analyzed without attention to sex. Existing media research on race accurately describes how Black masculinity is misrepresented as violent; Black men are disproportionately overrepresented as criminals and disproportionately underrepresented as victims of crime (Entman & Rojecki, 2000). This, however, does not provide a vivid understanding of how Black women are represented by media. Meyers sought to correct this oversight.

Like Cuklanz and Moorti, Meyers found that Black women were blamed for their attacks. Consistent with Chapter 5's discussion of truncated passives, many media stories presented women as the causes of the attacks, and the men who attacked them were dropped from the sentences. For example, the clause "lewd conduct on the part of women being groped and fondled" (reporter Paul Crawley, as quoted in Meyers, 2004, p. 110) elides *who* is doing the groping and fondling.

In addition to news coverage similarities, Meyers also found differences as a result of her intersectional analysis. She argues that the news coverage of Freaknik blamed African American women "for their own victimization and minimized the seriousness of the violence" by portraying them either as naïve visitors who placed themselves in harm's way or as "Jezebels whose lewd behavior provokes men to grope, fondle, and even rape" (p. 111). The dynamic of good girl–bad girl is not unique to portrayals of African American women, although the cultural history of the Jezebel creates a cultural presumption within primarily Euramerican audiences that African American women are more likely to be bad girls.

Media report acts of rape that occur not only in the United States but also in other countries, and those media reports interact with U.S. foreign policy. As the great power conflict between the United States and the Soviet Union waned, policy makers turned to other justifications for war, of which one was rape. A number of recent studies have examined the way in which media representations of violence against women, including rape, have been used as justification for intervention in places such as Kosovo and Afghanistan.

U.S. war rhetoric genders and sexes the people involved. It presents U.S. male warriors as benign, other countries' male warriors as violent and irrational, and women (regardless of the side) as "helpless bystanders" (Stables, 2003, p. 94). This narrative structure feeds into different reporting norms when it comes to wartime sexual violence. U.S. atrocities were systematically underreported or reported as "an aberration or an unfortunate byproduct of the horror of war" (p. 96). For other combatant countries, however, "rape becomes symbolic of the larger pattern of brutality visited by these militaristic societies" (p. 96). Kosovo demonstrates this.

Communication studies scholar Gordon Stables (2003) identifies three strategies in media coverage justifying aerial bombing of Kosovo in the spring of 1999: "First, accounts amplified the acts of violence as an important component of the crisis. Second, the representations utilized compelling historical narratives to explain the Serbs as a more familiar evil. Finally, the coverage emphasized the political geography of the Balkans, as an ethnic 'other' to explain the nature of the violence" (p. 98). Presenting the Serbs as premodern and barbaric meant that rape was a byproduct of a particular cultural heritage, not the result of masculinity. Given this, Stables argues that "instead of optimism" about how the media now seems to be attending to war violence targeted at women, "the war in Kosovo counsels scholars to examine closely representations of gendered violence because . . . national discourse may transform women's bodies into the symbolic battlefield of virtual conflicts" (p. 109). Media position women's bodies as in need of being saved and "American masculinity as chivalrous" (p. 103).

The challenge posed by these criticisms of mediated representations of rape is, then, how to create an ethical representation. It is difficult to enable a person who has not experienced rape to understand the trauma. Not until the 1988 film *The Accused* (based on an actual incident) was rape dealt with forthrightly in a mainstream Hollywood movie. The movie raises the issue of whether Jodie Foster's character, Sarah Tobias, deserved to be gang-raped by three men, given her provocative clothing and dancing; the movie made clear that she did not. However, vivid depictions of rape potentially repeat, commodify, or eroticize the trauma. When deciding whether to reproduce vivid narratives of rape, one should consider how those whose stories are told would want their stories told. Particularly when discussing sexual violence occurring abroad, "we need to be mindful of how rhetorical acts of witnessing may function as new forms of international tourism and appropriation," not as world traveling (Hesford, 2004, p. 121).

Research that focuses on detailed descriptions of media content is important. Such research helps people recognize the dominant trends in media instead of merely operating from the limited slice of media texts to which each person might be exposed. Similarly, media effects research, even with its limits, functions as a good place to start conversations about the effects media exposure indeed might have.

The Gaze(s)

The second prominent strand of media research focuses on media constructions of audience. Two parallel lines of research emerged in the 1970s to explain how visual media gender the practice of watching, create a legitimating gender ideology, influence gender identity, and structure audience expectations. The first theory focuses on the way media codes position audiences. The second theory uses psychoanalysis to explain how cinema's form spoke exclusively to a male spectator. It is important to note that both of these theories have generated serious critical responses; however, both have strongly influenced media research.

Ways of Seeing. In the 1970s, the British Broadcasting Company aired a television series titled *Ways of Seeing*. A book by the same name soon followed. John Berger's *Ways of Seeing* (1972) advances a series of claims that have influenced media scholarship. First, he argues that the invention of the camera drastically changed how human beings see. It "destroyed the idea that images were timeless" and challenged the viewer's belief that he (and Berger means *he*) was the center of the universe, a perspective created by paintings up until that time (p. 18). Berger argues that in European art, from the Renaissance onward, men were the presumed viewers (p. 64). He develops this argument in one of the book's most often-quoted passages:

> *Men act* and *women appear.* Men look at women. Women watch themselves being looked at. This determines not only most relations between men and women but also the relation of women to themselves. The surveyor of woman in herself is male: the surveyed female. Thus she turns herself into an object— and most particularly an object of vision: a sight. (p. 47)

The presumed sex of the viewer is male, and even when the viewer is female, she views herself through men's eyes. Thus, when women assess their bodies, they do so not from the perspective of another woman, but from the perspective of a man.

In case you do not believe that men long were presumed the "'ideal' spectator," try this experiment: Examine an image of a traditional nude (the images from the series are available at http://courses.washington.edu/englhtml/eng1569/berger/), and replace an image of a woman with the image of a man. Then, ask yourself, what does the transformation do, not only to the image, "but to the assumptions of a likely viewer" (p. 64)? (The traditional paintings of nudes also demonstrate how beauty standards have changed across time.) Berger's point is that the way the body is positioned, whether in paintings or in advertisements, employs a series of codes that audiences can read, even though they may not be conscious that they are decoding.

Berger's insights are useful insofar as they encourage those studying media to think about the ways audiences look. However, his work has limits. First, it explains ways of looking that are unique to Western art traditions. In the cross-cultural study of advertising discussed earlier (Frith et al., 2005), the authors argue that one reason why Western women's bodies are sexually objectified but Asian women's bodies are not is the Western art tradition. In contrast to Western art, "displaying the female body has not been the tradition in Chinese art" (p. 65); Chinese art is the form that influenced Hong Kong and Singapore. Thus, "traditions of 'gaze' may very well have developed differently in the East and the West" (p. 65).

Second, Berger's book predates important changes in the way men's bodies are presented in advertising. From Robert Mapplethorpe's art photography to Abercrombie & Fitch's advertising, men's bodies are increasingly playing a role. Susan Bordo (1999) explores how recent advertising images of men create gender tensions, stating that "men are not supposed to enjoy being surveyed *period*. It's feminine to be on display" (p. 173). However, images of men that have appeared since the 1990s, particularly in Calvin Klein underwear advertisements, do present men as on display. Such ads have led to an evolution in masculinity's meaning. Consistent with Berger, Bordo argues that "to be so passively dependent on the gaze of another person for one's sense of self-worth is incompatible with being a real man"; thus, "men and women are socially sanctioned to deal with the gaze of the Other in different ways" (pp. 172–173).

Third, "Berger's opposition of 'acting' and 'appearing,' . . . is something of a false duality—and always has been" because women's appearance involves immense action: "It takes time, energy, creativity, dedication. It can *hurt*" (Bordo, 1999, pp. 220–221). However, the fiction that appearance is act free persists. Few stars admit that their bodies have been surgically sculpted, and most magazine readers gleefully engage in the willing suspension of disbelief, accepting pictures as perfect reflections of the models even as most should be aware that virtually every image appearing in fashion magazines has been digitally altered.

Fourth, Berger's claims too easily slip from generalizations about how people look at representations (art, advertising) to how people look at each other. One must be careful about making generalizations based on representations and applying them to how human beings interact. Berger often slips from discussing media-produced "ways of seeing" to describing how real men look at real women in their everyday lives. The boundaries should be kept distinct; the gaze is a system that works when discussing realistic representation. It is not automatically reproduced in individual behavior.

THE GAZE

At about the same time that Berger's series and book appeared, media theorist Laura Mulvey (1975) published what would become one of the most frequently cited essays in media studies. Using psychoanalytic theory, Mulvey posits that cinema not only highlights woman's to-be-looked-at-ness but actually builds the way woman is to be looked at into the film itself. The way the camera, the audience, and the male character (with whom all spectators—male and female—identify) look at women reinforces the male as active and the female as passive. For Mulvey, the cinematic gaze is male. Mulvey's criticism applies to all mainstream cinema, and she believes that the only way to avoid the dominance of the male gaze was through avant garde film that undermines the system of representation.

Mulvey's theory is criticized because she identified a single, universal gaze: She assumed that there was only one White male gaze and that no possibility for a female or a non-White gaze existed. Others would challenge this, arguing that female (Gamman & Marshment, 1989; Kaplan, 1983) and transgender (Halberstam, 2005) gazes are possible, that people can read against the grain of the male gaze (de Lauretis, 1984; Walters, 1995), and that the focus of psychoanalysis on sexual difference as the fundamental organizing principle of human subjectivity was misplaced, in light of the centrality of race to identity (DiPiero, 2002). She also assumed that a lone media text directly and unilaterally affected the spectator at the moment of consumption, ignoring that multiple factors simultaneously influence the spectator, such as socialization, education, other texts, and peer pressure. The most trenchant criticism of Mulvey is provided by bell hooks (1992): "Feminist film theory rooted in an ahistorical psychoanalytic framework that privileges sexual difference actively suppresses recognition of race, reenacting and mirroring the erasure of black womanhood that occurs in films, silencing any discussion of racial difference—of racialized sexual difference" (p. 123).

Not only can multiple gazes exist, but Brenda Cooper (2000) argues that one can find a rejection of the dominant male gaze even in mainstream Hollywood films. Cooper argues that *Thelma & Louise* (1991) encourages viewers to identify not with the males on the screen but with the female figures who actively mocked and challenged patriarchal conventions. Cooper's analysis is bolstered by her earlier study (1999) of spectator responses, which found that men and women saw the film differently. Men tended to see the film as an example of unjustified male bashing (perhaps because they identified with the men in the film, few of whom were sympathetic), and women tended to see it as a commentary on women's marginalized social position (because they identified with the women in the film).

Cooper's study illustrates Condit's point about polyvalence; male and female audiences readings were polyvalent.

Despite the criticisms of Mulvey, her recognition of the gendered pleasures of the gaze continues to spark research. *Signs,* the premiere journal of feminist scholarship, recently published a special issue on feminist theories of visual culture. Every essay made clear the importance of intersectionality to understanding how the gaze operates. In order to answer the question, how do I look? one must think about "gender . . . as inextricably entwined (embodied, experienced, thought, and imagined) with other aspects of identity, including race and ethnicity, nationality, sexual orientation, and class" (Doyle & Jones, 2006, p. 608). In particular, Eve Oishi (2006) offers a theory of perverse spectatorship, which calls for attention to "the infinitely oblique and circuitous routes through which identification passes" (p. 649). Of course, being able to read or watch against the grain requires being able to identify the grain, and for that we have the writings of Berger and Mulvey to thank.

An Oppositional Gaze

Recognition of ways in which audiences are gendered/sexed and raced contributes importantly to one's understanding of the gendered/sexed and raced content of mediated communication. To be an active participant in media discourse about gender instead of a passive recipient of it, one must possess a heuristic vocabulary with which to critically discuss the content and the gaze. One cannot engage in creative readings of media unless one knows that such readings are necessary and possible. In her book on race and representation, bell hooks labels this an *oppositional gaze.*

Although hooks's *Black Looks* (1992) focuses mostly on race, her arguments apply to gender, sex, and sexual orientation as well. She argues that discussions of race need to expand beyond debates about good and bad representations to address the issue of standpoint. She asks, "From what political perspective do we dream, look, create, and take action?" (p. 4). Media's positioning of the audience is not determinative as long as audiences are conscious of media's attempt to position them. Audience members can reposition themselves. African Americans can refuse to look through White eyes. Women can refuse to look through men's eyes. LGBT people can refuse to look through straight eyes. A number of elements compose an oppositional gaze and a critical consciousness.

First, to embrace an oppositional gaze, one must "consider the perspective from which we look, vigilantly asking ourselves who do we identify with, whose image do we love" (hooks, 1992, p. 6). Even though hooks's call to action targets Blacks as an audience, hers is a call to all people. She challenges Blacks to unlearn their cherishing of hateful images of themselves. She challenges Whites as "the many non-black people who produce images and critical narratives about blackness and black people" to "interrogate their perspective"; otherwise, "they may simply recreate the imperial gaze—the look that seeks to dominate, subjugate, and colonize" (p. 7). Our point in highlighting one's positioning in relation to media is to encourage those with privilege to recognize that privilege. This does not mean, however, that one needs to identify as a victim (p. 14). Instead, it means that one should ask, to whom and for whom does this media representation speak? When one enjoys mediated depictions of sexual violence, with whom is one identifying—the perpetrator or the victim?

Second, one must recognize the degree to which she or he participates in culture. People are not merely passive audiences for the reception of media messages and images. Susan Bordo (1997) explains, "Unless one recognizes one's own enmeshment in culture, one is in no position to theorize about that culture or its effects on others" (p. 13). Recognizing the way in which people are "culture makers as well as culture consumers" enables each person to act to transform the culture (p. 15). Remember, we chose to not write about an all-powerful *the media*. Instead, we chose to write about *media* and the ways each person participates in the institution as both recipient and creator. However, we also chose to speak of media as an institution to highlight the way in which it is social and economic and presents hegemonic messages that require work to read from an oppositional perspective. We chose to talk about media as an institution to make clear that personal choices about gender are not sufficient to change the institution of gender or the gendered institution of media, nor do personal cultural choices necessarily translate into political action in the public sphere.

Our point in highlighting individual agency in relation to media representations is not to imply that each person individually controls the effect of media on herself or himself. An institutional focus makes clear that even those choices considered the most personal are influenced by larger social forces. Do you wear makeup or not? Do you get calf implants or not? Do you wear jeans or not? Like Bordo (1997), our call for critical consciousness is meant to celebrate "those choices that are undertaken in full consciousness that they are not only about 'creating' our own individual lives but constructing the landscape of our culture" (p. 16). A person's embrace of beauty ideals influences not only that person's body but others' bodies as well. Bordo explains, "Each of us shapes the culture we live in every moment of our lives, not only in our more public activities but also in our most intimate gestures and personal relationships, for example, in the way we model attitudes toward beauty, aging, perfection, and so on for our children, friends, students, lovers, colleagues" (p. 16).

Being critically conscious of the degree to which each person is enmeshed in culture also encourages one to be conscious of the inevitable contradictions produced by media. Beliefs and actions will not always cohere, in your bodies or in others' bodies. The point of critical consciousness is not to castigate those who claim to reject hegemonic masculinity but still love boxing, or those who condemn consumer culture yet still own more than 25 pairs of shoes. Instead, critical consciousness should enable one to make some sense of the multiple identifications offered and enable one to make changes when the contradictions become untenable.

Third, an oppositional gaze necessarily moves from social critique to political action. The goal in examining popular culture is not just to critique the image but to transform the image, to create alternatives, to find images that subvert, and to pose critical alternatives that move people beyond thinking merely about good or bad images (hooks, 1992). Cultural criticism becomes just another pastime if it is not linked to institutional change.

Fourth, an oppositional gaze is conscious of the way in which contemporary media engage in commodification—the selling of cultural, sexual, or gender difference in a way that supports institutionalized discrimination. For hooks (1992), one must recognize when presentations of ethnicity are not signs of inclusiveness but the production of "colorful ethnicity for the white consumer appetite that makes it possible for blackness to be commodified in unprecedented ways, and for whites to appropriate black culture without interrogating whiteness or showing concern for the displeasure of blacks" (p. 154). Some rap music videos demonstrate how particular representations of Black gender/sex are sold to White youth, often by White corporations for the benefit of White shareholders (Yousman, 2003). Rap videos, particularly those marketed to suburban White youth, present Black men and dark-skinned Black women as hypersexualized. Young White men's consumption of rap music and their embrace of the nonverbal and linguistic customs of hip-hop culture is not a sign of cultural inclusiveness, because this commodification of Blackness maintains an "ideology that is consistent with an acceptance of White economic, political and social supremacy" (p. 386). White youth obsession with Black culture is not a sign of progressive social change but rather a form of consuming the other, reconfirming our point in Chapter 6, that "prejudice and institutional racism are not one and the same" (p. 387), because "the particular nature of the images that White youth are consuming—images of Black youth who are violent or hostile, often unemployed and/or involved in criminal practices—may in fact reinforce, rather than challenge, the tendency of White youth" to support institutionalized racism (p. 387).

Media as Always Liberatory and Constraining

Given the polyvalence of media products and that each audience member is actively involved in the interpretation and reception of messages, even seemingly restrictive media forms can be used for liberatory purposes. Romance novels are one unexpected example of female audiences reading media texts in a way that resists hegemonic masculinities and docile femininities (Modleski, 1984; Radway, 1991).

As part of the high culture/low culture divide, romance novels were long dismissed as unworthy of study. However, their popularity indicates that something complex is happening. Initially critiqued as feeding women's masochistic tendencies and as a backlash against feminism (Douglas, 1980), media scholars now believe that romance novels targeted at women deserve serious study. English professor Tania Modleski (1998) argues that "women's fantasies did not simply reflect female masochism . . . popular feminine narratives do testify to women's resistance to patriarchal norms and involve heroine and reader in a complex negotiation of the line between fantasy and reality" (p. 39). Performance studies scholar Karen Mitchell (1996) confirms this negotiated reading of romances. Women she interviewed were interested in "liberated women seeking sensitive men as equal partners," instead of the stereotypical weak heroine and macho hero (p. 54). The women were active consumers and would sometimes "re-write" the novels' more disturbing depictions of passive femininity and masculine sexual violence. In romances, the women found some degree of liberation and empowerment, even as the novels reinscribed the fairy tale of the perfect heterosexual romance. It is this push and pull between liberation and constraint we now explore.

With every movement toward liberation, constraints are reinscribed, and with every image that appears restrictive, an oppositional reading is possible. Madonna provides a classic example. Madonna is best understood "as a site of contradiction," where her "gender play simultaneously challenges and reinforces gender roles" (Hallstein, 1996, p. 123). In this section, we work through a series of examples that highlight liberatory as well as constraining presentations of gender.

Although we ended the other chapters about institutions by emphasizing their liberatory potential, we depart from that pattern here. We wish to counteract people's tendency to think of all media products as cutting edge and forward thinking. Most critical cultural research demonstrates that even the most progressive-seeming *commercial* media products re-entrench dominant beliefs even as they appear to challenge them. In contrast, *noncommercial* media forms such as zines (Brouwer, 2005; Comstock, 2001), performance art (Demo, 2000), cyberspace (Flanagan & Booth, 2002), and National Public Radio (Foss & Foss, 1994) often are more empowering than constraining. In this chapter, we focus on commercial media forms, as they are the forms with which you are most likely to be familiar.

The examples in this section emphasize masculinity. Why? We want to remind you that gender in communication is not just about women and femininity but also about men and masculinity, women and masculinities, and men and femininities. Just as Whites often do not consider White a race, masculinity often is not considered a gender. Norms become unmarked. Thus, we intentionally and overtly mark masculinity as a gender and challenge the notion that *gender* means *women* (Dow & Condit, 2005). Given the burgeoning of masculinity studies in research on gender in media, this chapter becomes an ideal location in which to emphasize that gender means more than women. Of course, even as we focus on masculinity, issues of femininity and sexuality are necessarily implicated.

This section contains four themes. First, gender is constructed through media representations, and media representations of gender are always in flux. Second, the borders of genders are continually resecured by media representations in response to this change. Third, even progressive representations of gender can resecure traditional understandings of gender. Fourth, new technologies tend to replicate old gender dynamics.

Gender Is Constructed and Thus Is Always in Flux

One location in which media representations of gender appear increasingly destabilized is in the presentation of masculinity in U.S. and British men's magazines, such as *Maxim* and *GQ*. One might think that these magazines are bastions of he-man-ness. But another interpretation is possible. Although he primarily studied British magazines, Gauntlett (2002) argues that whether in the United States or United Kingdom, "the magazines really show men to be *insecure* and *confused* in the modern world, and seeking help and *reassurance,* even if this is (slightly) suppressed by a veneer of irony and heterosexual lust" (p. 167). As is true of all institutional discourse, "The discourses of masculinity which the magazines help to circulate can therefore, unsurprisingly, be both enabling and constraining" (p. 180).

Gauntlett believes that the discourses of masculinity in these contemporary magazines are distinctive because they recognize that masculinity is a social construction, not a cultural given. He believes the subject matter of "today's magazines for men are *all about* the social construction of masculinity" (p. 170). Masculinity is the subject matter because social forces have destabilized masculinity. Previously, "men didn't need lifestyle magazines because it was obvious what a man was, and what a man should do. . . . It is only in the modern climate, in which we are all aware of the many choices available to us, and are also aware of the feminist critique of traditional masculinity, and the fact that gender roles can and do change, that men have started to need magazines about how to be a man today" (p. 170). Gauntlett's hopeful read of men's magazines is tempered by his recognition that the U.S. *Maxim* is "slow and sometimes backwards" as it tries to figure out issues of masculine identity (p. 175).

The degree to which nationality and culture influence the construction of masculinity is evident in the presentation of masculinity in Japanese men's magazines. Portrayals of men in Japanese media encourage an increasingly feminized ideal man (Faiola, 2005; Takizawa, 2005). Feminization appears in the form of attractiveness encouraged in Japanese men, who are told to make themselves more appealing to women. The demands for attractiveness correspond with the increased offering of cosmetics for men. However, even as men embrace more feminine ideals, inequality between the sexes persists in Japan.

Like Gauntlett's readings of men's magazines, women's magazines are about the construction of femininity and contain locations for transgressive readings of gender. The magazine *Cosmopolitan,* in the form most people now recognize, was launched in 1964 in the United States by Helen Gurley Brown when she took over its editorship. The magazine, which many rightly condemn as offering restrictive representations of women's overly thin bodies, also contains transgressive elements. When launched by Gurley Brown, the magazine had an explicit sexual agenda, "for *Cosmo* was playing *Playboy* at its own game, seeing sexual pleasure as important, and suggesting that women were entitled to it. *Cosmo*'s assertion of women's rights to enjoy sex, and to talk about it, was quite radical, and this new discourse brought other changes—men, for example, were no longer treated with reverence, but could be seen as inadequate, or the butt of jokes" (Gauntlett, 2002, p. 53). However, like the complex masculinity contained in men's magazines, the femininity of *Cosmo* is a particular one—a heterosexual one.

Even when magazines are not as radical as the early *Cosmo,* readers do not always take all of a magazine's messages seriously but instead employ a "pick 'n' mix attitude . . . which might suggest that those who fear for the reader-victim of these publications are overemphasizing the power of the texts and underestimating the ability of readers to be selective and critical" (Gauntlett, 2002, p. 206). However, fashion magazines offer a limited range from which to pick. Women's magazines may be playful in their approach to makeup and clothing, but "they would never encourage women to step outside their carefully imagined boundaries of the 'sexy,' the 'stylish' and the 'fashionable'" (p. 206). This illustrates Condit's point about the limits of polysemy. While women may pick 'n' mix messages, a common, consistent message is presented: that a woman's self-worth is influenced by her looks, clothes, and accessories. Additionally, factors other than individual agency influence the reception of messages: (1) peer groups and (2) commodification. Peer groups strongly influence how messages are evaluated. In a study of girls at two middle schools, one predominantly White and the other predominantly Mexican American and African American, journalism professor Meenakshi Gigi Durham (1999) found that "girls *on their own* may be somewhat more able to critically examine and deconstruct media messages than in the peer group context" (p. 210). Thus, when cultural studies researchers claim that mediated messages are polysemous, they may be ignoring the fact that media consumption and interpretation often is a group activity, not an individual one. Oppositional readings of texts are delimited by the social structures reproduced in peer groups: "The peer group was shown to be a training ground where girls learned to use the mass media to acquire the skills of ideal femininity," although sometimes rejections of these norms could be voiced (p. 212).

Second, it is important to note the way in which agency itself is commodified. Even though *feminism* carries negative connotations to many, advertisers have embraced feminist viewpoints when advertising to women. Does this mean that media have embraced feminism's political beliefs? No. Instead, the hegemonic processes of media translate women's calls for independence and equality into "stylized commodity signs" (Goldman, Heath, & Smith, 1991, p. 333). In a study of the advertising in *Mademoiselle* magazine, researchers found that in the late 1980s advertisers began to play with variations of the male gaze and with ways to "address and position the female spectator" (p. 334). Advertisers targeted ads to women who considered themselves living in a postfeminist era, meaning that women presumed their social and legal equality even as they shunned the feminist label. Instead of ads urging women to buy a product in order to be desired by men and envied by women, ads now offer women ways to "reclaim the female body as a site for women's own pleasure and as a resource for her power in a broader marketplace of desire than marriage" (p. 335).

Later research confirms these findings. Media acknowledge that feminism exists and do so by taking the messages of feminism (economic, geographic, professional, and sexual freedom) and packaging them in the form of individualism and consumerism. Quite simply, "certain kinds of female agency are recognizably and profitably packaged as commodities" (Tasker & Negra, 2005, p. 107). Just as diversity often is sold as a commodity (as bell hooks has noted), so, too, is feminism. The summer 2006 advertising campaign for *Secret* deodorant, "50 years of strong women," is the latest example of the selling of feminist agency. One should not lose sight of the fact that commercial media are just that: *commercial.* They sell products to audiences and audiences to producers.

Even though many media representations reinforce traditional gender norms, "modern media has a more complex view of gender and sexuality than ever before" (Gauntlett, 2002, p. 90). Being able to see this complexity, even when it is not immediately apparent, depends on the development of a critical consciousness. Additionally, even though more complexity is present does not mean that hegemonic masculinity and subordinate femininity have been decentered. An analysis of news and popular movies demonstrates this.

Resecuring Genders' Borders: "Masculinity in Crisis"

Although Gauntlett celebrates the destabilization of masculinity, others worry that such instability is the sign of masculinity in crisis. In their review of discussions of masculinity across media forms, communication scholars Karen Ashcraft and Lisa Flores (2003) believe that "US representations of manhood converge on the claim that masculinity is in the midst of crisis" (p. 2). Whether masculinity is, in fact, in crisis is not the issue. Instead, the issue is that media present it as in crisis, and actions are called for as a result of that presentation. When masculinity "figures itself as in crisis and figures white men as vulnerable to attack," it can "justify the constant securing of its borders" (Dickinson & Anderson, 2004, p. 290). Although Gauntlett is correct that contemporary media possess a much more complex view of gender, this does not mean that the complexity is uniformly accepted and welcomed.

Much as muscular Christianity was a response to the perceived effemination of men at the end the 19th century, much popular culture at the end of the 20th century is a response to the "imminent collapse of the corporate man, over-civilized and emasculated by allied obligations to work and women. To rebuild this haggard creature," movies such as *Fight Club* (1999) and *In the Company of Men* (1997) turn to what Ashcraft and Flores label a "'civilized/primitive' masculinity, embodied by the hardened white man who finds healing in wounds" (p. 2). Men employ physical and psychological violence (their primitive side) to maintain or recapture their masculinity even in the world of business (their civilized side).

An analysis of fictional men in fictional movies seems like a strange place to discover what it means to be a "real" man; however, one can study masculinity not only by studying actual men but also by studying discourses about masculinity found in popular culture. The purpose of media analysis is not to determine whether the media representations are empirically accurate but to explore how such representations shape the social imagination. Regardless, "accomplishing gender necessarily entails performance, whether improvised in the mundane moments of everyday life or memorialized on screen for countless witnesses" (Ashcraft & Flores, 2003, p. 3).

In their analysis, Ashcraft and Flores pay particular attention to the way in which masculinity, like femininity, is "not a stable or unified phenomenon; its meanings shift over time and in relation to culture, context, and person," and it also "is inevitably raced and classed" (p. 3). They note that when hegemonic masculinity is discussed, authors often are referring to hegemonic *White* masculinity, even though race is not overtly mentioned; U.S. hegemonic masculinity is raced White. This is part of the power of hegemonic White masculinity: It "co-opts discourses of race, class, and sexuality without deposing its white, heterosexual, and middle-class footing" (p. 4).

Fight Club also illustrates how media forms criticized by religious and social conservatives actually may support, instead of undermine, the heteronormative ideal. Robert Westerfelhaus and Robert Alan Brookey's (2004) analysis of *Fight Club* explores how heteronormative values are pervasive even though the film is "self-consciously irreverent and seemingly antireligious" (p. 321). *Fight Club* initially celebrates the homosocial relationship between narrator Jack (Edward Norton) and Tyler (Brad Pitt) through subtextual eroticism, which is part of the film's theme of rebellion, but that relationship ultimately is violently rejected. Even as the film mocks many social institutions, it reinforces heteronormativity.

Progressive Representations Resecure Traditional Gender Norms: Mr. Mom and *Ellen*

As noted in the chapters on family and work, men in increasing numbers are becoming primary caregivers to children. This increase is reflected by a corresponding increase of news stories and movies featuring this "new" man. In a study of television news accounts of stay-at-home fathers televised from 1995 to 1999, communication studies professor Mary Douglas Vavrus (2002) found that although the stories did "represent a challenge to more traditional masculine identities depicted in media," they also tended to reinforce institutions that maintained gendered dichotomies: heterosexuality and the nuclear family (p. 353). Instead of representing stay-at-home fathers who are in homosexual relationships (statistically the largest group), stories focused on heterosexual men whose wives typically worked in high-paying professions. This is somewhat understandable, as very few families can afford to live on one salary, yet some stay-at-home fathers or single fathers who are primary caregivers come from different socioeconomic classes. The upside is that these stories did "nudge nurturance ever closer to incorporation within an ideal of hegemonic masculinity" (Vavrus, 2002, p. 368). However, given the reinscription of heterosexuality and the nuclear family, on balance a Mr. Mom story "poses little threat to traditional representations of masculinity" (p. 369).

Even apparently revolutionary media representations of sexuality tend to play into constraining norms. In 1997, the sitcom *Ellen* made television history when it became the first prime-time show to have an openly homosexual lead character. The significance of this should not be underestimated. However, the way in which the show handled Ellen's coming out limited its liberatory potential. Bonnie J. Dow (2001) argues that in the process of making her lesbianism visible, Ellen simply traded one power relation for another. Although she was no longer silenced as a lesbian, her new "out" speech still had to follow rules. First, her homosexuality had to be presented as relevant only in terms of its impact on her personal relations; the political oppression of LGBT peoples was reduced to a personal issue. Second, the most important relations a homosexual character has are with heterosexuals; the sexuality of homosexuals is not represented. Dow concludes that "it is not sexuality that has been repressed in television, but, rather, the *politics* of sexuality; . . . the secret being kept isn't homosexuality; it's homophobia and heterosexism" (p. 135).

New Technologies Replicate Old Gender Norms

Although many now take the Internet for granted, it is a relatively recent phenomenon. Email access originally was limited to those working in technical and academic fields; broad access and usage did not occur until the late 1980s. By the mid-1990s, the word *Internet* was common; in August 1996, the first version of Google was launched; and since 2002, Web-based tools have popularized blogs. When the capabilities of the Internet were first explored, many thought it would be free from discrimination; in cyberspace, no one would have a gender, race, nationality, ethnicity, religion, class, sex, or sexual orientation. However, the reality is that identity issues are present in the virtual world as much as in the corporeal, in terms of both access to and actual presence on the Web. Research on the Internet demonstrates that its egalitarian promise has not been realized.

Studies of the Internet contest its ability to function as the great equalizer. The U.S. Department of Commerce's National Telecommunications and Information Administration has regularly released comprehensive studies of U.S. Internet access titled *Falling Through the Net*. The 1999 report states, "Whites are more likely to have Internet access *at home* than Blacks or Hispanics are from *any* location" (U.S. Department of Commerce). Not only that, the way in which one uses the Internet is determined by one's demographic characteristics, which "not only determine *whether* and *where* one uses the Internet. Income, education, race, and gender, among other characteristics, strongly influence what a person does online" (n.p.). Those belonging to subordinated demographic groups are more likely to use the Internet in public places, such as schools or community centers, and are more likely to use it to take courses or conduct job searches. It is used as an instrument to enter the economic system of paid labor.

The last published report (U.S. Department of Commerce, 2000) indicates that even though digital inclusion has increased, "a digital divide remains or has expanded slightly in some cases" (p. xvi). Given the increasingly central role the Internet plays in education and business, access is no longer a luxury. Thus, those who lack access are increasingly at a disadvantage.

Even if one makes it online, the issues of race and sex still warrant consideration. Communication arts scholar Lisa Nakamura (2005) questions the belief that the Internet ought to be raceless; we additionally interrogate the idea that it should be sexless. Two questions should be answered: (1) Is the Internet raceless and sexless? (2) Should the Internet be raceless and sexless? Nakamura answers no to both questions in regard to race. We answer no to both questions in regard to sex.

Race is present on the Net. First, online race is presumed White, and there are "incentives for minorities to opt for default whiteness online" (p. 531). Second, race is commodified through identity tourism, wherein White men take on the gender persona of Asian men. Nakamura notes how many chat sites present themselves as race free (meaning that one should not overtly talk about one's race lest one be perceived divisive), yet the avatars (the icons used to represent the users) are clearly raced.

Sex also is present on the Net. The Pew Internet & American Life Project (Fallows, 2005) tracks women's and men's usage and has found that women's use is catching up to men's, although reasons for use differ (note that no study has controlled for gender rather than sex in usage studies). Men's use initially outstripped women's, but by 2000 the user population was evenly divided. Depending on age and race, in some categories women use the Internet more than men do. Young women are more likely than young men to be online, but older men are more likely than older women to be online, and Black women are more likely than Black men to be online. However, one must also account for frequency and intensity of use. Men go online more frequently than women and during any given day are more likely to access the Internet. Finally, men and women use the Internet for distinct reasons. Men tend to use it for information gathering and entertainment, whereas women tend to use it for communication (e.g., email) purposes. Such statistics demonstrate that the Internet, which initially appealed to men because of descriptions that highlighted its use as a tool of control for personal advancement and marketing, has evolved and has become appealing to women. It can also provide a location for artistic expression, humor, and social support (Warnick, 1999).

Interestingly, even when women and men are equally represented in online usage, that equality is not recognized. One of the first studies of gender/sex and blogging (Herring, Kouper, Scheidt, & Wright, 2004) notes that even though there are as many women and children weblog authors as male, contemporary discussions about weblogs in scholarly literature, media reports, and blogs themselves "tend to disproportionately feature adult, male bloggers" (para. 3). The researchers posited that because filter blogs, which are produced primarily by adult males, were analyzed most, the activities of women and teen bloggers were marginalized, "thereby indirectly reproducing societal sexism and ageism, and misrepresenting the fundamental nature of the weblog phenomenon" (para. 4).

Conclusion

The creativity and artistry involved in media creations opens spaces for creative performances of gender—within limits. Even as Hollywood is condemned for failing to live up to traditional family values, most dominant media images reinforce the gender binary of heteronormativity. However, even though the politics of much media are regressive, most people take pleasure in going to movies, reading novels, perusing magazines, and surfing the Web. The danger is not that people do these things but that they often do them uncritically. Audiences act as though they were passive recipients of media, not active participants in culture. The more one realizes that one can *talk back* to the screen, the page, or the picture, the more one realizes that one is not merely buying a commodity. The more one becomes an engaged member of the cultural conversation, the more one learns to employ an oppositional gaze. Condit (1989) explains that audience's complex relationship to media "is a consequence of the fact that humans, in their inherent character as audiences, are inevitably situated in a communication *system,* of which they are a part, and hence have some influence within, but by which they are also influenced" (p. 120). This chapter should make clear the ways in which people can engage in the active and dynamic practice of resistant readings of media and not be dupes. People can use "media texts to serve their own interests in unpredictable ways" (Dow & Condit, 2005, p. 457).

Although creative uses of media are important, an institutional approach to media also makes clear that they may be insufficient. First, media are ephemeral, making them a "fragile basis for lasting social change" (Dow, 2001, p. 137). Second, changes in representation do not necessarily translate into changes in policy (Budd et al., 1990). Although we believe that images, texts, and messages matter, we also want to clarify the limits of personalized politics; institutional-level change is required, and heightened consciousness of media images of women and men, masculinity and femininity, Whiteness and otherness does little if they are not translated into political action.

CHAPTER 12

One Last Look Through a Critical Gendered Lens

"Battle of the sexes," "opposite sex," "gender wars," "the war against boys." The typical approach to gender in communication reinforces the idea of a gender/sex binary. There are only two sexes—male and female—and they are opposite. There are only two genders—masculine and feminine—and men are masculine and women are feminine, and the more you are of one, the less you are of the other. Embedded within this gender/sex binary is heteronormativity. All are presumed heterosexual, and if one violates this presumption, then intense questions are raised about one's gender, and if one violates presumptions about one's gender, then questions are raised about one's sexual orientation. Here, at the end of this book, we hope you realize that understanding gender in communication is nowhere near that simple. In fact, accepting a heteronormative gender/sex binary is more likely to induce you to commit errors when you assess communicative exchanges.

Further complicating one's understanding of gender/sex in communication is the fact that gender is not an isolable component of a person's identity. Identity is intersectional. How one performs gender is inextricably influenced by one's race, class, sex, sexual orientation, physical ability, nationality, religion, education, work status, family, citizenship status, and every other identity ingredient that makes up who one is. A book about gender in communication is necessarily about much more than gender.

However, despite the complexities and fluidities of identity, many institutions are still structured around identity categories as if each were permanently fixed, unproblematically identifiable, and easily distinguished. For this reason, even though gender is complicated by other identity ingredients, it still is useful as a category of analysis when one is trying to understand the dynamics of gender in communication. Our goal in writing this textbook is to make clear that one cannot understand gender unless one also understands the complexity of each person's identity, the influences of institutions upon gender, and the way in which questions of power are woven throughout.

Thus, in this book we have *not* offered a list of differences between women's and men's communication patterns. It would simply be wrong, a categorical error, to talk about gender in communication by talking about differences between women's and men's communication patterns. The most up-to-date research demonstrates that looking for gender differences in communication by studying women as one group and men as another yields no meaningful results. Even though many tend to believe that men (as men) and women (as women) communicate differently, "the literature shows unstable, context-specific, relatively small, and variable effects" (Dow & Condit, 2005, p. 453). According to meta-analyses of research on gender in communication, biological sex tends to account for "a miniscule [*sic*] 1% of the variance in communication behaviors" (p. 453). *One percent.* Biological sex is not the determining element; rather, gender role characteristics are. It would be a waste of time to devote an entire book to explaining only 1% of communicative actions; however, if one approaches communication using a critical gendered lens, many more subtleties and complexities emerge, justifying the scope of this book.

Additional problems plague a differences approach. A focus on differences between women and men

- ignores the vast array of similarities among people;
- ignores the existence of intersex people;
- assumes that sex determines gender;
- ignores the differences among women and among men and thus fails to accurately account for the importance of issues such as race, class, and nationality.

As gender communication scholar John Sloop (2005) writes in his review of recent literature on sex, race, class, and gender, "a gender/sexuality project that avoids questions of, say, class and race, not only reinforces the larger material and economic ways in which class and racial borders are reinforced and delimited, but also provides a critique of gender/sexuality issues that has limited explanatory power" (p. 326).

Perhaps most importantly, a differences approach tends to ignore the issue of power and its offspring, violence. When one simply assumes that men and women are different, then one too easily explains away power inequalities as the natural outcome of differences. Our attention to violence throughout this book is intended to make clear that differences are rarely mere innocent cultural constructions. Instead, these constructions (e.g., man, woman, Black, White, rich, poor, citizen, noncitizen) have consequences. These consequences become clearest when one tracks issues such as rape, domestic violence, poverty, and genocide. Our point is not that men and masculinity are the cause of all society's ills. Instead, our point is that hegemonic masculinity and its celebration of violence as a solution to problems contributes to those ills.

We realize that ours is a complex approach to understanding gender in communication. We also realize that accounting for complexity is not easy. However, we do not consider this a drawback. We would rather be overly complex and get you thinking about gender diversity than overly simple and allow you to ignore important variables that influence human communication. Human beings are wonderfully complex, and so it makes sense that the identity ingredient of gender would be, too. As gender communication scholars Bonnie Dow and Celeste Condit (2005) make clear, "Sex and gender are not simply variables deserving incorporation in equations, but are complex factors that require careful, sustained attention to their formation and to the nonsimple ways in which they play out in human communication" (p. 454).

For this reason, we have tried to highlight moments of emancipation and liberation, as well as the moments of contradiction that accommodation breeds. Although institutional structures and social power create inequalities, those inequalities do not persist unchallenged. Despite grinding poverty, people live full lives. Despite oppression and subordination, people find ways to creatively express themselves. Despite constant threats of violence, people resist. In many cases, the acts of resistance use the very gender structures meant to subordinate. These acts of resistance are not without consequence, but for many the risk of backlash is not enough to deter them from finding ways to have livable lives. Of course, for many, accommodation is the selected path by which they find ways to live with the demands social institutions place upon them.

Although many gender scholars are criticized (if not condemned) for denying that differences exist, we believe that criticism is based on a misunderstanding of our (and others') argument. In recognizing gender diversity, we are not denying differences between women and men. Instead, our argument is that the range of differences is much greater than a gender binary placed upon the axis of sex difference would permit. There are not two genders that neatly correspond to two sexes. Instead, a multiplicity of genders exists, which intersects with, influences, and is influenced by the vast array of other identity ingredients. Nor does gender inhere within individuals in some immutable form; rather, gender is constructed through institutional, interpersonal, and public discourse, and these constructions demand and maintain expectations of gender differentiation. Thus, ours is not a rejection of difference but an accounting of far more differences and far more similarities than people usually think about. Our goal is not to get beyond gender/sex but to open up possibilities for more genders and sexes. We do not deny that differences exist; rather, we simply reject the notions that the differences can be understood solely as differences between women and men and that differences exist solely within individual women and individual men.

Because we operate from an assumption of gender diversity, we also want to make clear that all people have at their disposal a range of communication strategies, even though those strategies may not always neatly fit with the gender identity one is developing. As you have learned in other communication studies classes, adaptability and flexibility are the marks of a good communicator. The same is true when one considers gender in communication: Gender flexibility is good. Different places, different interpersonal relationships, and different times in a person's life will call for different gendered styles.

As important as personal choices about gender performance are, and as much as we want to empower people to exercise agency in their communication choices about gender, we also want to make clear that those choices exist in larger social and institutional structures. Choice is never totally free of external constraints. Some choices are more valued and more validated than others, such as choosing to have children in a traditional, heterosexual marriage. Some choices are easier to make because we recognize their possibilities, such as men's choices to be firefighters and women's to be nurses. Some choices are not seen as choices, because they participate in existing patterns and practices, such as women's wearing of skirts and men's wearing of slacks. However, other choices are devalued or condemned, such as the choice of a woman to be child free or of a man to be the primary caregiver to young children. Some choices seem impossible, such as the choice of women in the 1900s to speak publicly. Some choices are highlighted as choices, as people flaunting something, such as the choice of men to dress in skirts or the choice of homosexual couples to kiss in public. For these reasons, one cannot discuss personal choices about gender in communication without also discussing the public politics of sex and gender.

Accordingly, the development of a critical gendered lens becomes necessary through which to study public communication about gender and to study institutions that construct and maintain gender/sex. Attention to the way in which media messages reinforce and expand gender/sex is necessary. Understanding how communication patterns about work and welfare gender particular groups is essential. Exploring how public statements about religion define what it means to be (only) a man or a woman is important. Analysis of what gets to be considered a *family* helps one understand who gets to be considered fully human. And analysis of public discourse about education enables one to track the ways stereotypes about gender/sex are maintained.

Personal gender/sex politics, although essential and important, are not the whole story. Personal choices matter. But political choices matter, too, and one should not lose sight of them. Gender in communication is not just about interpersonal relationships—whether men and women can be friends or whether men are from Mars and women from Venus—but also about larger social structures and the way they interact with the realities of people's personal lives. It *does* matter who does the dishes, cleans the toilet, takes out the trash, and changes diapers. It also matters what the minimum wage is—or what a person would be paid to do those things for another person who is economically privileged enough to hire them done.

As we explained early in this book, our goal has not been to give you all the answers—the simple lists that make simple sense of everything around you. Instead, our goal has been to give you the skills to ask the complicated questions, to ask whether a pattern exists along gender or sex lines, to ask why people do things the way they do, to ask whether something can be changed, to ask for something to change, to ask whether gender alone really explains it all. Sex privilege exists, and race privilege exists, but class privilege can complicate both of them. In other words, more than sex difference, power seems to be one of the most important analytical categories; and in the capitalist, consumerist society of the contemporary United States, power means money. In the United States, a rich White woman often holds more power than a poor Black man. A rich Hispanic man often holds more power than a poor White man. However, statistically there are many more rich White men in the United States than any other category of rich people we might list. Future research on gender in communication must take into account race, class, citizenship, sexuality, and religion if it is to say anything meaningful about the human condition. Nowhere is this clearer than in studies of globalization.

The centrality of economics points to one of the most important and least understood factors that influence gender in communication in contemporary times: globalization. Scholarship is emerging that deals with the challenge of globalization to understanding culture, gender, and communication; detailed research on globalization and gender in communication is appearing in scholarly journals. Students of gender in communication must keep in mind, as they attempt to track the influences of power on gender in communication, that globalization has created "shifting fault lines of economic and cultural power"; these shifts are occurring at an unprecedented speed, and they produce "new configurations of power, and new planes of dis/empowerment that cannot be equated with any other period in history" (Shome & Hegde, 2002, p. 175). Communication scholars Raka Shome and Rada Hegde make clear that the effect of globalization is not to make the category of identity disappear. Instead, one should focus on "*how* identity becomes a matter of struggle" (p. 179). In other words, not only is identity itself complex, but identity alone is not the only axis of power.

Just as institutions create locations of constraint and empowerment so, too, does globalization (Shome & Hegde, 2002, p. 184). Thus, we leave you with even more questions to ask about gender in an age of globalized communication. You should ask about where locations of domination exist in a globalized world. You should ask where acts of resistance occur. But also you should ask how all these fit together to create understandings of culture, nation, and gender.

References

W e have taken some liberties with APA reference style. To help readers see the contributions of both women and men to our subject, we have included first names of authors where known. We feel this recognition is important. Although we recognize the artificiality of sex distinctions and the complexity of identity, we also realize that no matter how artificial, identity categories do matter. As M. Jacqui Alexander and Chandra Talpade Mohanty (1997) note, even as postmodernist theories attempt to pluralize and dissolve "the stability and analytic utility of the categories race, class, gender, and sexuality . . . the relations of domination and subordination that are named and articulated through the processes of racism and racialization still exist, and they still require analytic and political specification and engagement" (p. xvii).

Abbey, Antonia, Zawacki, Tina, Buck, Phillip O., Clinton, A. Monique, & McAuslan, Pam. (2001). Alcohol and sexual assault. *National Institute on Alcohol Abuse and Alcoholism (NIAAA) Alcohol Health and Research World, 25*(1). Retrieved April 24, 2006, from http://www.athealth.com/Practitioner/ceduc/alc_assault.html

Abbey, Antonio, Ross, L. T., McDuffie, D., & McAuslan, Pam. (1996). Alcohol, misperception, and sexual assault: How and why are they linked? In David M. Buss & Neil M. Malamuth (Eds.), *Sex, power, conflict: Evolutionary and feminist perspectives* (pp. 138–161). New York: Oxford University Press.

Acker, Joan. (1990, June). Hierarchies, jobs, bodies: A theory of gendered organizations. *Gender & Society, 4*(2), 139–158.

Acker, Joan. (1992). Gendered institutions: From sex roles to gendered institutions. *Contemporary Sociology, 21,* 565–569.

Adams, Michele, & Coltrane, Scott. (2005). Boys and men in families: The domestic production of gender, power, and privilege. In Michael S. Kimmel, Jeff Hearn, & Robert W. Connell (Eds.), *Handbook of studies on men and masculinities* (pp. 230–248). Thousand Oaks, CA: Sage.

Adherents.com. (2005, August 28). Major religions of the world ranked by number of adherents. Retrieved December 27, 2005, from http://www.adherents.com/Religions_By_Adherents.html

Adler, Leonore Loeb. (Ed.). (1991). *Women in cross-cultural perspectives.* Westport, CT: Praeger.

Adorno, Theodor W. (1991). *The culture industry: Selected essays on mass culture.* London: Routledge.

Adrian, Bonnie. (2003). *Framing the bride: Globalizing beauty and romance in Taiwan's bridal industry.* Berkeley: University of California Press.

Agbese, Aje-Ori. (2003, Spring). Maintaining power in the face of political, economic and social discrimination: The tale of Nigerian women. *Women and Language, 26*(1), 18–26.

Aguilar, Delia D., & Lacsamana, Anne E. (Eds.). (2004). *Women and globalization.* Amherst, NY: Humanity Books.

Alcoff, Linda. (1995). The problem of speaking for others. In Judith Roof & Robyn Weigman (Eds.), *Who can speak? Authority and critical identity* (pp. 97–119). Urbana: University of Illinois Press.

Alcoff, Linda, & Potter, Elizabeth. (Eds.). (1993). *Feminist epistemologies.* New York: Routledge.

Alexander, M. Jacqui, & Mohanty, Chandra Talpade. (Eds.). (1997). Introduction: Genealogies, legacies, movements. In *Feminist genealogies, colonial legacies, democratic futures* (pp. xiii–xlii). New York: Routledge.

Allen, Brenda J. (1995). "Diversity" and organizational communication. *Journal of Applied Communication Research, 23,* 143–155.

Allen, Brenda J. (1996). Feminist standpoint theory: A Black woman's (re)view of organizational socialization. *Communication Studies, 47*(4), 257–271.

Allen, Brenda J. (1998). Black womanhood and feminist standpoints. *Management Communication Quarterly, 11,* 575–586.

Allen, Katherine R., & Walker, Alexis J. (2000). Constructing gender in families. In Robert M. Milardo & Steve Duck (Eds.), *Families as relationships* (pp. 1–17). Chichester, England: Wiley & Sons.

Ambady, Nalini, Hallahan, Mark, & Rosenthal, Robert. (1995). On judging and being judged accurately in zero-acquaintance situations. *Journal of Personality and Social Psychology, 69,* 518–529.

American Association of University Women. (1992). *Shortchanging girls, shortchanging America: A call to action.* Washington, DC: Author.

American Association of University Women. (1993). *Hostile hallways: The AAUW survey on sexual harassment in America's schools.* Washington, DC: Author.

American Association of University Women. (1998). *Gender gaps: Where schools still fail our children.* Washington, DC: Author.

American Association of University Women. (2001). *Hostile hallways: Bullying, teasing, and sexual harassment in schools.* Washington, DC: Author.

American Association of University Women. (2006). *Drawing the line: Sexual harassment on campus.* Washington, DC: Author.

American Psychiatric Association. (2000). *Diagnostic and statistical manual of mental disorders* (4th ed., text rev.). Washington, DC: Author.

Andersen, Margaret L. (2006). *Thinking about women: Sociological perspectives on sex and gender* (7th ed.). Boston: Pearson Education, Allyn & Bacon.

Anderson, Kristin J., & Leaper, Campbell. (1998, August). Meta-analyses of gender effects on conversational interruption: Why, what, when, where, and how. *Sex Roles, 39*(3–4), 225–252.

Anderson, Kristin L., Umberson, Debra, & Elliott, Slinikka. (2004). Violence and abuse in families. In Anita L. Vangelisti (Ed.), *Handbook of family communication* (pp. 629–645). Mahwah, NJ: Erlbaum.

Angier, Natalie. (1999). *Woman: An intimate geography.* New York: Anchor Books.

Anzaldúa, Gloria. (1987). *Borderlands/La Frontera: The new Mestiza*. San Francisco: Aunt Lute Books.

Anzaldúa, Gloria. (1990). Bridge, drawbridge, sandbar or island: Lesbians-of-Color *hacienda alianzas*. In Lisa Albrecht & Rose M. Brewer (Eds.), *Bridges of power: Women's multicultural alliances* (pp. 216–231). Philadelphia: New Society Publishers.

Apple, R. W., Jr. (2001, October 15). A nation challenged: News analysis: Nature of foe is obstacle in appealing for sacrifice. *New York Times*, p. B1.

Ardener, Edwin. (1973). *Some outstanding problems in the analysis of events*. Paper presented at the meeting of the Association of Social Anthropologists' decennial conference, Oxford. Later published in Malcom Chapman (Ed.), *The voice of prophecy and other essays/Edwin Ardener* (pp. 105–108). Oxford, UK: Basil Blackwell.

Ardener, Shirley. (2005). Ardener's "muted groups": The genesis of an idea and its praxis. *Women and Language, 28*(2), 50–54.

Aries, Elizabeth. (1996). Men *and women in interaction: Reconsidering the differences*. New York: Oxford University Press.

Aries, Elizabeth. (2006). Sex differences in interaction: A reexamination. In Kathryn Dindia & Daniel J. Canary (Eds.), *Sex differences and similarities in communication* (2nd ed., pp. 21–36). Mahwah, NJ: Erlbaum.

Armstrong, Jeannette. (1990). Words. In The Telling It Book Collective (Ed.), *Telling it: Women and language across cultures* (pp. 23–30). Vancouver, British Columbia, Canada: Press Gang Publishers.

As G.I. Joe bulks up, concern for the 98-pound weakling. (1999, May 30). *New York Times*, p. 2.

Asen, Robert. (2003). Women, work, welfare: A rhetorical history of images of poor women in welfare policy debates. *Rhetoric & Public Affairs, 6*(2), 285–312.

Ashcraft, Karen Lee, & Flores, Lisa A. (2003, January). "Slaves with white collars": Persistent performances of masculinity in crisis. *Text and Performance Quarterly, 23*(1), 1–29.

Ashcraft, Karen Lee, & Mumby, Dennis K. (2004). *Reworking gender: A feminist communicology of organization*. Thousand Oaks, CA: Sage.

Ayotte, Kevin, & Husain, Mary E. (2005, Fall). Securing Afghan women: Neocolonialism, epistemic violence, and the rhetoric of the veil. *NWSA Journal, 17*(3), 112–133.

Bailey, Covert, & Bishop, Lea. (2001). *The complete fit or fat book: The phenomenal program that successfully guides you from fatness to fitness*. New York: Galahad.

Baldry, Anna C. (2003). Bullying in schools and exposure to domestic violence. *Child Abuse and Neglect, 27,* 713–732.

Bandura, Albert. (2002). Social cognitive theory of mass communication. In Jennings Bryant & Dolf Zillman (Eds.), *Media effects: Advances in theory and research* (2nd ed., pp. 121–153). Mahwah, NJ: Erlbaum.

Bandura, Albert, & Walters, Richard H. (1963). *Social learning and personality development*. New York: Holt, Rinehart & Winston.

Bannerji, Himani, Carty, Linda, Dehli, Kari, Heald, Susan, & McKenna, Kate. (1991). *Unsettling relations: The university as a site of feminist struggles*. Boston: South End Press.

Barnett, Rosalind, & Rivers, Caryl. (2004). *Same difference: How gender myths are hurting our relationships, our children, and our jobs*. New York: Basic Books.

Bate, Barbara. (1988). *Communication and the sexes*. Prospect Heights, IL: Waveland.

Bate, Barbara, & Bowker, Judy. (1997). *Communication and the sexes* (2nd ed.). Prospect Heights, IL: Waveland Press.

Baxter, Judith. (2002). Jokers in the pack: Why boys are more adept than girls at speaking in public settings. *Language and Education, 16*(2), 81–96.

Baxter, Judith. (2003). *Positioning gender in discourse: A feminist methodology.* Basingstoke, Hampshire, UK: Palgrave, Macmillan.

Baxter, Judith. (2006). Putting gender in its place: A case study on constructing speaker identities in a management meeting. In M. Barrett & M. J. Davidson (Eds.), *Gender and communications at work* (pp. 154–165). Aldershot, UK: Ashgate Publishing.

Baxter, Leslie A., & Montgomery, Barbara M. (1996). *Relating: Dialogues and dialectics.* New York: Guilford Press.

Bayard, Donn, & Krishnayya, Sateesh. (2001). Gender, expletive use, and context: Male and female expletive use in structured and unstructured conversation among New Zealand university students. *Women and Language, 24*(1), 1–15.

Baydar, Gülsüm, & Ivegen, Berfin. (2006, Spring). Territories, identities, and thresholds: The Saturday mothers phenomenon in Istanbul. *Signs, 31*(3), 689–716.

Begley, Sharon, & Murr, Andrew. (1995, March 27). Gray matters. *Newsweek,* pp. 48–54.

Belenky, Mary Field, Clinchy, Blythe McVicker, Goldberger, Nancy Rule, & Tarule, Jill Mattuck. (1986). *Women's ways of knowing: The development of self, voice, and mind.* New York: Basic Books.

Belkin, Lisa. (2003, October 26). The opt-out revolution [Electronic version]. *New York Times Magazine.* Retrieved March 3, 2006, from http://www.nytimes.com/2003/10/26/magazine/26WOMEN.html?ei=5007&en=02f8d75eb63908e0&ex=1382500800&partner=USERLAND&pagewanted=all&position

Bell, Leslie C. (2004). Psychoanalytic theories of gender. In Alice H. Eagly, Anne E. Beall, & Robert J. Sternberg, (Eds.), *The psychology of gender* (2nd ed., pp. 145–168). New York: Guilford Press.

Bell, Linda A. (2005, July). *Women-led firms and the gender gap in top executive jobs* (Discussion Paper No. 1689). Bonn, Germany: The Institute for the Study of Labor (IZA). Retrieved July 25, 2006, from http://ftp.iza.org/dp1689.pdf

Bellafante, Ginia. (2004, January 12). Two fathers, with one happy to stay at home. *The New York Times,* p. 1.

Bellah, Robert N. (1967, Winter). Civil religion in America. *Daedalus, 96,* 1–21.

Bem, Sandra. (1974). The measurement of psychological androgyny. *Journal of Counseling and Clinical Psychology, 42,* 155–162.

Berger, John. (1972). *Ways of seeing.* London: Penguin Books.

Berlant, Lauren, & Warner, Michael. (1995, May). What does queer theory teach us about X? *PMLA, 110*(3), 343–349.

Bernard, Jessie. (1972). *The future of marriage.* New York: Bantam Books.

Best, Deborah L., & Thomas, Jennifer J. (2004). Cultural diversity and cross-cultural perspectives. In Alice H. Eagly, Anne E. Beall, & Robert J. Sternberg (Eds.), *The psychology of gender* (2nd ed., pp. 296–327). New York: Guilford Press.

Biesecker, Barbara A. (1992, Winter). Towards a transactional view of rhetorical and feminist theory: Rereading Helen Cixous's "The Laugh of the Medusa." *Southern Communication Journal, 57*(2), 86–96.

The Black Scholar. (Ed.). (1992). *Court of appeal: The Black community speaks out on the racial and sexual politics of Thomas vs. Hill.* New York: Ballantine Books.

Blau, Francine D., & Kahn, Lawrence M. (2000, Fall). Gender differences in pay. *Journal of Economic Perspectives, 14*(4), 75–99.

Bloustien, Gerry. (2003). *Girl making: A cross-cultural ethnography on the processes of growing up female.* New York: Berghahn Books.

Blustain, Sarah. (2000, November). The new gender wars. *Psychology Today, 33,* 42.

Bonvillain, Nancy. (2003). *Language, culture, and communication: The meaning of messages* (4th ed.). Upper Saddle River, NJ: Prentice Hall.

Bordo, Susan. (1997). *Twilight zones: The hidden life of cultural images from Plato to O.J.* Berkeley: University of California Press.

Bordo, Susan. (1999). *The male body: A new look at men in public and private.* New York: Farrar, Straus & Giroux.

Borisoff, Deborah, & Merill, Lisa. (2003). Gender and nonverbal communication. In Larry A. Samovar & Richard E. Porter (Eds.), *Intercultural communication: A reader* (10th ed., pp. 269–278). Belmont, CA: Wadsworth.

Bornstein, Marc H. (1995). Parenting infants. In Marc H. Bornstein (Ed.), *Handbook of parenting: Vol. 3. Status and social conditions of parents* (pp. 3–26). Mahwah, NJ: Erlbaum.

Boushey, Heather. (2005, December). Are women opting out? Debunking the myth. Center for Economic and Policy Research. Retrieved March 6, 2006, from www.cepr.net/publications/opt_out_2005_11.pdf

Bradstock, Andrew, Gill, Sean, Hogan, Anne, & Morgan, Sue. (Eds.). (2000). *Masculinity and spirituality in Victorian culture.* New York: St. Martin's Press.

Brannon, Linda. (2005). *Gender: psychological perspectives* (4th ed.). Boston: Pearson Education.

Britton, Dana M. (1999). Cat fights and gang fights: Preference for work in a male-dominated organization. *The Sociological Quarterly, 40*(3), 455–474.

Brod, Harry. (1987). The case for men's studies. In Harry Brod (Ed.), *The making of masculinities: The new men's studies* (pp. 52–53). Boston: Allen & Unwin.

Brooker, Peter. (2003). *A glossary of cultural theory* (2nd ed.). New York: Oxford University Press.

Brooks, Meredith, & Peiken, Shelly. (1997). Bitch [Music lyrics]. Retrieved June 6, 2006, from http://www.musicfanclubs.org/meredithbrooks/bitc.html

Brouwer, Daniel C. (1998). The precarious visibility politics of self-stigmatization: The case of HIV/AIDS tattoos. *Text and Performance Quarterly, 18,* 114–136.

Brouwer, Daniel C. (2005, December). Counterpublicity and corporality in HIV/AIDS zines. *Critical Studies in Media Communication, 22*(5), 351–371.

Brown, Penelope, & Levinson, Stephen. (1978). Universals in language usage: Politeness phenomenon. In Esther N. Goody (Ed.), *Questions and politeness* (pp. 56–89). Cambridge, UK: Cambridge University Press.

Buchanan, Pat. (1992, August 17). Remarks by Republican presidential candidate Pat Buchanan. Republican National Convention. Retrieved October 6, 2006, from http://www.buchanan.org/pa-92-0817-rnc.html

Budd, Mike, Entman, Robert M., & Steinman, Clay. (1990, June). The affirmative character of U.S. cultural studies. *Critical Studies in Mass Communication, 7*(2), 169–184.

Burgett, Bruce. (2005). On the Mormon question: Race, sex, and polygamy in the 1850s and the 1900s. *American Quarterly, 57,* 75–102.

Burke, Kenneth. (1966). *Language as symbolic action: Essays on life, literature, and method.* Berkeley: University of California Press.

Burke, Kenneth. (1969). *A rhetoric of motives.* Berkeley: University of California Press.

Burn, Shawn Meghan. (2000). *Women across cultures: A global perspective.* Mountain View, CA: Mayfield.

Bush administration publicizes plight of Afghan women. (2001, November 16). *Feminist Daily News Wire.* Retrieved June 5, 2002, from http://www.feminist.org/news/newsbyte/uswirestory.asp?id=5948

Bush, George W. (2001–2002). *Weekly compilation of presidential documents.* Retrieved June 5, 2002, from http://www.frwebgate.access.gpo.gov/cgi-bin/multidb.cgi

Bush, Laura. (2001, November 17). Radio address by Laura Bush to the nation. Retrieved June 5, 2002, from http://www.whitehouse.gov/news/releases/2001/11/20011117.html

Butler, Judith. (1990a). *Gender trouble: Feminism and the subversion of identity.* New York: Routledge.

Butler, Judith. (1990b). Performative acts and gender constitution: An essay in phenomenology and feminist theory. In Sue-Ellen Case (Ed.), *Performing feminisms: Feminist critical theory and theatre* (pp. 270–282). Baltimore: John Hopkins University Press.

Butler, Judith. (1991). Imitation and gender insubordination. In Diana Fuss (Ed.), *Inside/out: Lesbian theories, gay theories* (pp. 13–31). New York: Routledge.

Butler, Judith. (1993). *Bodies that matter: On the discursive limits of "sex."* New York: Routledge.

Butler, Judith. (1997). *Excitable speech: A politics of the performative.* New York: Routledge.

Butler, Judith. (2004). *Undoing gender.* New York: Routledge.

Buzzanell, Patrice M. (Ed.). (2000). *Rethinking organizational and managerial communication from feminist perspectives.* Thousand Oaks, CA: Sage.

Buzzanell, Patrice M., & Liu, Meina. (2005, February). Struggling with maternity leave policies and practices: A poststructuralist feminist analysis of gendered organizing. *Journal of Applied Communication Research, 33*(1), 1–25.

Buzzanell, Patrice M., Sterk, Helen, & Turner, Lynn H. (Eds.). (2004). *Gender in applied communication contexts.* Thousand Oaks, CA: Sage.

Byne, William M. (2005). Why we cannot conclude sexual orientation is a biological phenomenon. In J. Kenneth Davidson & Nelwyn B. Moore (Eds.), *Speaking of sexuality* (2nd ed., pp. 245–248). Los Angeles: Roxbury.

Cahill, Larry. (2005, May). His brain, her brain. *Scientific American, 292*(5), 40–47.

Caiazza, Amy. (2005). Don't bowl at night: Gender, safety, and civic participation. *Signs, 30*(2), 1607–1631.

Calafell, Bernadette Marie. (2004). Disrupting the dichotomy: "Yo soy Chincana/o?" in the New Latina/o South. *The Communication Review, 7,* 175–204.

Calás, Marta B. (1992). An/other silent voice? Representing "Hispanic woman" in organizational texts. In Albert J. Mills & Peta Tancred (Eds.), *Gendering organizational analysis* (pp. 201–221). Newbury Park, CA: Sage.

Calás, Marta B., & Smircich, Linda. (2001). From 'the woman's' point of view: Feminist approaches to organization studies. In Stewart R. Clegg, Cynthia Hardy, & Walter N. Nord (Eds.), *Handbook of organization studies* (pp. 218–257). Thousand Oaks, CA: Sage.

Cameron, Deborah. (1996). The language-gender interface: Challenging co-optation. In Victoria L. Bergvall, Janet Mueller Bing, & Alice F. Freed (Eds.), *Rethinking language and gender research: Theory and practice* (pp. 31–53). London: Longman.

Cameron, Deborah. (1997). Performing gender identity: Young men's talk and the construction of heterosexual masculinity. In Sally Johnson & Ulrike Hanna Meinhof (Eds.), *Language and masculinity* (pp. 47–64). Oxford, England: Basil Blackwell.

Cameron, Deborah. (1998). Lost in translation: Non-sexist language. In Deborah Cameron (Ed.), *The feminist critique of language* (2nd ed., pp. 155–163). New York: Routledge.

Campbell, Anne. (1993). *Men, women and aggression.* New York: Basic Books.

Campbell, Karlyn Kohrs. (1973, February). The rhetoric of women's liberation: An oxymoron. *Quarterly Journal of Speech, 59,* 74–86.

Campbell, Karlyn Kohrs. (1989). *Man cannot speak for her* (Volumes 1 and 2). Westport, CT: Praeger.

Campbell, Karlyn Kohrs, & Burkholder, Thomas R. (1997). *Critiques of contemporary rhetoric* (2nd ed.). Belmont: Wadsworth.

Campbell, Lynn. (2006, August 7). Waterloo's "experiment." *The Des Moines Register,* pp. 1A, 3A.

Canary, Daniel J., & Hause, Kimberley S. (1993, Spring). Is there any reason to research sex differences in communication? *Communication Quarterly, 41*(2), 129–144.

Cancian, Francesca. M. (1987). *Love in America: Gender and self-development.* New York: Cambridge University Press.

Cancian, Francesca M. (1989). Love and the rise of capitalism. In Barbara J. Risman & Pepper Schwartz (Eds.), *Gender in intimate relationships* (pp. 12–25). Belmont, CA: Wadsworth.

Cancian, Francesca M., & Oliker, Stacey J. (2000). *Caring and gender.* Thousand Oaks, CA: Sage.

CCaplan, Paula J., & Caplan, Jeremy, B. (1999). *Thinking critically about research on sex and gender* (2nd ed.). New York: Longman.

Carbaugh, Dan. (2002). "I can't do that!" But I "can actually see around corners": American Indian students and the study of public "communication." In Judith N. Martin, Thomas K. Nakayama, & Lisa N. Flores (Eds.), *Readings in intercultural communication: Experiences and contexts* (pp. 138–149). Boston: McGraw-Hill.

Carroll, Janell L. (2005). *Sexuality now.* Belmont, CA: Wadsworth.

Catherine of Sienna. (1980). *The dialogue* (Suzanne Noffke, O.P., Trans.). New York: Paulist Press. (Original work published ca. 1378)

Centers for Disease Control and Prevention. (2005a, May 3). Births, marriages, divorces, and deaths: Provisional data for November 2004. *National Vital Statistics Reports, 53*(19).

Centers for Disease Control and Prevention. (2005b, October 24). Sexual violence: Fact sheet. National Center for Injury Prevention and Control. Retrieved October 29, 2005, from http://www .cdc.gov/ncipc/factsheets/svfacts.htm

Chapman, Mary, & Hendler, Glenn. (1999). Introduction. In Mary Chapman & Glenn Hendler (Eds.), *Sentimental men: Masculinity and the politics of affect in American culture* (pp. 1–18). Berkeley: University of California Press.

Chappell, David. (2004). *A stone of hope: Prophetic religion and the death of Jim Crow.* Chapel Hill: University of North Carolina Press.

Charchar, Fadi J. (2003). Y are men the weaker sex? *Endocrine Abstracts, 6.* Retrieved July 20, 2005, from http://www.endocrine-abstracts.org/ea/0006/ea0006s4.htm

Chen, Martha, Vanek, Joann, Lund, Francie, & Heintz, James. (2005). *Progress of the world's women 2005: Women, work and poverty.* New York: United Nations Development Fund for Women.

Chittister, Joan Sr., OSB. (2004, August 13). To the 'experts in humanity': since when did women become the problem? [Electronic version]. *National Catholic Reporter, 40*(36), 7.

Chodorow, Nancy. (1978). *The reproduction of mothering: Psychoanalysis and the sociology of gender.* Berkeley: University of California Press.

Chow, Irene Hau-Siu, & Ding, Daniel Z. Q. (2002). Moral judgement and conflict handling styles among Chinese in Hong Kong and PRC. *The Journal of Management Development, 21*(9), 666–679.

Christie-Mizell, C. André. (2003, Summer). Bullying: The consequences of interparental discord and child's self-concept. *Family Process, 42*(2), 237–251.

Cichocki, Nina. (2004, November). Veils, poems, guns, and martyrs: Four themes of Muslim women's experiences in Shirin Neshat's photographic work. *Thirdspace, 4*(1). Retrieved July 14, 2006, from http://www.iiav.nl/ezines/web/Thirdspace/2004/N01/thirdspace/4_1_Cichocki.htm

Cixous, Hélène. (1981). Castration or decapitation? *Signs, 7,* 41–55.

Cixous, Hélène. (1991). "*Coming to writing*" *and other essays* (Deborah Jenson, Ed.). Cambridge, MA: Harvard University Press.

Clemetson, Lynette. (2006, February 9). Work vs. family, complicated by race. *The New York Times*, p. G1.

Cloud, Dana L. (1998, Fall). The rhetoric of "family values": Scapegoating, utopia, and the privatization of social responsibility. *Western Journal of Communication, 62*(4), 387–419.

Cloud, Dana L. (2004). "To veil the threat of terror": Afghan women and the "clash of civilizations" in the imagery of the U.S. war on terrorism. *Quarterly Journal of Speech, 90*(3), 285–306.

Coates, Jennifer. (1996). *Women talk: Conversations between women friends.* Oxford: Basil Blackwell.

Coates, Jennifer. (1997). One-at-a-time: The organization of men's talk. In Sally Johnson & Ulrike Hanna Meinhof (Eds.), *Language and masculinity* (pp. 107–129). Oxford, UK: Basil Blackwell.

Coates, Jennifer. (2003). *Men talk: Stories in the making of masculinities.* Malden, MA: Basil Blackwell.

Code, Lorraine. (1991). *What can she know? Feminist theory and the construction of knowledge.* Ithaca, NY: Cornell University Press.

Cofer, Judith Ortiz. (1997). The story of my body. In Mary Crawford & Rhoda Unger (Eds.), *In our own words: Readings on the psychology of women and gender* (pp. 47–54). New York: McGraw-Hill.

Collins, Patricia Hill. (1986). Learning from the outsider within. *Social Problems, 33,* 514–532.

Collins, Patricia Hill. (1990). *Black feminist thought: Knowledge, consciousness, and the politics of empowerment.* Boston: Unwin Hyman.

Collins, Patricia Hill. (1994). Shifting the center: Race, class, and feminist theorizing about motherhood. In Donna Bassin, Margaret Honey, & Maryle Mahrer Kaplan (Eds.), *Representations of motherhood* (pp. 56–74). New Haven, CT: Yale University Press.

Collins, Patricia Hill. (1998). *Fighting words: Black women and the search for justice.* Minneapolis: University of Minnesota Press.

Coltrane, Susan. (1989). Household labor and the routine production of gender. *Social Problems, 36,* 473–490.

The compact edition of the Oxford English dictionary. (1971). Glasgow, Scotland: Oxford University Press.

Comstock, Michelle. (2001). Grrrl zine networks: Re-composing spaces of authority, gender, and culture. *JAC, 21*(2), 383–409.

Condit, Celeste Michelle. (1989, June). The rhetorical limits of polysemy. *Critical Studies in Mass Communication, 6*(2), 103–122.

Condit, Celeste Michelle. (1990). *Decoding abortion rhetoric: Communicating social change.* Urbana: University of Illinois Press.

Condit, Celeste Michelle. (1992). Post-Burke: Transcending the sub-stance of dramatism. *Quarterly Journal of Speech, 78,* 349–355.

Condit, Celeste Michelle. (1998). Gender diversity: A theory of communication for the postmodern era. In Judith S. Trent (Ed.), *Communication: Views from the helm for the 21st century* (pp. 177–183). Boston: Allyn & Bacon.

Connell, R. W. (1987). *Gender and power: Society, the person, and sexual politics.* Stanford, CA: Stanford University Press.

Connell, R. W. (1995). *Masculinities.* Berkeley: University of California Press.

Connell, R. W. (2000). *The men and the boys.* Berkeley: University of California Press.

Connell, R. W. (2005). *Masculinities* (2nd ed.). Berkeley: University of California Press.

Connell, R. W., & Messerschmidt, James W. (2005, December). Hegemonic masculinity: Rethinking the concept. *Gender & Society, 19,* 829–859.

Conquergood, Dwight. (1992, February). Review essay: Ethnography, rhetoric, and performance. *Quarterly Journal of Speech, 78*, 80–97.

Coontz, Stephanie. (1992). *The way we never were: American families and the nostalgia trap.* New York: Basic Books.

Coontz, Stephanie. (1997). *The way we really are: Coming to terms with America's changing family.* New York: Basic Books.

Coontz, Stephanie. (2006). *Marriage, a history: From obedience to intimacy, or how love conquered marriage.* New York: Penguin.

Cooper, Brenda. (1999, March). The relevancy and gender identity in spectators' interpretations of *Thelma and Louise. Critical Studies in Mass Communication, 16*(1), 20–41.

Cooper, Brenda. (2000, Fall). "Chick flicks" as feminist texts: The appropriation of the male gaze in *Thelma & Louise. Women's Studies in Communication, 23*(3), 277–306.

Craig, Julie. (2001). From motherless children to rhinestone cowgirls: At the crossroads of feminism and country music. *Bitch, 14,* 60–65+.

Crawford, Mary. (1995). *Talking difference: On gender and language.* London: Sage.

Crenshaw, Kimberlé. (1989). Demarginalizing the intersection of race and sex: A Black feminist critique of antidiscrimination doctrine, feminist theory and antiracist politics. *University of Chicago Legal Forum,* 139–167.

Crenson, Matthew A., & Ginsberg, Benjamin. (2002). *Downsizing democracy: How America sidelined its citizens and privatized its public.* Baltimore: Johns Hopkins University Press.

Crystal, David. (1997). *English as a global language.* Cambridge, UK: Cambridge University Press.

Cuklanz, Lisa M. (1996). *Rape on trial: How the mass media construct legal reform and social change.* Philadelphia: University of Pennsylvania Press.

Cuklanz, Lisa M. (1998). The masculine ideal: Rape on prime-time television, 1976–1978. *Critical Studies in Mass Communication, 15,* 423–448.

Cuomo, Chris J. (1996, Fall). War is not just an event: Reflections on the significance of everyday violence. *Hypatia, 11*(4), 30–45.

Curran, Sara R. (2000, Spring). Women, work, and gender relations in developing countries: A global perspective (review). *Signs, 25*(3), 960–966.

Dabbs, James M., Jr., & Morris, Robin. (1990). Testosterone, social class, and antisocial behavior in a sample of 4,462 men. *Psychological Science, 1,* 209–211.

Daly, Mary. (1987). *Websters' first new intergalactic wickedary of the English language.* Boston: Beacon Press.

Daniels, Arlene Kaplan. (1987). Invisible work. *Social Problems, 34*(5), 403–415.

Davis, Devra Lee, Gottlieb, Michelle B., & Stampnitzky, Julie R. (1998, April 1). Reduced ratio of male to female births in several industrial countries. *Journal of the American Medical Association, 279*(13), 1018–1023.

Davis, James Earl. (2001). Transgressing the masculine: African American boys and the failure of schools. In Wayne Martino & Bob Meyenn (Eds.), *What about the boys? Issues of masculinity in schools.* Buckingham, England: Open University Press.

de la Cruz, Sor Juana Inés. (1987). *La Respuesta.* In *A woman of genius* (Margaret Sayers Peden, Trans.). Salisbury, CT: Lime Rick Press. (Original work published 1701)

de Lauretis, Teresa. (1984). *Alice doesn't: Feminism, semiotics, cinema.* London: MacMillan.

DeFrancisco, Victoria. (1991). The sounds of silence: How men silence women in marital relations. *Discourse and Society, 2*(4), 413–424.

DeFrancisco, Victoria. (1997). Gender, power, and practice: Or putting your politics where your mouth is. In Ruth Wodak (Ed.), *Gender, discourse, and ideology* (pp. 37–56). London: Sage.

DeFrancisco, Victoria, & Chatham-Carpenter, April. (2000). Self in community: African American women's views of self-esteem. *The Howard Journal of Communications, 11*(2), 73–92.

DeFrancisco, Victoria, & O'Connor, Penny. (1995). A feminist critique of self-help books on heterosexual romance: Read 'em and weep. *Women's Studies in Communication, 18*(2), 217–227.

DeLuca, Kevin Michael. (1999). Unruly arguments: The body rhetoric of Earth First!, ACT UP, and Queer Nation. *Argumentation & Advocacy, 36,* 9–21.

DeMello, Margo. (2000). *Bodies of inscription: A cultural history of the modern tattoo community.* Durham, NC: Duke University Press.

Demo, Anne Teresa. (2000, Spring). The Guerrilla Girls' comic politics of subversion. *Women's Studies in Communication, 23*(2), 133–156.

Deutsch, Francine M. (2004). Strategies men use to resist. In Michael S. Kimmel & Michael A. Messner (Eds.), *Men's lives* (6th ed., pp. 469–475). Boston: Allyn & Bacon.

Dick, Gary. (2004). Men's relationships with their fathers: Comparing men who batter with non-violent men. *Journal of Emotional Abuse, 4,* 61–84.

Dicker, Roy, & Piepmeier, Alison. (Eds.). (2003). *Catching a wave: Reclaiming feminism for the 21st century.* Boston: Northeastern University Press.

Dickinson, Greg, & Anderson, Karrin Vasby. (2004, September). Fallen: O.J. Simpson, Hillary Rodham Clinton, and the re-centering of white patriarchy. *Communication and Critical/Cultural Studies, 1*(3), 271–296.

Dienhart, Anna. (1998). *Reshaping fatherhood: The social construction of shared parenting.* San Francisco: Sage.

Dindia, Kathryn. (2006). Men are from North Dakota, women are from South Dakota. In Kathryn Dindia & Daniel J. Canary (Eds.), *Sex differences and similarities in communication* (2nd ed., pp. 3–20). Mahwah, NJ: Erlbaum.

DiPiero, Thomas. (2002). *White men aren't.* Durham, NC: Duke University Press.

Doherty, William J., & Beaton, John M. (2004). Mothers and fathers parenting together. In Anita L. Vangelisti (Ed.), *Handbook of family communication* (pp. 269–286). Mahwah, NJ: Erlbaum.

Dolan, Kathleen. (2005, March). Do women candidates play to gender stereotypes? Do men candidates play to women? Candidate sex and issues priorities on campaign websites. *Political Research Quarterly, 58*(1), 31–44.

Dorman, Benjamin. (2006, Winter). Tokyo's Dr. Phil. *Religion in the News,* pp. 20–21+.

Douglas, Ann. (1980, August 30). Soft-porn culture. *The New Republic,* pp. 25–29.

Dow, Bonnie J. (1995, Spring). Feminism, difference(s), and rhetorical studies. *Communication Studies, 46,* 106–117.

Dow, Bonnie J. (1996). *Prime-time feminism.* Philadelphia: University of Pennsylvania Press.

Dow, Bonnie J. (2001, June). *Ellen,* television, and the politics of gay and lesbian visibility. *Critical Studies in Media Communication, 18*(2), 123–140.

Dow, Bonnie J. (2003). Feminism, Miss America, and media mythology. *Rhetoric & Public Affairs, 6,* 127–149.

Dow, Bonnie J., & Condit, Celeste. (2005, September). The state of the art in feminist scholarship in communication. *Journal of Communication, 55*(3), 448–478.

Dow, Bonnie J., & Tonn, Marie Boor. (1993). "Feminine style" and political judgment in the rhetoric of Ann Richards. *Quarterly Journal of Speech, 79,* 286–302.

Dowd, Nancy E. (2000). *Redefining fatherhood.* New York: New York University Press.

Doyle, Jennifer, & Jones, Amelia. (2006). Introduction: New feminist theories of visual culture. *Signs, 31*(3), 607–615.

Du, Shanshan. (2000). "Husband and wife do it together": Sex/gender allocation of labor among the Qhawqhat Lahu of Langcang, Southwest China. *American Anthropologist, 10*(3), 520–537.

DuBowski, Sandi Simcha (Director/Producer). (2003). *Trembling Before G-d* [Documentary]. Israel: Simcha Leib Productions and Turbulent Arts, presented in Association with Keshet Broadcasting Ltd.

Duffy, Mignon. (2005, February). Reproducing labor inequalities: Challenges for feminists conceptualizing care at the intersections of gender, race, and class. *Gender & Society, 19*(1), 66–82.

Durham, Meenakshi Gigi. (1999, Summer). Girls, media, and the negotiation of sexuality: A study of race, class, and gender in adolescent peer groups. *Journalism and Mass Communication Quarterly, 76*(2), 193–216.

Dworkin, Andrea. (1993). I want a twenty-four-hour truce during which there is no rape. In Emilie Eucwald, Pamela R. Fletcher, & Martha Roth (Eds.), *Transforming a rape culture* (pp. 11–22). Minneapolis, MN: Milkweed Editions.

Dworkin, Andrea, & MacKinnon, Catharine A. (1988). *Pornography & civil rights: A new day for women's equality.* Minneapolis: Organizing Against Pornography.

Eakins, Barbara Westbrook, & Eakins, R. Gene. (1978). *Sex differences in human communication.* Boston: Houghton Mifflin.

Eakins, Barbara Westbrook, & Eakins, R. Gene. (1988). Sex differences in nonverbal communication. In Larry A. Samovar & Richard Porter (Eds.), *Intercultural communication: A reader* (pp. 292–309). Belmont, CA: Wadsworth.

Eckert, Penelope. (2003). Language and gender in adolescence. In Janet Holmes & Miriam Meyerhoff (Eds.), *The handbook of language and gender* (pp. 381–400). Malden, MA: Basil Blackwell.

Eckert, Penelope, & McConnell-Ginet, Sally. (1992). Think practically and look locally: Language and gender as community-based practice. *Annual Review of Anthropology, 21,* 461–490.

Eckert, Penelope, & McConnell-Ginet, Sally. (1999). New generalizations and explanations in language and gender research. *Language in Society, 28,* 185–201.

Edwards, Renee, & Hamilton, Mark A. (2004, April). You need to understand my gender role: An empirical test of Tannen's model of gender and communication. *Sex Roles: A Journal of Research, 50*(7–8), 491–505.

Ehrenreich, Barbara. (1990). Are you the middle-class? In Margaret L. Andersen & Patricia Hill Collins (Eds.), *Race, class and gender: An anthology* (pp. 100–109). Belmont, CA: Wadsworth.

Ehrenreich, Barbara. (2001). *Nickel and dimed: On (not) getting by in America.* New York: Holt.

Eid, Paul. (2003, Summer). The interplay between ethnicity, religion, and gender among second-generation Christian and Muslim Arabs in Montreal. *Canadian Ethnic Studies Journal, 35*(2), 30–62.

Eisikovits, Edina. (1998). Girl-talk/boy-talk: Sex differences in adolescent speech. In Jennifer Coates (Ed.), *Language and gender: A reader* (pp. 42–54). Oxford, England: Basil Blackwell.

Ekman, Paul, & Friesen, Wallace V. (1975). *Unmasking the face: A guide to recognizing emotions from facial cues.* Englewood Cliffs, NJ: Prentice Hall.

Elgin, Suzette Haden. (2000). *Native tongue.* New York: The Feminist Press at City University of New York. (Original work published 1984)

Elgin, Suzette Haden. (2002). *The Judas rose: Native tongue II.* New York: The Feminist Press at City University of New York. (Original work published 1987)

Elgin, Suzette Haden. (2002). *Earthsong: Native tongue III.* New York: The Feminist Press at City University of New York. (Original work published 1993)

El Guindi, Fadwa. (1999). *Veil: Modesty, privacy, and resistance.* New York: Berg.

El Guindi, Fadwa. (2005a). Confronting hegemony, resisting occupation. In Faye V. Harrison (Ed.), *Resisting racism and xenophobia: Global perspectives on race, gender and human rights* (pp. 251–268). New York: AltaMira Press.

El Guindi, Fadwa. (2005b, June). Gendered resistance, feminist veiling, Islamic feminism [Electronic version]. *Ahfad Journal, 22*(1), 53–78.

Elias, Marilyn. (1992, August 3). Difference seen in brains of gay men. *USA Today,* p. 8D.

Elliston, Deborah A. (2000). Geographies of gender and politics: The place of difference in Polynesian nationalism. *Cultural Anthropology, 15*(2), 171–216.

Enloe, Cynthia. (1989). *Bananas, beaches, and bases: Making feminist sense of international politics.* Berkley: University of California Press.

Ensler, Eve. (2000). *The vagina monologues: V-Day edition.* New York: Villard.

Entman, Robert M., & Rojecki, Andrew. (2000). *The black image in the white mind.* Chicago: University of Chicago Press.

Esteva, Gustavo. (1992). Development. In Wolfgang Sachs (Ed.), *The development dictionary* (pp. 6–25). New York: Zed Books.

Evans, Lorraine, & Davies, Kimberly. (2000, February). No sissy boys here: A content analysis of the representation of masculinity in elementary school reading textbooks. *Sex Roles, 42*(3–4), 255–270.

Evans, Patricia. (1992). *The verbally abusive relationship: How to recognize it and how to respond.* Holbrook, MA: Bob Adams.

Everitt, Joanna. (2005). Gender, media, and politics: A critical review essay. *Political Communication, 22,* 387–416.

Fabj, Valeria. (1993). Motherhood as political voice: The rhetoric of the Mothers of Plaza de Mayo. *Communication Studies, 44,* 1–18.

Faiola, Anthony. (2005, September 22). Men in land of samurai find their feminine side: Marketing fosters shift in gender roles. *Washington Post,* p. A01.

Fallows, Deborah. (2005, December 28). *How women and men use the Internet.* Washington, DC: Pew Internet & American Life Project. Retrieved May 10, 2006, from http://www.pewinternet.org/PPF/r/171/report_display.asp

Faludi, Susan. (1991). *Backlash: The undeclared war against American women.* New York: Doubleday.

Faludi, Susan. (1999, October 14). *Scenes from the betrayal of the American man.* Speech delivered to the Commonwealth Club of California. Retrieved May 19, 2006, from http://gos.sbc.edu/f/faludi.html

Family Violence Prevention Fund. (2006). Domestic violence is a serious, widespread social problem in America: The facts. Retrieved April 7, 2006, from http://www.endabuse.org/resources/facts/

Fausto-Sterling, Anne. (1992). *Myths of gender: Biological theories about women and men* (2nd ed.). New York: Basic Books.

Fausto-Sterling, Anne. (2005). The bare bones of sex: Part 1—sex and gender. *Signs, 30,* 1491–1527.

Felski, Rita. (1989). *Beyond feminist aesthetics.* Cambridge, MA: Harvard University Press.

Felski, Rita. (2006). "Because it is beautiful": New feminist perspectives on beauty. *Feminist Theory, 7*(2), 273–282.

Feminist Majority Foundation. (2001–2005). *The Taliban & Afghan women: Background.* Retrieved July 20, 2002, from http://www.feminist.org/afghan/facts.html

Fenstermaker, Sarah, & West, Candace. (2002). *Doing gender: Doing difference.* Thousand Oaks, CA: Sage.

Ferguson, Ann Arnett. (2000). *Bad boys: Public schools in the making of Black masculinity.* Ann Arbor: University of Michigan Press.

Ferns, Ilse. (2000, September). Moral development during adolescence: A cross-cultural study. (South Africa). *Dissertation Abstracts International: Section B: The Sciences and Engineering, 61*(3-B), 1670.

Fischer, Agneta, H. (1993). Sex differences in emotionality: Fact or stereotype? *Feminism & Psychology, 3,* 303–318.

Fisher, Bonnie S., Cullen, Francis T., & Turner, Michael G. (2000). *The sexual victimization of college women.* Washington, DC: National Institute of Justice.

Fishman, Pamela. (1978). Interaction: The work women do. *Social Problems, 25,* 397–406.

Fiske, John. (1987). *Television culture.* New York: Methuen.

Fivush, Robyn, & Buckner, Janine P. (2000). Gender, sadness, and depression: The development of emotional focus through gendered discourse. In Agneta H. Fischer (Ed.), *Gender and emotion: Social psychological perspectives* (pp. 232–253). Cambridge, UK: Cambridge University Press.

Flanagan, Mary, & Booth, Austin. (Eds.). (2002). *Reload: Rethinking women & cyberculture.* Cambridge: MIT Press.

Flores, Lisa A. (1996, May). Creating discursive space through a rhetoric of difference: Chicana feminists craft a homeland. *Quarterly Journal of Speech, 82,* 142–156.

Floyd, Kory, & Morman, Mark T. (2003). Human affection exchange: II. Affectionate communication in father-son relationships. *The Journal of Social Psychology, 143*(5), 599–612.

Floyd, Kory, & Morman, Mark T. (Eds.). (2006). *Widening the family circle: New research on family communication.* Thousand Oaks, CA: Sage.

Fondas, Nanette. (1997). Feminization unveiled: Management qualities in contemporary writing. *Academy of Management Review, 22,* 257–282.

Foote, Shelly. (1989). Challenging gender symbols. In Claudia Brush Kidwell & Valerie Steele (Eds.), *Men and women: Dressing the part* (pp. 144–157). Washington, DC: Smithsonian Institution Press.

Foss, Sonja K., & Foss, Karen A. (1994, November). The construction of feminine spectatorship in Garrison Keillor's radio monologues. *Quarterly Journal of Speech, 80*(4), 410–426.

Foss, Sonja K., & Griffin, Cindy L. (1995, March). Beyond persuasion: A proposal for an invitational rhetoric. *Communication Monographs, 62,* 2–18.

Foucault, Michel. (1972). *The archaeology of knowledge and the discourse on language* (Rupert Swyer, Trans.). New York: Pantheon.

Foucault, Michel. (1980). *Power/knowledge* (Colin Gordon, L. Marshall, J. Mephan, & K. Soper, Trans.). New York: Pantheon.

Fox, Mary Frank. (2001). Women, science, and academia: Graduate education and careers. *Gender & Society, 15,* 654–666.

Francis, Becky, & Skelton, Christine. (2005). *Reassessing gender and achievement: Questioning contemporary key debates.* London: Routledge.

Francis, Leslie J. (1997). The psychology of gender differences in religion: A review of empirical research. *Religion, 27,* 81–96.

Franke, Katherine M. (1997, April). What's wrong with sexual harassment? *Stanford Law Review, 49,* 691–772.

Frankenberry, Nancy. (1994, Fall). Introduction: Prolegomenon to future feminist philoso-
     phies of religions. *Hypatia, 9*(4), 1–15.
Franklin, Benjamin. (1751). Observations concerning the increase of mankind, peopling of
     countries, etc. Retrieved July 15, 2005, from http://www.historycarper.com/resources/
     twobf2/increase.htm
Fraser, Nancy. (1992). Rethinking the public sphere. In Craig Calhoun (Ed.), *Habermas and
     the public sphere* (pp. 109–142). Cambridge: MIT Press.
Fraser, Nancy, & Gordon, Linda. (1994, Winter). A genealogy of *dependency:* Tracing a
     keyword of the U.S. welfare state. *Signs, 19*(2), 309–336.
Frawley, Timothy. (2005). Gender bias in the classroom: Current controversies and impli-
     cations for teachers. *Childhood Education, 81*(4), 221–228.
Frederick, David A., Fessler, Daniel M. T., & Haselton, Martie G. (2005). Do representations
     of male muscularity differ in men's and women's magazines? *Body Image, 2,* 81–86.
Fredrickson, Barbara L., & Roberts, Tomi-Ann. (1997). Objectification theory: Toward
     understanding women's lived experiences and mental health risks. *Psychology
     of Women Quarterly, 21,* 173–206.
Freeman, Sue J. M., & Bourque, Susan C. (2001). Leadership and power: New conceptions.
     In Sue J. M. Freeman, Susan C. Bourque, & Christine M. Shelton (Eds.), *Women on
     power: Leadership redefined* (pp. 3–24). Boston: Northeastern University Press.
Freire, Paulo. (1972). *Pedagogy of the oppressed.* London: Penguin.
Friedan, Betty. (1963). *The feminine mystique.* New York: Dell.
Friedman, Howard S., & Miller-Herringer, Terry. (1991, November). Nonverbal display
     of emotion in public and private: Self-monitoring, personality, and expressive cues.
     Journal of Personality and Social Psychology, 61(5), 766–775.
Frith, Hannah, & Gleeson, Kate. (2004). Clothing and embodiment: Men managing body
     image and appearance. *Psychology of Men and Masculinity, 5*(1), 40–48.
Frith, Katherine, Shaw, Ping, & Cheng, Hong. (2005, March). The construction of beauty:
     A cross-cultural analysis of women's magazine advertising. *Journal of Communication,
     55*(1), 56–70.
Frosh, Stephen, Phoenix, Ann, & Pattman, Rob. (2002). *Young masculinities: Understanding
     boys in contemporary society.* Hampshire, England: Palgrave.
Fulghum, Robert. (2004). *All I really need to know I learned in kindergarten* (15th ed.). New
     York: Ballantine Books.
Fyee, Kristen. (2006, March 2). *Wolves in sheep's clothing: A content analysis of children's
     television.* Parents Television Council. Retrieved August 24, 2006, from http://www.
     parentstv.org/PTC/publications/reports/childrensstudy/childrensstudy.pdf
Gadpaille, Warren J. (1975). *The cycles of sex.* New York: Charles Scribner's Sons.
Gaffney, Edward McGlynn, Jr. (1990). Politics without brackets on religious convictions:
     Michael Perry and Bruce Ackerman on neutrality. *Tulane Law Review, 64,* 1143–1194.
Gage, Matilda Joslyn. (1980). *Women, church, and state* (Sally Roesch Wagner, Ed.).
     Watertown, MA: Persephone Press. (Original work published 1893)
Galvin, Lathleen M. (2006). Gender and family interaction: Dress rehearsal for an impro-
     visation? In Bonnie J. Dow & Julia T. Wood (Eds.), *The SAGE handbook of gender and
     communication* (pp. 41–55). Thousand Oaks, CA: Sage.
Gamman, Lorraine, & Marshment, Margaret. (Eds.). (1989). *The female gaze: Women as
     viewers of popular culture.* Seattle, WA: The Real Comet Press.
Gans, Herbert J. (1999). *Popular culture and high culture: An analysis and evaluation of taste*
     (Rev. ed.). New York: Basic Books.

Gao, Ge, & Ting-Toomey, Stella. (1998). *Communicating effectively with the Chinese.* Thousand Oaks, CA: Sage.

Gauntlett, David. (2002). *Media, gender and identity.* London: Routledge.

Gearhart, Sally Miller. (1979). The womanization of rhetoric. *Women's Studies International Quarterly, 2,* 195–201.

Gergen, Kenneth J. (1994). *Realities and relationships: Soundings in social construction.* Cambridge, MA: Harvard University Press.

Gerschick, Thomas J., & Miller, Adam Stephen. (2004). Coming to terms: Masculinity and physical disability. In Michael S. Kimmel & Michael A. Messner (Eds.), *Men's lives* (6th ed.). Boston: Allyn & Bacon.

Gerson, Kathleen. (2004, August). Understanding work and family through a gendered lens. *Community, Work and Family, 7*(2), 163–178.

Gibbons, Sheila. (Ed.). (2005, December). Industry statistics. *Media Report to Women.* Retrieved April 21, 2006, from http://www.mediareporttowomen.com/statistics.htm

Giffney, Noreen. (2004). Denormatizing queer theory: More than (simply) lesbian and gay studies. *Feminist Theory, 5*(1), 73–78.

Gillespie, Dair L., & Leffler, Ann. (1983). Theories of nonverbal behavior: A critical review of proxemics research. In Randall Collins (Ed.), *Sociological theory* (pp. 120–154). San Francisco: Jossey-Bass.

Gilligan, Carol. (1982). *In a different voice: Psychological theory and women's development.* Cambridge, MA: Harvard University Press.

Gilmore, Sean. (1995). Sports sex: A theory of sexual aggression. In Helen Sterk & Lynn Turner (Eds.), *Difference that makes a difference: Examining research assumptions in gender issues.* Westport, CT: Greenwood.

Gilmore, Sean (Writer), & Terek, Shirley (Producer). (1990). *Sport Sex* [documentary]. Meadville, PA.

Goffman, Erving. (1955). On facework: An analysis of ritual elements in social interaction. *Psychiatry, 18,* 213–231.

Goffman, Erving. (1963). *Behavior in public places: Notes on the social organization of gatherings.* New York: Free Press.

Goffman, Erving. (1979). *Gender advertisements.* New York: Harper & Row.

Goldberg, Carey. (2005, June 27). Test reveals gender early in pregnancy: Ethicists fear use in sex selection. *The Boston Globe,* p. A1.

Goldberg, Gertrude Schaffner, & Kremen, Eleanor. (1990). *The feminization of poverty: Only in America?* Westport, CT: Praeger.

Goldman, Robert, Heath, Deborah, & Smith, Sharon L. (1991). Commodity feminism. *Critical Studies in Mass Communication, 8*(3), 333–351.

Goldsmith, Daena J., & Fulfs, Patricia A. (1999). You just don't have the evidence: An analysis of claims and evidence in Deborah Tannen's *You just don't understand.* In Michael E. Roloff (Ed.), *Communication yearbook* (Vol. 22, pp. 1–49). Thousand Oaks, CA: Sage.

Gonzales, Angela A., & Kertesz, Judy. (2001). Engendering power in Native North America. In Dana Vannoy (Ed.), *Gender mosaics* (pp. 43–52). Los Angeles: Roxbury.

Goodall, H. L. (Bud). (2000). *Writing the new ethnography.* Walnut Creek, CA: AltaMira Press.

Gooden, Angela M., & Gooden, Mark A. (2001). Gender representation in notable children's picture books: 1995–1999. *Sex Roles, 45,* 89–101.

Goodwin, Marjorie Harness. (1999). Constructing opposition within girls' games. In Mary Bucholtz, A. C. Liang, & Laurel A. Sutton (Eds.), *Reinventing identities: The gendered self in discourse* (pp. 388–410). New York: Oxford University Press.

Gordon, Elizabeth. (1997). Sex, speech, and stereotypes: Why women use prestige speech forms more than men. *Language and Society, 26,* 47–63.

Gordon, Sarah A. (2001). "Any desired length": Negotiating gender through sports clothing, 1870–1925. In Philip Scranton (Ed.), *Beauty and business: Commerce, gender, and culture in modern America.* New York: Routledge.

Gottman, John, M. (1994). *What predicts divorce? The relationship between marital processes and marital outcomes.* Hillsdale, NJ: Erlbaum.

Gottman, John M., & Silver, Nan. (1999). *The seven principles for making marriage work.* New York: Random House.

Grabe, Shelly, & Hyde, Janet Shibley. (2006). Ethnicity and body dissatisfaction among women in the United States: A meta-analysis. *Psychological Bulletin, 132*(4), 622–640.

Graham-Bermann, Sandra, & Brescoll, Victoria. (2000). Gender, power, and violence: Assessing the family stereotypes of the children of batterers. *Journal of Family Psychology, 14,* 600–612.

Gramsci, Antonio, Rosenthal, Raymond, & Rosengarten, Frank. (1993). *Letters from prison.* New York: Columbia University Press.

Gray, Herman. (1995). Black masculinity and visual culture. *Callaloo, 18*(2), 401–405.

Gray, John. (1992). *Men are from Mars, women are from Venus: A practical guide for improving communication and getting what you want in your relationship.* New York: HarperCollins.

Greenberg, Julie A. (1999, Summer). Defining male and female: Intersexuality and the collision between law and biology. *Arizona Law Review, 41,* 265–328.

Greenberger, Marcia D., & Brake, Deborah L. (1996, July 5). The VMI decision: Shattering sexual stereotypes. *The Chronicle of Higher Education, 42*(43), A52.

Greene, Kathryn, & Krcmar, Marina. (2005, March). Predicting exposure to and liking of media violence: A uses and gratifications approach. *Communication Studies, 56*(1), 71–93.

Gregg, Nina. (1993). Politics of identity/politics of location: Women workers organizing in a postmodern world. *Women's Studies in Communication, 16*(1), 1–33.

Gring-Pemble, Lisa M. (2003). Legislating a "normal, classic family": The rhetorical construction of families in American welfare policy. *Political Communication, 20,* 473–498.

Grogan, Tamara. (2003). *Boys and girls together: Improving gender relationships in K-6 classrooms.* Greenfield, MA: Northeast Foundation for Children.

Gudykunst, William, B., & Ting-Toomey, Stella. (1988). *Cultural and interpersonal communication.* Newbury Park, CA: Sage.

Guerrilla Girls. (1995). *Confessions of the Guerrilla Girls.* New York: HarperPerennial.

Gunning, Isabelle R. (1997). Arrogant perception, world traveling, and multicultural feminism: The case of female genital surgeries. In Adrien Katherine Wing (Ed.), *Critical race feminism: A reader* (pp. 352–360). New York: New York University Press.

Gurian, Michael, & Stevens, Kathy. (2005). *The mind of boys: Saving our sons from falling behind in school and life.* San Francisco: Jossey-Bass.

Haag, Pamela. (2005, February 11). Navigating the new subtleties of sex-discrimination cases in academe. *The Chronicle of Higher Education, 51*(23), B20.

Haddock, Shelley A., Zimmerman, Toni Schindler, & Lyness, Kevin P. (2003). Changing gender norms: Transitional dilemmas. In Froma Walsh (Ed.), *Normal family processes: Growing diversity and complexity* (3rd ed., pp. 301–336). New York: Guilford Press.

Hadewijch. (1980). *The complete works* (Mother Columba Hart, O.S.B., Trans.). New York: Paulist Press. (Original work published ca. mid-1200s).

Halberstadt, Amy G., & Saitta, Martha B. (1987). Gender, nonverbal behavior, and perceived dominance: A test of the theory. *Journal of Personality and Social Psychology, 53,* 257–272.

Halberstam, Judith. (1998). *Female masculinity.* Durham, NC: Duke University Press.

Halberstam, Judith. (2005). *In a queer time & place.* New York: New York University Press.

Hall, Donald E. (Ed.). (1994). *Muscular Christianity: Embodying the Victorian age.* Cambridge, UK: Cambridge University Press.

Hall, Judith A. (1984). *Nonverbal sex differences: Communication accuracy and expressive style.* Baltimore: Johns Hopkins University Press.

Hall, Judith A. (2006). How big are nonverbal sex differences? The case of smiling and nonverbal sensitivity. In Kathryn Dindia & Daniel J. Canary (Eds.), *Sex differences and similarities in communication* (2nd ed., pp. 59–82). Mahwah, NJ: Erlbaum.

Hall, Judith A., Carter, Jason D., & Horgan, Terrance G. (2000). Gender differences in nonverbal communication of emotion. In Agneta H. Fischer (Ed.), *Gender and emotion: Social psychological perspectives* (pp. 97–117). Cambridge, UK: Cambridge University Press.

Hall, Judith A., Halberstadt, A. G., & O'Brien, C. E. (1997). Subordination and nonverbal sensitivity: A study and synthesis of findings based on trait measures. *Sex Roles, 37,* 295–317.

Hall, Kira. (1995). Lip service on the fantasy lines. In Kira Hall & Mary Bucholtz (Eds.), *Gender articulated: Language and the socially constructed self* (pp. 183–216). New York: Routledge.

Hall, Kira. (2000). Performativity. *Journal of Linguistic Anthropology, 9*(1–2), 184–187.

Hall, Stuart. (1989). Ideology and communication theory. In Brenda Dervin, Larry Grossberg, Barbara O'Keefe, & Ellen Wartella (Eds.), *Rethinking communication theory* (Vol. 1, pp. 40–52). Newbury Park, CA: Sage.

Hallstein, D. Lynn O'Brien. (1996). Feminist assessment of emancipatory potential and Madonna's contradictory gender practices. *Quarterly Journal of Speech, 82,* 125–141.

Hancock, Ange-Marie. (2004). *The politics of disgust: The public identity of the welfare queen.* New York: New York University Press.

Hand, Jeanne A., & Sanchez, Laura. (2000). Badgering or bantering? Gender differences in experience of, and reactions to, sexual harassment among U.S. high school students. *Gender & Society, 14,* 718–746.

Hanke, Robert. (1998, May). Theorizing masculinity with/in the media. *Communication Theory, 8*(2), 183–203.

Harding, Sandra. (1995). Subjectivity, experience, and knowledge: An epistemology from/for Rainbow Coalition politics. In Judith Roof & Robyn Weigman (Eds.), *Who can speak? Authority and critical identity* (pp. 120–136). Urbana: University of Illinois Press.

Harding, Sandra. (1998). *Can feminism be multicultural?* Ithaca, NY: Cornell University Press.

Harding, Sandra, & Hintikka, Merrill. (Eds.). (2003). *Discovering reality: Feminist perspectives on epistemology, methodology, and the philosophy of science.* Dordrecht, The Netherlands: Kluwer Academic. (Original work published 1983)

Hardman, M. J. (1986). Data source marking in the Jaqi languages. In Wallace Chafe & Johanna Nichols (Eds.), *Evidentiality: The linguistic coding of epistemology* (pp. 113–136). Norwood, NJ: Ablex.

Hardman, M. J. (1999, Spring). Why we should say "women and men" until it doesn't matter any more. *Women and Language, 22*(1), 1–2.

Harmon, Mary R. (2000). Gender/language subtexts as found in literature anthologies: Mixed messages, stereotypes, silences, erasure. In M. J. Hardman & Anita Taylor (Eds.), *Hearing many voices* (pp. 75–85). Cresskill, NJ: Hampton.

Harris, Angela. (1997). Race and essentialism in feminist legal theory. In Adrien Katherine Wing (Ed.), *Critical race feminism: A reader* (pp. 11–26). New York: New York University Press.

Harris, Judith. (2003, December 7). If shoe won't fit, fix the foot? Popular surgery raises concern. *New York Times*, pp. A1, A36.

Harter, Lynn M. (2004, May). Masculinity(s), the agrarian frontier myth, and cooperative ways of organizing: Contradictions and tensions in the experience and enactment of democracy. *Journal of Applied Communication Research, 32*(2), 89–118.

Harvey, Adia M. (2005, December). Becoming entrepreneurs: Intersections of race, class, and gender at the Black beauty salon. *Gender & Society, 19*(6), 789–808.

Hazard, Mrs. B. (1910, June). New York State Association opposed to woman suffrage. *The Chautauquan*, pp. 84–89.

Hearn, Jeff. (1993). Emotive subjects: Organizational men, organizational masculinities and the (de)construction of "emotions." In Stephen Fineman (Ed.), *Emotion in organizations* (pp. 142–166). London: Sage.

Hearn, Jeff. (1994). The organization(s) of violence: Men, gender relations, organizations, and violences. *Human Relations, 47*, 731–754.

Hecht, Michael A., & LaFrance, Marianne. (1998). License or obligation to smile: The effect of power and sex on amount and type of smiling. *Personality and Social Psychology Bulletin, 24*, 1332–1342.

Hegde, Radha Sarma. (1995). Recipes for change: Weekly help for Indian women. *Women's Studies in Communication, 18*(2),177–188.

Hegel, George Wilhelm Friedrich. (1807). *The phenomenology of mind* (J. B. Braille, Trans.). Germany: Wurtzburg & Bamberg.

Held, David, & McGrew, Anthony (Eds.). (2000). *The global transformation reader*. Cambridge, UK: Polity Press.

Helgeson, Vicki S. (1994). Relation of agency and communion to well-being: Evidence and potential explanations. *Psychological Bulletin, 116*(3), 412–428.

Helweg-Larsen, Marie, Cunningham, Stephanie J., Carrico, Amanda, & Pergram, Alison M. (2004). To nod or not to nod: An observational study of nonverbal communication and status in female and male college students. *Psychology of Women Quarterly, 28*, 358–361.

Hendriks, Alexandra. (2002, March). Examining the effects of hegemonic depictions of female bodies on television: A call for theory and programmatic research. *Critical Studies in Media Communication, 19*(1), 106–123.

Henley, Nancy. (1977). *Body politics: Power, sex, and nonverbal communication*. Englewood Cliffs, NJ: Prentice Hall.

Henley, Nancy. (1995). Body politics revisited: What do we know today? In Pamela J. Kalbfleisch & Michael J. Cody (Eds.), *Gender, power and communication in human relationships* (pp. 27–61). Hillsdale, NJ: Erlbaum.

Henley, Nancy, & Kramarae, Cheris. (1991). Gender, power, and miscommunication. In Nikolas Coupland, Howard Giles, & John M. Wiemann (Eds.), *"Miscommunication" and problematic talk* (pp. 18–43). Newbury Park, CA: Sage.

Hennessy, Rosemary. (1995). Subjects, knowledges, . . . and all the rest: Speaking for what. In Judith Roof & Robyn Weigman (Eds.), *Who can speak? Authority and critical identity* (pp. 137–150). Urbana: The University of Illinois Press.

Herbst, Claudia. (2004). Lara's lethal and loaded mission: Transposing reproduction and destruction. In Sherrie A. Inness (Ed.), *Action chicks: New images of tough women in popular culture* (pp. 21–46). New York: Palgrave MacMillan.

Herring, Susan C., Kouper, Inna, Scheidt, Lois Ann, & Wright, Elijah L. (2004). Women and children last: The discursive construction of weblogs. In Laura Gurak, Smiljana Antonijevic, Laurie Johnson, Clancy Ratliff, & Jessica Reyman (Eds.), *Into the blogosphere: Rhetoric, community, and culture of weblogs*. Retrieved August 13, 2004, from http://blog.lib.umn.edu/blogosphere/women_and_children.html

Hesford, Wendy S. (2004). Documenting violations: Rhetorical witnessing and the spectacle of distant suffering. *Biography, 27*(1), 104–144.

Hewlett, Sylvia Ann, & Luce, Carolyn Buck. (2005, March). Off-ramps and on-ramps: Keeping talented women on the road to success. *Harvard Business Review,* pp. 43–54.

Hildegard of Bingen. (1990). *Scivias* (Mother Columba Hart & Jane Bishop, Trans.). New York: Paulist Press. (Original work published ca. 1151/1152).

Hill, Shirley, A. (2002). Teaching and doing gender in African American families. *Sex Roles, 47*(11/12), 493–506.

Hines, Caitlin. (1999). Rebaking the pie: The woman as dessert metaphor. In Mary Bucholtz, A. C. Liang, & Laurel A. Sutton (Eds.), *Reinventing identities: The gendered self in discourse* (pp. 145–162). New York: Oxford University Press.

Hines, Melissa. (2004). Androgen, estrogen, and gender: Contributions of the early hormone environment to gender-related behavior. In Alice H. Eagly, Anne E. Beall, & Robert J. Sternberg (Eds.), *The psychology of gender* (2nd ed., pp. 9–37). New York: Guilford Press.

Hochschild, Arlie Russell. (1983). *The managed heart: Commercialization of human feelings.* Berkeley: University of California Press.

Hochschild, Arlie Russell. (1997). *The time bind: When work becomes home and home becomes work.* New York: Henry Holt.

Hochschild, Arlie Russell. (2003). *The second shift* (2nd ed.). New York: Avon Books.

Hofstede, Geert. (Ed.) (1998). *Masculinity and femininity: The taboo dimension of national cultures.* Thousand Oaks, CA: Sage.

Holland, Dorothy C., & Eisenhart, Margaret A. (1990). *Educated in romance.* Chicago: University of Chicago Press.

Hollander, Anne. (1978). *Seeing through clothing.* New York: Viking Press.

Holmes, Janet. (1995). *Women, men, and politeness.* London: Longman.

Holmes, Janet. (1997). Story-telling in New Zealand women's and men's talk. In Ruth Wodak (Ed.), *Gender and discourse* (pp. 263–293). London: Sage.

Hondagneu-Sotelo, Pierette, & Avila, Ernestine. (1997, October). "I'm here but I'm there": The meanings of Latina transitional motherhood [Electronic version]. *Gender & Society, 11*(5), 548–569.

hooks, bell. (1984). *Feminist theory: From margin to center.* Boston: South End Press.

hooks, bell. (1989). *Talking back: Thinking feminist, thinking black.* Boston: South End Press.

hooks, bell. (1992). *Black looks: Race and representation.* Boston: South End Press.

hooks, bell. (1993). *Sisters of the yam: Black women and self-recovery.* Boston: South End.

hooks, bell. (1994). *Teaching to transgress: Education as the practice of freedom.* New York: Routledge.

hooks, bell. (1995). Appearance obsession: Is the price too high. *Essence, 26,* 69–71.

HopKins, Mary Frances. (1995, May). The performance turn—and toss. *Quarterly Journal of Speech, 81,* 228–236.

Hopper, Robert. (2003). *Gendering talk.* East Lansing: Michigan State University Press.

Horkheimer, Max, & Adorno, Theodor W. (1972). *Dialectic of enlightenment* (John Cumming, Trans.). New York: Herder and Herder.

Horwitz, Linda Diane. (1998). *Transforming appearance into rhetorical argument: Rhetorical criticism of public speeches of Barbara Jordan, Lucy Parsons, and Angela Y. Davis.* Doctoral dissertation, Northwestern University.

Horwitz, Linda, Kowal, Donna, & Palczewski, Catherine Helen. (In press). Women anarchists and the feminine ideal: Voltairine de Cleyre, Emma Goldman, and Lucy Parsons. In Martha Soloman Watson (Ed.), *The rhetoric of nineteenth century reform.* Dearborn: Michigan State University Press.

Houston, Marsha. (2000). Multiple perspectives: African American women conceive their talk. *Women and Language, 23*(1), 11–17.

Houston, Marsha. (2004). When Black women talk with White women: Why the dialogues are difficult. In Alberto Gonzalez, Marsha Houston, & Victoria Chen (Eds.), *Our voices: Essays in culture, ethnicity, and communication* (4th ed., pp. 119–125). Los Angeles: Roxbury.

Hunt, Lynn. (Ed.). (1993). *The invention of pornography.* New York: Zone Books.

Hyde, Janet Shibley. (2005). The gender similarities hypothesis. *American Psychologist, 60*(6), 581–592.

Hyde, Janet S., & Plant, Elizabeth A. (1995). Magnitude of psychological gender differences: Another side to the story. *American Psychologist, 50,* 159–161.

Ingoldsby, Bron B., & Smith, Suzanna. (Eds.). (2006). *Families in multicultural perspective* (2nd ed.). New York: Guilford Press.

Ingraham, Chrys. (1999). *White weddings: Romancing heterosexuality in popular culture.* New York: Routledge.

Inness, Sherrie A. (Ed.). (2004). *Action chicks: New images of tough women in popular culture.* New York: Palgrave MacMillan.

International Society for Prevention of Child Abuse and Neglect. (2004). *World perspectives on child abuse* (6th ed.). Chicago: ISPCAN. Retrieved July 6, 2006, from http://www.ispcan.org/documents/ISPCANWorldPerspectives2004.pdf

The International Stepfamily Foundation. (2006, October). Retrieved October 1, 2006, from http://www.istepfamily.com

Irigaray, Luce. (1985a). *Speculum of the other woman* (Gillian C. Gill, Trans.). Ithaca, NY: Cornell University Press.

Irigaray, Luce. (1985b). *This sex which is not one* (Catherine Porter, Trans.). Ithaca, NY: Cornell University Press.

Irons, Jenny. (1998). The shaping of activist recruitment and participation: A study of women in the Mississippi civil rights movement. *Gender & Society, 12*(6), 692–709.

Ivy, Diane K., & Backlund, Phil. (2004). *GenderSpeak: Personal effectiveness in gender communication* (3rd ed.). Boston: McGraw-Hill.

Jablonsky, Thomas. (1994). *The Home, Heaven, and Mother Party: Female anti-suffragists in the United States, 1868–1920.* Brooklyn, NY: Carlson.

Jablonsky, Thomas. (2002). Female opposition: The anti-suffrage campaign. In Jean H. Baker (Ed.), *Votes for women: The struggle for suffrage revisited* (pp. 118–129). New York: Oxford University Press.

Jackson, Debra. (2003). Broadening constructions of family violence: Mothers' perspectives of aggression from their children. *Child and Family Social Work, 8,* 321–329.

Jackson, Ronald L., II, & Dangerfield, Celnisha L. (2003). Defining Black masculinity as cultural property: Toward an identity negotiation paradigm. In Larry A. Samovar & Richard E. Porter (Eds.), *Intercultural communication: A reader* (pp. 120–130). Belmont, CA: Wadsworth.

Jamieson, Kathleen Hall. (1988). *Eloquence in an electronic age: The transformation of political speechmaking.* New York: Oxford University Press.

Jamieson, Kathleen Hall. (1995). *Beyond the double bind: Women and leadership.* New York: Oxford University Press.

Japan's feminine falsetto falls right out of favor. (1995, December 13). *New York Times,* pp. A1, A4.

Jhally, Sut. (Producer/Writer/Editor). (1995). *DreamWorlds II* [Videotape]. (Available from Media Education Foundation, 26 Center Street, Northampton, MA 01060).

Johnson, Fern. (1996). Friendship among women: Closeness in dialogue. In Julia T. Wood (Ed.), *Gendered relationships: A reader* (pp. 79–94). Mountain View, CA: Mayfield.

Johnson, Fern. (2000). *Speaking culturally: Language diversity in the United States.* Thousand Oaks, CA: Sage.

Johnson, Michelle Kirtley, Weaver, James B., III., Watson, Kittie W., & Barker, Larry B. (2000). Listening styles: Biological or psychological differences. *International Journal of Listening, 14,* 32–46.

Johnson, Patrice D. (2002, April 5). Linguistic profiling. *The Black Commentator, 1.* Retrieved July 21, 2005, from http://www.blackcommentator.com/linguistic_profiling_pr.html

Jorgensen-Earp, Cheryl. (1990). The Lady, the Whore, and the Spinster: The rhetorical use of Victorian images of women. *Western Journal of Speech Communication, 54*(1), 82–98.

Journal of Marriage and the Family. (2001). Inside cover. *63*(1).

Julian of Norwich. (1978). *Showings* (Edmund Colledge, O. S. A. & James Walsh, S. J., Trans.). New York: Paulist Press. (Original work published ca. 1393).

Kachru, Braj B. (Ed.). (1982). *The other tongue: English across cultures.* Oxford, England: Pergamon Press.

Kane, Emily W. (2006). "No way my boys are going to be like that!" Parents' responses to children's gender nonconformity. *Gender & Society, 20*(2), 149–176.

Kanter, Rosabeth Moss. (1977). *Men and women of the corporation.* New York: Basic Books.

Kaplan, E. Anne. (1983). Is the gaze male? In Ann Snitow, Christine Stansell, & Sharon Thompson (Eds.), *Powers of desire: The politics of sexuality* (pp. 309–327). New York: Monthly Review Press.

Katz, Jackson. (1999). *Tough guise: Violence, media and the crisis of masculinity* [Videotape]. Northampton, MA: Media Education Foundation.

Katz, Jackson. (2003). *Wrestling with manhood: Boys, bullying and battering* [Videotape]. Northampton, MA: Media Education Foundation.

Kaw, Eugenia. (1997). "Opening" faces: The politics of cosmetic surgery and Asian American women. In Mary Crawford & Rhoda Unger (Eds.), *In our own words: Readings on the psychology of women and gender* (pp. 55–73). New York: McGraw-Hill.

Keenan, Elinor. (1974). Norm-makers and norm-breakers: Uses of speech by men and women in a Malagasy community. In Richard Bauman & Joel Sherzer (Eds.), *Explorations in the ethnography of speaking* (pp. 125–143). New York: Cambridge University Press.

Kellerman, Kathy. (1992). Communication: Inherently strategic and primarily automatic. *Communication Monographs, 59,* 288–300.

Kelly, Terri. (2005). From lingua franca to global English. *Global Envision* [Website]. Retrieved July 20, 2005, from http://www.globalenvision.org/library/8/655/

Kennedy, Randall. (2002). *Nigger: The strange career of a troublesome word.* New York: Pantheon Books.

Kerber, Linda K. (2005, March 18). We must make the academic workplace more humane and equitable. *The Chronicle of Higher Education,* pp. B6–B9.

Kerns, Leslie M. (2001). A feminist perspective: Why feminists should give the reasonable woman standard another chance. *Columbia Journal of Gender and Law, 10,* 195–230.

Kiesling, Scott Fabius. (2005). Homosocial desire in men's talk: Balancing and re-creating cultural discourses of masculinity. *Language in Society, 34*(5), 695–726.

Kikoski, John F., & Kikoski, Catherine Kano. (1999). *Reflexive communication in the culturally diverse workplace.* Westport, CT: Praeger.

Kilbourne, Jean. (1994). Toward a new model for the prevention of eating disorders. In Patricia Fallon, Melanie A. Katzman, & Susan C. Wooley (Eds.), *Feminist perspectives in eating disorders.* New York: Guilford Press.

Kilbourne, Jean (Creator), & Jhally, Sut (Director, Editor, Producer). (2000). *Killing us softly 3* [Videotape]. (Available from Media Education Foundation, 26 Center Street, Northampton, MA 01060)

Kimmel, Michael. (2000). *The gendered society.* New York: Oxford University Press.

Kimmel, Michael. (2003). Masculinity as homophobia. In Estelle Disch (Ed.), *Reconstructing gender: A multicultural anthology* (3rd ed., pp. 103–109). Boston: McGraw-Hill.

Kimmel, Michael S. (2004). *The gendered society* (2nd ed.). New York: Oxford University Press.

Kingsley, Charles. (1857). *Two years ago.* Cambridge, England: Macmillan.

Kirtley, Michelle D., & Weaver, James B., III. (Fall, 1999). Exploring the impact of gender role self-perception on communication style. *Women's Studies in Communication, 22*(2), 190–204.

Kissling, Elizabeth Arveda. (1991). Street harassment: The language of sexual terrorism. *Discourse and Society, 2*(4), 451–60.

Kivel, Paul. (2002). *Uprooting racism: How White people can work for racial justice* (Rev. ed.). Gabriola Island, British Columbia, Canada: New Society Publishers.

Klassen, Chris. (2003, November). Confronting the gap: Why religion needs to be given more attention in women's studies. *Thirdspace: A Journal for Emerging Feminist Scholars, 3*(1). Retrieved July 25, 2006, from http://www.thirdspace.ca/articles/klassen.htm

Kleinfeld, Judith. (1998). *The myth that schools shortchange girls: Social science in the service of deception.* Washington, DC: The Women's Freedom Network. Retrieved October 2006 from http://www.uaf.edu/northern/schools/download.html

Klopf, Donald W., & McCroskey, James C. (2007). *Intercultural communication encounters.* Boston: Pearson Allyn & Bacon.

Knapp, Mark L., & Hall, Judith A. (2002). *Nonverbal communication in human interaction* (5th ed.). Belmont, CA: Wadsworth.

Kochman, Thomas. (1990). Force fields in Black and White. In Donald Carbaugh (Ed.), *Cultural communication in intercultural contact* (pp. 193–194). Hillsdale, NJ: Erlbaum.

Kohlberg, Lawrence. (1966). A cognitive-developmental analysis of children's sex-role concepts and attitudes. In Eleanor E. Maccoby (Ed.), *The development of sex differences* (pp. 82–173). Stanford, CA: Stanford University Press.

Kowal, Donna. (1996). *The public advocacy of Emma Goldman: An anarcho-feminist stance on human rights.* Doctoral dissertation, University of Pittsburgh.

Kowal, Donna M. (2000). One cause, two paths: Militant vs. adjustive strategies in the British and American women's suffrage movements. *Communication Quarterly, 48,* 240–255.

Kowalczyk, Liz. (2001, September 28). Patriotic purchasing. Americans are being urged to spend, but analysts doubt the strategy will have an impact in the long run. *The Boston Globe,* p. C1.

Kraditor, Aileen S. (1965). *The ideas of the woman suffrage movement, 1890–1920.* New York: W. W. Norton.

Kramarae, Cheris. (1981). *Women and men speaking: Frameworks for analysis.* Rowley, MA: Newbury House.

Kramarae, Cheris. (1992). Harassment and everyday life. In Lana Rakow (Ed.), *Women making meaning: New feminist directions in communication* (pp. 100–120). New York: Routledge.

Kramarae, Cheris, & Spender, Dale. (1992). Exploding knowledge. In Cheris Kramarae & Dale Spender (Eds.), *The knowledge explosion: Generations of feminist scholarship* (pp. 1–26). New York: Teachers College Press.

Kramarae, Cheris, & Treichler, Paula A. (1992). *Amazons, bluestockings and crones: A feminist dictionary* (2nd ed.). London: Pandora Press.

Kramer, Laura. (2005). *The sociology of gender: A brief introduction* (2nd ed.). Los Angeles: Roxbury.

Kristeva, Julia. (1980). *Desire in language: A semiotic approach to literature and art* (Thomas Gora, Alice Jardine, & Leon S. Roudiez, Trans.; Leon S. Roudiez, Ed.). New York: Columbia University Press. (Original work published 1977)

Kroløkke, Charlotte, & Sørensen, Anne Scott. (2006). *Gender communication theories and analyses: From silence to performance.* Thousand Oaks, CA: Sage.

Krueger, Christine L. (2000). Review of *Women of faith in Victorian culture* and *Women's theology in nineteenth-century Britain. Victorian Studies, 43*, 178–181.

Kyratzis, Amy, & Guo, Jiansheng. (2001). Preschool girls' and boys' verbal conflict strategies in the U.S. and China: Cross-cultural and contextual considerations. *Research on Language and Social Interaction, Special Issue: Gender Construction in Children's Interactions: A Cultural Perspective, 4*(1), 45–74.

Lacan, Jacques. (1998). *The four fundamental concepts of psychoanalysis. The seminar of Jacques Lacan, Book 11.* (1st American ed.). New York: W. W. Norton.

Ladd, Tony, & Mathisen, James A. (1999). *Muscular Christianity: Evangelical Protestants and the development of American sport.* Grand Rapids, MI: Baker.

LaFrance, Marianne. (2002). Smile boycotts and other body politics. *Feminism and Psychology, 12*(3), 319–323.

LaFrance, Marianne, & Hecht, Marvin A. (2000). Gender and smiling: A meta-analysis. In Agenta H. Fischer (Ed.), *Gender and emotion: Social psychological perspectives* (pp. 118–142). Cambridge, UK: Cambridge University Press.

Lakoff, George. (2002). *Moral politics* (2nd ed.) Chicago: University of Chicago Press.

Lakoff, George. (2003, September 1). Framing the Dems. *The American Prospect.* Retrieved September 2, 2006, from www.prospect.org/print/V14/8/lakoff-g.html

Lakoff, George, & Johnson, Mark. (1980). *Metaphors we live by.* Chicago: University of Chicago Press.

Lakoff, Robin. (1975). *Language and woman's place.* New York: Harper & Row.

Laner, Mary Riege, & Ventrone, Nicole A. (2000). Dating scripts revisited. *Journal of Family Issues, 21*, 488–500.

Latouche, Serge. (1993). *In the wake of the affluent society: An exploration of post-development.* New York: Zed Books.

Lawrence, Charles R., III. (1993). If he hollers let him go: Regulating racist speech on campus. In Mari J. Matsuda et al. (Eds.), *Words that wound* (pp. 53–88). Boulder. CO: Westview Press.

Leaper, Campbell. (2000a). Gender, affiliation, assertion and the interactive context of parent-child play. *Developmental Psychology, 36*, 381–393.

Leaper, Campbell. (2000b). The social construction and socialization of gender. In Patricia H. Miller & Ellin Kofsky Scholrick (Eds.), *Towards a feminist developmental psychology* (pp. 127–152). New York: Routledge.

Leaper, Campbell, Anderson, Kristin, J., & Sanders, Paul. (1998). Moderators of gender effects on parents' talk to their children. *Developmental Psychology, 34*(1), 3–27.

Lee, Lin-Lee. (2004). Pure persuasion: A case study of *Nüshu* or "Women's Script" discourses. *Quarterly Journal of Speech, 90*, 403–421.

Lee, Valerie E., Croninger, Robert G., Linn, Eleanor, & Chen, Xiangiei. (1996). The culture of sexual harassment in secondary schools. *American Educational Research Journal, 33*(2), 383–417.

Lee, Yun-Suk, & Waite, Linda J. (2005, May). Husbands' and wives' time spent on house-work: A comparison of measures. *Journal of Marriage and Family, 67*(2), 328–336.

LePoire, Beth A., Burgoon, Judy K., & Parrott, Roxanne. (1992). Status and privacy restor-ing communication in the workplace. *Journal of Applied Communication Research, 4*, 419–436.

Lindsey, A. Elizabeth, & Zakahi, Walter, R. (2006). Perceptions of men and women depart-ing from conversational sex-role stereotypes. In Kathryn Dindia & Daniel J. Canary (Eds.), *Sex differences and similarities in communication* (2nd ed., pp. 281–298). Mahwah, NJ: Erlbaum.

Lindsey, Eric W., & Mize, Jacquelyn. (2001). Contextual differences in parent-child play: Implications for children's gender role development. *Sex Roles, 44*(3/4), 155–176.

Lippa, Richard. (1998). The nonverbal display and judgment of extraversion, masculinity, femininity, and gender diagnosticity: A lens model analysis. *Journal of Research in Personality, 32*, 80–107.

Livia, Anna, & Hall, Kira. (1997). "It's a girl!" Bringing performativity back to linguistics. In Anna Livia & Kira Hall (Eds.), *Queerly phrased: Language, gender, and sexuality* (pp. 3–20). New York: Oxford University Press.

Loewen, James W. (1995). *Lies my teacher told me: Everything your American history text-book got wrong.* New York: New Press.

Longley, Robert. (2004, September 1). Gender wage gap widening, census data shows: First decline in women's real earnings since 1995. Retrieved March 1, 2006, from http://usgovinfo.about.com/od/censusandstatistics/a/paygapgrows.htm

Lont, Cindy. (2001). The influence of media on gender images. In Dana Vannoy (Ed.), *Gender mosaics* (pp. 114–122). Los Angeles: Roxbury.

Lorber, Judith. (1994). *Paradoxes of gender.* New Haven, CT: Yale University Press.

Lorde, Audre. (1984). *Sister outsider.* Trumansberg, NY: The Crossing Press.

Loseke, Donileen, R., & Kurz, Demie. (2005). Men's violence toward women is the serious social problem. In Donileen R. Loseke, Richard J. Gelles, & Mary M. Cavanaugh (Eds.), *Current controversies on family violence* (pp. 79–95). Thousand Oaks, CA: Sage.

Lovaas, Karen E. (2003). Speaking to silence: Toward queering nonverbal communication. In Gust A. Yep, Karen E. Lovaas, & John P. Elia (Eds.), *Queer theory and communica-tion: From disciplining queers to queering the discipline(s)* (pp. 87–107). Binghamton, NY: Harrington Park Press.

Lovejoy, Meg. (2001). Disturbances in the social body: Differences in body image and eating problems among African American and White women. *Gender & Society, 15*, 239–261.

LSA Resolution on the Oakland "Ebonics" Issue. (1997, July 1). Approved by members attending the 71st Annual Business Meeting, Chicago, Illinois, January 3, 1997; adopted by LSA membership in a mail ballot, July 1, 1997. Retrieved July 25, 2006, from https://lsadc.org/info/lsa-res-ebonics.cfm

Lynch, Annette. (1999). *Dress, gender, and cultural change: Asian American and African American rites of passage.* Oxford, UK: Berg.

Lynn, Loretta. (1973). The pill [Music lyrics]. Retrieved June 8, 2006, from http://www.musicsonglyrics.com/L/lorettalynnlyrics/lorettalynnthepilllyrics.htm

Lytton, Hugh, & Romney, David M. (1991). Parents' differential socialization of boys and girls: A meta-analysis. *Psychological Bulletin, 109*, 267–296.

Maccoby, Eleanor E. (1998). *The two sexes: Growing up apart, coming together.* Cambridge, MA: Harvard University Press.

Maccoby, Eleanor, E., & Jacklin, C. N. (1974). *The psychology of sex differences.* Stanford, CA: Stanford University Press.

MacGeorge, Erina L., Graves, Angela R., Feng, Bo, Gillihan, Seth J., & Burleson, Brant. (2004). The myth of gender cultures: Similarities outweigh differences in men's and women's provision of and responses to supportive communication. *Sex Roles, 50*(3–4), 143–175.

MacKinnon, Catharine A. (1987). *Feminism unmodified: Discourses on life and law.* Cambridge, MA: Harvard University Press.

MacKinnon, Catharine A. (1993). *Only words.* Cambridge, MA: Harvard University Press.

MacKinnon, Catharine A. (2005). *Women's lives, men's laws.* Cambridge, MA: Harvard University Press.

MacKinnon, Catharine A., & Dworkin, Andrea. (1997). *In harm's way: The pornography civil rights hearings.* Cambridge, MA: Harvard University Press.

Madden, Tracey E., Barrett, Lisa Feldman, & Pietromanaco, Paula R. (2000). Sex differences in anxiety and depression: Empirical evidence and methodological questions. In Agneta H. Fischer (Ed.), *Gender and emotion: Social psychological perspectives* (pp. 277–298). Cambridge, UK: Cambridge University Press.

Majors, Richard. (2001). The cool pose, how Black men present themselves as a spectacle of self-expression and agency, by adopting the cool pose. In Stephen M. Whitehead & Frank J. Barrett (Eds.), *The masculinities reader* (pp. 209–218). Cambridge, UK: Polity Press.

Majors, Richard, & Billson, Janet Mancini. (1992). *Cool pose: The dilemmas of Black manhood in America.* New York: Lexington Books.

Malamuth, Neil M., & Donnerstein, Edward (Eds.). (1984). *Pornography and sexual aggression.* Orlando, FL: Academic Press.

Maltz, Daniel, N., & Borker, Ruth. (1982). A cultural approach to male-female miscommunication. In John J. Gumperz (Ed.), *Language and social identity* (pp. 196–216). Cambridge, UK: Cambridge University Press.

Mansbridge, Jane. (1998). Feminism and democracy. In Anne Phillips (Ed.), *Feminism & politics* (pp. 142–158). New York: Oxford University Press.

Maracle, Lee. (1989, Spring). Moving over. *Trivia: A Journal of Ideas, 14*(Part II), 9–12.

Marecek, Jeanne, Crawford, Mary, & Popp, Danielle. (2004). On the construction of gender, sex, and sexualities. In Alice H. Eagly, Anne E. Beall, & Robert J. Sternberg (Eds.), *The psychology of gender* (2nd ed., pp. 192–216). New York: Guilford Press.

Martin, Jane Rolland. (1991). The contradiction and the challenge of the educated woman. *Women's Studies Quarterly (1–2),* 8–27.

Martin, Judith N., & Nakayama, Thomas K. (2004). *Intercultural communication in contexts* (3rd ed.). Boston: McGraw-Hill.

Martin, Patricia Yancey. (2003). "Said and done" versus "saying and doing": Gendering practices, practicing gender at work. *Gender & Society, 17*(3), 342–366.

Martin, Patricia Yancey. (2004, June). Gender as social institution. *Social Forces, 82*(4), 1249–1273.

Martyna, Wendy. (1980a). Beyond the "he/man" approach: The case for nonsexist language. *Signs, 5,* 482–493.

Martyna, Wendy. (1980b). The psychology of the generic masculine. In Sally McConnell-Ginet, Ruth Borker, & Nelly Furman (Eds.), *Women and language in literature and society* (pp. 69–78). New York: Praeger.

Martyna, Wendy. (1983). Beyond the he/man approach: The case for nonsexist language. In Barrie Thorne, Cheris Kramarae, & Nancy Henley (Eds.), *Language, gender, and society* (pp. 25–37). Rowley, MA: Newbury House.

Mascia-Lees, Frances E., & Black, Nancy Johnson. (2000). *Gender and anthropology.* Prospect Heights, IL: Waveland Press.

Massachusetts Association Opposed to the Further Extension of Suffrage to Women. (1912, October). *Opinions of eminent persons against woman suffrage* [Pamphlet]. Boston: Author.

Mastracci, Sharon H. (2004). *Breaking out of the pink-collar ghetto: Policy solutions for non-college women.* Armonk, NY: M. E. Sharpe.

Matsuda, Mari. J. (1993). Public response to racist speech: Considering the victim's story. In Mari J. Matsuda, Charles R. Lawrence, III, Richard Delgado, & Kimberlè Williams Crenshaw (Eds.), *Words that wound* (pp. 17–51). Boulder, CO: Westview Press.

Matsuda, Mari J., Lawrence, Charles R., III, Delgado, Richard, & Crenshaw, Kimberlè Williams. (Eds.). (1993). *Words that wound.* Boulder, CO: Westview Press.

Matthews, Glenna R. (1992). *The rise of public woman: Woman's power and woman's place in the United States, 1630–1970.* New York: Oxford University Press.

Mattingly, Carol. (2002). *Appropriate[ing] dress: Women's rhetorical style in nineteenth-century America.* Carbondale: Southern Illinois University Press.

May, Steven K. (1997, November). *Silencing the feminine in managerial discourse.* Paper presented at the annual meeting of the National Communication Association, Chicago.

Mayer, Tamar. (Ed.). (2000). *Gender ironies of nationalism: Sexing the nation.* London: Routledge.

McCall, Leslie. (2005). The complexity of intersectionality. *Signs, 30,* 1771–1800.

McClintock, Anne. (1997). "No longer in a future heaven": Women and nationalism in South Africa. In Anne McClintock, Aamir Mufti, & Ella Shohat (Eds.), *Dangerous liaisons: Gender, nation, and postcolonial perspectives* (pp. 89–112). Minneapolis: University of Minnesota Press.

McClure, E. B. (2000). A meta-analysis review of sex differences in facial expression processing and their development in infants, children, and adolescents. *Psychological Bulletin, 126,* 424–453.

McConnell, Allen R., & Fazio, Russell H. (1996). Women as men and people: Effects of gender-marked language. *Personality and Social Psychology Bulletin, 22*(10), 1004–1013.

McConnell, Allen R., & Gavanski, I. (1994, May). *Women as men and people: Occupation title suffixes as primes.* Paper presented at the 66th Annual Meeting of the Midwestern Psychological Association, Chicago.

McElhinny, Bonnie S. (1992). "I don't smile much anymore": Affect, gender, and the discourse of Pittsburgh police officers. In Kira Hall & Birch Moonwomon (Eds.), *Locating power: Proceedings of the 1992 Berkeley Conference on Women and Language* (pp. 386–403). Berkeley, CA: Berkeley Women and Language Group.

McElhinny, Bonnie S. (1998). "I don't smile much anymore": Affect, gender and the discourse of Pittsburgh police officers." In Jennifer Coates (Ed.), *Language and gender: A reader* (Vol. 2, pp. 309–327). Malden, MA: Basil Blackwell.

McKay, Jim, Messner, Michael A., & Sabo, Donald F. (Eds.). (2000). *Masculinities, gender, relations, and sports.* Thousand Oaks, CA: Sage.

McLoughlin, Merrill, Shryer, Tracey L., Goode, Erica E., & McAuliffe, Kathleen. (1988, August 8). Men vs. women. *U.S. News and World Report,* pp. 50–56.

McNair Barnett, Bernice. (1993). Invisible Southern Black women leaders in the movement: The triple constraints of gender, race, and class. *Gender & Society, 7*(2), 162–182.

Mead, George Herbert. (1934). *Mind, self & society from the standpoint of a social behaviorist.* (Charles W. Morris, Ed.). Chicago: The University of Chicago Press.

Mead, Margaret. (1968). *Sex and temperament in three primitive societies.* New York: Dell. (Original work published 1935)

Mehrabian, Albert. (1972). *Nonverbal communication.* Chicago: Aldine-Atherton.

Mehrhof, Barbara, & Kearon, Pamela. (1971/1973). Rape: An act of terror. In Anne Koedt, Ellen Levine, & Anita Rapone (Eds.), *Radical feminism* (pp. 228–233). New York: Quadrangle.

Mercer, Kobena. (1994). *Welcome to the jungle: New positions in Black cultural studies.* London: Routledge.

Messerschmidt, Jasmes W. (1996). Managing to kill: Masculinities and the space shuttle *Challenger* explosion. In Cliff Cheng (Ed.), *Masculinities in organizations* (pp. 29–53). Thousand Oaks, CA: Sage.

Messner, Michael S. (2004). *The gendered society* (2nd ed.). New York: Oxford University Press.

Metts, Sandra. (2006). Gendered communication in dating relationships. In Bonnie J. Dow & Julia T. Wood (Eds.), *The SAGE handbook of gender in communication* (pp. 25–40). Thousand Oaks, CA: SAGE.

Meyers, David. (2004). *Psychology* (7th ed.). New York: Worth.

Meyers, Marian. (2004, June). African American women and violence: Gender, race, and class in the news. *Critical Studies in Media Communication, 21*(2), 95–118.

Michaud, Shari L., & Warner, Rebecca M. (1997). Gender differences in self-reported response in troubles talk. *Sex Roles: A Journal of Research, 37*(7–8), 527–541.

Miedzian, Myriam. (1993). How rape is encouraged in American boys and what we can do to stop it. In Emilie Buchwald, Pamela R. Fletcher, & Martha Roth (Eds.), *Transforming a rape culture* (pp. 153–164). Minneapolis, MN: Milkweed Editions.

Millenium Campaign. (2004). About the goals. Goal 3. Retrieved October 10, 2006, from http://www.millenniumcampaign.org/site/pp.asp?c=grKVL2NLE&b=186382

Miller, Casey, & Swift, Kate. (1993). Foreword. In Jane Mills, *Womanwords: A dictionary of words about women* (pp. ix–xii). New York: Henry Holt.

Mills, Jane. (1993). *Womanwords: A dictionary of words about women.* New York: Henry Holt.

Mills, Rosemary S. L., Nazar, Jane, & Farrell, Heather M. (2002). Child and parent perceptions of hurtful messages. *Journal of Social and Personal Relationships, 19,* 731–754.

Mills, Sara. (2003). *Gender and politeness.* Cambridge, UK: Cambridge University Press.

Mink, Gwendolyn. (1995). *The wages of motherhood: Inequality in the welfare state, 1917–1942.* Ithaca, NY: Cornell University Press.

Minsky, Rosalind. (1998). *Psychoanalysis and culture: Contemporary states of mind.* New Brunswick, NJ: Rutgers University Press.

Mischel, Walter. (1966). A social learning view of sex differences in behavior. In Eleanor E. Maccoby (Ed.), *The development of sex differences* (pp. 93–106). Stanford, CA: Stanford University Press.

Mitchell, Karen S. (1996). Ever after: Reading the women who read (and re-write) romances. *Theatre Topics, 6*(1), 51–69.

Mizokami, Yuki. (2003). Ambiguous boundary between women's and men's speech in the Japanese language in the use of polite expressions. *Studia Linguistica, 16,* 105–126.

Modleski, Tania. (1984). *Loving with a vengeance: Mass-produced fantasies for women.* New York: Routledge.

Modleski, Tania. (1998). *Old wives tales and other women's stories.* New York: New York University Press.

Mohanty, Chandra Talpade. (2003). *Feminism without borders.* Durham, NC: Duke University Press.

Moi, Toril. (1985). *Sexual/textual politics: Feminist literary theory.* London: Methuen.

Monsour, Michael. (2006). Communication and gender among adult friends. In Bonnie J. Dow & Julia T. Wood (Eds.), *The SAGE handbook of gender in communication* (pp. 75–70). Thousand Oaks, CA: Sage.

Moorti, Sujata. (2002). *Color of rape: Gender and race in television's public spheres.* New York: State University of New York Press.

Morgan, Marcyliena. (1999). No woman no cry: Claiming African American women's place. In Mary Bucholtz, A. C. Liang, & Laurel A. Sutton (Eds.), *Reinventing identities: The gendered self in discourse* (pp. 27–45). New York: Oxford University Press.

Morman, Mark T., & Floyd, Kory. (2006). The good son: Men's perceptions of the characteristics of sonhood. In Kory Floyd & Mark T. Morman (Eds.), *Widening the family circle: New research on family communication* (pp. 37–55). Thousand Oaks, CA: Sage.

Morrison, Toni. (Ed.). (1992). *Race-ing justice, en-gendering power: Essays on Anita Hill, Clarence Thomas and the construction of social reality.* New York: Pantheon Books.

Moss, Peter, & Deven, Fred. (Eds.). (1999). *Parental leave: Progress or pitfall?* The Hague: Netherlands. Interdisciplinary Demographic Institute.

Moya, Paula M. L. (1997). Postmodernism, "realism," and the politics of identity: Cherríe Moraga and Chicana feminism. In M. Jacqui Alexander & Chandra Talpade Mohanty (Eds.), *Feminist genealogies, colonial legacies, democratic futures* (pp. 125–150). New York: Routledge.

Muehlenhard, Charlene L., Goggins, Mary F., Jones, Jayne M., & Satterfield, Arthur T. (1991). Sexual violence and coercion in close relationships. In Kathleen McKinney & Susan Spreecher (Eds.), *Sexuality in close relationships* (pp. 155–176). Hillsdale, NJ: Erlbaum.

Mulac, Anthony. (1998). The gender-linked language effect: Do language differences really make a difference? In Dan J. Canary & Katherine Dindia (Eds.), *Sex differences and similarities in communication: Critical essays and empirical investigations of sex and gender in interaction* (pp. 127–153). Mahwah, NJ: Erlbaum.

Mulac, Anthony, Wiemann, John M., Widenmann, Sally J., & Gibson, Toni W. (1988). Male/female language differences and effects in same-sex and mixed-sex dyads: The gender-linked language effect. *Communication Monographs, 55,* 315–335.

Mulvey, Laura. (1975). Visual pleasure and narrative cinema. *Screen, 16*(3), 6–18.

Mumby, Dennis K. (2001). Power and politics. In Fredric M. Jablin & Linda L. Putnam (Eds.), *The new handbook of organizational communication: Advances in theory, research, and methods* (pp. 585–623). Newbury Park, CA: Sage.

Murphy, John. (2003). "Our mission and our moment": George W. Bush and September 11th. *Rhetoric & Public Affairs, 6*(4), 607–632.

Murray, Patty. (2005). Biography. *Patty Murray* [Website]. Retrieved July 18, 2005, from http://www.pattymurray.com/biography.php

Muscio, Inga. (2002). *Cunt: A declaration of independence.* New York: Seal Press.

Nadasen, Premil. (2005). *Welfare warriors: The welfare rights movement in the United States.* New York: Routledge.

Nakamura, Lisa. (2005). Head-hunting on the Internet: Identity tourism, avatars, and racial passing in textual and graphic chat spaces. In Raiford Guins & Omayra Zaragoza Cruz (Eds.), *Popular culture: A reader* (pp. 520–533). Thousand Oaks, CA: Sage.

Nakayama, Thomas K., & Krizek, Robert L. (1999). Whiteness as a strategic rhetoric: In Thomas K. Nakayama & Judith N. Martin (Eds.), *Whiteness: The communication of social identity* (pp. 87–106). Thousand Oaks, CA: Sage.

Nanda, Serena. (1996). Hijras: An alternative sex and gender role in India. In Gilbert Herdt (Ed.), *Third sex, third gender: Beyond sexual dimorphism in culture and history* (pp. 373–415). New York: Zone Books.

Nanda, Serena. (2000). *Gender diversity: Crosscultural variations.* Prospect Heights, IL: Waveland Press.

Narayanan, Vasudha. (2003). Hinduism. In Arvind Sharma & Katherine K. Young (Eds.), *Her voice, her faith: Women speak on world religions* (pp. 11–58). Boulder, CO: Westview Press.

National Association for Single Sex Public Education. (2006a). Advantages for girls. NASSPE website. Retrieved October 1, 2006, from http://www.singlesexschools.org/advantages-forgirls.htm

National Association for Single Sex Public Education. (2006b). Learning style differences, extracted from from Sax, Leonard, M.D., Ph.D. *Why gender matters* (2005). NASSPE website. Retrieved October 1, 2006, from http://www.singlesexschools.org/research-learning.htm

National Clearinghouse on Child Abuse and Neglect Information. (2004). Child abuse and neglect fatalities: Statistics and interventions. Retrieved July 6, 2006, from http://www.childwelfare.gov/pubs/factsheets/fatality.pdf

National Education Association Research. (2003). *Status of the American public school teacher 2000–2001.* Washington, DC: NEA.

National Organization for Women. (2006). *Violence against women in the United States.* Retrieved April 4, 2006, from http://www.now.org/issues/violence/stats.html

Nettle, Daniel, & Romaine, Suzanne. (2000). *Vanishing voices: The extinction of the world's languages.* New York: Oxford University Press.

Newman, Michael. (1992). Pronominal disagreements: The stubborn problem of singular epicene antecedents. *Language in Society, 21,* 447–475.

Ng, Sik Hung. (1990). Androcentric coding of *man* and *his* in memory by language users. *Journal of Experimental Social Psychology, 26,* 455–464.

Nichols, Patricia. (1983). Linguistic options and choices for Black women in the rural South. In Barrie Thorne, Cheris Kramarae, & Nancy Henley (Eds.), *Language, gender, and society* (pp. 54–68). Rowley, MA: Newbury House.

Norton, Robert. (1983). *Communication style: Theory, applications, and measures.* Beverly Hills, CA: Sage.

Oakland School Board approves Black English program and sparks national debate [Electronic version]. (1997, January 13). *Jet, 91,* 12.

Oakley, Ann. (1981). *Woman's work: The housewife, past and present.* New York: Pantheon.

Ogasawara, Yuko. (1998). *Office ladies and salaried men: Power, gender, and work in Japanese companies.* Berkeley: University of California Press.

Oishi, Eve. (2006). Visual perversions: Race, sex, and cinematic pleasure. *Signs, 31*(3), 641–674.

Okamoto, Shigeko. (1995). "Tasteless" Japanese: Less "feminine" speech among young Japanese women. In Kira Hall & Mary Bucholtz (Eds.), *Gender articulated: Language and the socially constructed self* (pp. 297–328). New York: Routledge.

O'Kelly, Lisa. (2004, June 6). It beats working: Women fought hard for the right to be working mothers—but now many want to step off the career ladder and swap the boardroom for full-time motherhood. Is this the failure of one movement or the beginning of another? *The Observer (London),* p. 1.

Olian, JoAnne. (Ed.). (1995). *Everyday fashions 1909–1920: As pictured in Sears catalogues.* New York: Dover.

Olivardia, Roberto. (2001). Why now? How male body image is closely tied to masculinity and changing gender roles. *Society for the Psychological Study of Men and Masculinity Bulletin, 6*(4), 11–12.

Olivardia, Roberto, & Pope, Harrison, G., Jr. (1997). Eating disorders in men: Prevalence, recognition, and treatment. *Directions in Psychiatry, 17,* 41–51.

Olivardia, Roberto, Pope, Harrison, G., Jr., Borowiecki, John J., III, & Cohane, Geoffrey. (2004). Biceps and body image: The relationship between muscularity and self-esteem and eating disorder symptoms. *Psychology of Men and Masculinity, 5*(2), 112–120.

Olson, Loreen. (2002, Winter). Exploring "common couple violence" in heterosexual romantic relationships. *Western Journal of Communication, 66*(1), 104–129.

Olson, Loreen, N., & Lloyd, Sally A. (2005). "It depends on what you mean by starting it": An exploration of how women define initiation of aggression and their motives for behaving aggressively. *Sex Roles, 53*(7/8), 603–617.

Orbe, Mark P. (1998, February). From the standpoint(s) of traditionally muted groups: Explicating a co-cultural communication theoretical model. *Communication Theory, 8*(1), 1–26.

Orbe, Mark P., & Harris, Tina M. (2001). *Interracial communication: Theory into practice.* Belmont, CA: Wadsworth.

Orenstein, Peggy. (1994). *School girls: Young women, self-esteem, and the confidence gap.* New York: Doubleday.

Palczewski, Catherine Helen. (1993). Public policy argument and survivor testimony: Pro-ordinance conservatives, confession, mediation, and recuperation. In Raymie E. McKerrow (Ed.), *Argument and the postmodern challenge: Proceedings of the eighth SCA/AFA conference on argumentation* (pp. 461–467). Annandale, VA: SCA.

Palczewski, Catherine Helen. (1995). Voltairine de Cleyre: Sexual pleasure and sexual slavery in the 19th century. *National Women's Studies Association Journal, 7,* 54–68.

Palczewski, Catherine Helen. (1996). Bodies, borders and letters: Gloria Anzaldúa's "Speaking in tongues: A letter to 3rd world women writers." *The Southern Communication Journal, 62,* 1–16.

Palczewski, Catherine Helen. (2001, Summer). Contesting pornography: Terministic catharsis and definitional argument. *Argumentation and Advocacy, 38,* 1–17.

Palczewski, Catherine Helen. (2002). Keynote address: Argument in an off key. In G. Thomas Goodnight et al (Eds.), *Communicative reason and communication communities* (pp. 1–23). Washington, DC: National Communication Association.

Palczewski, Catherine Helen. (2005, November). The male Madonna and the feminine Uncle Sam: Visual argument, icons, and ideographs in 1909 anti-woman suffrage postcards. *The Quarterly Journal of Speech, 91*(4), 365–394.

Parker, Patricia S. (2003). Control, resistance, and empowerment in raced, gendered, and classed work contexts: The case of African American women. *Communication Yearbook, 27,* 257–291.

Parkin, Wendy. (1993). The public and the private: Gender, sexuality and emotion. In Stephen Fineman (Ed.), *Emotion in organizations* (pp. 167–189). London: Sage.

Parrenas, Rhacel Salazar. (2001). *Servants of globalization: Women, migration and domestic work.* Stanford, CA: Stanford University Press.

Parsons, Talcott, & Bales, Robert, F. (1955). *Family, socialization and interaction process.* Glencoe, IL: The Free Press.

Pateman, Carole. (1989). *The disorder of women: Democracy, feminism and political theory.* Stanford: Stanford University Press.

Patterson, Charlotte J. (1995). Families of the lesbian baby boom: Parents' division of labor and children's adjustment. *Developmental Psychology, 31,* 115–123.

Patterson, Charlotte J. (2000). Family relationships of lesbian and gay men. *Journal of Marriage and the Family, 62,* 1052–1069.

Paulos, John Allen. (1995). *A mathematician reads the newspaper.* New York: Basic Books.

Payack, Paul JJ. (2005). The number of words in the English language. *The Global Language Monitor* [Website]. Retrieved July 20, 2005, from http://www.languagemonitor.com/wst_page7.html

Penelope, Julia. (1990). *Speaking freely.* New York: Pergamon Press.

Pennington, Dorothy L. (2003). The discourse of African American women: A case for extended paradigms. In Ronald L. Jackson & Elaine B. Richardson (Eds.), *Understanding African American rhetoric* (pp. 293–307). New York: Routledge.

Peplau, Letitia Anne, & Beals, Kristin P. (2004). The family lives of lesbians and gay men In Anita L. Vangelisti (Ed.), *Handbook of family communication* (pp. 233–248). Mahwah, NJ: Erlbaum.

Peplau, Letitia Anne, & Spalding, Leah R. (2000). The close relationship of lesbians, gay men, and bisexuals. In Clyde Hendrick & Susan S. Hendrick (Eds.), *Close relationships: A source book* (pp. 111–123). Thousand Oaks, CA: Sage.

Perry, William G. (1970). *Forms of intellectual and ethical development in the college years.* New York: Holt, Rinehart & Winston.

Petchesky, Rosalind P. (1997). Spiraling discourses of reproductive and sexual rights: A post-Beijing assessment of international feminist politics. In Cathy J. Cohen, Kathleen B. Jones, & Joan C. Tronto (Eds.), *Women transforming politics* (pp. 569–587). New York: New York University Press.

Peterson, Gary W., Bodman, Denise Ann, Bush, Kevin R., & Madden-Derdich, Debra. (2000). Gender and parent-child relationships. In David H. Demo, Katherine R. Allen, & Mark A Fine (Eds.), *Handbook of family diversity* (pp. 82–104). New York: Oxford University Press.

Peterson, Lori West, & Albrecht, Terrance L. (1999). Where gender/power/politics collide: Deconstructing organizational maternity leave policy. *Journal of Management Inquiry, 8,* 168–181.

Pheterson, Gail. (Ed.). (1989). *A vindication of the rights of whores.* Seattle, WA: Seal Press.

Piaget, Jean. (1965). *The moral judgment of the child.* New York: Free Press.

Pilkington, Jane. (1998). Don't try and make out that I'm nice! The different strategies women and men use when gossiping. In Jennifer Coates (Ed.), *Language and gender: A reader* (254–269). Oxford, UK: Basil Blackwell.

Pipher, Mary B. (1994). *Reviving Ophelia: Saving the selves of adolescent girls.* New York: Putnam.

Plant, E. Ashby, Kling, Kristen C., & Smith, Ginny L. (2004). The influence of gender and social role on the interpretation of facial expressions. *Sex Roles: A Journal of Research, 51*(3–4), 187–197.

Pope, Harrison G., Jr., Gruber, Amanda J., Choi, Precilla, Olivardia, Roberto, & Phillips, Katharine A. (1997). Muscle dysphoria: An underrecognized form of body dysmorphic disorder. *Psychosomatics, 38,* 548–557.

Pope, Harrison G., Jr., Phillips, Katharine A., & Olivardia, Roberto. (2000). *The Adonis complex: The secret crisis of male body obsession.* New York: Simon & Schuster.

Popenoe, Rebecca. (2004). *Feeding desire: Fatness, beauty and sexuality among a Saharan people.* London: Routledge.

Preston, Cheryl B. (2003, Spring). Women in traditional religions: Refusing to let patriarchy (or feminism) separate us from the source of our liberation. *Mississippi College Law Review, 22,* 185–214.

Price, Janet, & Shildrick, Margrit. (Eds.). (1999). *Feminist theory and the body: A reader.* New York: Routledge.

Price, Joshua M. (2002). The apotheosis of home and the maintenance of spaces of violence. *Hypatia, 17*(4), 39–70.

ProEnglish. (n.d.). Who we are: All about ProEnglish. Retrieved March 26, 2005, from http://www.proenglish.org/main/gen-info.htm

Purnell, Thomas, Idsardi, William, & Baugh, John. (1999). Perceptual and phonetic experiments on American English dialect identification. *Journal of Language and Social Psychology, 18*, 10–30.

Putney, Clifford. (2001). *Muscular Christianity: Manhood and sports in Protestant America, 1880–1920.* Cambridge, MA: Harvard University Press.

Queen, Robin M. (1997). "I don't speak spritch": Locating lesbian language. In Anna Livia & Kira Hall (Eds.), *Queerly phrased: Language, gender, and sexuality* (pp. 214–232). New York: Oxford University Press.

Quinn, Beth A. (2002, June). Sexual harassment and masculinity: The power and meaning of "girl watching." *Gender & Society, 16*(3), 386–402.

Radway, Janice A. (1991). *Reading the romance: Women, patriarchy, and popular literature.* Chapel Hill: University of North Carolina Press.

Rakow, Lana. (1986). Rethinking gender research in communication. *Journal of Communication, 36*, 11–26.

Ramey, Estelle. (1976). Men's cycles (they have them too you know). In Alexandra G. Kaplan & Joan P. Bean (Eds.), *Beyond sex-role stereotypes* (pp. 137–142). Boston: Little, Brown.

Ratzinger, Cardinal Joseph (2004). Letter to the Bishops of the Catholic Church on the Collaboration of Men and Women in the Church and in the World. Retrieved December 22, 2006, from http://www.wf-f.org/BenedictXVI.html

Reardon, Betty A. (1985). *Sexism and the war system.* New York: Teachers College Press.

Reay, Diane. (2001). Spice girls, nice girls, girlies, and tomboys: Gender discourse, girls' cultures and femininities in the primary classroom. *Gender and Education, 13*(2), 153–166.

Reed, Cheryl L. (2004, October 10). "Supermoms" draw line in sandbox; Today's mothers are dropping out of the work force by the thousands: 'Ideally, everyone would have this choice.' *Chicago Sun-Times,* p. 24.

Reiss, David. (2000). *The relational code: Deciphering genetic and social influences on adolescent development.* Cambridge, MA: Harvard University Press.

Renegar, Valerie R., & Sowards, Stacey K. (2003). Liberal irony, rhetoric, and feminist thought: A unifying third wave feminist theory. *Philosophy and Rhetoric, 36*(4), 330–352.

Rennison, Callie, M. (2003). *Intimate partner violence, 1993–2001.* Washington, DC: U.S. Department of Justice, Bureau of Justice Statistics.

Rich, Adrienne. (1979). *On lies, secrets, an silence.* New York: W. W. Norton.

Rich, Adrienne. (1980). Compulsory heterosexuality and lesbian existence. *Signs, 5,* 631–660.

Rich, Adrienne. (1986). *Blood, bread, and poetry: Selected prose 1979–1985.* New York: W. W. Norton.

Risman, Barbara J. (1998). *Gender vertigo: American families in transition.* New Haven, CT: Yale University Press.

Robinson, James H. (2003). Communication in Korea: Playing things by eye. In Larry A. Samovar & Richard E. Porter (Eds.), *Intercultural communication: A reader* (10th ed., pp. 57–64). Belmont, CA: Wadsworth.

Robnett, Belinda. (1996). African-American women in the civil rights movement, 1954–1965: Gender, leadership, and micromobilization. *American Journal of Sociology, 101*(6), 1661–1693.

Romanes, George J. (1887). Mental differences between men and women. *Nineteenth Century, 21,* 654–672.

Roof, Judith, & Weigman, Robyn. (Eds.). (1995). *Who can speak? Authority and critical identity*. Urbana: University of Illinois Press.

Roscoe, Will. (1987). Bibliography of berdache and alternative gender roles among North American Indians. *Journal of Homosexuality, 14*, 3–4.

Rosen, Karen H. (1996). The ties that bind women to violent premarital relationships. In Dudley D. Cahn & Sally A. Lloyd (Eds.), *Family violence from a communication perspective* (pp. 151–176). Thousand Oaks, CA: Sage.

Rothenberg, Paula S. (Ed.). (2001). *Race, class, and gender in the United States: An integrated study* (5th. ed.). New York: Worth.

Rothschild, Joyce, & Davies, Celia. (1994). Organizations through the lens of gender: Introduction to the special issue. *Human Relations, 47*, 583–590.

Ruane, Janet M., & Cerulo, Karen M. (2004). *Second thoughts: Seeing conventional wisdom through the sociological eye* (3rd ed.). Thousand Oaks, CA: Pine Forge Press.

Rubin, Gayle. (1984). Thinking sex: Notes for a radical theory of the politics of sexuality. In Carole Vance (Ed.), *Pleasure and danger: Exploring female sexuality* (pp. 267–319). London: Victor Gollancz.

Rubinstein, Ruth P. (2001). *Dress code: Meaning and messages in American culture* (2nd ed.). Boulder, CO: Westview Press.

Ruddick, Sara. (1989). *Maternal thinking*. New York: Ballantine Books.

Rutter, Virginia, & Schwartz, Pepper. (2000). Gender, marriage, and diverse possibilities for cross-sex and same-sex pairs. In David H. Demo, Katherine R. Allen, & Mark A. Fine (Eds.), *Handbook of family diversity* (pp. 59–81). New York: Oxford University Press.

Sadker, David. (2002). An educator's primer on the gender war. *Phi Delta Kappan, 84*(3), 235–241.

Sadker, David, & Sadker, Myra. (1994). *Failing at fairness: How America's schools cheat girls*. New York: Simon & Schuster.

Sadker, David, & Zittleman, Karen. (2005). Closing the gender gap—again! Just when educators thought it was no longer an issue, gender bias is back in a new context. *Principal, 84*(4), 18–22.

Sagrestano, Lynda M., Heavey, Christopher L., & Christensen, Andrew. (2006). Individual differences versus social structural approaches to explaining demand-withdraw and social influence behaviors. In Kathryn Dindia & Daniel J. Canary (Eds.), *Sex differences and similarities in communication* (2nd ed., pp. 379–395). Mahwah, NJ: Erlbaum.

Sandler, Bernice R., Silverberg, Lisa A., & Hall, Roberta M. (1996). *The chilly classroom climate: A guide to improve the education of women*. Washington, DC: National Association for Women in Education.

Sandnabba, N. Kenneth, & Ahlberg, Christian. (1999). Parents' attitudes and expectations about children's cross-gender behavior. *Sex Roles, 40*, 249–263.

Sanger, Kerran L. (1995). Slave resistance and rhetorical self-definition: Spirituals as strategy. *Western Journal of Communication, 59*(3), 177–192.

Sapir, Edward. (1958). The status of linguistics as a science. In David G. Mandelbaum (Ed.), *Edward Sapir: Culture, language and personality*. Berkeley: University of California Press. (Original work published 1929)

Sassen, Saskia. (1998). *Globalization and its discontents*. New York: New Press.

Sax, Leonard. (2005). *Why gender matters: What parents and teachers need to know about the emerging science of sex differences*. New York: Doubleday.

Schram, Sanford F. (1995). *Words of welfare: The poverty of social science and the social science of poverty*. Minneapolis: University of Minnesota Press.

Schriver, Kristina. (2003, Spring). Rhetorical pathologies and gender difference: An ideological examination of cultural discourse in Faulkner v. The Citadel. *Women's Studies in Communication, 26*(1), 27–60.

Schroeder, Pat. (1999). *24 years of house work . . . and the place is still a mess: My life in politics.* Kansas City, MO: Andrews McMeel.

Schulz, Muriel R. (1975). The semantic derogation of woman. In Barrie Thorne & Nancy Henley (Eds.), *Language and sex: Difference and dominance* (pp. 64–75). Chicago: Newbury House.

Schwartz, Barbara K., & Cellini, Henry R. (1995). Female sex offenders. In Barbara K. Schwartz & Henry R. Cellini (Eds.), *The sex offender: Corrections, treatments and legal practices* (Vol. 1, pp. 5:1–5:22). Kingston, NJ: Civic Research Institute.

Scully, Diane. (1990). *Understanding sexual violence: A study of convicted rapists.* Boston: Unwin Hyman.

Sells, Laura R. (1993). Maria W. Miller Stewart. In Karlyn Kohrs Campbell (Ed.), *Women public speakers in the United States, 1800–1925* (pp. 339–349). Westport, CT: Greenwood Press.

Sheldon, Amy. (1990). Pickle fights: Gendered talk in preschool disputes. *Discourse Processes, 13*(1), 5–31.

Shelton, Beth Anne, & John, Daphne. (1996). The division of household labor. *Annual Review of Sociology, 22,* 299–322.

Shields, Stephanie A. (2000). Thinking about gender, thinking about theory: Gender and emotional experience. In Agneta H. Fischer (Ed.), *Gender and emotion: Social psychological perspectives* (pp. 3–23). Cambridge, UK: Cambridge University Press.

Shifrin, Donald. (1998, August). Three-year study documents nature of television violence. *AAP News.* Retrieved May 8, 2006, from http://www.aap.org/advocacy/shifrin898.htm

Shiller, Peggy. (2005, February 28). Off-ramps and on-ramps: Keeping women on the road to success. Center for Work-Life Policy. Retrieved March 3, 2006, from www.worklife policy.org/pdfs/news-pr10.pdf

Shivdas, Meena M. (2000). Alternative assessment of women and media based on NGO reviews of Section J, Beijing Platform for Action. *WomanAction.* Retrieved April 26, 2006, from http://www.womenaction.org/csw44/altrepeng.htm#recommend

Shome, Raka. (1996, February). Postcolonial interventions in the rhetorical canon: An "other" view. *Communication Theory, 6*(1), 40–59.

Shome, Raka, & Hegde, Radha S. (2002, June). Culture, communication, and the challenge of globalization. *Critical Studies in Media Communication, 19*(2), 72–189.

Simonds, Cheri J., & Cooper, Pamela J. (2001). Communication and gender in the classroom. In Leslie P. Arliss & Deborah J. Borisoff (Eds.), *Women and men communicating: Challenges and changes* (2nd ed., pp. 232–253). Prospect Heights, IL: Waveland.

Sloop, John M. (2004). *Disciplining gender: Rhetorics of sex identity in contemporary U.S. culture.* Amherst: University of Massachusetts Press.

Sloop, John M. (2005, August). In a queer time and place and race: Intersectionality comes of age. *Quarterly Journal of Speech, 91*(3), 312–326.

Smith, Craig R. (1995, Winter). Dan Quayle on family values: Epideictic appeals in political campaigns. *Southern Communication Journal, 60*(2), 152–164.

Smith, Jason K. (2002). *Counter-hegemonic masculinity in hip hop music: An analysis of The Roots' construction of masculinity in their music and in the media culture.* Master's thesis, University of Hartford, West Hartford, CT.

Solomon, Martha. (1987). *Emma Goldman.* Boston: Twayne.

Sommer, Robert. (1959). Studies in personal space. *Sociometry, 22,* 247–260.

Sommers, Christina Hoff. (2000). *The war against boys: How misguided feminism is harming our young men.* New York: Simon & Schuster.

Spender, Dale. (1985). *Man made language* (2nd ed.). London: Routledge and Kegan Paul.

Spender, Dale. (1989). *Invisible women: The schooling scandal.* London: The Women's Press.

Spivak, Gayatri Chakravorty. (1988). Can the subaltern speak? In Cary Nelson & Lawrence Grossberg (Eds.), *Marxism and the interpretation of culture* (pp. 271–313). Urbana: University of Illinois Press.

Spivak, Gayatri Chakravorty. (1996). *The Spivak reader* (Donna Landry & Gerald MacLean, Eds.). New York: Routledge.

Spivak, Gayatri Chakravorty. (2004). Terror: A speech after 9–11. *Boundary 2, 31,* 81–111.

Spurgas, Alyson Kay. (2005, August). Body image and cultural background. *Sociological Inquiry, 75*(3), 297–316.

Stables, Gordon. (2003, March). Justifying Kosovo: Representations of gendered violence and U.S. military intervention. *Critical Studies in Media Communication, 20*(1), 92–115.

Stacey, Jackie. (1989). Desperately seeking difference. In Lorraine Gamman & Margaret Marshment (Eds.), *The female gaze: Women as viewers of popular culture* (pp. 112–129). Seattle, WA: Real Comet Press.

Stapleton, Karyn. (2003). Gender and swearing: A community practice. *Women and Language, 26*(2), 22–33.

Statham, Anne, Richardson, Laurel, & Cook, Judith A. (1991). *Gender and university teaching: A negotiated difference.* Albany: State University of New York Press.

Stein, Nan. (2003). Bullying or sexual harassment? The missing discourse of rights in an era of zero tolerance. *Arizona Law Review, 45,* 783–799.

Stein, Nan. (2005). Still no laughing matter: Sexual harassment in K–12 schools. In Emilie Buchwald, Pamela Fletcher, & Martha Roth (Eds.), *Transforming a rape culture* (Rev. ed., pp. 57–74). Minneapolis, MN: Milkweed Editions.

Stephens, Mitchell. (1998). *The rise of the image, the fall of the word.* New York: Oxford University Press.

Sterk, Helen M. (1989, September). How rhetoric becomes real: Religious sources of gender identity. *The Journal of Communication and Religion, 12,* 24–33.

Stockard, Jean, & Johnson, Miriam. (1980). *Sex roles.* Englewood Cliffs, NJ: Prentice Hall.

Stokoe, Elizabeth, & Smithson, Janet. (2001). Making gender relevant: Conversation analysis and gender categories in interaction. *Discourse & Society, 12*(2), 217–244.

Story, Louise. (2005a, September 20). Many women at elite colleges set career path to motherhood. *The New York Times,* p. 1.

Story, Louise. (2005b, September 23). Background: Reporting on the aspirations of young women. *New York Times on the Web.* Retrieved March 3, 2006, from Lexis/Nexis.

Stratta, Terese M. Peretto. (2003). Cultural expressions of African American female athletes in intercollegiate sports. In Anne Bolin & Jane Granskog (Eds.), *Athletic intruders: Ethnographic research on women, culture and exercise.* Albany: State University of New York Press.

Straus, Erwin W. (1966). *Phenomenological psychology.* New York: Basic Books.

Stringer, Jeffrey L., & Hopper, Robert. (1998, May). Generic *he* in conversation. *Quarterly Journal of Speech, 84,* 209–221.

Strong, Bryan, DeVault, Christine, & Sayad, Barbara W. (1999). *Human sexuality: Diversity in contemporary America.* Mountain View, CA: Mayfield.

Subrahmanian, Ramya. (2005). *Promising practices and implications for scaling up girls' education: Report of the UN girls' education initiative South Asia workshop help in Chandigarh, India, 20–22 September 2004.* London: Commonwealth Secretariat.

Suomi, Stephen J. (1997). Nonverbal communication in nonhuman primates: Implications for the emergence of culture. In Ullica Segerstråle & Peter Molnár (Eds.), *Nonverbal communication: Where nature meets culture* (pp. 131–150). Mahwah, NJ: Erlbaum.

Suzette Haden Elgin. (2004). Retrieved April 1, 2006, from http://www.sfwa.org/members/elgin/

Swain, Jon. (2005). Masculinities in education. In Michael S. Kimmel, Jeff Hearn, & R. W. Connell (Eds.), *Handbook of studies on men and masculinities* (pp. 213–229). Thousand Oaks, CA: Sage.

Swain, Scott. (1989). Covert intimacy: Closeness in men's friendships. In B. J. Risman & Pepper Schwartz (Eds.), *Gender and intimate relationships* (pp. 71–86). Belmont, CA: Wadsworth.

Swann, Joan. (2003). Schooled language: Language and gender in educational settings. In Janet Holmes & Miriam Meyerhoff (Eds.), *The handbook of language and gender.* Malden, MA: Basil Blackwell.

Takizawa, Shoko. (2005, Spring). Cultural feminization of Japanese men. *Transcending Silence* . . . Retrieved July 6, 2006, from http://www.albany.edu/ws/journal/journal_05/takizawa3.html

Talbot, Mary M. (1998). *Language and gender.* Cambridge, UK: Polity Press.

Tanenbaum, Leora. (2000). *Slut! Growing up female with a bad reputation.* New York: HarperCollins.

Tannen, Deborah. (1984). *Conversational style: Analyzing talk among friends.* Norwood, NJ: Ablex.

Tannen, Deborah. (1990). *You just don't understand: Women and men in conversation.* New York: William Morrow.

Tannen, Deborah. (1994a). *Gender and discourse.* New York: Oxford University Press.

Tannen, Deborah. (1994b). *Talking from 9 to 5.* New York: Avon Books.

Tasker, Yvonne, & Negra, Dianne. (2005, Winter). In focus: Postfeminism and contemporary media studies. *Cinema Journal, 44*(2), 107–110.

Tavris, Carol. (1992). *The mismeasure of woman.* New York: Simon & Schuster.

Taylor, Anita, & Perry, Linda A. M. (2001, Fall). Paradoxes: No simple matter. *Women and Language, 26*(2), 1–6.

Taylor, Ella. (1991). *Prime-time families: Television culture in postwar America.* Berkeley: University of California Press.

Thie, Marilyn. (1994, Fall). Epilogue: Prolegomenon to future feminist philosophies of religions. *Hypatia, 9*(4), 229–240.

Thomas, William. (1995). *Scorched earth: The military's assault on the environment.* Philadelphia: New Society Press.

Thorne, Barrie. (1993). *Gender play: Girls and boys in school.* New Brunswick, NJ: Rutgers University Press.

Thorne, Barrie. (2003). Girls and boys together . . . but mostly apart: Gender arrangements in elementary schools. In Estelle Disch (Ed.), *Reconstructing gender: A multicultural anthology* (pp. 369–386). Boston: McGraw-Hill.

Thurner, Manuela. (1993, Spring). "Better citizens without the ballot": American anti-suffrage women and their rationale during the progressive era. *Journal of Women's History, 5*(1), 33–60.

Tickner, J. Ann. (1992). *Gender in international relations.* New York: Columbia University Press.

Tobin, Allen J., & Dusheck, Jennie. (1998). *Asking about life.* Ft. Worth, TX: Saunders College.

Tonn, Mari Boor. (1996, February). Militant motherhood: Labor's Mary Harris "Mother" Jones. *Quarterly Journal of Speech, 82,* 1–21.

Tracy, Karen. (2002). *Everyday talk: Building and reflecting identities.* New York: Guilford Press.

Travis, Cheryl Brown, Meginnis, Kayce L., & Bardari, Kristin M. (2000). Beauty, sexuality and identity: The social control of women. In Cheryl Brown Travis & Jacquelyn W. White (Eds.), *Sexuality, society, and feminism* (pp. 237–272). Washington, DC: American Psychological Association.

Trethewey, Angela. (2001, November). Reproducing and resisting the master narrative of decline: Midlife professional women's experiences of aging. *Management Communication Quarterly, 15*(2), 183–226.

Trethewey, Angela, & Ashcraft, Karen L. (2004, May). Practicing disorganization: The development of applied perspectives on living with tension. *Journal of Applied Communication Research, 32*(2), 81–88.

Trujillo, Nick. (1991). Hegemonic masculinity on the mound: Media representations of Nolan Ryan and American sports culture. *Critical Studies in Mass Communication, 8,* 290–308.

Turner, Caroline S. (2003). Incorporation and marginalization in the academy: From border toward center for faculty of color? *Journal of Black Studies, 34,* 112–125.

Turner, Lynn, & West, Richard. (2004). *Introducing communication theory: Analysis and application* (2nd ed.). Boston: McGraw-Hill.

Turner, Lynn H., & West, Richard. (Eds.). (2006a). *The family communication sourcebook.* Thousand Oaks, CA: Sage.

Turner, Lynn, & West, Richard. (2006b). *Perspectives on family communication* (3rd ed.). Boston: McGraw-Hill.

Turner, Terisa E., & Brownhill, Leigh S. (2004, January-March). Why women are at war with Chevron: Nigerian subsistence struggles against the international oil industry. *Journal of Asian and African Studies, 39*(1–2), 63–94.

Tyrangiel, Josh. (2006, May 29). In the line of fire. *Time, 167*(22), 60–65.

Tyson, Ann Scott. (2005, May 26). Bid to limit women in combat withdrawn. *The Washington Post,* p. A01.

Understanding Islam and the Muslims. (n.d.). *USC-MSA compendium of Muslim texts.* Retrieved November 9, 2005, from http://www.usc.edu/dept/MSA/introduction/understandingislam.html

Unger, Rhoda. (1979). Toward a redefinition of sex and gender. *American Psychologist, 34,* 1085–1094.

Unger, Rhoda, & Crawford, Mary. (1992). *Women and gender: A feminist psychology.* Philadelphia: Temple University Press.

United Nations Fourth World Conference on Women. (1995). *Beijing Declaration and Platform for Action.* Violence against women. Retrieved December 21, 2005, from http://www.un.org/womenwatch/daw/beijing/platform/violence.htm

U.S. Bureau of the Census. (2006, January 31). Father's Day: June 19. *Facts for Features.* Retrieved February 28, 2006, from http://www.census.gov/Press-Release/www/releases/archives/facts_for_features_special_editions/004706.html

U.S. Department of Commerce, National Telecommunications and Information Administration. (1999, July). Internet access and usage. In *Falling through the net: Defining the digital divide* (part 2). Retrieved July 5, 2006, from http://www.ntia.doc.gov/ntiahome/fttn99/part2.html

U.S. Department of Commerce, National Telecommunications and Information Administration. (2000, October). Falling through the net, toward digital inclusion. Retrieved August 26, 2006, from http://www.ntia.doc.gov/ntiahome/fttn00/contents00.html

U.S. Department of Education, National Center for Educational Statistics. (2003). *Digest of educational statistics 2002.* Washington, DC: Government Printing Office.

U.S. Department of Health and Human Services. (2005, September). *Violence against women: Domestic and intimate partner violence.* Womenshealth.gov. Retrieved April 11, 2006, from http://www.4woman.gov/violence/domestic.cfm

U.S. Equal Opportunity Employment Commission. (2005, March 2). Sexual harassment. Retrieved February 21, 2006, from http://www.eeoc.gov/types/sexual_harassment.html

U.S. General Accounting Office. (2002, January). *A new look through the glass ceiling: Where are the women? The status of women in management in ten selected industries.* Washington, DC: Author.

Vacek, Edward. (2005, March). Feminism and the Vatican [Electronic version]. *Theological Studies, 66*(1), 159–177.

Vaid, Urvashi. (1995). *Virtual equality.* New York: Anchor Books.

Valdes, Francisco. (1995, January). Queers, sissies, dykes, and tomboys: Deconstructing the conflation of "sex," "gender," and "sexual orientation" in Euro-American law and society. *California Law Review, 83,* 3–128.

van Dijk, Teun A. (1995). Editorial: The violence of text and talk. *Discourse and Society, 6*(3), pp. 307–308.

Vannoy, Dana. (Ed.). (2001). *Gender stratification: Social interaction and structural accounts.* Los Angeles: Roxbury.

Vavrus, Mary Douglas. (2002, September). Domesticating patriarchy: Hegemonic masculinity and television's "Mr. Mom." *Critical Studies in Media Communication, 19*(3), 352–375.

Vida, Vendela. (1999). *Girls on the verge: Debutante, dips, drive-by, and other initiations.* New York: St. Martin's Press.

Vingerhoets, Ad, & Scheirs, Jan. (2000). Sex differences in crying: Empirical findings and possible explanations. In Agneta H. Fischer (Ed.), *Gender and emotion: Social psychological perspectives* (pp. 143–165). Cambridge, UK: Cambridge University Press.

Vuola, Elina. (2002). Remaking universals? Transnational feminism(s) challenging fundamentalist ecumenism. *Theory, Culture and Society, 19*(1–2), 175–195.

Walker, Alexis J. (1999). Gender and family relationships. In Marvin Sussman, Suzanne K. Steinmetz, & Gary W. Peterson (Eds.), *Handbook of marriage and the family* (2nd ed., pp. 439–474). New York: Plenum Press.

Wallis, Claudia. (2004, March 22). The case for staying home: Caught between the pressures of the workplace and the demands of being a mom, more women are sticking with the kids [Electronic version, Cover story]. *Time, 163*(12), p. 50+.

Walters, Suzanna Danuta. (1995). *Material girls: Making sense of feminist cultural theory.* Berkeley: University of California Press.

Ward, L. Monique. (2005, Fall). Children, adolescents, and the media: The molding of minds, bodies, and deeds. *New Directions for Child and Adolescent Development, 109,* 63–71.

Ward, L. Monique, & Rivadeneyra, Rocio. (1999, August). Contributions of entertainment television to adolescents' sexual attitudes and expectations: The role of viewing amount versus viewer involvement. *The Journal of Sex Research, 36*(3), 237–249.

Warner, Michael. (2002). *Publics and counterpublics.* New York: Zone.

Warnick, Barbara. (1999, March). Masculinizing the feminine: Inviting women online ca. 1997. *Critical Studies in Mass Communication, 1,* 1–19.

Weatherall, Ann. (1998). Re-visioning gender and language research. *Women and Language, 21*(1), 1–9.

Weatherall, Ann. (2002). *Gender, language and discourse.* London: Routledge.

Weber, Max. (1947). *The theory of social and economic organizations* (A. M. Henderson & Talcott Parsons, Trans.). New York: Oxford University Press.

Welsh, Sandy, Carr, Jacquie, MacQuarrie, Barbara, & Huntley, Audrey. (2006, February). "I'm not thinking of it as sexual harassment": Understanding harassment across race and citizenship. *Gender & Society, 20*(1), 87–107.

Welter, Barbara. (1976). *Dimity convictions: The American woman in the nineteenth century.* Athens: Ohio University Press.

West, Candice, & Zimmerman, Don H. (1983). Small insults: A study of interruptions in cross-sex conversations between unacquainted persons. In Barrie Thorne, Cheris Kramarae, & Nancy Henley (Eds.), *Language, gender, and society* (pp. 103–119). Rowley, MA: Newbury House.

West, Candice, & Zimmerman, Don H. (1987). Doing gender. *Gender & Society, 1,* 125–151.

West, Richard, & Turner, Lynn H. (2004). *Introducing communication* (2nd ed.). Boston: McGraw-Hill.

Westerfelhaus, Robert, & Brookey, Robert Alan. (2004, July/October). At the unlikely confluence of conservative religion and popular culture: *Fight Club* as heteronormative ritual. *Text and Performance Quarterly, 24*(3–4), 302–326.

Whitam, Frederick, L., Daskalos, Christopher, Sobolewski, Curt G., & Padilla, Peter. (1998). The emergence of lesbian sexuality and identity cross-culturally: Brazil, Peru, the Philippines, and the United States. *Archives of Sexual Behavior, 27*(1), 31–57.

Whitam, Fredrick, L., Diamond, Milton, & Martin, James. (1993). Homosexual orientation in twins: A report on 61 pairs and three triplet sets. *Archives of Sexual Behavior, 22*(3), 187–207.

Whitehead, Stephen M. (2002). *Men and masculinities: Key themes and new directions.* Cambridge, UK: Basil Blackwell.

Wiehl, Lis. (2002, Spring). "Sounding Black" in the courtroom: Court-sanctioned racial stereotyping. *Harvard Blackletter Journal, 18,* 185–210.

Wilson, Elizabeth, & Ng, Sik Hung. (1988). Sex bias in visual images evoked by generics: A New Zealand study. *Sex Roles, 18,* 159–168.

Wilson, Robin. (2004, October 29). Reports show difficulty of sex-discrimination lawsuits. *The Chronicle of Higher Education,* p. A12.

Wing, Adrien Katherine. (1997). Brief reflections toward a multiplicative theory of praxis and being. In Adrien Katherine Wing (Ed.), *Critical race feminism: A reader* (pp. 27–34). New York: New York University Press.

Witt, Linda, Paget, Karen M., & Matthews, Glenna. (1994). *Running as a woman: Gender and power in American politics.* New York: The Free Press.

Wolf, Naomi. (1991). *The beauty myth: How images of beauty are used against women.* New York: Anchor Books.

Wood, Julia. (2001). The normalization of violence in heterosexual romantic relationships: Women's narratives of love and violence. *Journal of Social and Personal Relationships, 18*(2) 239–261.

Wood, Julia. (2005). *Gendered lives: Communication, gender and culture* (6th ed.). Belmont, CA: Wadsworth.

Wood, Julia. (2007). *Gendered lives: Communication, gender and culture* (7th ed.). Belmont, CA: Wadsworth.

Wood, Julia, & Dindia, Kathryn. (1998). What's the difference? A dialogue about differences and similarities between women and men. In Daniel J. Canary & Kathryn Dindia

(Eds.), *Sex differences and similarities in communication: Critical essays and empirical investigations of sex and gender in interaction* (pp. 19–39). Mahwah, NJ: Erlbaum.

World Health Organization. (2002, October 2). First ever Global Report on Violence and Health released. Retrieved October 29, 2005, from http://www.who.int/mediacentre/news/releases/pr73/en/

World Health Organization. (2005a). *WHO multi-country study on women's health and domestic violence against women*. Geneva, Switzerland: Author.

World Health Organization. (2005b, November 24). Landmark study on domestic violence. Retrieved April 11, 2006, from http://www.who.int/mediacentre/news/releases/2005/pr62/en/index.html

Wright, Paul H. (1982). Men's friendships, women's friendships, and the alleged inferiority of the latter. *Sex Roles, 8,* 1–20.

Wright, Paul H. (2006). Toward an expanded orientation to the comparative study of women's and men's same-sex friendships. In Daniel J. Canary & Kathryn Dindia (Eds.), *Sex differences and similarities in communication* (2nd ed., pp. 37–58). Mahwah, NJ: Erlbaum.

Wurtzel, Elizabeth. (1998). *Bitch: In praise of difficult women*. New York: Doubleday.

Wysham, Daphne. (2002, October). Women take on oil companies in Nigeria. *Economic Justice News Online, 5*(3). Retrieved July 14, 2005, from http://www.50years.org/cms/ejn/story/82

Yaeger-Dror, Malcah. (1998). Factors influencing the contrast between men's and women's speech. *Women and Language, 21*(1), 40–46.

Yang, Li-Shou, Thornton, Arland, & Fricke, Thomas. (2000). Religion and family formation in Taiwan: The decline of ancestral authority. In Sharon K. Houseknecht & Jerry G. Pankhurst (Eds.), *Family, religion, and social change in diverse societies* (pp. 121–146). Cambridge: Oxford University Press.

Yanowitz, Karen L., & Weathers, Kevin J. (2004). Do boys and girls act differently in the classroom? A content analysis of student characters in educational psychology textbooks. *Sex Roles, 51*(1–2), 101–107.

Young, Iris Marion. (1990). *Throwing like a girl and other essays in feminist philosophy and social theory*. Bloomington: Indiana University Press.

Young, Iris Marion. (1997). *Intersecting voices: Dilemmas of gender, political philosophy, and policy*. Princeton, NJ: Princeton University Press.

Young, Shelagh. (1989). Feminism and the politics of power: Whose gaze is it anyway? In Lorraine Gamman & Margaret Marshment (Eds.), *The female gaze: Women as viewers of popular culture* (pp. 173–188). Seattle, WA: Real Comet Press.

Yousman, Bill. (2003, November). Blackophilia and blackophobia: White youth, the consumption of rap music, and white supremacy. *Communication Theory, 13*(4), 366–391.

Yuval-Davis, Nira. (1997). *Gender and nation*. London: Sage.

Yuval-Davis, Nira. (1999). The 'multi-layered citizen': Citizenship in the age of 'globalization.' *International Feminist Journal of Politics, 1*(1), 119–136.

Zack, Naomi. (1998). *Thinking about race*. Belmont, CA: Wadsworth.

Zaeske, Susan. (1995). The "Promiscuous Audience" controversy and the emergence of the early women's rights movement. *Quarterly Journal of Speech, 81,* 191–207.

Zimmerman, Toni Schindler, Haddock, Shelley A., & McGeorge, Christine R. (2001). Mars and Venus: Unequal planets. *Journal of Marital and Family Therapy, 27*(1), 55–68.

Zompetti, Joseph P. (1997). Toward a Gramscian critical rhetoric. *Western Journal of Communication, 61*(1), 66–86.

Index

About the Authors

Victoria Pruin DeFrancisco, Ph.D., is a Professor of Communication Studies and affiliate faculty in Women's Studies at the University of Northern Iowa. She teaches courses in gender, intercultural, and interpersonal communication. Victoria comes from a close Italian American family and has five siblings. She is married and has stepchildren and grandchildren who call her Nana and remind her every day why she wrote this book.

Catherine Helen Palczewski, Ph.D., is a Professor of Communication Studies, Director of Debate, and affiliate faculty in Women's Studies at the University of Northern Iowa. She teaches courses in the rhetoric of social protest, argumentation, and political communication. One side of her family tree makes her a second-generation Polish American citizen, and the other makes her eligible to be a member of the Daughters of the American Revolution.

This book was a truly coauthored endeavor. The fun, sweat, work, and joy were equally shared. The name order on the cover and title page are accidental.